INTRODUCING UBUNTU: DESKTOP LINUX

BRIAN PROFFITT

THOMSON
———————— ✳ ————————™
COURSE TECHNOLOGY
Professional ■ Technical ■ Reference

ISBN-10: 1-59863-415-1
ISBN-13: 978-1-59863-415-0
Library of Congress Catalog Card Number: 2007927292
Printed in the United States of America
08 09 10 11 12 TW 10 9 8 7 6 5 4 3 2 1

Publisher and General Manager, Thomson Course Technology PTR:
Stacy L. Hiquet

Associate Director of Marketing:
Sarah O'Donnell

Manager of Editorial Services:
Heather Talbot

Marketing Manager:
Mark Hughes

Acquisitions Editor:
Mitzi Koontz

Marketing Assistant:
Adena Flitt

Project Editor and Copy Editor:
Marta Justak

Technical Reviewer:
Kurt Wall

PTR Editorial Services Coordinator:
Erin Johnson

Interior Layout Tech:
ICC Macmillan Inc.

Cover Designer:
Mike Tanamachi

CD-ROM Producer:
Brandon Penticuff

Indexer:
Sharon Shock

Proofreader:
Gene Redding

THOMSON

COURSE TECHNOLOGY

Professional ■ Technical ■ Reference

Thomson Course Technology PTR,
a division of Thomson Learning Inc.
25 Thomson Place
Boston, MA 02210
http://www.courseptr.com

Be excellent to each other.

ACKNOWLEDGMENTS

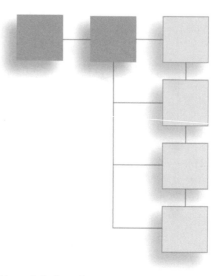

It goes without saying that you would not be holding this book in your hands had not some very talented and creative people lent their skills to help me get this done in what may be record time.

I can never express enough gratitude to my editors. For those of you who think this brilliant writing is the sole product of my fevered work, you would be wrong. So I thank Marta Justak, Kurt Wall, and Gene Redding profusely for their hard work. I would also extend my sincerest thanks to Mark Shuttleworth and Malcolm Yates of Canonical; Joe Eckert and Lauree Ostrofsky from Baker Communications Group; and Aurelia Negrerie from Linspire. They all took time out from their busy days to help a poor author at their door, looking for information, and this book is much better for their efforts.

They say no man is an island. I am fortunate enough to have three spectacular women in my life who know how to treat me right (or drive me insane, depending on the time of day). My wife and two wonderful daughters get the big thanks and smooches for putting up with me squirreled away in the basement office (a.k.a. "The Cave") for days at a stretch.

About the Author

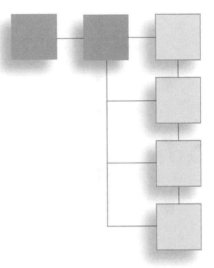

Brian Proffitt has been Managing Editor of *Linux Today* (linuxtoday.com), a premier news and information site about all things Linux and Open Source, as well as four other Linux Web sites for Jupitermedia Corp. since 2002. He is the author of numerous books on computer technology, mostly on Linux, but with a Mac and Windows book thrown in just for variety. He is also the author of a student guide on Plato. A black belt in tae kwon do and a private pilot, he enjoys spending time with his family in his home in northern Indiana.

Contents

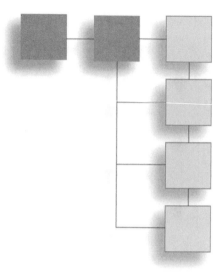

INTRODUCTION

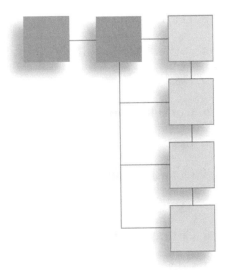

Many people think of Ubuntu as an operating system that is way over their heads—that only techies can use this strange, arcane OS with the funny name.

For all of you who have been having these thoughts, this book is here to tell you that this is simply not the case. Ubuntu, and Linux, in general, have become very easy for everyday home and business users to install and use.

Now you can find out for yourself, in just one weekend, how easy it is to get started using Ubuntu and discover that there is life beyond Vista.

Is This Book for You?

Introducing Ubuntu: Desktop Linux is for anyone who wants to get started using Ubuntu, specifically Ubuntu 7.04, and only has one computer at their home or business on which to install this new operating system. Think of this book as a personal tutorial, a one-on-one class with an expert user of Ubuntu. You get to stay in the comfort of your own home or office and learn how to do the following things:

- Use Ubuntu as a sole operating system or have it happily co-exist with Windows.

- Gather information about your system to assess your system's capability to use Ubuntu.

- Learn about the many versions of Linux and the entire Ubuntu family.

- Install the Ubuntu operating system.

- Deal with any unusual installation issues.

- Configure your PC to boot to Ubuntu and Windows.

- Examine the GNOME interfaces.

- Create a customized desktop.

- Explore the Ubuntu filesystem.

- Connect to the Internet.

- Add a printer to your PC.

- Add additional hardware to your PC.

- Install software using the Synaptic Package Manager.

- Explore some of the essential tools packaged with Ubuntu.

- Examine and configure Firefox to browse the Internet and use Evolution to read your e-mail and manage your appointments.

- Use OpenOffice.org 2.2 as your preferred office suite.

- Troubleshoot any installation and configuration issues that may pop up.

What's on the CD

There's not a lot you need to start using Ubuntu: basically, just the software and an Intel-based PC. It does not even have to be a new PC. Ubuntu works well on older PCs, and it has much better performance on those PCs than Windows XP, and also on older machines the new Vista operating system won't even touch.

Ubuntu is a free-of-charge distribution of Linux, which means that anyone with a broadband Internet connection (like a cable modem or DSL line) and a "writeable" CD-ROM drive can download the whole package and create his own CD-ROM. This is free, except for the cost of the blank disc.

For people who don't want to spend much money and don't have access to a big Internet pipe, there is a second option. A few companies download each new version as it is released, create hundreds of CD-ROMs containing the complete Ubuntu distribution, and then sell them for a low cost.

Much of the preparation for installation is discussed in Chapters 1 and 2. You should definitely read these chapters first so you can get ready for the rest of your exploration of Ubuntu.

This book details how to find and download your own copy of the Ubuntu operating system, which is useful for any version of Ubuntu. We also thought it would be a good idea to make it even easier and include a free, licensed copy of Ubuntu right in the back of the book. On the CD you will find a complete copy of Ubuntu 7.04, "Feisty Fawn," ready to install.

On that CD, besides the Ubuntu operating system, you will find copies of

- OpenOffice.org, a full-featured office suite for Ubuntu and Windows

- Firefox, the popular browser that beats Internet Explorer on speed and reliability

- Evolution, a robust messaging and contact management application

PART I

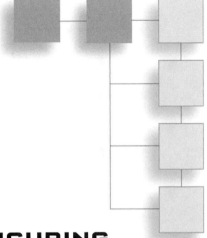

INSTALLING AND CONFIGURING UBUNTU

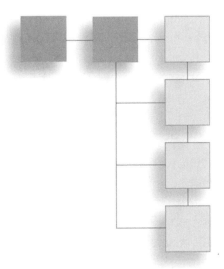

CHAPTER 1

WHAT IS UBUNTU?

It's got a weird name, at least to Western ears. But for people all over the world, Ubuntu may represent the best alternative to the Windows operating system seen to date.

That's the nickel-tour synopsis of Ubuntu, the free operating system that can run on just about any PC. But to really explain what Ubuntu is, we'll need to take a step back and examine the origins of the software from which Ubuntu sprang: GNU/Linux.

In this chapter, we'll explore the origins of Linux, learning about its many different types, of which Ubuntu is just one aspect. Then we'll look into the more recent history of this branch of Linux, Ubuntu, which is directly descended from Debian. In the process, we'll learn how the first and only South African cosmonaut decided to marry an old Bantu concept to a new operating system.

What Is Linux?

You might be asking yourself, why bother with a history lesson? No one kicks off a book on how to use Windows or Mac OS X with a detailed biography of Bill Gates or Steven Jobs. In this case, understanding the origins of Ubuntu is to understand the functionality of Ubuntu itself.

Besides, it's a good story, which you can read while you're installing Ubuntu on your own PC.

A Brief History of Linux

The beginnings of Ubuntu actually began in a place very far away from South Africa: the much colder climes of Helsinki, Finland. It was there, in 1991, that a young computer science student at the University of Helsinki put the word out to an online newsgroup asking for input on a new operating system he was building for his home PC: a copy of the Minix operating system that, until then, could only be run on big, high-end machines.

That was in August. By the next month, the first version was released with no public announcement; only the group working with the student was privy to the release. On October 5, 1991, version 0.02 of the brand-new code was publicly announced. The rest, as they say, is history. The student, Linus Torvalds, based his master's thesis on the project, now dubbed *Linux*.

By the end of the decade, Linux was found on thousands of computers around the world, serving in many capacities, most notably as the operating system on which most Web site software runs. Current estimates show anywhere from 70–80 percent of the world's Web sites run on top of some version of Linux. Linus himself still serves as project manager for the Linux kernel—the very heart of the operating system—even as businesses ranging from IBM to neighborhood churches use the Linux operating system every day.

Linux has grown to a multibillion dollar a year business, which is not bad for a piece of code that is available absolutely free of charge to anyone who wants it.

That's no typo: Linux is indeed free, and in more than one sense of the word. This is understandably puzzling to many new to this operating system, since the concept of making money from something that's free seems counterintuitive. How does this work? To answer, let's take a look at how Linux is put together.

How Linux and Windows Are Nothing Alike

When looking at Linux, invariably comparisons are made to its strongest competitor, Microsoft Windows. It's a fair comparison, since Windows sits on over 90 percent of desktops in the world and has made its company, Microsoft, arguably the richest company on the planet. When you look at each operating system side-by-side, they look quite a bit alike: there are menus, windows, icons, toolbars—all of the familiar visual cues that most people take for granted when they use a computer these days. When you crack open the hood, however, you will find that Linux and Windows are nothing alike.

Modularity

Let's revisit the work of young Linus. What he and his fellow contributors were working on was not an operating system in the way you think of Windows or Mac OS X. He was working on what it known as the kernel: the tiny, but powerful, core that lies at the center of all things Linux. But an operating system is not just a kernel: There is software to talk to keyboards, mice, screens, the Internet, installed applications, not to mention the software that makes all of those pretty nifty-looking windows, icons, and menus. Underneath all of that, though, is the kernel: the piece of software that organizes all of the tasks a human being needs a computer to do and coordinates it into instructions the computer can understand.

Linux is not the only operating system with an operating system at its core; all operating systems have kernels, even Windows. But not all kernels are created equal.

To illustrate, think of a kernel as a child's connecting toy block. It's self contained, and other blocks can be easily attached to it. In fact, in this example, other blocks certainly do, like the block that displays the computer's output on the screen or the block that controls the network card that lets the computer talk to the Internet. All the blocks connect rather neatly to the kernel block, which is only slightly bigger than the rest of the blocks, because it's not doing all of the work— the other blocks are. The whole thing put together is what we know as the Linux operating system.

By contrast, the Windows kernel is also a connecting block, but it's much bigger than the blocks that connect to it. It's nearly as big as all of Linux itself, and that's just the Windows kernel. The reason for this size disparity is because the Windows kernel is so interconnected to its helper applications that essentially all the blocks are welded into one monster piece. Other blocks can connect to this kernel, but only in very specific ways. (In fact, to really play up the analogy, in Linux the blocks can be any color or shape you want; in Windows the blocks are all the same shade and very similar in shape.)

This difference in structure quickly reveals some of the more obvious benefits of Linux over Windows: because individual "blocks" are small and you never use them all at the same time, this means that in the real world Linux doesn't need as many machine resources as Windows to run efficiently. In fact, Linux runs very well on PCs that Windows would just putter on.

Nowhere is this difference more apparent than with the newest Windows operating system, Vista, which requires a lot of hardware resources—so much so that many potential Vista users are looking at significant upgrade costs just to get their machines Vista-ready. Or they are looking to buy all new machines altogether.

Security

Another big difference in the two operating systems' makeup is in their security. It is a documented fact that there are tens of thousands of Windows viruses, Trojans, and worms out there: a veritable zoo of malicious software designed to cause damage to your data, copy it for others to abuse, or even take over your computer so it can be used to attack other computers. On the other hand, there are only about 500 known Linux viruses, and none of them has ever been let loose in the wild.

Why such a big gap? One could argue that since the Windows operating system is on such a vast majority of the world's desktops, it is a bigger target for malicious software writers, and that's certainly a good reason. But the way Windows operating systems are constructed may also have something to do with it. Recall our analogy: The Windows connecting bricks are all basically the same shape and the same color. In real terms, that means that if one of the blocks gets affected by something bad, then it's much easier for the rest of the blocks to be affected by the same thing.

In Linux, this is not usually going to happen, because it is made up of so many different kinds of blocks. It is possible that someone could "take over" the block that runs an Internet browser on Linux, but that's all a bad coder is likely going to get. In Windows, a similar takeover of the browser could lead to total appropriation of the machine.

Finally, there is one more important difference between Windows and Linux: Because of the modular nature of Linux, it can be run on pretty much any kind of computer in any kind of machine. You can find Linux running on everything from supercomputers like IBM's Big Blue/L to TiVos to mobile phones to wristwatches.

This works this way because Linux is modular all the way down through the kernel. Not only is the operating system made up of blocks, but the kernel itself also is modular in nature. If you want Linux to run on a mobile phone, you don't need the part of the kernel that runs a mouse, so it's just taken out. Removing the parts they don't need leaves hardware engineers with a kernel that can be run just for their device, whether it is big or small.

Naturally, this doesn't matter to users of Ubuntu that much. They will use the "generic" version of the Linux kernel, with all of the special applications that the developers of Ubuntu have decided to ship. All for free.

Yes, there's that word again. Free. When you acquire Ubuntu, it, and most of the applications that with it, are free of charge. You don't have to pay a cent. How does that work?

The Meaning of Free Software

Before Linus Torvalds decided to put together the school project that would eventually shake the IT world's foundations, there was a young software developer toiling away at a school a whole ocean away: the Massachusetts Institute of Technology in Cambridge, MA. The developer's name was Richard M. Stallman, and in his work at MIT's Artificial Intelligence Lab, he came up with a pretty nifty idea. Software, he reasoned, should be free for all to use. Not just free of charge, but free to share. He not only thought up this idea, but he also implemented it by creating a set of free tools perfect for the creation of a new, free operating system. Everything an infant operating system needed was included, except a kernel. He called this set of tools GNU, an acronym you will see a lot of while working with Ubuntu. It means, in a clever, geeky, recursive play on words, *GNU's not UNIX*.

At the same time, beyond the wordplay, Stallman did some really radical: he created a free software license.

All software created is released under some sort of license. A license dictates how a piece of software can be sold, copied, and used. Much of the software that you have used until now, such as Windows, has what is known as a proprietary license. It states—in exquisitely long legalese—that you, the user, can use one copy of Windows. You can't copy it and sell it to anyone else. Nor are you allowed to see or otherwise manipulate the code that made Windows. To do so would bring certain doom upon you. Or worse, lawyers.

What Stallman proposed was a license that would be a mirror image of proprietary licenses. His original idea went something like this:

- You have the freedom to run the program, for any purpose.

- You have the freedom to change the program to suit your needs. This means that you can have the source code, which is the actual human instructions used to put an application together.

- You have the freedom to redistribute copies of the program, either for free or for a fee.

- You have the freedom to redistribute changed copies of the original program.

Those are the four basic principles found in the license Stallman created, the GNU General Public License, or GPL for short. This license was written to guarantee that once software is made free under this license, it will always stay that way.

Free, in this context, means free of charge and also free of restrictions to share and change. A very common euphemism heard around the Linux community is that the GPL is "free as in beer and free as in freedom."

To break this down in nontechnical and nonlegal terms, here's what the GPL means: Here's the software. Here's the source code. Do what you want with it. If you improve it, make sure you include all of the source code with your improvements and pass it along. Don't ever try to keep other people from getting your improvements to the source code. We can tell you to do this because we wrote the software, and these are the terms under which we're willing to let you have it.

In a less litigious society, this could be broken down even further to: "Be excellent to each other."

How the GPL became tied to Linux was really a matter of practicality. Torvalds had his kernel but none of the tools that would make that kernel into a real operating system (think engine without the gears, wheels, shafts, and axles that make a car). The GNU tools were ready to go, but they had no kernel. In a classic "you've got your chocolate in my peanut butter" flash of inspiration, Torvalds modified the GNU tools so they would run with his Linux kernel, and poof! the Linux operating system was born.

Because of the close interplay of the GNU tools and the Linux kernel, Torvalds decided to adopt GNU's GPL license for the kernel as well. This interplay is also why you will often see the operating system referred to as "GNU/Linux" and the kernel just as "Linux." Purists, Stallman the most vocal, believe that adding "GNU/" to the Linux name reflects the huge contribution the GNU tools made to the birth of the GNU/Linux operating system.

Whether people back this stance or not, the common accepted term for the kernel and the operating system is "Linux," which is what this book will use unless referring to a version of Linux that specifically uses "GNU/Linux" in its official name.

Now you know how the free part of Linux works. But with all that freedom, how does anyone still make money in the Linux business? Well, if you recall from that list of principles that formed the basis of the GPL, the third item said that one could redistribute GPL software as desired, either free or for a fee. This means that companies are allowed to package Linux (or other free software) and sell it to whoever is willing to buy it.

Okay, but where's the money? Why would a user pay money for something that's free?

There are two reasons, actually. The first is convenience. While Linux and all of its components are free to acquire, getting all of this software and putting it together is not always something someone wants to do. To return to our analogy, you could buy the box of connecting blocks and put Linux together on your own, but that takes time and not a little technical expertise.

Instead, you could pay a company that has already put Linux together for you to download from the Internet or buy it in a nice box, complete with instruction manual. Whatever you prefer. Such a company or organization has created what's known as a Linux distribution. All distributions are slightly different from each other, but they're all still Linux.

The second reason someone would pay for something free is for support. After you buy software, many companies will offer free or fee-based technical support, such as a phone number or Web site for you to use to get questions answered. Linux is no different; in fact, Linux companies depend on support fees to generate their revenue.

It should be noted at this point that Ubuntu isn't going to charge you money every time you need some help. Ubuntu doesn't ask for support fees from single users or even smaller commercial users. Instead, Ubuntu asks for fees from larger companies who have decided to use Ubuntu in their organization. For such customers, having a support contact isn't a luxury—it's a necessity.

Now you know the secret to making money with Linux: don't charge for the software itself—charge for the services you can provide with the software.

So who puts all of this code together? And why do they do it? It's not always to earn a living, as you might expect.

Distributions of All Shapes and Sizes

In the very beginning, there was one distribution of Linux, known as *MCC Interim Linux*. Its singular status didn't last long. Very soon, there was a handful of distributions. Today, nearly 16 years later, there are upwards of 200 distributions. No one knows the exact number, since new ones are being created every week, and old ones are being allowed to languish into obscurity.

Where to Find Distributions

For an up-to-date inventory of Linux distributions, visit DistroWatch (www.distrowatch.com).

Whatever the exact number, there are a lot of distributions out there, and they all fall into one of two categories: commercial or noncommercial.

The commercial distributions exist for a pretty self-explanatory reason: Someone wants to make money, either a company or a group of developers. These distributions tend to be the most well known of the Linux distributions, though they are not necessarily the most influential.

Distributions in this category include Red Hat Enterprise Linux, SUSE Linux Enterprise Server, Mandriva Linux, Linspire, Turbolinux, and Xandros. Those are the more commercially successful distributions; it is by no means a complete list.

Noncommercial distributions are generally run as not-for-profits, if they are well organized, or even as a hobby for one of a group of developers. The motivation for developers is varied. Some want to create something meaningful. Some do it to earn extra money (some nonprofit distributions do receive some funding through voluntary support and donations). Some want to have fun coding. Whatever the reason, developers have made noncommercial distributions very popular and extremely influential among all Linux developers.

Noncommercial distributions include Debian GNU/Linux, Slackware Linux, Fedora, openSUSE, SimplyMEPIS, and Freespire. Just to give you an idea of how influential noncommercial distributions can be, know that SimplyMEPIS, Freespire, Linspire, and Xandros are among the many Linux distributions (commercial or otherwise) based on what has become the most popular non-commercial distribution today: Debian GNU/Linux.

As has Ubuntu.

What Ubuntu Is

If you were to ask under which category Ubuntu fell, technically the answer would have to be commercial, if only because its development is ultimately funded by the United Kingdom company Canonical Ltd. It's a hard thing to define, though, since community involvement in Ubuntu development is so intense. In fact, this involvement is a good reason why Ubuntu has become so popular. With so much user involvement, backed by corporate funding, Ubuntu has been able to become one of the most user-friendly Linux distributions available today.

There is more to it, of course. And it starts back in 1993, when one Purdue University student decided that he had a better way to put Linux together.

The Debian Connection

When Ian Murdock started the Debian Linux release in August 1993, the whole idea of a distribution was still very new. At the time, there were just five other distributions available, and in his opinion, none of them were very good. He actually cited one of them, the Softlanding Linux System (SLS), as a reason why something like Debian (which takes its name from his first name and his wife's name Deb) was needed because it was full of errors and bugs.

Older Than Dirt

Interestingly, an offshoot of SLS that came out one month prior to Debian was Slackware Linux. The Slackware Linux developers must have gotten something right, because it holds the distinction of being the oldest surviving Linux distribution. Debian GNU/Linux is the second oldest.

Murdock's focus on the free aspects of software eventually led him to rename the distribution Debian GNU/Linux. But there were more than cosmetic name changes at work as the first version of Debian was developed over the next few years. The preference for free software carries through the entire Debian Project to this day. This is one of the reasons Debian is unique among the Linux distributions: Only free software is included as part of the official released code.

Other distributions are willing to include software that isn't free, but not Debian. If it's not licensed under the GPL, the software isn't "in" the core release. You can still get non-free stuff (drivers, say), it just isn't part of the core distribution. The Debian Project says it best: "As a service to our users, we also provide packages in separate sections that cannot be included in the main distribution due to either a restrictive license or legal issues."

Another distinction Debian has is its relatively slow production cycle, mostly due to its very meticulous quality control processes. Most Linux distributions come out with a new version every six to eight months; Debian has a new release scheduled for 2007, but the last release came out in the summer of 2005, and the release before that came out nearly three years earlier. Of course, as slow as these releases are, users of Debian know that what they get when they install the software will be very, very stable. So what if you might celebrate a birthday or two in-between releases?

Debian's other quality is how it manages software installations. Using a tool known as *apt-get*, Debian users can download not only the software they desire but also every other piece of software the desired application might need to run correctly. It also keeps track of everything you have installed, so whenever there's an update, you get the latest and greatest version of the code automatically installed with just one command.

Debian's stability and free nature have made it a very desirable platform for other distributions to use as a base. But there's always room for improvement in some people's minds. Thus was born Ubuntu.

The Canonical Connection

In 1995, South African entrepreneur Mark Shuttleworth launched Thawte Consulting, a company that was created to design and build super-secure servers for worldwide sale, as well as to provide certificates that would prove that someone on the Internet was who he claimed to be. The server side of the business didn't do too well, mostly due to U.S. cryptography laws that prevented the purchasing of non-U.S. servers of this nature. But the certificate side did really well—especially when Verisign came along in 1999 and bought the company for $575 million.

With the money, Shuttleworth was able to fund a lot of free software projects in South Africa, as well as indulge in a little bit of travel: In 2002, he became the second private citizen and first African to travel in space when he visited the International Space Station.

Ultimately, Shuttleworth founded the private firm Canonical, which sponsors, among other things, the Ubuntu distribution.

Shuttleworth tried this venture as a Debian-based distribution because of his familiarity with working with Debian when he started Thawte. He'd clearly benefited from Debian, and now it was time to give back to the Debian Project. And what better way to give back than to improve it?

Shuttleworth named his new project *Ubuntu,* which is a Bantu word for a traditional African concept that loosely translates into "humanity towards others." It is a philosophy where kindness towards other people isn't an effort—it simply is. The Ubuntu distribution reflects that concept through its simple, balanced approach to providing cutting edge software that upholds the ideals of free software.

For example, one of the aspects that Shuttleworth didn't like about Debian was the slow production cycle. To change that, he decided that his new distribution, Ubuntu, would come out every six months in April and October. He and his team also streamlined the development process by organizing the developers into community teams and reducing the total number of applications included in the Ubuntu distribution (2,000), relative to Debian GNU/Linux (10,000). Fewer applications greatly decreased the complexity of the quality control process and subsequently the time involved in the whole production process.

Another way that Shuttleworth wanted to improve Debian was to send back any improvements made in Ubuntu's packages to Debian. Even though Ubuntu makes up only a fifth of Debian's packages, he thought that Ubuntu's quality check would help speed Debian's development process along.

Finally, while Ubuntu would try to uphold the free software ideals of Debian, it wouldn't strictly do so. Just like Debian, nonfree, proprietary applications would be available for Ubuntu users to install if they wanted to.

The Community Connection

If you talk to anyone who has been exposed to Ubuntu for any length of time, you will almost certainly hear about the pervasiveness and strength of the Ubuntu community. More than just developers, the Ubuntu community is made up of users, documenters, designers, and developers working together not only to build a better product, but also to make sure it's easy to use.

Web sites, mailing lists, conferences—all are aspects of how the Ubuntu teams work together to produce their product. They also do a very good job of explaining how Ubuntu works, as you will see later in this book. According to the Ubuntu community site, "Membership in the Ubuntu community recognizes participants for a variety of contributions, from code to artwork, advocacy, translations and organizational skills. If you are active in the Forums, or submitting icons or sounds or artwork, then you are eligible for Membership, which gives you a say in the governance of the project."

That kind of participatory community is nothing new to Linux, but what is notable is the efficiency and openness of the Ubuntu community. This community is an enormous strength of Ubuntu, one in which users will benefit from often.

It would be difficult to pin down why the Ubuntu community, among all the other free and open source software communities, is so strong and vibrant. Many participants in the project cite Canonical's real willingness to listen to the community as a major draw.

A Cosmonaut's View

In order to better understand the importance that community and Canonical bring to Ubuntu, I sat down with Canonical's founder Mark Shuttleworth for an interview prior to the release of Ubuntu 7.04.

Proffitt: *Everybody says that the community structure is the biggest benefit of working with Ubuntu. Would you agree with that assessment?*

Shuttleworth: I'd hope so; I mean, we set out very much to build something that lived up to the free stuff the communities expect and would like to see in the Linux distribution. And at the same time to bring to the project a similar level of commercial expertise and quality that you might expect from a more commercial project. And so what we seek to do is to create the fusion of community and commerce, something that is self sustained but is freely available and lives up to the sort of ideals of the free software community. So when people say that they really like working with the Ubuntu community, I think that's exactly the kind of feedback I'd like to hear.

Proffitt: *Right.*

Shuttleworth: And then when there are issues conversely in the community, it's something that we take very seriously and want to sort out right away.

Proffitt: *How do you go about achieving that fusion?*

Shuttleworth: I think part of the process is letting go of control and understand that okay, we can accept that since we're doing this in partnership with people who are coming at this from all sorts of different cultures, from 10 different time zones, from different backgrounds, and so on it's much harder to predict exactly what we're going to get in six months' time or in a year's time. Now I don't want to make the project sound completely sort of unguided and ungoverned—quite the reverse, right? There's a very strong commitment to the process itself. So we know once we're going to get the release, we know very strongly how we can manage that, and we can manage very strongly the resources that we put into it. This is now far bigger than Canonical, and so a lot of what goes into a release is determined through this consensus building process with the community.

Proffitt: *How hard is it to keep up with the release base strategy that you have? That's also been another positive point for Ubuntu—the regular release cycle. How hard has that been to kind of keep that framework going?*

Shuttleworth: It is tough—but it also is a great privilege every six months to be able to bring to the world the very latest and greatest stuff that the free software community is producing. And I'm very conscious of the fact that when people talk about Ubuntu, they're really (99 percent of the time) talking about a piece of the software that has been written by other communities, like OpenOffice and Apache and Firefox and so on. And each of those other communities is constantly working to improve and innovate that particular piece of software. It's kind of our responsibility to provide a sufficient conduit every six months to the outside world of what that group is working on. So it's quite a responsibility for us; we want to make sure that every six months what we [send] out as a new release of Ubuntu really represents the best of what all of those communities have done. I think we are kind of ambassadors for free software—for other people's work in free software.

Proffitt: *I'd like to back up a little bit and talk about your initial reasons for getting into the business of Linux, so to speak. What was your first exposure to the Linux operating system?*

Shuttleworth: Gee, that goes back the early '90s. I was a student at the University of Cape Town, and I was really trying to come to understand the Internet and to get my own computer hooked up to the Internet through the university.

It turned out that this just couldn't be done using Windows, and it could be done very easily with Linux. And that turned into a love affair, which really allowed me to explore the Internet at a very early stage and then build a small business, which was quite successful. Having done that, I then felt that one of the goals that I could set [for] myself was essentially to try and bring that same experience of empowerment to people who weren't quite as technically interested as I was.

At the time I was studying IT and passionate about the Internet and was willing to devote a tremendous amount of time and effort to getting into the guts of it. But it seemed to me that free software shouldn't be just about empowering the people that have sort of an extreme self-reliance, effectively; it should also be about empowering people who are at the completely opposite end of the spectrum, like people in countries who have financial constraints associated with technology and their access to technology, and also people who simply want something that's reliable and cost effective. So this is a way for me to give back to the community that made it possible for me to be successful in the first place and to try and [give away] that empowerment.

Proffitt: *In press reports you obviously are very active in getting the Shuttleworth Foundation out to help underdeveloped nations and regions.*

Shuttleworth: Right.

Proffitt: *And you personally, too.*

Shuttleworth: I have a very strong philanthropic need to feel that the work that we're doing is going to have a profound impact in parts of the world that won't otherwise get this kind of assistance. That's kind of one target market; there are really three.

One is the philanthropic market—people for whom the availability of something like Ubuntu is binary. It makes something profoundly possible that just isn't possible any other way. It's freely available, so there's no financial barrier, and it's easy for them to use. That's the first group, and that's a very important group for me personally.

Then there are developers—people who will express some of their creativity and their innovation through free software. If we can shift more and more of the brainpower in the world so that the smartest people in the world are saying hey, I've got an idea, and they are expressing that in the free software world rather than in the proprietary software world, then that's a profound impact.

The other thing that I want to do is make it sustainable. It's very important to me that we actually show that it's possible to create something that has a life apart from just my philanthropy towards it—something that is economically sustainable even though the product itself is entirely free. This applies in the commercial market as well—enterprises and data centers and also in call centers and other kinds of infrastructure. They are very important markets as well.

So, there's [the] three different groups that we try to address the needs of in each release.

Proffitt: *Well, speaking of new releases, you've got one coming out very soon. For the readers of this book, can you in brief describe some of the new features of Ubuntu and how it's going to look and be more effective than other desktop operating systems?*

Shuttleworth: Sure, and perhaps it would help if I sort of broke it down into things that are relevant to each of those three groups.

Proffitt: *Sure.*

Shuttleworth: For the folks who are not power users of technology, the next release, 7.04, has a lot more work to make things sort of just work out of the box—particularly around networking. On install, we're installing a utility which effectively gives you a visual indicator of all of the wireless networks around you, called *Network Manager,* to make it really easy to log onto a particular network or shift to a different network. It intelligently deals with changes in your network configuration.

So, for example, if you plug into the LAN and then disconnect, it will auto-matically look for wireless LANs that you've been on before, and that's a step towards making Ubuntu a more mobile, more sort of knowledge-worker friendly platform.

On the development side, we have a whole series of hooks now to identify problems in applications and to connect the person who is experiencing that problem directly to the developers. So if an application crashes, we have the ability to ask the user if they want to send all the details of that crash to a central database. We can pass those details onto the developer communities that are actually working on that project. So we can start providing much deeper and richer insight for the developers in the free software community as to how [the applications are] going wrong, where they're crashing, etc.

Some of those issues will be caused by changes that we made as part of this Ubuntu process of packing up and so on, but in many cases, the information is still extremely useful for the upstream. We're hoping that that's something that developers get excited about—that they will now have a very easy way to get very large-scale testing, quality assurance feedback, from millions and millions of Ubuntu users.

On the enterprise side, we have a few more people working on server-side features, so things like clustering and sort of higher availability setups are easier to do in this next release: more kinds of super stuff that addresses the needs of the folks in the supercomputer market, as well as just folks running large-scale data centers. Quite a few companies now are putting Ubuntu on servers, so we're putting more work into the infrastructure that makes it easy to deploy and manage those services. It's a fun thing for everybody.

Proffitt: *Okay, excellent. Your three-tiered approach—is that something that is going to be an ongoing feature of Ubuntu?*

Shuttleworth: Well, you know it would be wrong to simplify things just down to those three tiers.

Proffitt: *Sure.*

Shuttleworth: Ubuntu is also a series of communities within the overall project. So you have groups like the Edubuntu project, and they've got a release coming out where they've done a lot of work on classroom management, with this next release of Edubuntu, which is part of Ubuntu 7.04. It's going to be a new release of Edubuntu 7.04, and it will be a lot easier for teachers to coordinate work across the classroom so they can see more easily what a particular student is looking at or what they're doing. They can pass work more easily to a student or get all the students' computers turned on or off, and so on. So each of these different communities will have its own highlights and focal points.

The Xubuntu guys have a release that's coming out that's focused very much on sort of low-end computers, and it's sort of very lightweight, very efficient, and very fine. So it would be kind of wrong for me to characterize those three target groups as the only groups that the Ubuntu project is interested in serving. And there's also room for smaller, more focused communities to slide in underneath the border of the Ubuntu umbrella.

Proffitt: *I'm glad you brought those up because I wanted to talk about those next. About those different flavors of Ubuntu that you mentioned, Edubuntu and Kubuntu and Xubuntu—was that part of the original plan you had for the Ubuntu distribution, or did they sort of grow organically?*

Shuttleworth: No, the original plan was to create something that met the needs of the desktop user and then to take that to the point where it could be commercially sustainable. That clearly pointed to the desktop and clearly pointed to the server sort of environment. Some of these other groups that have kind of spontaneously sprung up inside of Ubuntu have been quite surprising. For example, the multimedia crowd with the Ubuntu Studio and the education crowd—it's been very gratifying to see communities saying okay, this is an umbrella project that we really identify with, and we think we can collaborate with it efficiently. We want to be part of it. So it's certainly scaled really well beyond what I had imagined it would.

Proffitt: *One last question before I let you go. The people that are going to be reading this book are going to be brand new users and maybe have never even seen a Linux distribution before. What you would say to a new Ubuntu user about why Ubuntu is something that they should use versus another operating system?*

Shuttleworth: What I'll say is that the real power of free software comes in two places: The first is in the ability to have complete control over how your infrastructure works and to go as far as reshaping some of the components themselves if it doesn't meet your needs. That's obviously something that people who see themselves as potential power users are going to be interested in because they will have run up against the limits and frustrations associated with the platform that is closed to them.

On the other side of the spectrum are folks who will probably be a bit nervous about taking on some things that are still in the early adoption phase. To them I would say that the thing they should most look for is the ability to connect with other people who are having a similar experience. And that really represents the essence of all of this, which is the community around the project as much as the project itself. Your experience of Ubuntu will be that much greater if you participate in the forum, if you hop online and talk with other users, if you find a niche where you can exchange ideas with other people who are interested in solving similar sorts of problems as you. So to them I would say come onboard. Welcome onboard.

Conclusion

In this chapter, you learned quite a bit about the history of the operating system you are about to install. This is important because if you understand where Ubuntu came from and how it is put together, you will understand the capabilities and the limitations of this popular operating system.

In Chapter 2, we'll spend some very important time making a plan for your Ubuntu installation. Will you use it exclusively or dual-boot your machine with Windows? Is your hardware going to be compatible with Ubuntu, or will you need to plan for some finagling to get everything to run smoothly? The beginnings of these answers will be explored in the next chapter.

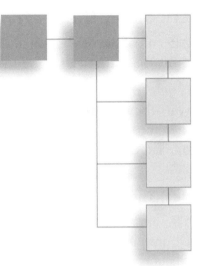

CHAPTER 2

BEFORE YOU INSTALL UBUNTU

You've made the decision: After hearing about this phenomenon known as *Ubuntu* from friends, family, or maybe the IT staff down at the office, you are going to try it out for yourself.

But installing an operating system is not as simple as installing an application like Photoshop or Firefox. While the Ubuntu developers have made the process as painless as possible, there's no getting around the fact that putting a new operating system on a PC is not something that should be done lightly. Unless you just bought the computer at the store and took it out of its box, there will be existing data on the machine that you will want to save.

Also, while Ubuntu is ultimately safer and faster than a Windows-based operating system, it's not perfect—sometimes things can go wrong. To prevent problems, a little prevention up front is well worth the time.

In this chapter, you'll do all the fact-finding and planning needed to successfully pull off your own installation of Ubuntu. Specifically, you will:

- Learn about the different flavors of Ubuntu and decide which is best for you.

- Discover how to obtain a copy of Ubuntu for yourself.

- Gather information about your computer to assess how well it will run with Ubuntu.

- Prepare your system for single or multiple operating systems.

Choosing the Right Ubuntu

After all of the discussion about all those different kinds of Linux, I'm sure you're thinking that at least it's nice there's just one Ubuntu.

If only. But not to worry. The differences between the versions are not so great—your choice at this point will really just come down to personal preference. And the nice thing is that you can switch to other Ubuntu flavors if you want to try one later.

Yes, There's More than One

You almost could say that Ubuntu is a victim of its own popularity. Because Ubuntu is so efficient and easy to use (among Linux distributions), developers of all persuasions have taken a good thing and molded it into something they prefer even more. These variations of Ubuntu follow a six-month release cycle (though they might be offset by a few days here and there). Most of the differences between the flavors of Ubuntu are purely cosmetic.

While this book will focus on the original Ubuntu, it won't hurt to take a quick look at the other variations, in case you see something you'd like to try later.

Desktop Environments

Before we discuss the differences between the flavors of Ubuntu, it would be a good idea to discuss *what* is different—specifically, the graphical interfaces that users work with when they work with any kind of Linux.

Most computer users are used to seeing just one graphical interface when they run their PCs. Windows XP and Vista Home Edition users get to use the basic Windows interface, Vista premium editions use the fancier Aero interface, and OS X users use Aqua. Graphical interfaces are the technical name for the windows, menus, and icons that so many computer users have grown accustomed to.

In these operating systems, you get the interface that comes with the OS. You can change the colors and the sizes of some items (bigger icons, for instance), but at the end of the day, you're still using the same interface.

In Linux, this is not the case: There are literally dozens of interfaces for you to choose from. This goes back to the whole modular nature of Linux. Unlike Vista, the interface applications are separate from the core operating system. So if something creates a glitch on a Linux interface, known as a *desktop environment,* the core operating system is not affected.

These desktop environments do more than just look different; they are managed by completely different tools, and each carries its own set of specialized applications. For example, a text editor (like Windows Notepad) called *Gedit* is available for the GNOME desktop environment, and in the

K Desktop Environment (KDE) the same kind of editor is known as *Kate.* (The first letter of an application is often a clue to the preferred environment for that application.)

Confusing? It shouldn't be. The good news is that applications for one desktop environment usually work in other environments without a hitch. (The author, for instance, prefers to work in KDE but won't part with the Gedit editor. The two work together quite well.)

Ubuntu

Ubuntu is the primary version amongst the Ubuntu "family" of variations, the one on which all the others are based.

One of Ubuntu's main characteristics is that it uses, by default, the GNOME desktop environment. GNOME, along with its predecessor KDE, is one of the most popular desktop environments around for Linux and other UNIX-based operating systems. It's often regarded as an easier-to-use environment, with fewer controls to worry about. Free software purists prefer it for the totally free nature of the code that is used to build GNOME (see Figure 2.1).

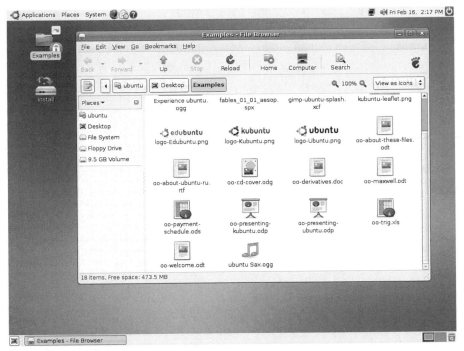

Figure 2.1
The Ubuntu desktop, featuring the Nautilus file manager.

Figure 2.2
The Kubuntu desktop, featuring the Konqueror file manager/browser.

Kubuntu

Kubuntu was the first "alternate" flavor of Ubuntu created, and as you might have guessed from the name, it features the KDE. KDE came before GNOME, but quite a few people in the Linux community don't like it because initially it was built with the help of nonfree code (the Debian Project initially would not ship releases with KDE). The GNOME project was started as a result of this concern. Today, the code in KDE is more open, and those objections have been rendered moot.

Kubuntu makes exclusive use of KDE and its attendant applications, as shown in Figure 2.2.

Xubuntu

This Ubuntu flavor uses the Xfce environment, a simple and fast environment based on the old UNIX CDE environment. It is the latest officially supported flavor of Ubuntu. Xfce takes a bit of getting used to because the graphic

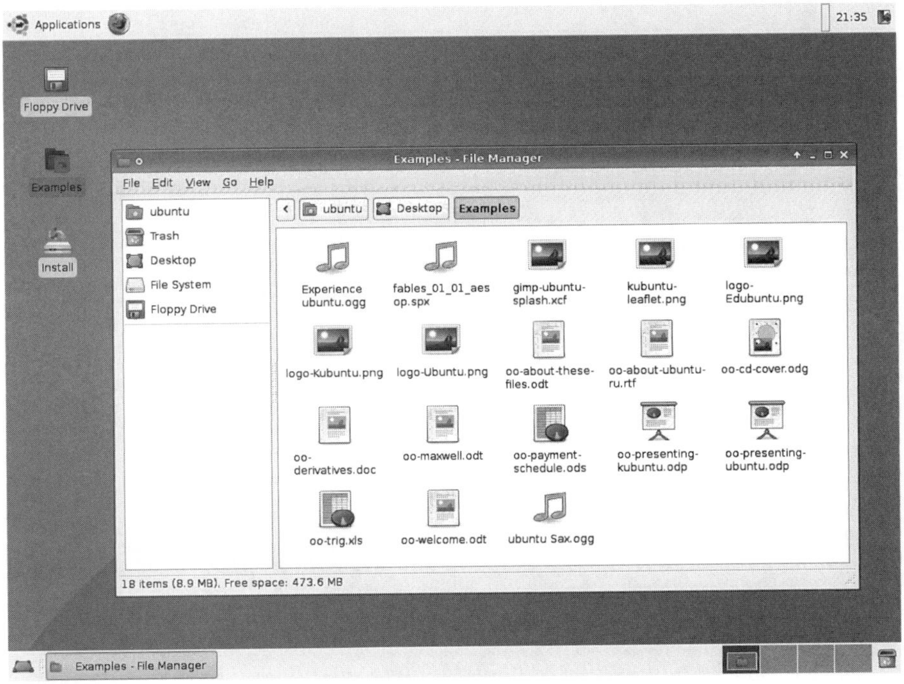

Figure 2.3
The Xubuntu desktop, featuring the Thunar file manager.

interface tools are a bit less intuitive than the more robust GNOME and KDE environments.

This gives Xubuntu the added advantage of not being as resource hungry as other Linux distributions and makes it ideal for running on slower, older PCs (see Figure 2.3).

Edubuntu

Unlike the other three official Ubuntu flavors, Edubuntu is not different because of its look or feel. Edubuntu's differences lie in the content and tools it provides to users.

Edubuntu is often referred to as the "kid's Ubuntu," and indeed, the addition of educational and gaming software certainly matches that description. But the overall goal of the project is to provide an easy-to-use distribution for all ages of students. According to the project's home page, "the current version of Edubuntu is aimed at classroom use, and future versions of Edubuntu will expand to other educational usage, such as university use."

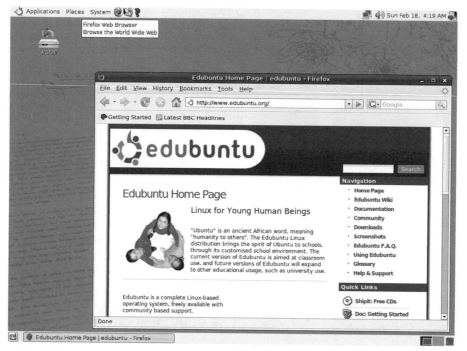

Figure 2.4
The Edubuntu desktop, featuring the Firefox browser.

As you can see in Figure 2.4, Edubuntu runs a GNOME desktop, with the differences mostly in the set of educational applications that ships with the distribution. These include various language, science, and math learning tools.

The Unofficial Flavors

The popularity of Ubuntu has led to the creation of a few "unofficial" flavors, each tailored to a very specific audience. The unofficial label is a bit misleading, as it might imply that there's something shady about these software offerings. On the contrary, as with all things Linux, people are free to do as they please with free software.

What makes these flavors unofficial is the decision by the main Ubuntu development team not to provide support for these versions. It takes a lot of work to put together, release, and then maintain a Linux distribution. The Ubuntu developers have to manage four. To add more would be difficult, even with the financial and logistical support of Canonical.

So if you choose to try one of these *distros*, don't look for support from the Ubuntu team (although they are typically similar enough to the core Ubuntu distro that what works as a solution in Ubuntu could work as a solution for these flavors).

What Is This "Distro"?

"Distro" is geek-speak for "distribution."

As of the printing of this book, there are seven unofficial released Ubuntu flavors. Four are modeled for users of a particular faith, one is very security oriented, one features another type of light-on-its-feet desktop, and one just includes everything.

In the religion category, there is Ubuntu CE, which stands for Christian Edition. It, like Edubuntu, is very similar to the main Ubuntu distribution. Ubuntu CE features a number of Christian-friendly applications, including a robust Bible study application (see Figure 2.5). Ubuntu CE has found an audience beyond faithful Christians, too, as it includes a powerful parental control tool to monitor and block unwanted Internet surfing.

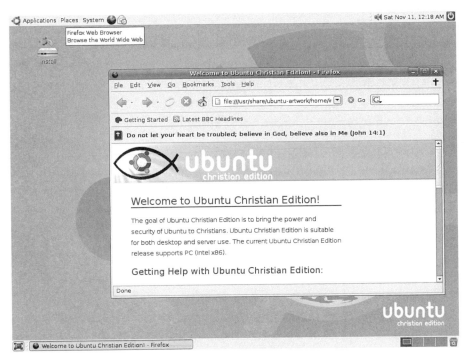

Figure 2.5
The Ubuntu CE desktop, featuring the Firefox browser.

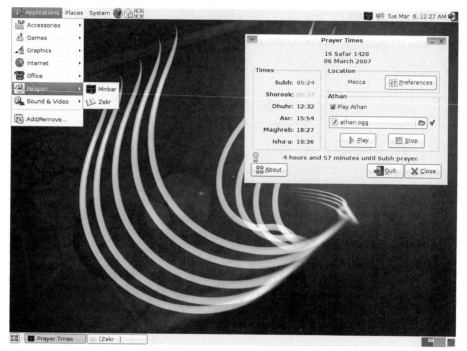

Figure 2.6
The UbuntuME desktop, featuring the Minbar prayer time application.

Another represented faith is Islam, with the new UbuntuME (Muslim Edition). Similar to Ubuntu, it features the GNOME desktop (though in an esthetically pleasing theme with green hues). Like Ubuntu CE, it includes useful tools for the faithful, including a prayer time application, a Quran study tool, and Arabic learning software (see Figure 2.6). It is the latest addition to the unofficial lineup.

A decidedly different flavor of Ubuntu, released not long after Ubuntu CE, is Ubuntu SE, with the S standing for "Satanic." A GNOME-based offering, this flavor of Ubuntu isn't really a separate offering. It doesn't offer anything different in the way of application content. It is just a set of specific GNOME themes that give this desktop—if you'll pardon the pun—a very hot, red look (see Figure 2.7).

Rounding out the collection of faith-oriented flavors is the Ubuntu Christmas Edition, which is perhaps the only seasonal flavor of Ubuntu (or Linux distribution, for that matter). This version, which debuted in 2006, has all of the appearances of just having a few extra holiday themes (see Figure 2.8), but under the hood are a great many applications not normally included in the general release of Ubuntu, because of their nonfree nature. No longer available, it has evolved into a new iteration of Ubuntu. But one wonders if it will appear again next December.

Figure 2.7
The Ubuntu SE desktop, featuring the Firefox browser.

In the category of alternative desktop offerings, there's Fluxbuntu. Fluxbuntu is very lightweight, as it features the Fluxbox window manager. A window manager is what desktop environments use to handle basic interface functionality, but they can also be run by themselves. Their appearance can be stark (as seen in Figure 2.9), but since very few system resources are devoted to handling the graphics, what you end up with is a very fast machine, no matter how old it is.

If security is your thing, you might want to look into nUbuntu (Network Ubuntu). It's a very light flavor of Ubuntu that does not include things like office applications or desktop environments. Like Fluxbuntu, nUbuntu runs Fluxbox as an interface, and what it includes in its application set is very sophisticated security and forensic tools (see Figure 2.10).

Finally, there's the one Ubuntu version that supposedly has it all: Ubuntu Ultimate Edition. Based on its predecessor Ubuntu Christmas Edition, UUE throws in every free and nonfree app its creators could think of for its users to have the most robust set of tools possible. Due to some licensing issues, it doesn't have everything, but it does a pretty good job (see Figure 2.11).

Figure 2.8
The Ubuntu Christmas Edition desktop.

That's all of the unofficial flavors—thus far. By the time this books hits the shelves, there may be more. And that's part of the beauty of Ubuntu: There's something out there for everyone.

What's with the Zoo?

Spend a little time working with Ubuntu (in any flavor), and you will likely hear some strange terms. Like "Dapper" or "Warty" or even "Edgy Eft." It's as if someone is describing some sort of weird zoo. Fear not—there aren't any exotic animals wandering around the world of Ubuntu...just some interesting code names.

As mentioned in Chapter 1, "What Is Ubuntu?," a new version of Ubuntu is released every six months, specifically in April and October. To note this, the version numbers for Ubuntu are not incrementally sequential. They don't go from 1.0, to 2.0, to 3.0, or whatever. Instead, the version numbers reflect the year

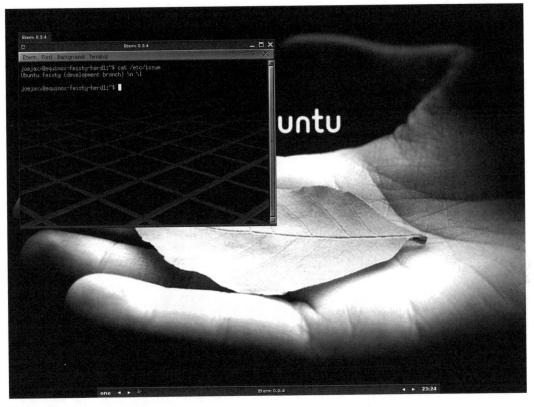

Figure 2.9
The Fluxbuntu desktop, featuring the Eterm application.

and month of the actual release. Hence, the most recent version of Ubuntu, which came out in April 2007, is version 7.04. When the next version comes out in October 2007, it will be version 7.10.

But version numbers can be a bit boring, especially for the freewheeling developers of Linux and Ubuntu. So beginning with version 4.10, which was the first Ubuntu release, code names were assigned to each release. Table 2.1 lists the code names and their version number.

You probably noticed the odd numbering for the June 2006 release, Dapper Drake. Dapper is different from the other Ubuntu releases because Canonical chose that release to implement something new: Long Term Support (LTS). To make Ubuntu more attractive to corporate users, who might be dissuaded by Ubuntu's normal 18-month support plan, Canonical decided to delay the release of Dapper by two months, giving it a more stringent quality control process.

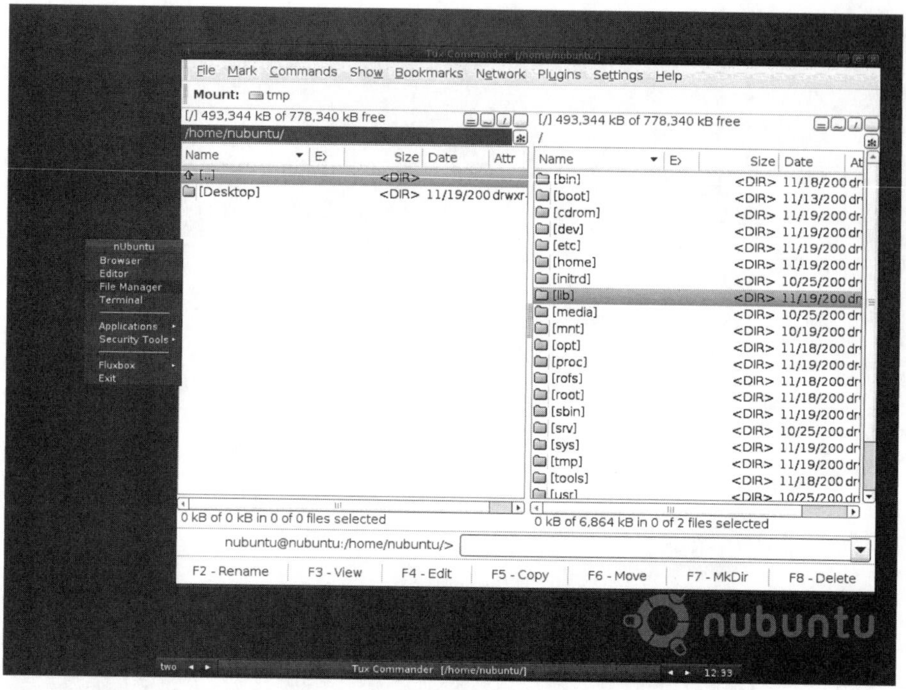

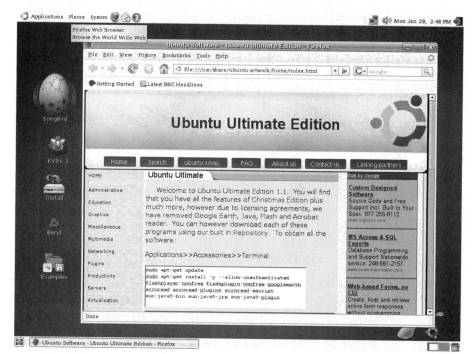

Figure 2.10
The nUbuntu desktop, featuring the Tux Commander file manager.

Figure 2.11
The Ubuntu Ultimate Edition desktop, featuring the Firefox browser.

Table 2.1 Ubuntu Code Names

Release Date	Version Number	Code Name
October 2004	4.10	Warty Warthog
April 2005	5.04	Hoary Hedgehog
October 2005	5.10	Breezy Badger
June 2006	6.06 LTS	Dapper Drake
October 2006	6.10	Edgy Eft
April 2007	7.04	Feisty Fawn
October 2007	7.10	Gutsy Gibbon

The end result was the most stable version of Ubuntu to date: 6.06 LTS. Dapper will be supported by Canonical until June 2009 for desktop installations and June 2011 for server installations.

Know What You Want Your PC to Do

With all of these choices for Ubuntu, it's pretty easy to get hung up on which one to pick. For the purposes of this particular book, the recommended flavor is going to be the main Ubuntu distribution itself. Beyond simplicity, there are a couple of good reasons for going with Ubuntu:

- **GNOME is a good first step.** Since GNOME is the default desktop environment on Ubuntu, this makes Ubuntu a good beginner's choice. GNOME is not as robust as other desktop environments, but it is simple to configure and has some fantastic eye candy.

- **Everything is available.** Choosing Ubuntu will not exclude you from the features of the other flavors. You can install software, change the look and feel, whatever you'd like.

For general desktop and small business use, Ubuntu is the recommended version to start with—at least until you get your feet wet.

The only exception to this suggestion is for users who are interested in installing Ubuntu in an academic setting. In this case, you might want to check out Edubuntu first. Edubuntu also uses GNOME, so most of the material covered in this book will apply to this flavor, if you want to look at it. The additional educational software is certainly worth exploring.

Getting Ubuntu

We've covered the menu of Ubuntu flavors; now it's time to order.

The simplest way to acquire Ubuntu is to use the CD included with this book. It contains a full-featured copy of Ubuntu 7.04, no different from anything you will download from the Internet.

Of course, sometimes CDs get damaged or lost. Or you may want to download future editions of Ubuntu. If that's the case, then the rest of this chapter will be useful to you to learn how to acquire Ubuntu.

Another easy way of obtaining Ubuntu is to purchase a select Dell desktop or laptop that comes with Ubuntu already installed. Dell began selling these pre-loaded Ubuntu machines in the summer of 2007.

Barring these options, getting your hands on Ubuntu is not as simple as driving down to the computer store and buying a boxed set of software. Very few Linux distributions are sold as retail, and Ubuntu is not one of them. Nor will it come already installed on a new computer, like Windows or OS X. No, Ubuntu is free, but you will need to invest some time in obtaining it.

Before you begin, let's review what you will need to lay your hands on a copy of Ubuntu if you don't have access to the CD from this book. At a *minimum*, you will need a working CD drive and at least a dial-up connection to the Internet. That's because this is all you need to get online and order a copy of Ubuntu sent to you (either free or at a very low cost).

Now, if you have broadband Internet access and a working CD or DVD burner drive, you can download the software and create your own CD. It takes a little time, but it's faster than waiting for the disc to arrive in the mail. Whatever you choose, getting Ubuntu is pretty simple.

Download Ubuntu

Downloading software has become a much more common practice than it used to be. The advent of broadband, plus some technological tricks to get the software into smaller packages so downloads won't take as long, has made this practice more common. If you have fast access to the Internet, this is the way to go.

Narrowband Options

It should be noted that the converse is also true: If you don't have broadband access, it is *not* recommended that you download Ubuntu for installation. You can do it, but on a standard 56 K dial-up connection it will take just over 29 hours at top speed. If you don't want to do this, see the "Getting a CD" section later in this chapter.

When you download Ubuntu, you are actually downloading what is known as an ISO image. A disc image (whether for CD or DVD) is analogous to a picture of all of the different 1s and 0s that will make up the contents of the disc you will eventually create. The advantage to this approach is you only have to download one (really big) file, instead of all of the hundreds of files that make up Ubuntu. The disadvantage is that you have to get a special application to create a CD from a disc image (which we'll discuss in the "Burning CDs/DVDs" section later).

Let's begin the acquisition process.

Via the Web

Getting Ubuntu from the Web is easy and (most notably) free. Except for the cost of the CD you will be burning later and your time, which won't be much, you'll soon have a full-featured operating system installed on your PC.

To begin, open your favorite Internet browser. In this book, the Firefox browser is being used, since it is free software, like Linux, and is a very robust application.

Where You're Coming From

As mentioned in the Introduction, it is assumed that you are using Windows XP before you implement Ubuntu.

1. Surf to the Ubuntu Web site at http://www.ubuntu.com (see Figure 2.12).

2. Click the Download link. The Get Ubuntu page will open (see Figure 2.13).

3. Click the Ubuntu 7.04 Desktop Edition radio button.

4. Click the appropriate computer type radio button. Typically, you should select the Standard Personal Computer option.

Figure 2.12
The Ubuntu home page.

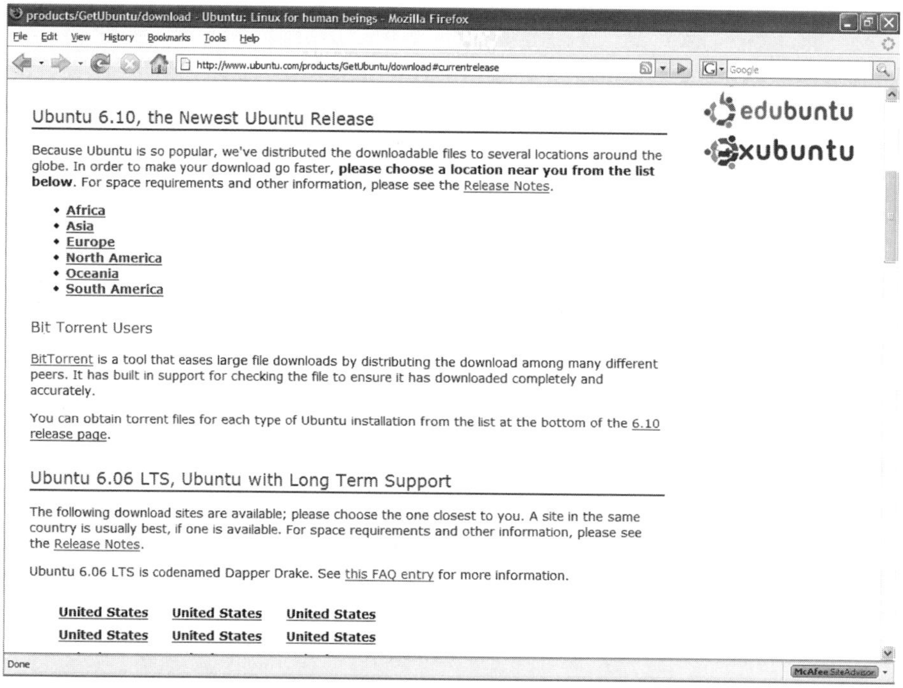

Figure 2.13
The Get Ubuntu page.

5. Select the appropriate Location option.

6. Click the link for the site that is closest to you. A list of download options will appear.

Local versus Global

Even though the Internet is a global network, and you could download your copy of Ubuntu from anywhere on the planet, it is still better to be as "local" as possible for any big download. The fewer network nodes (sort of like railroad yards for the Internet) a signal has to go through, the faster it is for you.

7. Click the Start Download link. Your browser will open the Opening ubuntu-7.04-desktop-i386.iso dialog box (see Figure 2.14).

8. Click the Save to Disk radio button.

9. Click OK. The download process will begin, and the file will be saved to the default location on your Windows PC.

Via Bittorrent

Even on a broadband connection, downloading a nearly 700 MB file is going to take some time. On the average day, this will be about 15 minutes, give or take. But if you are trying to get this disc image file when everyone else is trying to do the same thing, the time involved can stretch to hours as your browser patiently waits its turn to pull down the file, bit by bit.

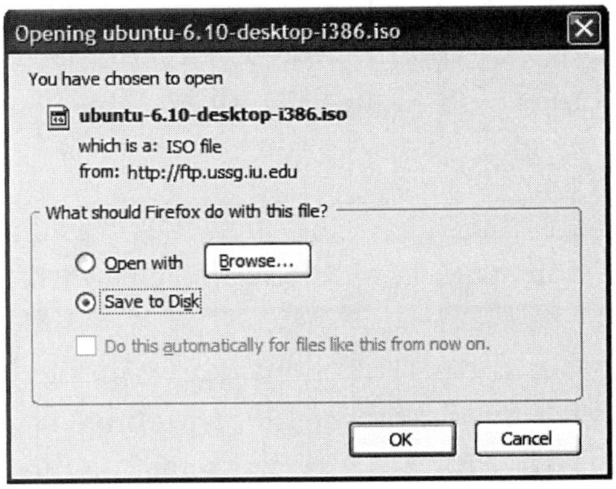

Figure 2.14
Your browser asks what you want to do with the image (.iso) file.

There is a way to download the file that typically avoids the traffic jams sometimes found at central file servers, using a relatively new method known as *Bittorrent*.

You may have heard of Bittorrent in the news or technology media outlets, because it is often (and erroneously) regarded as a tool for software pirates to download and transfer their illicit wares. Actually, there are many legitimate uses for Bittorrent: Downloading a Linux distribution like Ubuntu is certainly one of them.

Here's how it works: Instead of downloading files from a central server, Bittorrent downloads are shared by all of the people who want to obtain those files. At least one of the users in this group (known as a *swarm*) has all of the files. That is the seed computer. In a Bittorrent download, all of the computers in the swarm query each other and find out what parts of the download each machine has. If my computer needs part 863 of file 42, and computer B has it, I will download it from him. If my box has part 567 of file 23 and computer B needs it, it will download the piece of the file from me. If nobody in the swarm has it yet, a computer queries the seed computer, gets the needed piece of the file, and shares it with the rest of the swarm.

In this method, known as peer-to-peer or distributed downloading, no one computer has the burden of being the source for a given file or files. The traffic load is shared among all the members of the swarm. The neat thing is, that as more computers in the swarm acquire 100 percent of the files they need, those machines in turn become seeds. In this way, the process actually gets faster as time goes on.

There are many Bittorrent clients available for the three major operating systems, and you may have one already. One that can be recommended is Azureus, a robust Bittorrent client that can be used on Linux, OS X, and Windows. It's also (as a huge bonus), an open source software product.

Getting Azureus

To obtain your copy of Azureus, visit http://azureus.sourceforge.net with your favorite browser.

After you obtain a copy of Azureus, or any other Bittorrent client, you will need to find and download what's known as a *tracker file*. A tracker file, which is very small, tells your Bittorrent application where seeds and swarms that have the files you need are on the Internet.

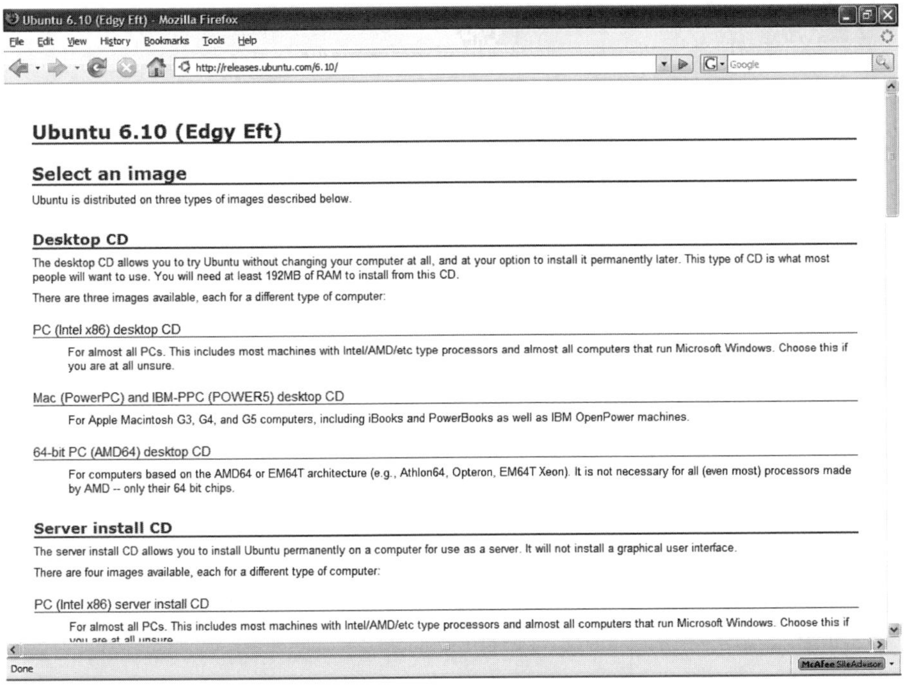

Figure 2.15
The Ubuntu Releases page.

Locating a Bittorrent tracker file is pretty simple, since Ubuntu keeps a list of them on its site. You just have to make sure you get the right file.

1. Surf to the Ubuntu Releases page at http://releases.ubuntu.com/7.04/ (see Figure 2.15).

2. Scroll down to the bottom of the page. A very detailed list of files will appear (see Figure 2.16).

3. Click the ubuntu-7.04-desktop-i386.iso.torrent link. Your browser will open the Opening ubuntu-7.04-desktop-i386.iso.torrent dialog box.

The Right Stuff

It is important that you click the correct link in this operation; clicking just the ".iso" link will start downloading the whole image file. Be sure that you click the ".iso.torrent" file link. Also, be sure "i386" appears in the name of the file, if you have a regular PC. If your PC happens to be 64-bit, click "ubuntu-7.04-desktop-amd64.iso.torrent".

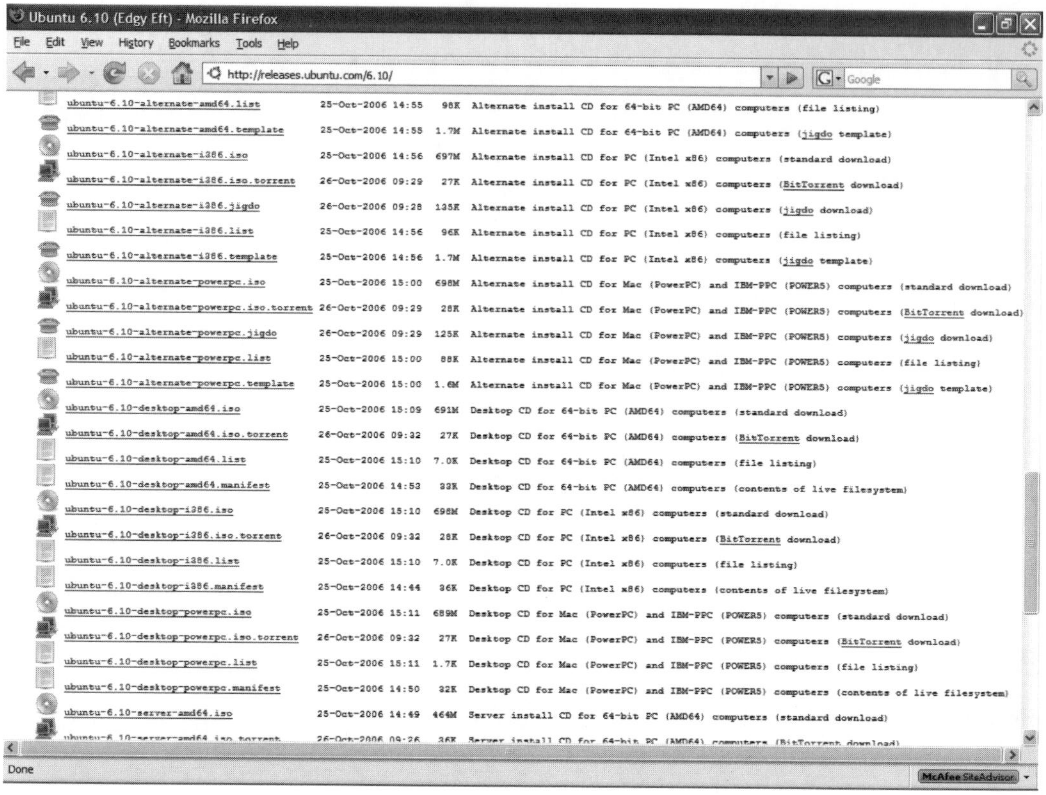

Figure 2.16
A multitude of files to download.

4. Click the Save to Disk radio button.

5. Click OK. The download process will begin, and the tracker file will be saved to the default location on your Windows PC.

After you have the tracker file, open your Bittorrent client and use the file to start your download of the actual image file. Using Azureus, this is a very simple process.

1. Open the Azureus application (see Figure 2.17).

2. Click the Open Torrents icon. The Open Torrents dialog will appear (see Figure 2.18).

3. Click the Add Files button. The Choose the Torrent File dialog box will open.

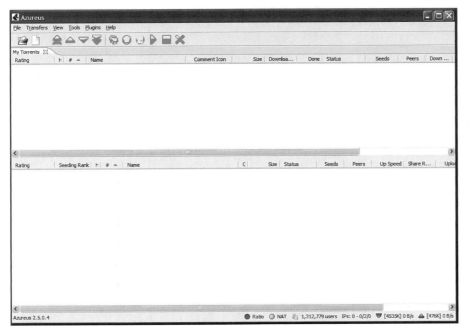

Figure 2.17
The Azureus application.

4. Navigate to the folder where the Ubuntu tracker (.torrent) file is saved.

5. Select the tracker file.

6. Click Open. The dialog box will close, and the information about the torrent contents will appear in the Open Torrents dialog box (see Figure 2.19).

7. Click OK. The Bittorrent download process will begin, and the image file will be saved to the specified location on your Windows PC.

Give and Take

Don't be a leech! This is what people who just download what they need and then turn off the Bittorrent application are called. The best way for torrent downloads to work is if you continue to share the download after you acquire the files. Your client should have a notation of share ratio—the amount of torrent uploaded compared to the amount downloaded. You should not stop the torrent process until that ratio is at least greater than 1.000, meaning that you have shared your files at least one complete time. The good news is, uploading is a much slower process than downloading, so leaving it on won't affect the rest of your Internet surfing very much.

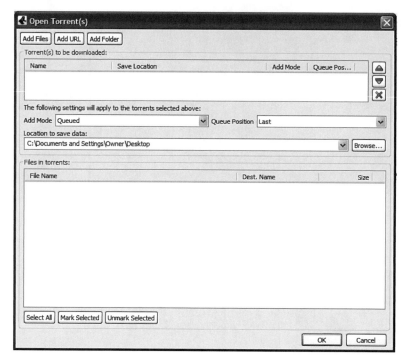

Figure 2.18
The Open Torrents dialog box.

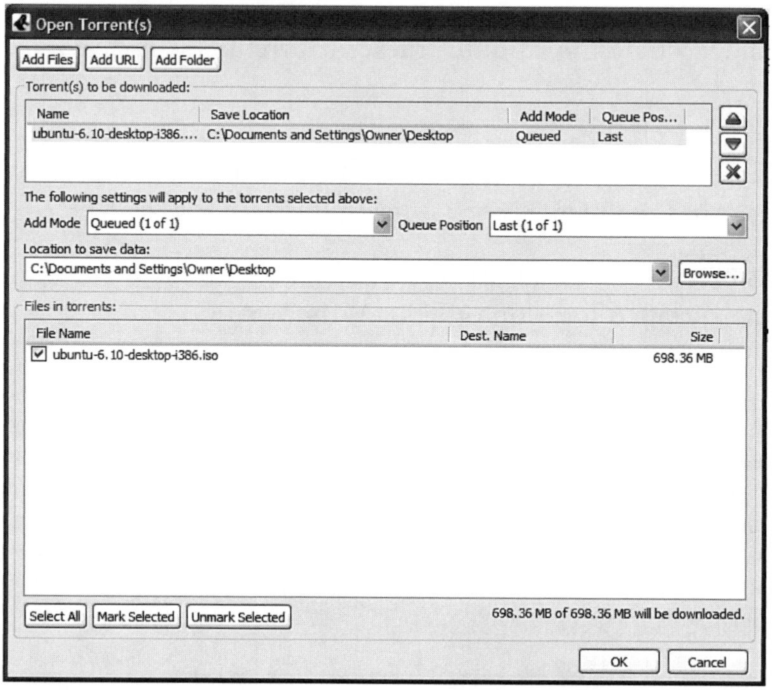

Figure 2.19
The files contained in your torrent can be examined.

Burning CDs

In whatever manner you get the Ubuntu image file to your computer, eventually you will need to create the actual CD you will use to install Ubuntu.

While Windows and OS X each have the capability to burn files onto a CD, burning an image file to a CD correctly is something that needs a separate application. There are many such applications out there, and most newer PCs that are sold with a CD-R burner device may already have such a helper application preloaded on the PC when it was purchased. Check your Windows application menu and see if it's there.

Even if you don't have such an application, it's easy to find them on the Internet. The application that Ubuntu recommends for Windows users is a free program called *Infra Recorder,* which can be found at http://infrarecorder.sourceforge.net/. If you download and install Infra Recorder, follow these steps to burn the image file onto a CD-R disc.

1. Insert a blank CD-R or CD-RW disc into your CD burner drive.

2. Open the Infra Recorder application (see Figure 2.20).

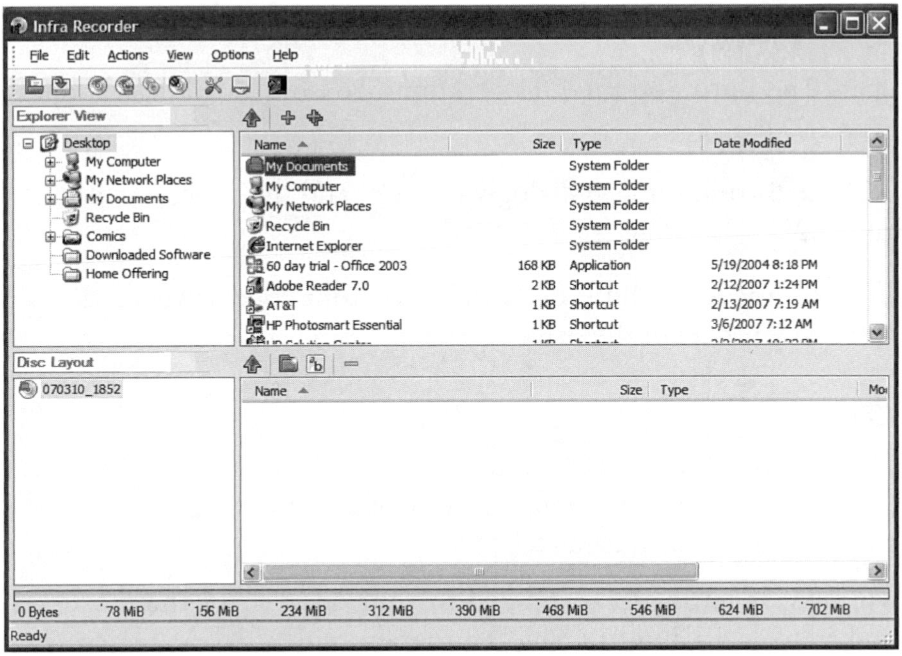

Figure 2.20
The Infra Recorder application.

Figure 2.21
The configuration settings for burning the image file to CD.

3. Click the Actions | Burn Image menu command. The Open dialog box will appear.

4. Navigate to the folder where the Ubuntu image file is saved.

5. Select the image file.

6. Click Open. The Burn ubuntu-7.04-desktop-i386.iso dialog box will open (see Figure 2.21).

7. Click OK. The Burning Image dialog will open, and the process will start (see Figure 2.22).

8. When finished, the new Ubuntu CD will eject from your drive. Click OK and remove the disc from the drive.

Getting a CD

If you don't have a broadband connection, or if all of the previous instructions seemed like a lot of work, you can obtain a copy of an Ubuntu CD that will be mailed right to your home or business.

There are two ways of getting CDs shipped to your door. First, the most economic method is to use Ubuntu's ShipIt program and order a free copy of

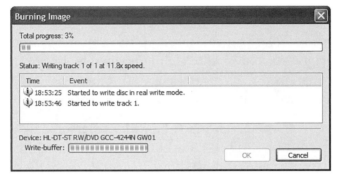

Figure 2.22
Burning the image file.

Ubuntu. This method, while free, is rather slow—it can take many weeks to receive a shipped Ubuntu CD.

Still, such a great deal deserves to be mentioned. All you need to do is point your browser to http://shipit.ubuntu.com. There, just click the "I want to request CDs of Ubuntu 7.04 (Feisty Fawn)" release link. You will then be asked to create a Launchpad account, from which you can order the free CDs.

Launchpad is Canonical's development community portal that allows community members to work on various Ubuntu-related projects. Signing up will merely include you in that community and enable you to participate in the ShipIt program.

Getting Kubuntu or Edubuntu

For free Dapper versions of Kubuntu, visit https://shipit.kubuntu.org. For Edubuntu, see https:// shipit.edubuntu.org.

Remember, the ShipIT program claims that shipping times take up to 6–10 weeks, so be patient.

If you want something a little faster or want the latest and greatest version of Ubuntu, you can purchase it for a nominal fee that will cover the cost of making the CD and shipping it to you. The best place to find a location near you that will sell new Ubuntu CDs is on the GetUbuntu page, located at www.ubuntu.com/ getubuntu/purchase. The page displays a concise list of sites where you can order a CD or DVD for your system.

Installation Preparation

You have the CD burned and ready. Now you can insert it into your drive and launch the installation process, right? Sure, if you're feeling invincible. But even the most avid Linux user knows that no software is perfect, and something could always go wrong.

Unless you are installing Ubuntu on a brand-new machine with no personal data on it, you should always back up your files so you can get to them later, whether something goes wrong or right. Even if you are installing a new machine, there are still some steps you need to take prior to installation.

Gathering Information about Your System

Ubuntu is a very robust operating system, and on most computers, it will install without a problem. But if there is a problem, it will likely be because Ubuntu did not recognize a piece of hardware on your PC.

There are various reasons why this happens, perhaps the biggest one being that there are so many different kinds of hardware out in the world that it is impossible for even the hard-working Ubuntu and Linux developers to keep up with them all. In a world where most hardware companies care only about working with Windows, the companies' developers generally don't spend time writing software drivers that will allow their devices to work on Linux. Fortunately, as Linux becomes more prevalent (thanks to easy-to-use distributions like Ubuntu), quite a few companies are seeing the error of this plan and are now working on Linux drivers.

There are still gaps in hardware coverage, unfortunately, and while most times those gaps are able to be closed with some work on the user's part, it helps if you know ahead of time.

Hardware Issues

Hardware concerns will be covered in Chapter 7, "Making Things Work."

If you're like most people, you may know the superficial information about your PC, like: "19-inch monitor, CD/DVD drive, printer, USB ports . . ." etc. To get a proper list for compatibility issues with Ubuntu, you will need to dig a little further. For some, this can be the most intimidating part of the installation, but really, it's not too bad.

As you begin examining your computer, you will first notice that a lot of the information you need to know is right there in front of you. Your monitor, for instance, is sitting on your table or desk with its brand name and model displayed on the front or back. Likely, the same is true for your printer and any other external devices you might have. You'll want to take note of both the brand name and model as they appear on the device.

In addition to identifying external devices, you'll need to determine what's actually inside your computer. One place to start is by displaying a list of devices as identified by your existing operating system. Windows XP and Vista use a built-in applet called the Device Manager to list known devices.

In Windows XP, open the Device Manager using the steps outlined here.

1. Click the Start button on the Windows taskbar; then select Control Panel. The Control Panel window will appear.

2. Click the Printers and Other Hardware icon. The Printers and Other Hardware page will open.

3. Click the System icon (located on the left side of the Control Panel window). The System Properties dialog will open (see Figure 2.23).

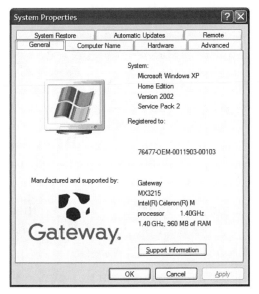

Figure 2.23
The System Properties dialog box is the home of the Device Manager.

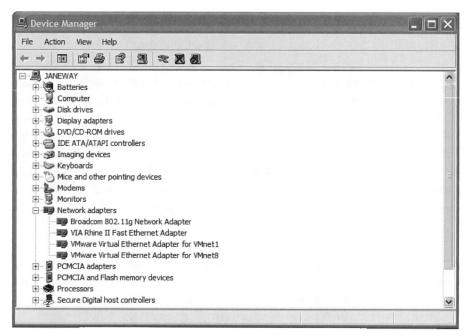

Figure 2.24
The Device Manager will show you nearly every hardware device used by your computer (at least as identified by your current operating system).

4. Click the Hardware tab. The Hardware page will be displayed.

5. Click the Device Manager button. The Device Manager, which lists the inner workings of your computer, will appear as shown in Figure 2.24.

Now you need to do some old-fashioned detective footwork. Your computer may (or may not) actually use a device for each of the device types listed in the Device Manager. For example, to determine what kind of CD-ROM drive is installed in your computer, first expand the DVD/CD-ROM drives list by clicking its expansion control (the little plus sign in a box) shown in Figure 2.25.

As you can see in Figure 2.25, this computer has one CD-ROM drive, with a rather cryptic label. To find out more about a device, double-click the desired device. The Properties dialog box for the CD-ROM drive appears (see Figure 2.26).

This is a classic example of a device that has been made to conform to Windows' standards—so much so that Windows does not care who manufactured it. As far as Windows is concerned, this is just a standard CD-ROM drive. It is still a good

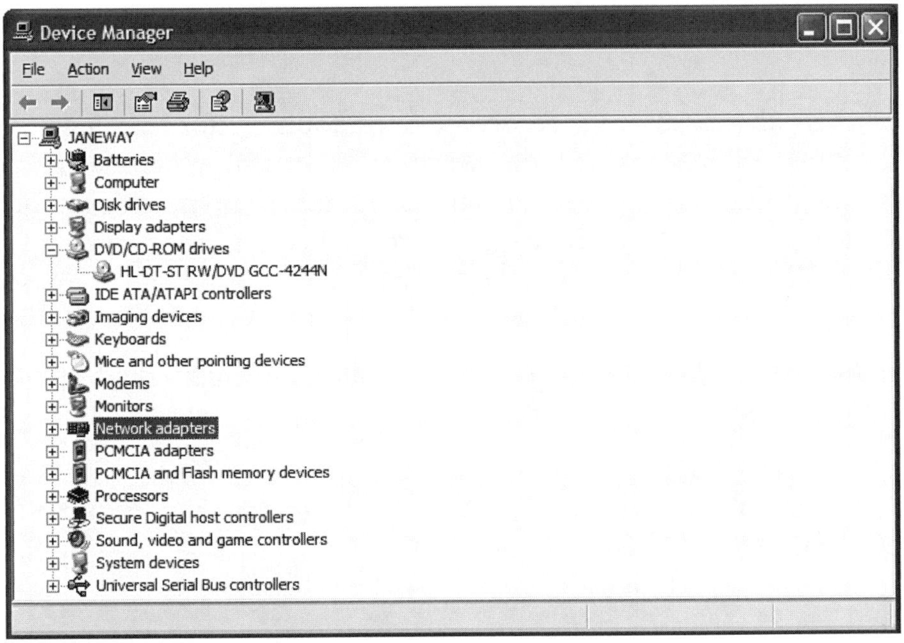

Figure 2.25
Open a list of devices by clicking the expansion box.

Figure 2.26
Not too much information here, but every little bit helps.

idea to record the nongeneric information, in case there is a hiccup later with Ubuntu.

You may find that other books urge readers to keep a journal for tracking and recording all of their PC's hardware along with any other issues that may arise while installing Ubuntu. This approach has merit, but there's no need to get out the pencil and paper. In the Device Manager, there is a Print icon you can use to just print out all of the information Windows knows about the hardware on your PC.

You will find this printed document full of very technical information—most of which you will not need. Still, it saves time writing it all down.

To successfully install Ubuntu and troubleshoot it later if problems arise, the most important information you need is for those devices that make your computer most operable, as listed in Table 2.2.

Table 2.2 Important Hardware Information Needed for Ubuntu Installation/Troubleshooting

Hardware	Information Needed
CPU	Manufacturer, Model, Speed
Motherboard	Manufacturer, Model
Buses	Manufacturer, Model
Memory (RAM)	Size
Video Card	Manufacturer, Model, Video RAM size, Chipset
Sound Card	Manufacturer, Model
Monitor	Manufacturer, Model, Horizontal and Vertical Synchronization Rates
Hard Drive	Manufacturer, Model, Size, Type (SCSI vs. IDE)
Network Card	Manufacturer, Model
CD-ROM Drive	Manufacturer, Model, Size
Floppy Drive	Manufacturer, Model, Size
Modem	Manufacturer, Model, Transmission Speed
Printer	Manufacturer, Model
Mouse	Manufacturer, Model, Type (PS/2, Serial, or USB)
Keyboard	Manufacturer, Model, Number of Keys, Language
SCSI Card and Devices	Manufacturer, Model, Type of Device Controlled
IDE Adapters	Manufacturer, Model, Type of Device Controlled

Most of the information you require is included in the Device Manager output you printed, but not all. For example, you can locate information on the amount of RAM installed on your computer by clicking the General tab in the System Properties dialog box. Another option might be to right-click the hard drive icon displayed in My Computer and select the Properties option to see how large your drive space is. A little detective work will go a long way toward making your Ubuntu installation easier.

Backing Up Your Data

After you have ascertained your hardware setup, you will need to take the next step to get your computer ready for the installation: backing up the data on your PC.

It is always a good idea to back up your valuable data, guarding against system catastrophe. At the very least, you'll want your data protected from power surges, virus attacks, computer theft, or anything else that could affect your ability to access the data on your machine.

Installing Ubuntu certainly can't be classified as a catastrophic event. But depending on how you are going to be changing your hard drive's partitions or perhaps even formatting your hard drive, these events can and will erase data completely.

The first thing you should decide is what data should be backed up. That really depends on what you want to do in your Ubuntu installation. Especially if you plan to perform a dual boot (running Windows and Ubuntu on the same PC), then you will need to make sure you've safeguarded most of your Windows data.

Completely Replacing Windows

Even if you plan to completely remove Windows and install Ubuntu in its place, there is still merit to saving your data files. Most files created in Windows can be opened in Ubuntu, such as graphic files (GIFs, JPEGs, PNGs) and Adobe Acrobat (PDF) files. In addition, Microsoft Office files can even be opened, compliments of a great office suite application called *OpenOffice.org* that is fully Office compatible. You'll need to save, not back up, these files if you plan to use them on your Ubuntu machine, though. Ubuntu will not be able to read a

Windows backup file. If this is the case, use an external hard drive or a Flash memory stick (also known as a *thumb drive*) and directly save your data files to such a device using Windows Explorer. You will be able to use Ubuntu to retrieve them later.

Prepping for Dual Boot

If you are planning on dual booting your machine, a backup operating system is needed to ensure that you can still get to your Windows side in case something goes wrong with the setup. Most computer applications these days use huge amounts of disk space, primarily because today's big hard drives enable them to do so. Backing up your data and your application files is, therefore, a big job. If you have sufficient storage capacity (such as one of those external hard drives or a really big Flash memory stick), then it is recommended you back up your entire hard drive.

For those of you who do not have a sufficient large-capacity device to hold an entire drive's worth of data, then just back up your data files. Your data files are the documents, spreadsheets, drawings, and other files that you have created over time on your computer. If you do run into trouble, you can restore your system by first reinstalling your operating system and your applications using your original disks and then restoring your archived personal data files.

If you have never used a backup program, you will find them easy to use. Many backup programs are available, including an excellent one found with Norton System Utilities. The principles for backup utilities are pretty much the same: locate and identify the files you want to archive, specify the location of the new archive file, and then create the file. Restoration is simply the reverse of this action.

Microsoft Windows has its own utility for backup that can be used to archive your data. The next steps describe how to work with the Windows Backup utility.

1. Click Start | All Programs | Accessories | System Tools | Backup. The Backup or Restore Wizard application will open (see Figure 2.27).

2. Click Next. The Backup or Restore page will appear, as shown in Figure 2.28.

Figure 2.27
Microsoft's Backup utility.

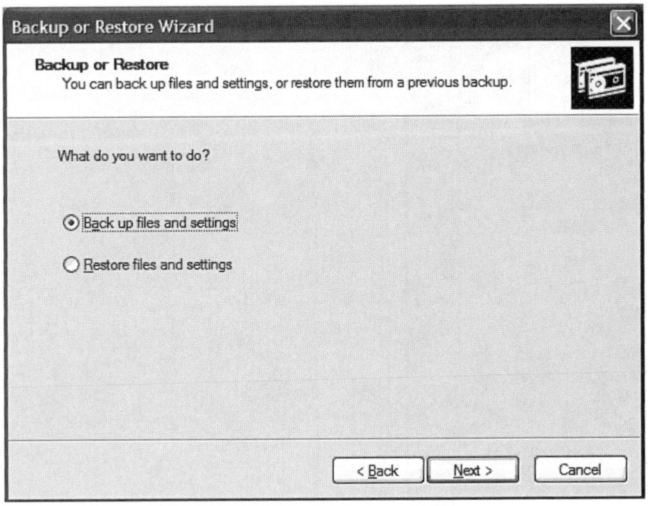

Figure 2.28
Backing up or restoring?

3. Click the Back Up Files and Settings radio button and then click Next. The What to Back Up page will appear (see Figure 2.29).

4. Here you can choose to back up your entire set of computer files, or you can choose to back up only selected files. Select the Let Me Choose What to Back

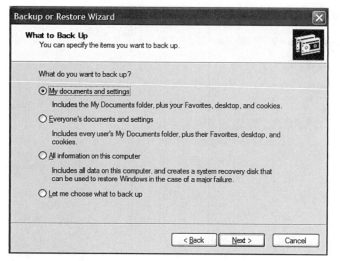

Figure 2.29
You can select what files you want to back up.

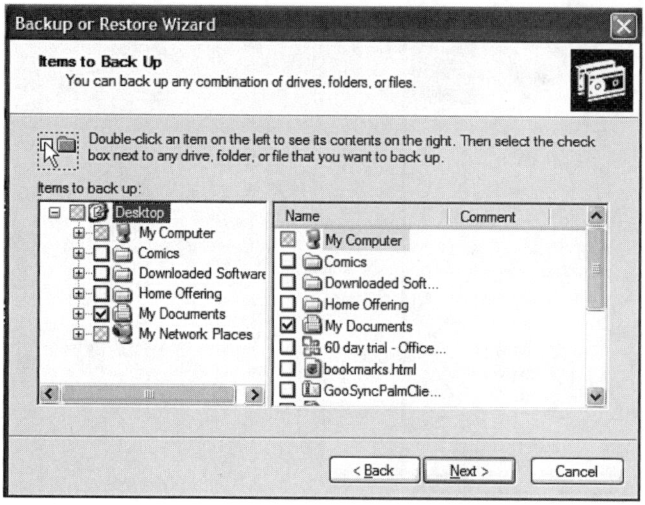

Figure 2.30
You can select all or part of a folder's contents.

Up radio button; then click Next. The Items to Back Up page appears (see Figure 2.30).

Backing it All Up

If you have the storage space, go ahead and click the All Information on This Computer radio button and proceed with the remaining steps of the Backup or Restore Wizard.

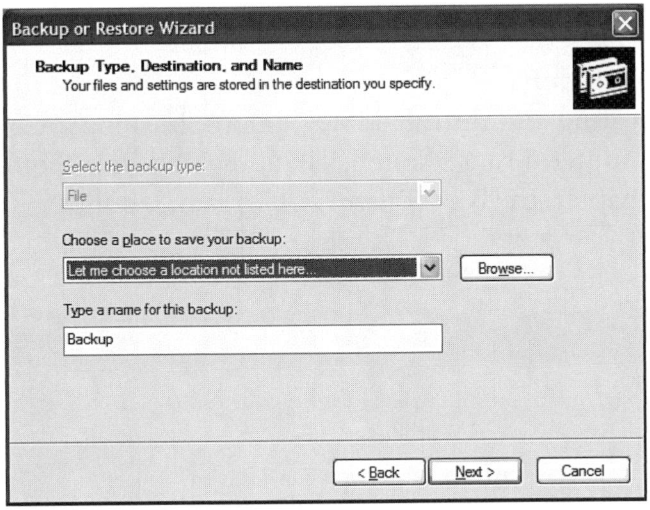

Figure 2.31
Choose where to store the backup file.

5. On the left side of the dialog box, select the check boxes for the drives and folders you want to back up. As necessary, use the expansion icons in the directory listing to view subfolders. Note that selecting a folder automatically selects all of the files within the folder. Alternatively, select or clear the check boxes for the specific files you want to include or exclude from the file list on the right side of the dialog box.

6. Click Next. The Backup Type, Destination, and Name page will appear (see Figure 2.31).

7. Choose your preferred location and type a file name for your backup file. When complete, click Next to continue. The final page will appear.

Where to Save

Make sure you save this information on a drive other than your hard drive. Secondary hard drives and external hard drives are good places.

8. Click Finish. The backup process will begin.

Make sure the backup file is stored away from your hard drive. As you will see in the next section, big changes are coming to your drive.

Conclusion

In this chapter, you learned the essential steps in preparing your machine for installing Ubuntu, including locating and downloading Ubuntu, burning a CD or DVD, and prepping your computer for installation. That preparation is about to pay off, because in the next chapter, the big moment has arrived: Ubuntu will very shortly be running on your computer.

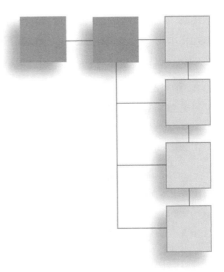

CHAPTER 3

INSTALLING UBUNTU

Now comes the moment of truth. You've done the homework, figured out how you want to install your copy of Ubuntu, and you're ready to go.

This chapter won't disappoint you. Its sole goal is to walk you through the installation process using the Ubiquity graphical installer. Along the way, you will:

- Discover how to explore Ubuntu—without installing it.

- Choose which option will be best for you: installing Ubuntu alone or alongside another operating system.

- Journey step-by-step through the installation process.

- Create one or more users for your Ubuntu machine.

Try Before You Buy

This section may leave you scratching your head and wondering why you just went through all of the preparation in Chapter 2, "Before You Install Ubuntu." Be patient, there's a method to my madness.

Since Ubuntu 6.06 LTS (Dapper Drake), all official versions of Ubuntu have been available to users as a LiveCD version. "LiveCD" is the label for operating systems that can be booted and run *right from the CD itself*. Without installation.

This means that when you insert your Ubuntu CD into the disc drive and restart your computer, it will automatically begin running on your computer without putting any new files or touching pre-existing data on your machine. It just starts up and runs.

So why, you ask, should I bother installing Ubuntu at all? I can just run it from the CD. Well, this is true, and many people do—especially when they are using someone else's PC and don't want to use the pre-existing operating system. Why use Windows on your friend's computer when you can just insert your Ubuntu LiveCD and have a more familiar environment ready to go?

The first issue is speed: Running any operating system from the CD drive means it will be a much slower process. Data has to be pumped in constantly from the drive, and only the fastest drives will give you any kind of decent user experience.

If your system is low on RAM, performance of the LiveCD will take an even bigger hit. When an operating system and its applications run, they use the RAM memory as a workspace to perform their operations. The more memory that's available, the more efficiently the apps will run. But once there are a lot of applications running, the RAM gets filled up. To keep up with the demand, the operating system uses space on the disk drive known as *swap space* to help fulfill memory needs. This is why you will hear your hard drive churning away when you're running a lot of stuff on your computer. Using swap space is slower, but it gets the job done.

When to Upgrade the RAM

If you hear your hard drive working a lot—even when you are using just one or two applications, it's probably time to consider getting more RAM installed on your machine. It not only speeds your operations up, but it will save a lot of wear and tear on your hard drive.

When you run a LiveCD, however, the swap space option does not apply, since Ubuntu from the CD won't touch your drive's data. If your system does not have a lot of RAM installed, be prepared for a slow LiveCD operation.

Slow operation notwithstanding, the advantages of the LiveCD are that it lets you take your operating system with you, as mentioned before, and—something that benefits you right now—it lets you try Ubuntu before you "buy" it. Buy, in this case, means install.

Everything in the LiveCD instance of Ubuntu matches what you would get if you installed Ubuntu onto your PC. All you need to do is insert the disc into your CD drive and reboot your PC.

You will see a text menu on a black screen asking you what you want to do. The preselected option is Boot or Install, so you don't have to do anything else. After a bit more of a wait (another disadvantage of using LiveCDs), Ubuntu will eventually come up on your screen, as shown in Figure 3.1.

If, at this point, you want to explore the Ubuntu operating system, you are invited to skip ahead to Chapter 4, "Desktop Basics," to begin your exploration.

If you are ready to go ahead and install Ubuntu, there is one more issue that needs to be addressed: whether you share your PC with Windows.

Figure 3.1
The Ubuntu LiveCD desktop.

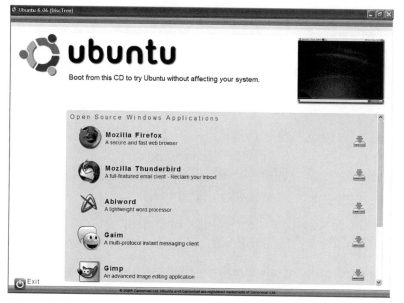

Figure 3.2
Open source goodness for your Windows.

Something for Everyone

One extra bonus that's contained on the Ubuntu CD is something that Windows users will definitely get a benefit from: a collection of free and open source software applications that will run on the Windows platform. All you have to do is insert the CD into the drive during an active Windows session, and the DiscTree window will appear, listing the available apps (see Figure 3.2).

These are all very mature applications, and they're all free for you to install and try out. If you do plan on keeping a Windows partition running, it is highly recommended that you use these applications, if only to maintain continuity with the applications that will be installed with Ubuntu.

One or Two Operating Systems?

Now comes the time where you have a really important decision to make. Like all important decisions, you should weigh your options carefully. You must decide whether you are going to run Ubuntu alone on your PC, or whether you want to retain Windows and be able to switch back and forth between it and Ubuntu. This section will examine the pros and cons of each side of the decision and give you tips on what to do if you decide to dual boot your system.

Making Room for Multiple Operating Systems

There are several pros and cons for using multiple operating systems on one computer. The cons include the headaches of installing two or more operating systems on a machine, resulting in more limited hard drive space available for each of the operating systems.

But the benefits of using multiple operating systems are huge. For instance, you will have the ability to run all of the programs available for each of the operating systems you'll have on your PC. You will also be able to use all of the hardware your PC has. Finally, you'll save money by not needing to buy another PC.

It is recommended that dual booting is the way you should go—especially if you have Windows applications that you just can't part with and which have no counterparts in Ubuntu. This option gives you the benefits of using Ubuntu without a lot of investment in time or money.

If you decide to include Ubuntu on your PC in addition to Windows, you will need to make room for it on your hard drive. But making room on your hard drive for Ubuntu is a far different operation than making room for the latest computer game. You will need to create a brand new *partition* from which Ubuntu will operate.

Here is a crash course in disk partitions and why you can't write data to a disk without them.

Why Partition?

Imagine the bee, buzzing around your garden. If you were to follow this bee back to its home, you would find a seemingly chaotic mass of buzzing insects, each looking as if they aimlessly wander about with nothing better to do than hang out and buzz.

But as we all know, bees all have a specific purpose, working together for the collective benefit of the hive. One group of bees has the job of taking care of all of the cute little baby bees after the queen lays her eggs. Now, think back to your science classes: Where are the baby bees raised?

If you said the honeycomb, you're right. If you're wondering what this has to do with partitions, hang on.

The honeycomb is an ingenious device composed of hexagonal cells made of beeswax, where honey and bee larvae are stored for safekeeping. Ponder this:

How would the bees get by if they did not have honeycombs? The answer is they wouldn't.

Keeping the honeycombs in mind, you can apply this analogy to how data is stored on a disk drive. Data, you see, cannot be stored on a drive without some sort of structure already in place for the data to be organized.

When data is placed on a drive, it is written into this structure, called a *filesystem* in the Linux community. A filesystem is the format in which data is stored—a honeycomb of cells if you will, where each little piece of data gets placed.

Computers being computers, it's a little more complicated than that. Data for a single file, for example, does not get stored in data blocks that sit right next to each other. The data may be stored in data blocks 456, 457, and 458 and then block 6,134, then block 7,111, and so on. (This is an oversimplification, but you get the idea.) It's the job of the filesystem to track where each file resides so that when you send a command to work with a file, the filesystem knows all of the separate blocks where the file is stored.

Because of all of this file tracking and retrieving, computer engineers came up with the idea of keeping the filesystems small, even on large hard drives. So the idea of partitions came into play. Basically, the partition is a virtual barrier that tells the filesystem: "You used to be able to write to blocks 1–25000 all over the disk, but now you're only allowed to write to blocks 1–17500. A second filesystem will write to blocks 17501–25000, so hands off!"

Thus, you have partitions. And each partition can use a different filesystem. As an analogy, honeycombs created by honeybees are different than those created by wasps—similar structure but different outcomes.

If your PC contains a typical installation of Windows, your Windows filesystem is contained within one big partition that covers your entire hard drive. This leaves no room for another partition and a new filesystem. Remember, even if you have gigabytes of empty space on your drive, this space, like files and directories, may be scattered throughout the drive and still belongs to the Windows partition.

The easiest method to add a partition to your existing hard drive filesystem is to use a third-party application. This shoves your existing partition into a single, smaller collection of data blocks, leaving truly contiguous empty and unstructured (unformatted) space elsewhere in the drive where you can install a partition in which Ubuntu can reside.

Back Up Your Data

Before you use any tool to manipulate or create partitions, back up or save your data to an alternate physical drive. Please.

Partitions Ubuntu Will Need

When Ubuntu is installed, it uses an eight-step application known as *Ubiquity* to accomplish the task. When Ubiquity detects another operating system on your computer, it will ask you whether you will want to replace the contents of your entire hard drive or perform a manual partition operation.

This is the choice point that will determine if you have a single Ubuntu operating system on your computer or multiple ones (Ubuntu and Windows). The mechanics of how to go through this procedure will be outlined in the "Partition Settings" section later in this chapter. For now, there are recommendations that should be passed on to new Ubuntu users.

In Windows systems, the filesystem is oriented towards a key root directory that is based on the drive letter of the hard drive. For most primary drives, that drive letter is "C," so the root directory in Windows is denoted as C:\. Other drives have root directories (D:\, E:\, etc.), too. The root directories are always tied to the physical drive or partition, and all the subdirectories (or subfolders as they're called in Windows) are directly descended from the root directory on the same physical drive. C:\Documents and Settings\Brian\My Documents will always be located on the primary (C:\) drive or partition.

The filesystems in Ubuntu are a bit more flexible. For instance, the common path for a user's home directory is /home/<username>. The "home" is a subdirectory of the root folder, which is denoted in Linux-based systems as "/". So, in the author's case, the home directory is /home/bproffitt. Here's the default directory structure for an Ubuntu machine.

```
/
/bin
/boot
/cdrom
/dev
/etc
/home
/initrd
/lib
```

```
/media
/mnt
/opt
/proc
/rofs
/root
/sbin
/srv
/sys
/tmp
/usr
    /var
```

Odd names aside, it looks similar to a set of Window folders, doesn't it? A bunch of directories in a nice tree pattern, all located on the same partition. Except while this listing reflects the typical Ubuntu filesystem, it does not mean all of these directories are located on the same partition.

That is because of a unique UNIX filesystem property known as *mount points*. If you want, you can decide to put any directory on any drive or partition, and Ubuntu's file management will seamlessly copy, retrieve, save, or delete files wherever they are physically located.

Using the author's system as an example, the root (/) directory's mount point is located on /dev/hda2, which denotes the third partition ("2") of the primary ("a") hard drive (''dev/hd''). But the mount point for the /home directory (and all of its subdirectories) is located on /dev/hda3, a completely separate partition. The advantages to this are that the personal data that belongs to the author will always be stored on a separate partition, which means that if ever it were necessary to migrate to another Linux distribution or perform a clean installation of a future version of Ubuntu, that personal data would always be preserved and the files accessible though the /home directory in Ubuntu's filesystem.

You can mount different directories of the Ubuntu filesystem on any partition or drive, even different drives, if your PC is so equipped.

When you use Ubiquity's partitioning tool to set up your drive, it is obvious that you will need to devote some space to your existing Windows operating system and some to Ubuntu. How much? The easy answer is simply to divide your drive in half, with each OS getting a fair share of the pie. Many other factors may play into making that choice differently.

If, for example, you have a small drive upon which Windows is taking up a lot of space, then you will need to be conservative with your Ubuntu installation.

Space Available

You will need at least 3GB of disk space to handle an average Ubuntu installation. Figure at least 2 more GB of storage space, unless you have some sort of networked storage devices available.

While you are considering the amount of space you will need to set aside for Ubuntu, also make sure that you have enough to allocate for swap space on your drive. It is often hard to determine how much swap space to create, because different users need differing amounts based on the type of work they do. If you work with a lot of really big files (graphics, desktop publishing), you should set your swap space memory to be pretty high, such as double your system's RAM capacity. For most users, the rule of thumb is that the swap should equal 1.5 times your RAM. No matter what you choose, it is important to remember not to set swap space at more than 2 GB; Ubuntu, like most operating systems, doesn't handle anything higher.

Running Ubiquity

For older versions of Ubuntu—and, indeed, for older versions of any Linux distribution—starting an installation was a matter of inserting the CD into the drive and rebooting your system. The installation application would be presented as a choice on the initial menu, and once selected, off the installation would go.

Today, with the LiveCD option for Ubuntu, starting the installation is even less strenuous. As you may have noticed in Figure 3.1, there is a nice little Install icon on the desktop when you run the Ubuntu LiveCD. After you double-click that icon, the Ubiquity installation application will start.

Ubiquity is a seven-step installation routine that begins with a Language Setup screen, detailed in the next section.

Let's walk you through what happens, so you will know what to expect.

Language Settings

One of the excellent benefits of developing free software around the world is the really good language support. Ubuntu is certainly a beneficiary of this. Step 1 of Ubiquity (shown in Figure 3.3) lists the 57 different language options (plus one nonlocalization option that defaults to English) available to Ubuntu users.

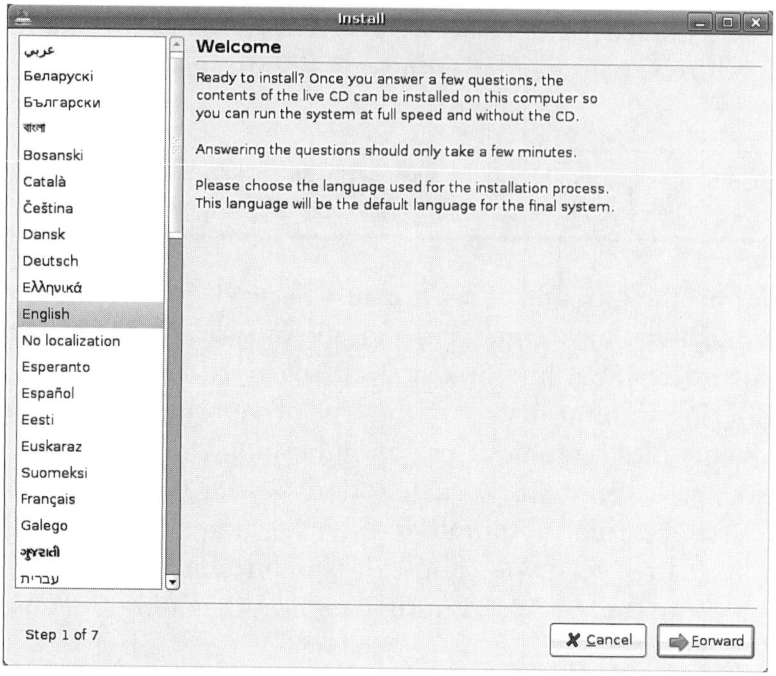

Figure 3.3
The many languages of humanity.

Clearly, some of these are not understandable to everyone, unless you're a linguist. The basic rule here is simple: If you can't understand the language option, don't select it.

Do select the appropriate language for you; then click Continue to move to Step 2.

Time Zone Settings

Step 2 of Ubiquity displays a map of the world, with which you can determine your proper time zone settings (see Figure 3.4).

If you want to use the map, first guide the mouse to your local region. Notice that the mouse cursor has changed to a magnifying glass with a plus sign. Clicking the desired region will zoom in (albeit slowly) to that region, as shown in Figure 3.5.

Don't Get Lost

If you accidentally zoom in on the wrong region, right-click on the map to return to the whole-world view.

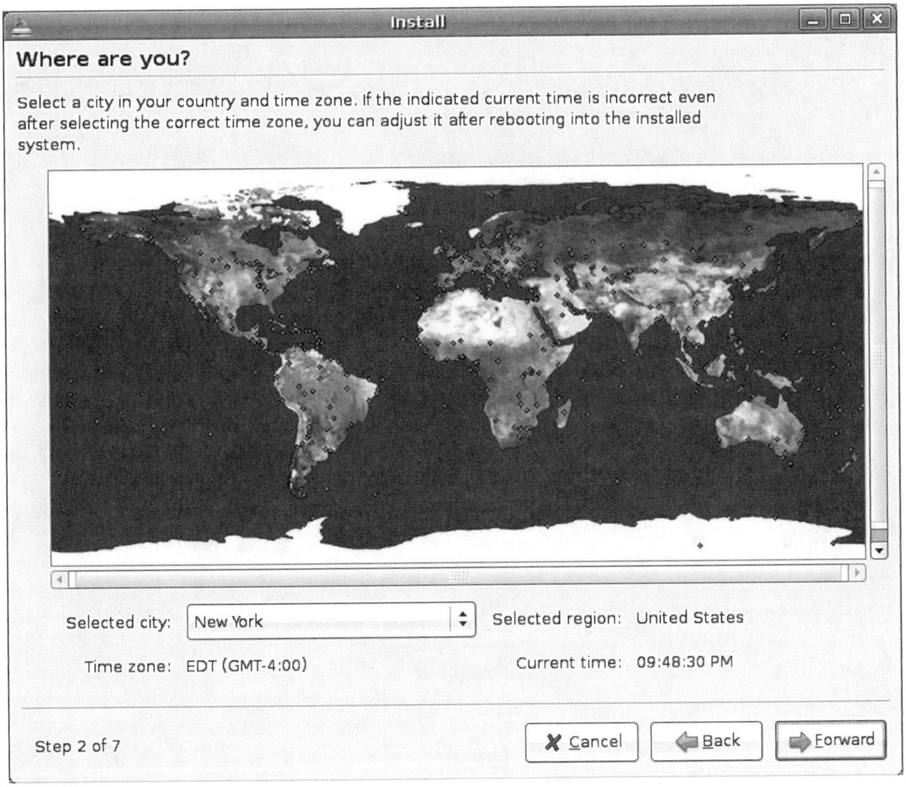

Figure 3.4
Finding yourself with Ubuntu.

Click the city closest to your location that's still in your same time zone. The city will appear in the Selected City drop-down list at the bottom of Ubiquity. If you clicked on the wrong city, just try again.

Confirm that you have the correct city selected and the time zone is also correct. Click Forward to proceed to Step 3.

Save Some Daylight

In 2007, the U.S. and Canada extended their observance of Daylight Savings Time from March 11–November 4, 2007. The latest version of Ubuntu has been updated to reflect these changes, as well as recent changes in the state of Indiana's observance of DST.

Keyboard Settings

You might think a keyboard is a keyboard, but around the world, and even within nations, there are many variations in the way people input their words into a PC.

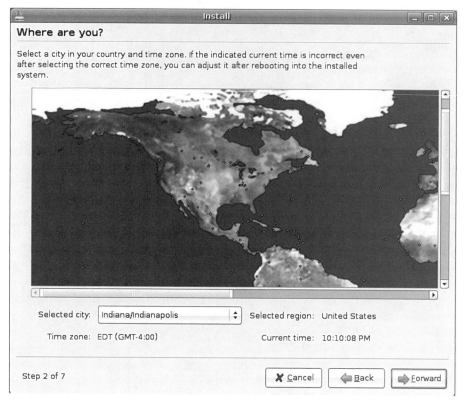

Figure 3.5
Narrowing down your geographic choices.

Step 3 of Ubiquity, displayed in Figure 3.6, shows all of the different keyboards supported by Ubuntu.

The selected keyboard is the default keyboard setting based on the language selection you made in Step 1. If you are unsure of what kind of keyboard you are using, leave this default option selected. Otherwise, select the appropriate keyboard and then click Forward to advance to Step 4.

Partition Settings

Now comes the most important part of the Ubiquity process: selecting your partition options.

By default, Ubiquity has selected the option to use the entire disk to install Ubuntu (see Figure 3.7). Before you leave that option selected and click Continue, let's review what that means.

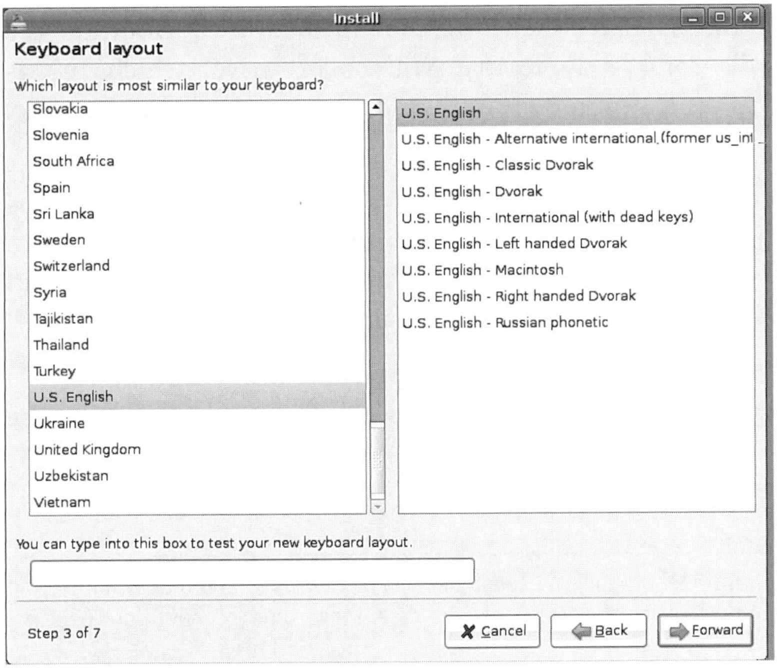

Figure 3.6
It's not just a QWERTY world out there.

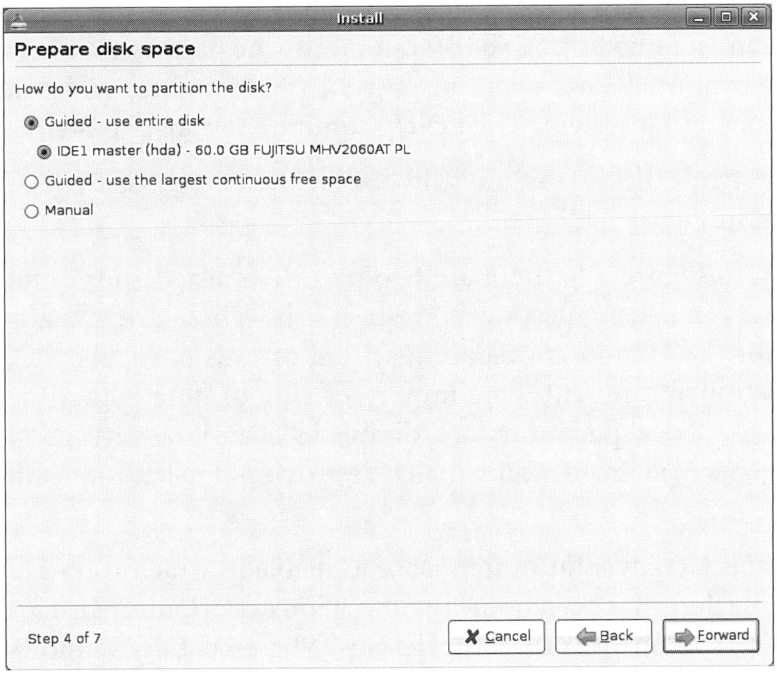

Figure 3.7
Caution: partitioning ahead.

Using the entire disk means that when you are finished with Ubquity, the installation process will completely format your hard drive, which means that everything that was on it (Windows and your personal data) will be gone. Forever.

If you read Chapter 2 and backed up all of your system's files, then this will be only a minor headache as you restore what was overwritten by the Ubuntu installation process. If you did not back up your Windows partition, and you did not want to format your entire drive, this will be akin to a major disaster.

So, and it cannot be stressed enough, be sure that you want to totally replace Windows and your personal data with Ubuntu before you select the Guided - Use Entire Disk option.

Save Your Personal Files

Many new users think that somehow their personal files will be preserved and that Windows will automatically be transformed to Ubuntu. This is not the case. Make sure you have your personal files safely backed up.

If this is what you really want to do, leave the Entire Disk option selected, click Continue, and move to Step 6.

Otherwise, click the Manual radio button so you can specify the partition settings that will let you keep your Windows operating system (and its data) and run Ubuntu as a separate operating system. Then click Continue to move to Step 5.

After scanning your system's disks, Ubiquity will display the current settings of your system, as shown in Figure 3.8.

In the example shown in Figure 3.8, there are two partitions listed (hda2 and hda1) that use the fat32 and ntfs filesystems, respectively. These are actually two drive partitions for the Windows operating system on this particular PC. Your machine may be much different. One important clue to note is that the Format check boxes for these partitions are disabled. That is a very good thing because it prevents you from accidentally destroying a partition with data in it.

On this machine, there is already a lot of free space available in which to install Ubuntu (because this machine has been home to other Linux distributions). This will probably not be the case on your machine, because 99 percent of Windows installations completely fill up a hard drive's partitions.

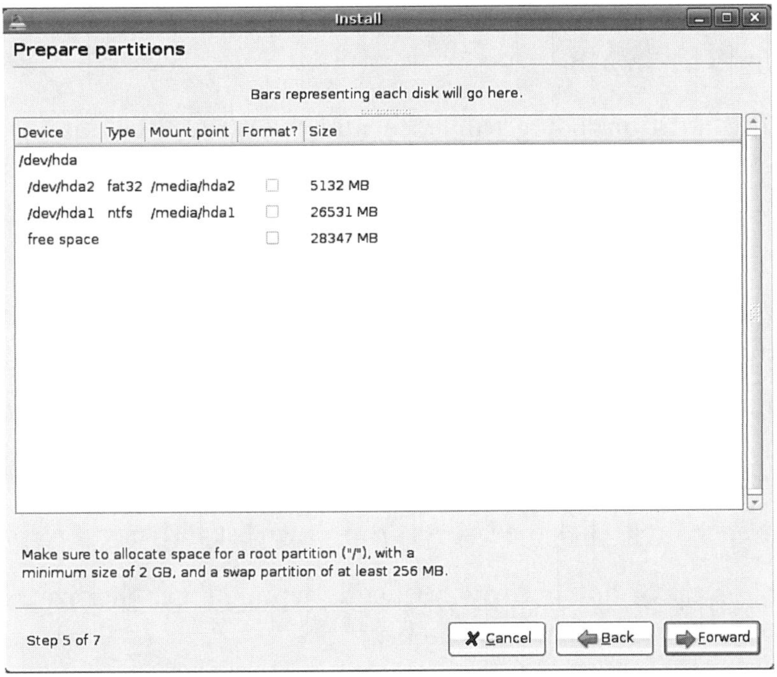

Figure 3.8
One existing partitioning scheme.

To create free space, you will need to resize existing partitions, making them smaller so that free space will be created from what room is left on the disk. Before you begin this, remember that you should not shrink your Windows partitions too small, because they'll become too small for the existing data on that partition. (Don't worry, Ubiquity will warn you if you try to go too small.)

To resize a partition, follow these steps.

1. Right-click the partition you want to resize. A pop-up menu will appear.

2. Click Edit. The Edit Partition dialog box will open (see Figure 3.9).

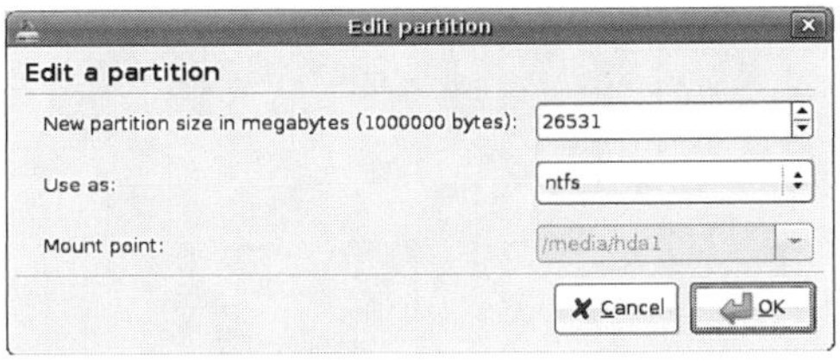

Figure 3.9
Editing a partition's size.

3. Using the combobox up or down arrow or just by typing, enter the size you want the partition to be, in MB.

4. Click OK. The Edit Partition dialog will close, and the Write Previous Changes message box will appear (see Figure 3.10).

5. Click Continue. The partition will be resized to your specifications.

After the right amount of free space is created, you will need to create some partitions to house your Ubuntu installation.

1. Right-click the free space line. A context menu will appear.

2. Click New. The Create Partition dialog box, shown in Figure 3.11, will open.

3. To set up the swap space first, click the Use As drop-down list and select Swap.

4. Using the combobox up or down arrow or just by typing, enter the size in MB that you want the swap partition to be.

5. Click OK. The disk will be rescanned, and the new swap partition will appear.

6. Right-click free space again. A context menu will appear.

Figure 3.10
Confirming a resize operation.

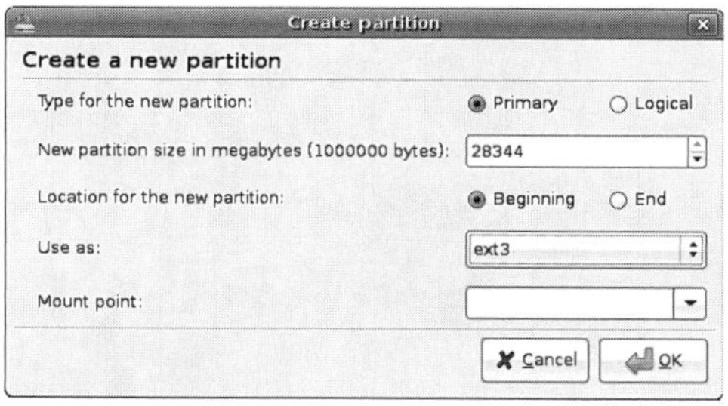

Figure 3.11
Creating a new partition.

7. Click New. The Create Partition dialog box will open.

8. Confirm the Primary Partition option is set.

9. Using the combobox up or down arrow or just by typing, enter the size in MB that you want the root partition to be.

10. Select the type of filesystem you want to format the drive with in the Use As field. (The default ext3 filesystem is perfectly suitable for nearly all users.)

11. Enter / in the Mount Point field. This will create the all-important root mount point.

12. Click OK. The disk will be rescanned, and the new partition will appear.

13. If you did not take up all available free space with the root partition, repeat Steps 6–12 to create additional partitions with varying sizes and mount points. When finished, your partitions could look similar to those displayed in Figure 3.12.

14. Click Forward to advance to Step 6.

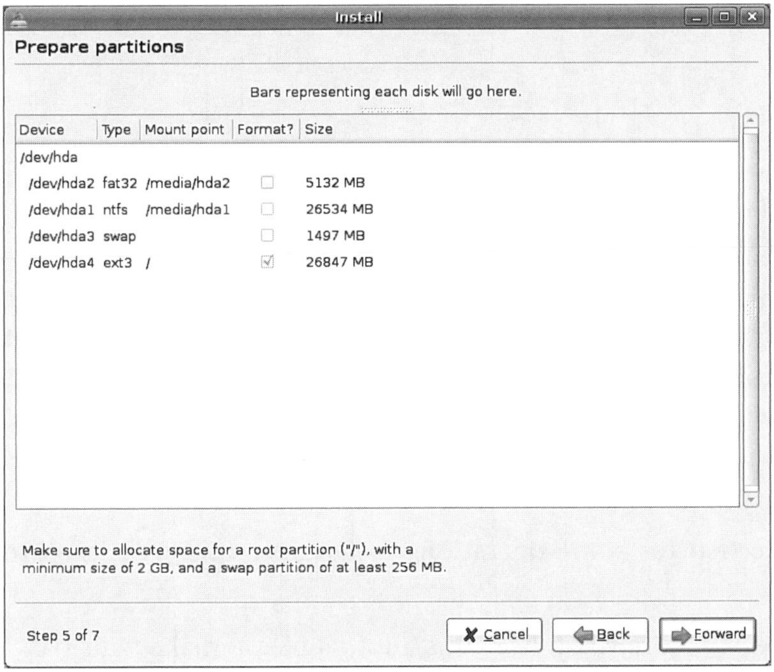

Device	Type	Mount point	Format?	Size
/dev/hda				
/dev/hda2	fat32	/media/hda2	☐	5132 MB
/dev/hda1	ntfs	/media/hda1	☐	26534 MB
/dev/hda3	swap		☐	1497 MB
/dev/hda4	ext3	/	☑	26847 MB

Figure 3.12
One possible partitioning scheme.

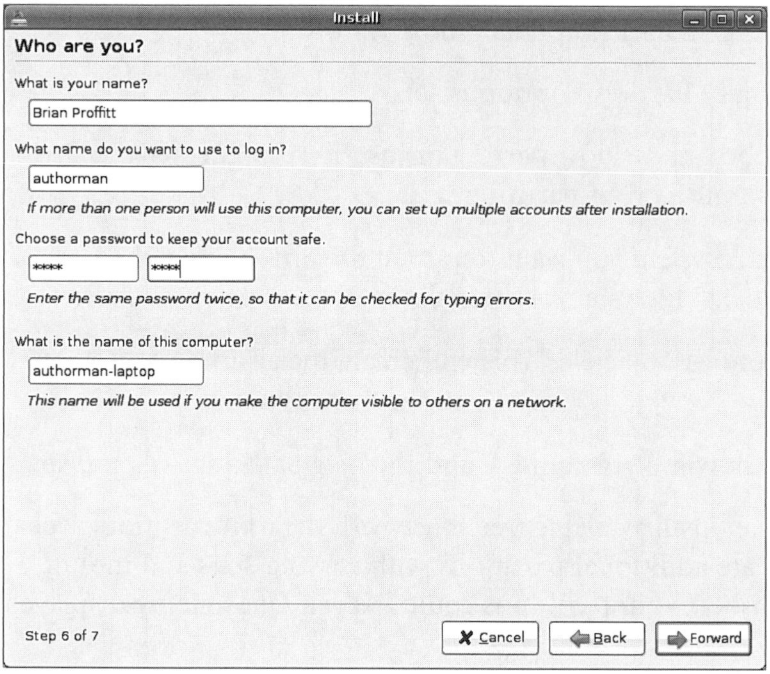

Figure 3.13
Tell Ubuntu who you are.

User Settings

Now that the hard part's done, you will be able to finish the Ubuntu installation in no time. In Step 6, you merely need to enter your personal information, including name, preferred user ID, and password (see Figure 3.13).

Most of this is straightforward information and easy to fill in. A couple of caveats for you to follow: First, never make your user ID any variation of the word "root." Accidentally coming in as the root user will give you a lot of privileges on your Ubuntu machine. While that may sound good, it is most assuredly not. Root, or superuser, accounts have the capability to damage many files at once, whereas regular users are not granted such access.

Superuser access is needed for some operations in Ubuntu, and we'll explore those later.

The second thing, and you surely will hear this a lot, is please make your password hard to guess. Use letters and numbers in combinations that don't make up words or proper names. Such passwords are easier to crack. One favorite scheme is to use the first letter of the words in a refrain from your favorite song. You should get a suitably hardened password.

Once you fill in the information, click Forward to conclude in Step 7.

Reviewing the Settings

In this final step, you have one last chance to review the settings you have made during the Ubiquity installation procedure. Review these setting carefully, especially the partition settings.

If anything does not match what you need, click the Back button to step through the Ubiquity stages and re-enter the corrected information.

When you are satisfied with the settings, click Install. The automated installation procedure will begin. When it is complete, in anywhere from 15 minutes to an hour, depending on your PC, you will be asked to remove the CD from the CD drive. After a system restart, Ubuntu will be installed on your machine.

Conclusion

In this chapter, you reviewed the installation steps for getting Ubuntu on your PC. Special attention was paid to the partitioning settings, because this is the one part of the installation where there is a potential for important data loss.

Now that Ubuntu is installed, it's time to take the grand tour of this excellent operating system in Chapter 4, "Desktop Basics."

CHAPTER 4

DESKTOP BASICS

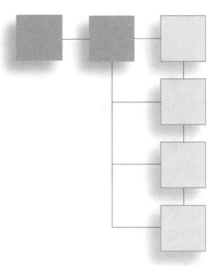

One of the first things new users notices about the Ubuntu desktop is its muted tones. Some users are a little more blunt: "It's . . . brown . . ." they may mutter, less than enthusiastically.

Indeed, given the glitz and glam of many of today's graphic environments, the default color scheme of Ubuntu is rather sedated. But there is a good reason: The various shades of brown reflect the various shades of humanity, which the spirit of Ubuntu embraces. All human skin pigmentation, if you think about it, is just some shade of brown.

While brown is (literally) everyone's color, it may not be your preference for a desktop. Not to worry: There are so many ways to customize your desktop, and not just through color, you will hardly know where to begin.

This chapter will provide guidance on how to begin the process of making your Ubuntu desktop truly your own.

In this chapter, you will:

- Learn more about the development of the GNOME desktop.

- Ensure that your monitor is set at the best resolution.

- Discover how to modify settings for various desktop elements.

- Navigate the GNOME desktop.

Understanding the GNOME Desktop

First, it's not "gnome," like those odd little blue-coated, red-hatted critters that run around the Scandinavian countryside. It's "guh-nome," heavy on the "g" and light on the "uh."

GNOME (GNU Network Object Model Environment) is the product of Miguel de Icaza, a Mexican computer engineering student who took one look at the KDE environment and really liked what he saw—until he discovered the nonfree code sitting (at the time) within it.

De Icaza, a devoted follower of the free software ideals, decided that what was needed in Linux was a similar desktop environment that had none of the then-perceived licensing limitations of KDE.

GNOME first debuted in August 1997, when de Icaza first made the announcement about the project he was working on in the comp.os.linux.announce newsgroup. By December of that same year, the first workable test version was made available to the Linux community. It would not be until March of 1999 that version 1.0 would be released to the general public, but by then the word had gotten out, and thousands of free software devotees climbed on board the GNOME bandwagon.

GNOME, like KDE, is a desktop environment. It is not a window manager, like Enlightenment or Metacity. Window managers control the look and feel of the windows, menus, and other visual components of a graphic interface. Desktop environments include window managers and provide a specific platform for applications to operate within. If an application is written for a desktop environment, therefore, it can tap into a wide range of common features with other applications in that environment.

In the Linux community, GNOME is lauded for more than its free software status. It has generally been regarded as more aesthetically pleasing than KDE, as the themes available for GNOME have more of an eye-candy appeal. (Recent versions of KDE dispute this, which you will learn if you ever try Kubuntu.)

Beyond the look of GNOME, de Icaza has pushed new boundaries for the perception of free software in the corporate world. A year after the release of GNOME 1.0, de Icaza partnered with several major corporations to form the GNOME Foundation—a nonprofit organization dedicated to the ideal of keeping GNOME development moving forward in a rapid and open way.

The GNOME Foundation, with high-powered members such as Sun Micro-systems, HP, and IBM (not to mention Canonical), wants to make GNOME *the* interface for Linux and make that interface very easy for users to adapt to.

One of the major hurdles to people using Linux has been the perception that it is too hard to use, a perception that the GNOME Foundation wants to change. By offering software developers a stable and communicative environment within which to create new GNOME apps, the GNOME Foundation serves as an incubator of sorts for bringing more user-friendly applications to the GNOME interface.

It is for many of these same reasons that Ubuntu's default desktop is GNOME. Let's take a brief tour and learn how to change the look of the desktop along the way.

Desktop Settings and Features

When you look at the GNOME desktop, you will see how simple and clean it is (see Figure 4.1). That's because the interface designers decided to present just the tools you need in as unobtrusive a way as possible. No "Recycle Bin" or "My Document" icons will be found here—unless you want them.

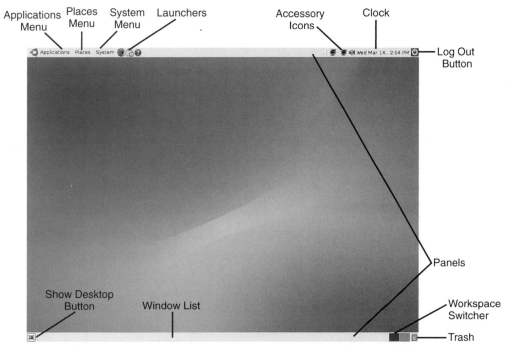

Figure 4.1
The Ubuntu GNOME desktop.

Figure 4.2
The Applications menu.

Some of the elements of the desktop will be familiar in function to you if you have used Windows or OS X in the past. Some controls and features will be less familiar, but once you get an idea of how they work, this will soon pass.

- **Applications Menu.** This menu is very similar in form and function to the Start menu in Windows. In this menu, many of the applications installed on your Ubuntu machine can be found, arranged by category (see Figure 4.2).

- **Places Menu.** This menu will allow you to quickly navigate to specific directories on your machine and others, depending on how you configure it (see Figure 4.3).

- **System Menu.** The System menu is an important component of the desktop, giving the user access to a variety of configuration settings, as well as Quit and Restart options and general Help access (see Figure 4.4).

- **Panels.** The Panels in Ubuntu are where a lot of Ubuntu controls (menus, launchers, switchers, and so on) reside. Panels can be customized to have different locations, sizes, and appearances, which will be discussed in the "Panels" section later in this chapter.

Figure 4.3
The Places menu.

Figure 4.4
The System menu.

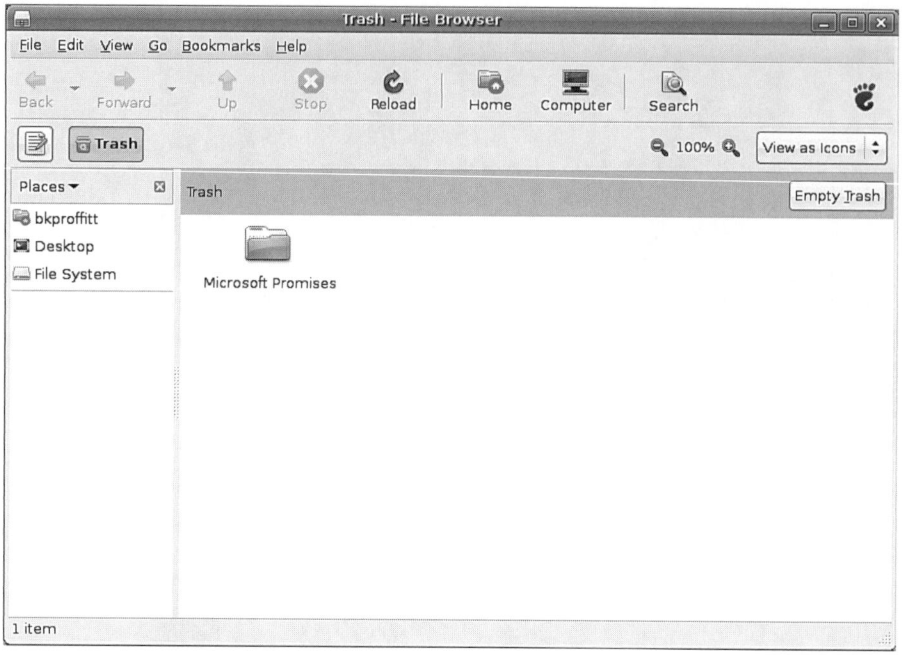

Figure 4.5
The Trash folder.

- **Trash.** The Trash icon is a placeholder for the Trash folder on your Ubuntu PC. When you delete files on the desktop, they aren't permanently deleted; they are sent to this folder. To see the contents of Trash, click the icon (see Figure 4.5). If you want to permanently rid yourself of the files in Trash, click the Empty Trash button.

- **Workspace Switcher.** This control is unique to most distributions of Linux with robust desktop environments like GNOME. Instead of just one desktop, you can actually have more than one, each with its own set of open applications, icons—even looks. For further information, see the "Workspaces" section later in this chapter.

- **Window List.** Similar to the Windows taskbar or the OS X dock, the Window list will display all of the running applications and windows in Ubuntu (see Figure 4.6).

- **Show Desktop Button.** This button has a very simple, yet useful, function. When clicked, all open windows on the desktop are immediately minimized. Very handy if you have a lot of open applications and need to get to a launcher on the desktop (refer to Figure 4.1).

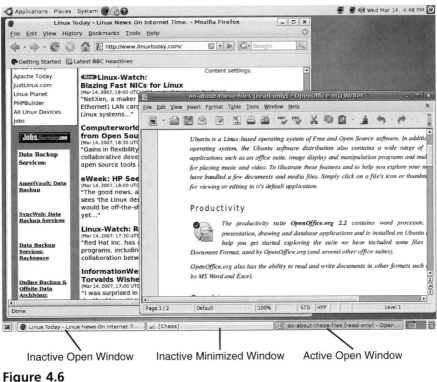

Figure 4.6
An active Window list.

- **Launchers.** Icons in Ubuntu are stilled called icons, but if they have the assignment of launching something, such as an application, file, or folder, then they are called *launchers*. Launchers can appear on the desktop or in desktop panels.

- **Accessory Icons.** Some icons don't just launch something; they're there to tell the user something, too, such as whether the computer is connected to a network.

- **Clock.** The name pretty much says it all: a panel accessory that informs users of the time and date. It does more, such as tap into Evolution, Ubuntu's personal information management application, for access to current appointments and tasks.

- **Log Out Button.** This panel accessory starts the logout or shutdown process when clicked.

There's more, much more to the GNOME desktop than just these features listed here. But these are the basics you will need to know first, as you continue your exploration of this new interface. Now it's time to learn how to customize the desktop and make it more your own.

All Your Own

The settings that will be explored in this chapter will only affect the user making the setting changes. Other users will be unaffected by these changes, unless otherwise noted.

Resolution

The screen resolution in Ubuntu is not strictly a desktop function, since changing the size of the screen resolution actually affects everything in Ubuntu, not just the desktop. Still, before you do anything else, let's see if you can make your viewing experience better.

Screen resolution is tech shorthand for the number of pixels displayed on the screen at any one time. It is usually denoted as width × height, in pixels. So, a common resolution of 800 × 600 displays 800 pixels of graphic information across your monitor screen and 600 pixels down (for a total of 480,000 pixels on the whole screen). That's a lot of pixels, but, truth be told, 800 × 600 is a bit below average in terms of today's powerful graphics cards and monitors.

These days, resolutions of 1024 × 768 are more common, and on the widescreen monitors hitting the retail shelves, 1280 × 1024 is a good resolution, and 1600 × 1200 is not unheard of.

The net effect of these resolutions settings is, the higher the resolution, the more pixels can fit on a screen. The more pixels, the smaller the objects on the screen will look. Thus, with a higher resolution, you can fit more information and windows on your screen, and the image itself will be sharper and have more detail.

When Ubuntu is first installed, it typically does a good job of probing your monitor and graphics card and figuring out which resolution is the best fit for your hardware's capabilities. There is a lot of hardware out there, though, and sometimes Ubuntu misses the mark. Before moving on to specific desktop settings, let's check the resolution.

As you can see in Figure 4.7, the resolution for the desktop shown is a bit low—objects are very large, and there's not a lot of screen "real estate" available. Your monitor may be able to handle something larger.

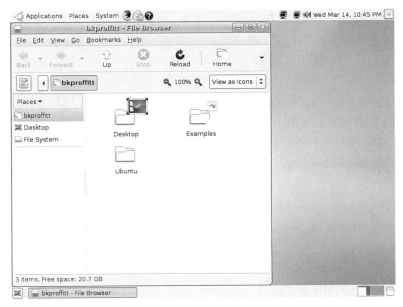

Figure 4.7
An 800 × 600 desktop resolution.

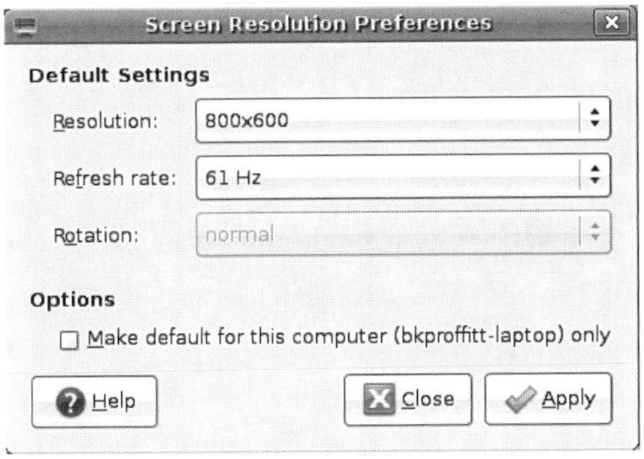

Figure 4.8
You say you want a resolution.

Changing this is easy, just use the steps outlined below.

1. Click the System | Preferences | Screen Resolution menu command. The Screen Resolution Preferences dialog box will open (see Figure 4.8).

2. Click the Resolution drop-down list and select a resolution value higher than the current one.

3. Click Apply. The desktop resolution will be changed.

4. A message box will appear asking if you want to keep this resolution. Confirm your choice.

Menus

One of the nicer features of Ubuntu is its capability to edit the contents of menus to include exactly what you want. Ubuntu does a good job of including the most frequently used applications in its menus, but there may be some that you would like to have in the menus for more ready access, not to mention some commands you would like to remove.

Configuring Ubuntu's menus is relatively simple. And, while you're doing so, you may learn about even more applications you didn't know Ubuntu had.

1. Right-click any menu in the GNOME panels. A context menu will appear.

2. Click Edit menus. The Main Menu dialog box will open (see Figure 4.9).

3. Click a submenu item in the Menus column. Items in italic print are currently not visible on any menu. The contents of that submenu will be displayed in the Items column.

Figure 4.9
Configuring menu contents.

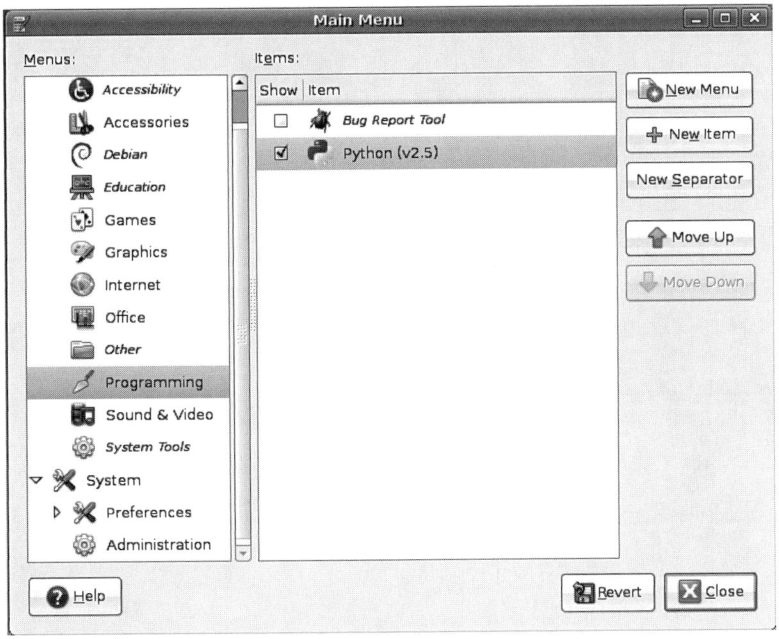

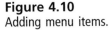

Figure 4.10
Adding menu items.

4. To add an item to a menu, click the check box next to that item in the Items column. The item will be selected (see Figure 4.10).

5. To move an item, click the item you want to move. The Move Up and Move Down buttons will become active.

6. Click Move Up. The menu item will move one place up in its list.

7. Click Close. The menus will reflect your changes.

Not only can you make items visible and move them around, but you can also add items to menus.

1. To add a new item, navigate to the submenu where you want the item to be and click New Item. The Create Launcher dialog box will open (see Figure 4.11).

2. Type the name of the application you want to add in the Name field.

3. Type the command used to start the program in the Command field.

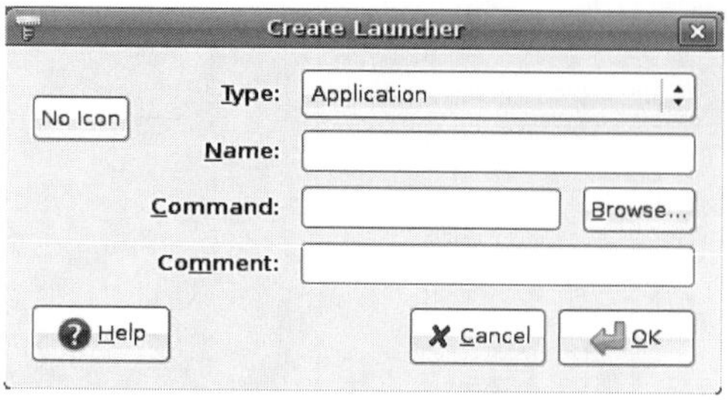

Figure 4.11
The Create Launcher dialog box.

Figure 4.12
Looking for icons.

Choosing an Application

You can use the Browse button to open the Choose an Application dialog box and navigate to the appropriate command. Many applications are found in the /usr/bin or /usr/sbin directories.

4. To add an icon, click the No Icon button. The Browse Icons dialog box will open (see Figure 4.12).

5. Click a desired icon and then click OK. The selected icon will appear in the Create Launcher dialog box.

6. Click OK. The Create Launcher dialog box will close, and the new menu item will appear in the Item column of the Main Menu dialog.

7. Click Close. The menus will reflect your changes.

Figure 4.13
Creating a new submenu.

To add a new submenu to your menu selection, proceed with these steps:

1. Click the top-level menu where you want your new submenu to be.

2. Click New Menu. The Directory Properties dialog box will open (see Figure 4.13).

3. Type the name of the application you want to add in the Name field.

4. To add an icon, click the No Icon button. The Browse Icons dialog box will open.

5. Click a desired icon and then click OK. The selected icon will appear in the Directory Properties dialog box.

6. Click Close. The Directory Properties dialog box will close, and the new submenu item will appear in the Menu column of the Main Menu dialog.

7. Click Close. The menus will reflect your changes.

Panels

Menus aren't the only thing that can be customized in Ubuntu. In fact, when you come right down to it, it's a lot easier to list the elements in Ubuntu that aren't customizable in some way.

Panels are no exception. The panels are the gray horizontal bars at the top and bottom of the Ubuntu desktop that contain various tools and menus. At least, that's how they start out. But after a little bit of tweaking, you will soon discover that gray, horizontal, top, and bottom are all just loose concepts. The panels can look like nearly anything and be located in different places. It all depends on you.

One quick change you can make is relocating any panel.

1. Right-click and hold the mouse cursor on a panel. The cursor will change to a gripping hand.

Figure 4.14
Moving a panel.

2. Drag the cursor to another edge of the screen. The panel will move to that edge.

3. Release the mouse button. The panel is fixed in its new position (see Figure 4.14).

Like menus, items can be added or removed from panels. Three categories of items can be added to a panel: a tool, such as an accessory or monitoring tool, an Application Launcher from the Applications menu, or a custom Application Launcher. We can walk through all of these in just a few steps, starting with a GNOME tool.

1. Right-click the panel to which you want to add an item. A context menu will appear.

2. Click Add to Panel. The Add to Panel dialog box will open (see Figure 4.15).

3. Click the item you would like to add. The item is selected.

4. Click Add. The item will appear in the panel (see Figure 4.16).

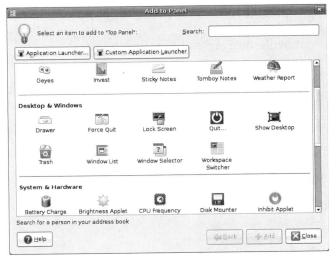

Figure 4.15
Adding items to a panel.

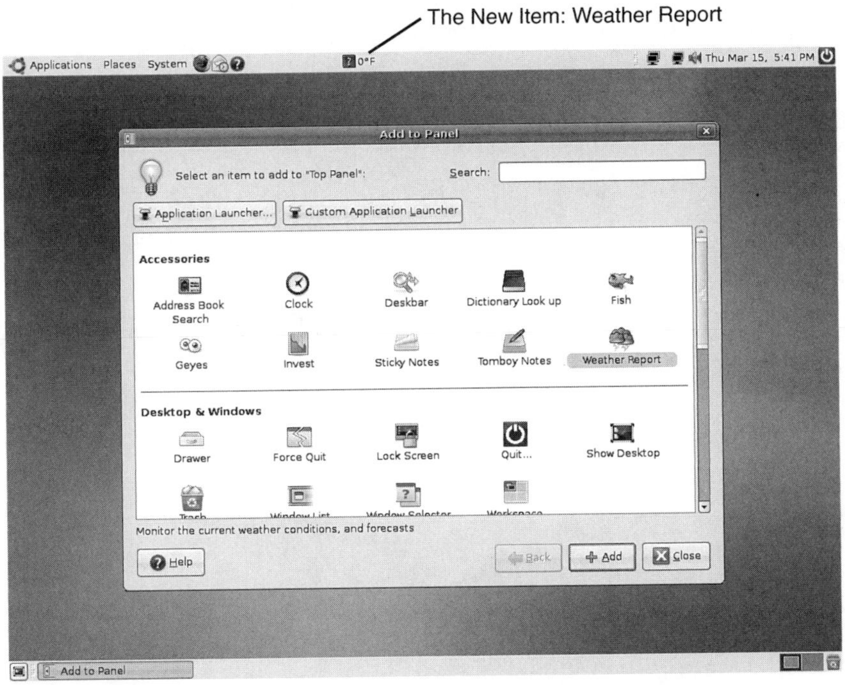

The New Item: Weather Report

Figure 4.16
A new item, almost ready.

5. To move the item, right-click its icon. A context menu will appear.

6. Click Move. The mouse cursor will change to a gripping hand.

7. Move the mouse cursor left or right across the screen. The panel item will move in a corresponding fashion.

8. When the item is positioned in the correct place, click the item. The item will be in the desired position.

9. Click Close. The Add to Panel dialog box will close.

Adding an application is just as simple. You can choose from any app on the Application menu or run your own.

1. Right-click the panel to which you want to add an item. A context menu will appear.

2. Click Add to Panel. The Add to Panel dialog box will open.

3. Click Application Launcher. The contents of the Application menu will appear in the central window (see Figure 4.17).

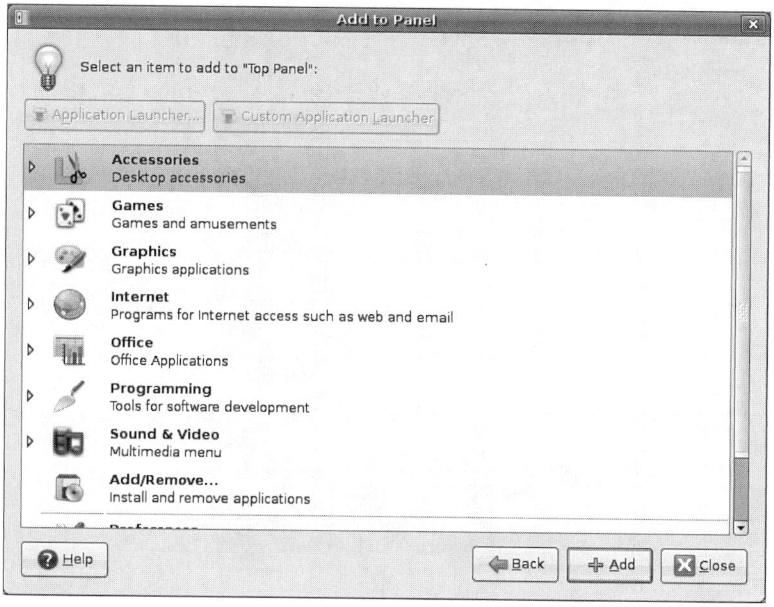

Figure 4.17
Any item on the Application menu can be added.

4. Click the expansion arrow (triangle) to expand a group of applications.

5. Click the application you would like to add. The application is selected.

6. Click Add. The application item will appear in the panel.

7. To move the item, right-click its icon. A context menu will appear.

8. Click Move. The mouse cursor will change to a gripping hand.

9. Move the mouse cursor left or right across the screen. The panel item will move in a corresponding fashion.

10. When the item is positioned in the correct place, click the item. The item will be in the desired position.

11. Click Close. The Add to Panel dialog box will close.

You don't have to be limited to just the apps in the Application menu; just use the Custom Application Launcher tool.

1. Right-click the panel to which you want to add an item. A context menu will appear.

2. Click Add to Panel. The Add to Panel dialog box will open.

3. Click Custom Application Launcher. The Create Launcher dialog box will appear.

4. Type the name of the application you want to add in the Name field.

5. Type the command used to start the program in the Command field.

6. To add an icon, click the No Icon button. The Browse Icons dialog box will open.

7. Click a desired icon and then click OK. The selected icon will appear in the Create Launcher dialog box.

8. Click OK. The Create Launcher dialog box will close, and the new menu item will appear in the panel.

9. To move the item, right-click its icon. A context menu will appear.

10. Click Move. The mouse cursor will change to a gripping hand.

11. Move the mouse cursor left or right across the screen. The panel item will move in a corresponding fashion.

12. When the item is positioned in the correct place, click the item. The item will be in the desired position.

13. Click Close. The Add to Panel dialog box will close.

To remove an item from a panel is a much faster process.

1. Right-click the item you want to delete. A context menu will appear.

2. Click Remove from Panel. The item will be deleted from the panel.

If the look of the panels is not something you can aesthetically appreciate, there's good news: You can change the panel look very quickly.

1. Right-click the panel to which you want to add an item. A context menu will appear.

2. Click Properties. The Panel Properties dialog box will open (see Figure 4.18).

3. Click the Background tab.

4. Click the Solid Color radio button. The color options will become active, as shown in Figure 4.19.

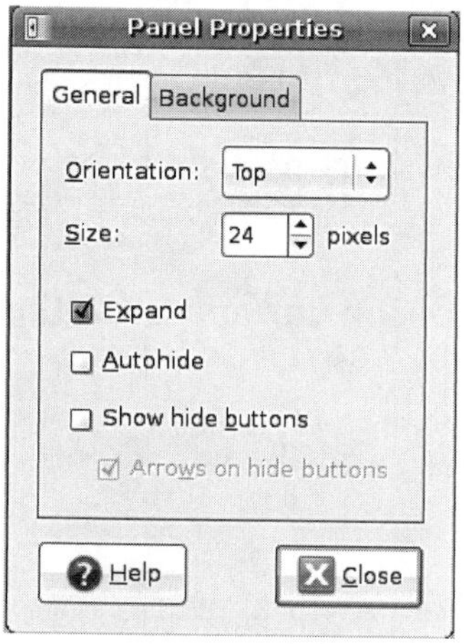

Figure 4.18
The Panel Properties dialog box.

Figure 4.19
Choose your panel's color.

Figure 4.20
A transparent panel.

5. Click and drag the Style slide towards the Transparent setting. The panel will become more transparent.

6. Click Close. The Panel Properties dialog box will close, and the panel will have become rather clear (see Figure 4.20).

See-Thru Panels

Making a panel transparent is only one change you can make in the Panel Properties dialog box. Try experimenting with different colors, shading, and background images in the Background tab. In the General tab, you can adjust the panel's size, set it to Autohide, or even reduce its width.

Mouse and Keyboard

During the installation process, you were able to define the type of keyboard you were using. While it is unlikely that Ubiquity got it wrong, there may come a time when you will swap keyboards or add a new user who prefers to plug in his own unique input device. And you were never given any options to set your mouse settings.

As you play with the Ubuntu desktop, let's take the time to see where such settings can be configured.

First, let's see how the mouse can be configured. You might think that there's not much to change with a mouse, but you may be surprised.

Click the System | Preferences | Mouse menu command. The Mouse Preferences dialog box will open (see Figure 4.21).

- On the Buttons page, you can set your mouse to be left-handed (which switches the button operations) and set the time between double-clicks—something very useful for those users with slower reflexes.

- On the Pointers page, shown in Figure 4.22, you can select a specific mouse theme and activate a control that will highlight the mouse on the screen when you press the Ctrl button on your keyboard.

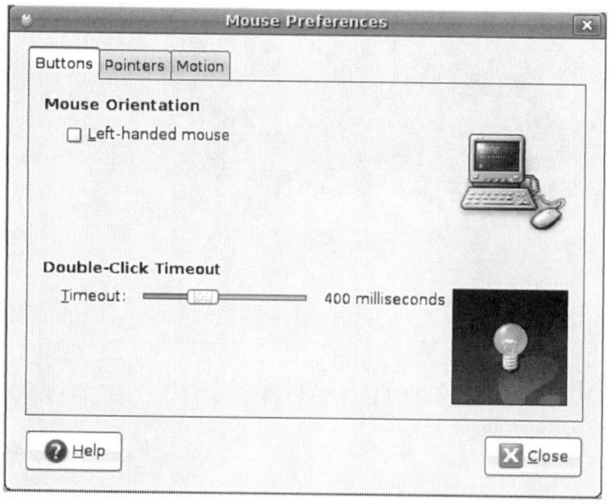

Figure 4.21
Everything a mouse needs but the cheese.

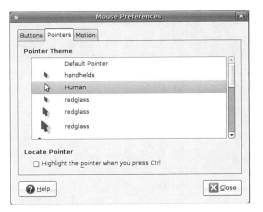

Figure 4.22
Choosing a pointer theme.

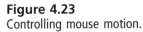

Figure 4.23
Controlling mouse motion.

- On the Motion page, acceleration and sensitivity of the mouse can be set, as well as the range a mouse can have when it is dragging and dropping desktop objects (see Figure 4.23).

The keyboard for your Ubuntu can also get a lot of attention, with features you may not have heard of before, but make perfect sense once you use them. To access the keyboard configurations, click the System | Preferences | Keyboard menu command. The Keyboard Preferences dialog box will open (see Figure 4.24).

- On the Keyboard page, the response time of repeating keys and cursor blinks can be set.

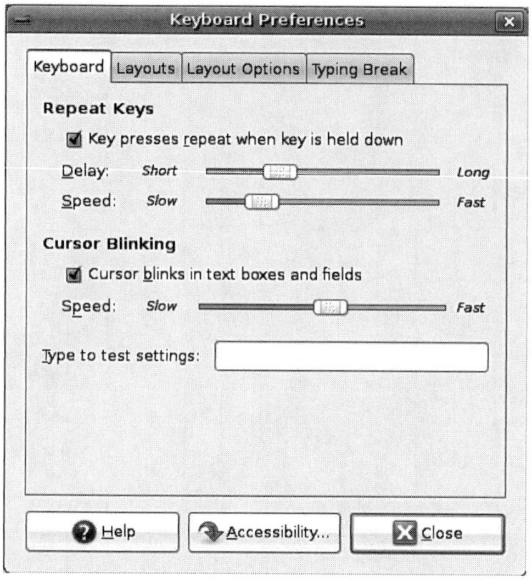

Figure 4.24
Basic keyboard settings.

Figure 4.25
Choosing a keyboard layout.

■ On the Layouts page, you can select your keyboard type as you did in the installation of Ubuntu and add additional keyboard configurations (see Figure 4.25).

■ On the Layout Options page, various options can be applied to certain keys on your specific layout by clicking on the expansion arrows and then selecting the appropriate radio buttons (see Figure 4.26).

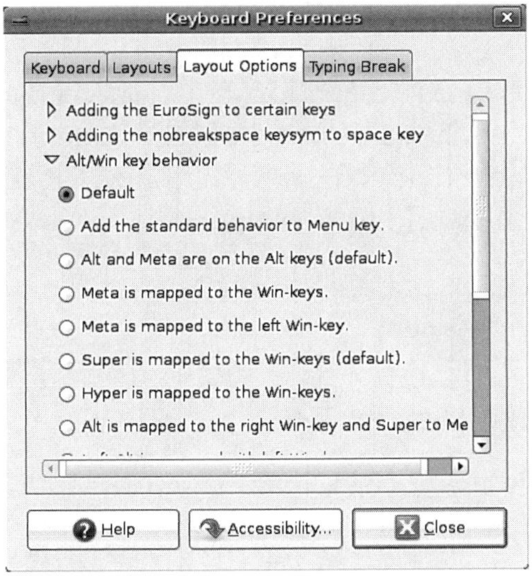

Figure 4.26
Many keymapping options are available.

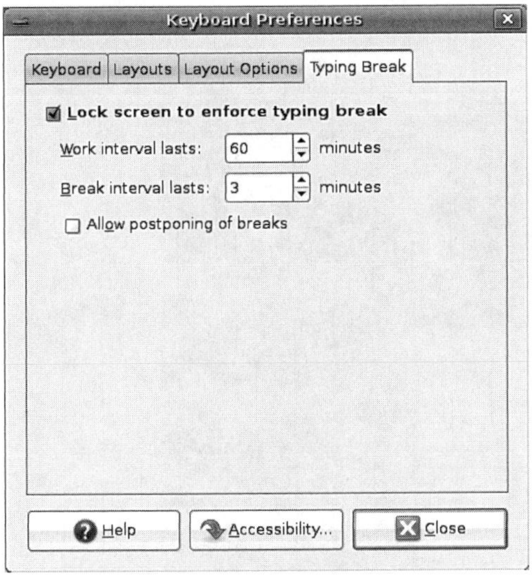

Figure 4.27
A feature for your health.

- On the Typing Break page, you can force the keyboard to lock itself and make you take a break at any given interval (see Figure 4.27). This may seem like a time waster, but regular breaks help prevent repetitive stress injuries that often come with excessive typing.

Time and Date

The Clock accessory that runs in your panel is pretty straightforward: It shows the date and the time. You can, if you want, set it manually. But the really punctual people among you might be interested to know that you can synchronize Clock to match the atomic clocks maintained by the world's governments.

System Time and Date

All time and date settings will affect every user on the system.

1. Right-click the Clock. A context menu will appear.

2. Click Adjust Date & Time. Immediately the screen will dim, and an administrative password dialog box will open (see Figure 4.28).

The Secret Password

The administrative password is the password that belongs to the administrative user for an Ubuntu PC. By default, that's the first user who installed Ubuntu. For more on user account management, see the "Setting Up User Accounts" section in Chapter 7, "Making Things Work."

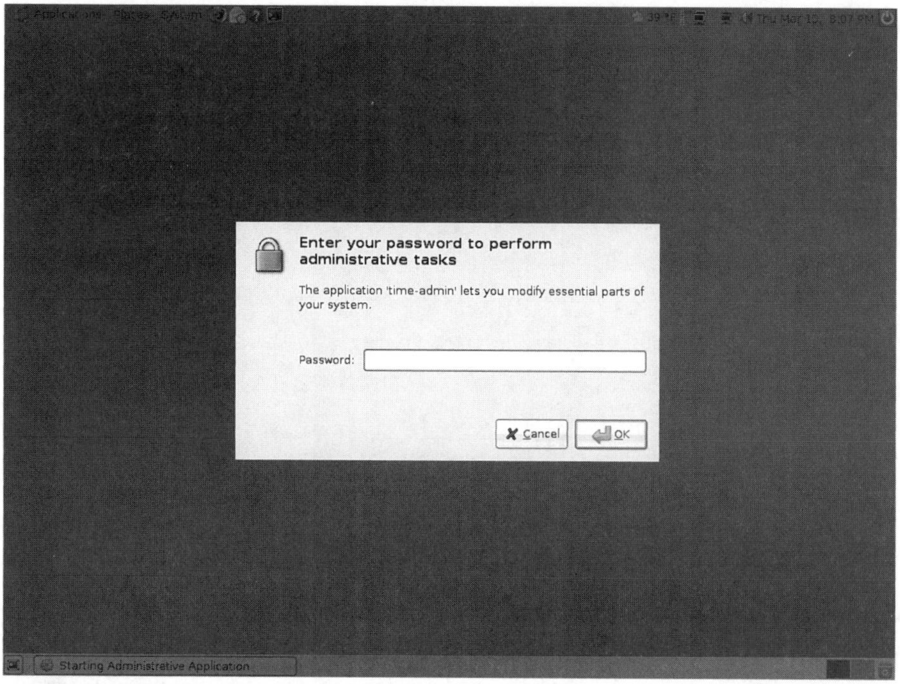

Figure 4.28
Administrative tasks require an admin password.

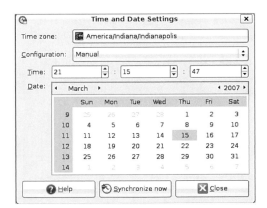

Figure 4.29
Setting your clock.

3. Type in the administrative password and click OK. The desktop will unlock, and the Time and Date Settings dialog box will open (see Figure 4.29).

4. Settings on the Clock can be done manually with the controls in this dialog box. To set your clock via a public or private atomic clock time server, click the Configuration drop-down list and select Keep Synchronized with Internet Servers.

Check Your Connection

If you want your PC to be auto synchronized, you will need to be able to connect to the Internet.

If this is the first time you have tried to synchronize your Clock, you will get a message box that warns that NTP support is not installed. NTP stands for Network Time Protocol, which is simply the language your computer uses to talk to the various time servers in the world. If you see this warning and are currently connected to the Internet, click the Install NTP Support button, and the correct software will be installed. (If you are not currently connected, click Cancel and try to synchronize again later when you are online.)

Once NTP support is installed, and you choose the Keep Synchronized configuration, the Time and Date Settings dialog box will be altered to reflect just three fields, as shown in Figure 4.30.

To finish this operation, click the Select Servers button to open the Time Servers dialog box (see Figure 4.31).

Figure 4.30
Autosetting your clock.

Figure 4.31
International timekeepers.

You may check off as many servers as you'd like, though a lot is not needed. You should select more than one, in case one server is offline for some reason. Make sure that you click servers near you, since locality makes for a faster signal, and be sure to select the pool.ntp.org setting, so you don't overload individual time servers.

Click Close to shut down the Time Servers dialog box; then click Close to close the Time and Date Settings dialog box. Your Clock will be synchronized upon booting your system.

Workspaces

Something that most Windows users haven't seen yet is the workspaces on the GNOME desktop. Workspaces are virtual desktops, in that each workspace can contain its own windows, icons, and running applications. By default, Ubuntu gives you two workspaces to start working with, but you can add a lot more if need be.

Workspaces are ideal for those users who need to separate one set of tasks from another. For instance, a certain author will keep all the applications involved with writing a book in one workspace and the applications used for his day job in another workspace.

To switch between workspaces, simply click the workspace you want to view in the Workspace Switcher in the lower right panel. You can control the number of workspaces by following the steps below.

1. Right click the Workspace Switcher. A context menu will appear.

2. Click Preferences. The Workspace Switcher Preferences dialog box will appear, as shown in Figure 4.32.

3. To change the number of workspaces, type the number you want in the Number of Workspaces field. A new workspace will be added to the switcher.

4. To give each workspace a unique name, slowly click the default name twice; then type a new name. The names will be changed.

5. Click the Show workspace names in the Switcher check box. The Switcher will display the new names, as shown in Figure 4.33.

6. Click Close. The Workspace Switcher Preferences dialog box will close.

Figure 4.32
Control the number of workspaces.

Figure 4.33
Workspaces can have proper names.

To open windows in workspaces, either you can navigate to a workspace and open the application there, or you can move any window to a workspace in just one step. Simply click the Window Menu icon in the upper-left corner of any open window and select the Move to Another Workspace menu. Then click the destination workspace for this window.

Window Dressing

Like custom cars, people seem to love to customize their PCs with the flashiest themes and colors. And for the best eye candy bang for your buck, very few desktop environments compare with the GNOME desktop. So for the sheer enjoyment of it, let's touch on how to start tricking out your Ubuntu ride.

Backgrounds

Backgrounds are the easiest thing to change in Ubuntu, although unfortunately to save space on the installation CD, there are only two backgrounds included, both brown abstracts. It would therefore be a good idea to get a background first from another source, such as the Internet or a personal graphic file.

Figure 4.34
Changing wallpapers is easy.

Decorator's Tip

One of the best places to find beautiful wallpaper art for your Ubuntu PC is the Wallpapers section: GNOME-Look at http://www.gnome-look.org. Be sure to visit the section that matches your desktop's resolution.

1. Right-click anywhere on the desktop. A context menu will appear.

2. Click Change Desktop Background. The Desktop Background Preferences dialog box will appear (see Figure 4.34).

3. If you see a desired wallpaper, click it. The Ubuntu background will immediately update.

4. To use another file for wallpaper, click Add Wallpaper. The Add Wallpaper dialog box will open.

5. Navigate to and select the file you want to use for wallpaper.

6. Click Open. The Add Wallpaper dialog box will close, and the new wallpaper will appear, already selected in the Desktop Wallpaper window.

7. Click Finish. The dialog box will close, and your new wallpaper will be displayed (see Figure 4.35).

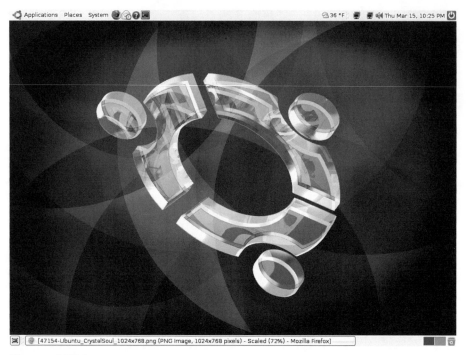

Figure 4.35
The only limit is your imagination.

Themes

Themes are used in Ubuntu to change whole color and window schemes at one time. They are very fun to play with, and even if you download a theme from the Internet, you can customize any part of it to make it truly unique.

To load a new theme, follow these steps.

1. Click the System | Preferences | Theme menu command. The Theme Preferences dialog box will open (see Figure 4.36).

2. Click a desired theme. The theme's settings will be reflected immediately on the Ubuntu desktop (see Figure 4.37).

3. To change part of a theme, click the Customize button. The Theme Details dialog box will open (see Figure 4.38).

4. Explore the detail controls and see what happens. When finished, click Close. If you made any changes, the theme will be displayed as a Custom theme.

Figure 4.36
Ubuntu has varying themes to choose from.

Figure 4.37
Themes are applied instantly.

5. Click Save Theme. The Save Theme As dialog box will appear.

6. Enter a name and description for the theme and click Save. The new theme will be saved in the list of themes.

7. Click Close. The theme will now be set.

Figure 4.38
You can change any part of a theme.

Themes R' Us

Like wallpapers, many excellent themes can be found at the GNOME-Look Web site.

Conclusion

In this chapter, we took a tour of the Ubuntu interface itself, the GNOME desktop. You have seen that it is very similar to Windows and OS X desktops, although there are some important differences.

There is a lot to see and play with in the GNOME desktop, and before you continue on to the next chapter, you are invited to take a moment and do just that: play. Then we'll get to the important business of any PC, which is connecting to the Internet.

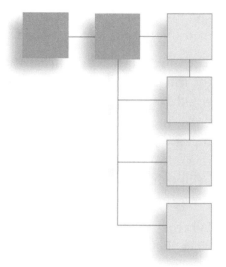

CHAPTER 5

GETTING ONLINE

Now that you have run through some of the basic configuration steps for your Ubuntu PC, its time to take a look at how you can get Ubuntu talking to other computers, namely through that ubiquitous medium of the twenty-first century, the Internet.

In this chapter, you will learn how to configure Ubuntu to connect to the Internet through:

- A home or office network.

- Broadband cable/DSL modems.

- Dial-up connections.

- Wirelessly via WiFi.

How to Get on the Internet

Much has been said about the Internet this past couple of decades. Although much hoopla and hype have been associated with this—the largest of all public computer networks—it should be noted that the Internet is not even close to being finished, even in developed nations.

The growth of the Internet (thus far) is in many ways similar to the growth of the telephone in the United States in the late nineteenth century. For the first five years of its commercial existence, the telephone was in about 10 percent of

U.S. households. In five more years, it was in 50 percent of American homes. And in another five years, it was in 90 percent of all U.S. homes.

The Internet matches this growth pattern fairly closely. By 1994, five years after the Internet broke out of its purely academic setting, connections to the Internet could be found in about 10 percent of U.S. homes. Now, 13 years later, the pervasiveness of Internet access in the United States has reached over 70 percent. Incredible as it may seem, the United States is only at about the three-quarter mark toward full Internet usage. (The Internet's presence in other nations is behind in terms of percentages, but perhaps only because the U.S. had a head start; the pattern of growth remains the same.)

Whether you are one of the new kids on the Internet block or have been surfing since the days of Mozilla, you will find the Internet is becoming less of a place to play and more of a place to work. Everyday people are turning to the Internet to handle banking needs, shop for holiday gifts, and talk to friends and family through Web-based phone services.

The history of Linux and the Internet is an intertwined one. Linux's predecessor, UNIX, was *the* operating system upon which the Internet was built. In fact, much of the syntax of the Internet ("http://," FTP commands, forward slashes for directory separators) is directly derived from UNIX line commands, which in turn can be found in Ubuntu today.

So it should come as no surprise that Ubuntu provides a rich set of Internet tools for access. All you have to do is get yourself connected.

Getting to the Internet is fairly simple these days. Broadband access is provided by a variety of carriers, which boils down to cable from the cable companies or digital subscriber line (DSL) access from the phone companies. Within some cities, wireless access to the Internet is freely or cheaply available in some neighborhoods. Offices and retail buildings are almost always wired for network access for tenants. And there's always narrowband access: when your computer's modem dials up the Internet on a regular phone line.

Ubuntu can handle them all—often seamlessly.

Configuring Connections

For the most part, Ubuntu comes Internet ready. Which means if you plug in some kind of cord to your computer that's connected on its other end to the

Internet, chances are pretty good that Ubuntu will recognize what's going on and go ahead and make that connection for you.

Still, there are some parts of the process that might need your help. Dial-up, for instance. Dialing up to the Internet is not a complicated business for Ubuntu— but figuring out how to use the modem that came with your computer could present a hurdle, since many modem manufacturers don't have Linux drivers to operate them. Wireless connections can be tricky sometimes as well, for the same lack of drivers for WiFi cards.

Most of these situations have been discovered, however, and solutions are finding their way into Ubuntu. In the next sections, we'll step through the processes of connecting to the Internet, no matter which method you prefer. In Chapter 7, "Making Things Work," we'll review the troubleshooting techniques needed in case something doesn't work as planned.

Dial-Up

The "language" of the Internet is called TCP/IP (Transmission Control Protocol/ Internet Protocol). This language is how data is sent from your computer to a Web server computer in, say, South Africa.

Even though TCP/IP is a UNIX-based product, Ubuntu needs additional protocol help connecting to the Internet through a dial-up connection. TCP/IP, after all, does not transmit the IP (Internet Protocol) data packets through serial lines very well—serial lines like those in modems, for example.

To get all of the data packets through a modem, an additional protocol, PPP, is used, which is a UNIX invention. With its predecessor, SLIP, they were both developed to connect UNIX computers to the Internet, and PPP was later adopted by Microsoft for use in Windows. Ubuntu has absolutely no problems handling PPP.

While dial-up, or narrowband, connections comprise fewer than 20 percent of all Internet connections—a number that falls every year—it is still prevalent enough that you should know how to use it. Many broadband Internet accounts, DSL especially, will provide you with dial-up access to use in case the main DSL connection is under repair, or you are traveling and need to access the Internet from another location.

Here's how to start the dial-up process. Before you begin, you should have your Internet service provider (ISP) information in hand, specifically your username, password, and the phone number to dial.

1. Click System | Administration | Network. You will be asked to provide your administrative password.

2. Enter your password. The Network Settings dialog box (see Figure 5.1) will appear.

3. Click Modem Connection; then click the Properties button. The Settings for Interface ppp0 dialog box will open, as shown in Figure 5.2.

Figure 5.1
The Network Settings dialog box.

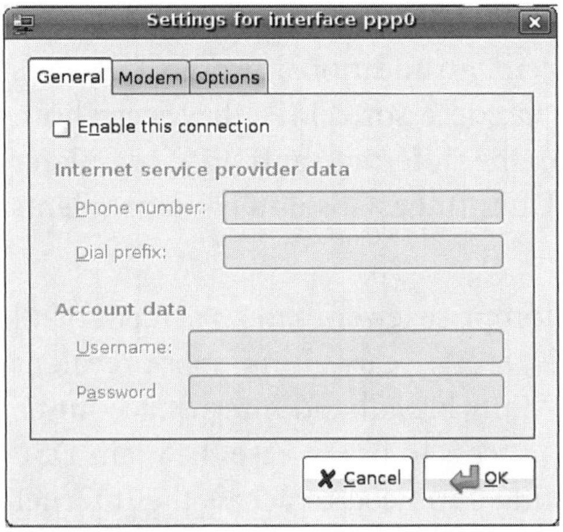

Figure 5.2
Configuring dial-up settings.

4. Click the Enable This Connection check box.

5. Type the dial-in number in the Phone Number field.

6. Type your ISP username and password in the appropriate fields. Your information should be similar to that shown in Figure 5.3.

7. Click the Modem tab. The Modem page will appear (see Figure 5.4).

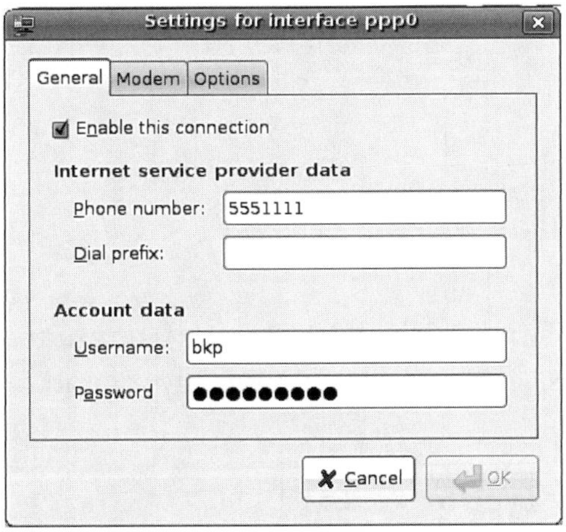

Figure 5.3
Example of dial-up settings.

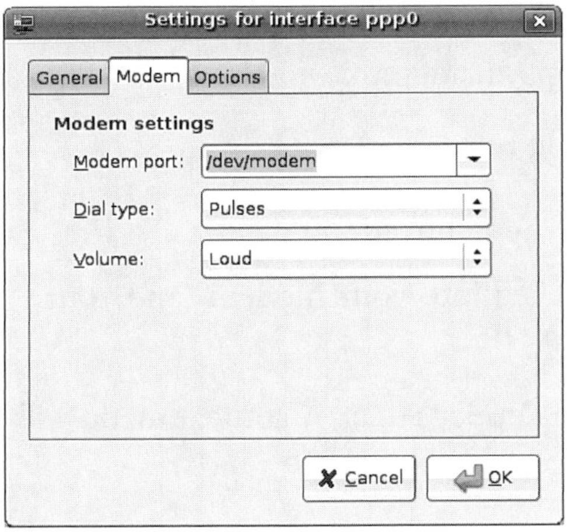

Figure 5.4
Setting your specific modem's device.

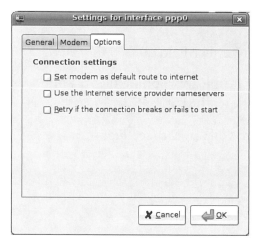

Figure 5.5
Selecting custom modem options.

8. Select a value in the Modem Port field. This sets the pathway for Ubuntu to find your modem when the time comes. /dev/modem is typically a good port setting.

9. If you use a touch-tone phone, set Dial Type to Tones.

10. Click the Options tab. The Options page will appear (see Figure 5.5).

11. Click the Use the Internet Service Provider Name Servers check box.

12. Click the Retry if the Connection Breaks or Fails to Start check box.

13. Click OK. The Settings for Interface ppp0 dialog box will close.

14. Click Close. The Network Settings dialog box will close.

Now all that you need to do is start the dial-up connection.

1. Make sure that your phone cord is plugged into your modem (and your modem is connected to your computer).

2. Click the Network Manager applet in the upper panel. A context menu will appear (see Figure 5.6).

3. Click Dial Up Connections | Connect to ppp0 via Modem. The modem will automatically dial up and connect to the Internet.

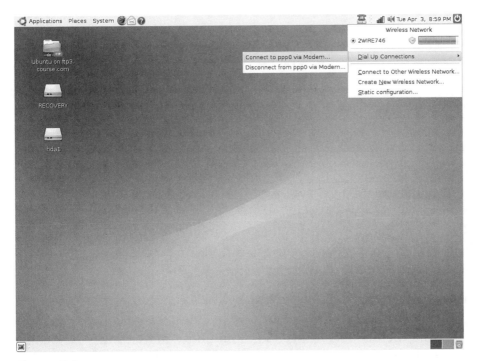

Figure 5.6
Starting the dial-up.

Disconnecting a dial-up connection is just as simple.

1. Make sure that your phone cord is plugged into your modem (and your modem is connected to your computer).

2. Click the Network Manager applet in the upper panel. A context menu will appear.

3. Click Dial Up Connections | Disconnect to ppp0 via Modem. The modem will disconnect from the Internet.

The Scoop on Internal Modems

Presumably your modem was correctly recognized by Ubuntu, and all of these steps went smoothly. Unfortunately, if your modem is inside your computer, then it is likely that things did not go as well. Internal modems, also called *winmodems,* are notorious for not working for Ubuntu and other Linux distributions, because of the lack of Linux support by the modem manufacturers. This is not to say, however, that using an internal modem is not possible. See the "Modems" section in Chapter 7 for the steps needed to get internal modems up and running.

DSL

DSL is one of the two main forms of broadband used in the U.S. today, the other being cable. There are, of course, other ways of getting broadband into your home, such as broadband cellular, satellite, fiber optic, or municipal WiFi. But in many cases, these methods are not common or far too expensive to justify using them.

DSL uses the same copper phone lines that run into your home or business; in fact, you can make a voice phone call and still maintain Internet access on the same line at the same time. This is because a DSL line sends the digital "Internet" signal at frequencies that are far above the range of human hearing. Once the signal gets back to the phone company, the voice and the network signals are split by a switcher, with the voice signal routed to the person on the other end of your conversation and the network signal sent out to the Internet.

There is, though, a catch to all of this techno-brilliance: Because of the very high frequencies involved, a digital signal in a DSL line can only travel a short distance in the wires before degrading, about one and a quarter miles. So people who live or work in rural settings are unable to enjoy DSL—at least until their phone company gets a switcher near their location.

There are two types of DSL modems that a phone company will provide you. One is the older type, which acts like a traditional modem that you have to connect and disconnect to the Internet as the need arises. The newer models of DSL modem essentially behave as routers: They are always connected to the Internet and manage that connection with onboard software.

Connecting with this latter type of modem, known as an *Ethernet DSL modem,* is very straightforward: Computers are connected to the DSL modem/router via network cable or by WiFi, and the Ethernet DSL modem/router handles all the rest. In fact, you can visit the next section, "LAN/Cable," to proceed with connecting to the Internet.

The older types of DSL modems are known as USB modems because they connect to your PC through the USB port. These, unfortunately, are not ideal for any broadband connection on any computer—Ubuntu, Windows, or otherwise. That's because PCs are designed with hardware (network interface cards or NICs) made specifically to go out and talk to other computers. Using a USB port to accomplish this is like asking your nose to start speaking instead of your mouth.

This is the one place in the book where you are strongly encouraged not to use a piece of hardware. This is because of the limitations of the hardware itself, not Ubuntu. If your computer doesn't have a NIC, they can be purchased and installed relatively cheaply. If your telephone carrier didn't give you an Ethernet modem, ask for one.

If you are unwilling or unable to switch from a USB modem, there are a number of Web sites dedicated to helping you get your modem to work with Ubuntu, the best of them being at https://help.ubuntu.com/community/UsbAdslModem/.

LAN/Cable

Most broadband connections in the home or office these days will connect to your PC's NIC port through what's known as a Local Area Network (LAN). The cable used (known in the IT biz as *Cat 5 or Cat 6 wire*) looks like a phone cord, with a rectangular head that plugs into a matching port on your network router and your PC. Another term you have heard bandied about is *Ethernet,* which describes the specific kind of network you are plugged into, namely many PCs connected to one central router.

The router is the heart of your network, and it is important to keep it running nice and smoothly. Make sure that it's got plenty of ventilation, a steady stream of power, and updated software. A happy router is a functioning router.

Routers and PCs speak to each other via the TCP/IP protocol described earlier in this chapter. And because no phones are involved, there's no need to apply additional software to translate anything to PPP or anything else a phone line needs.

What's nice about using a LAN or Ethernet connection is that nine times out of ten, it just works. Plugging the Cat 5 cable into your PC tells Ubuntu to start the software running to get you connected to the network.

A router has two main functions. First, it acts as a switchboard, sending and receiving signals from the PCs on the network with great speed. Second, to keep these signals straight, the router is often responsible for assigning each PC or device that's connected to the network a unique IP address.

An IP address is a unique combination of four numbers (1.2.3.4) that belongs to only one device on a network at a time. Users can specify their own IP address if they want, but often the router does it for them by using a tool known as *DHCP,* which automatically assigns IP addresses to a device whenever it is physically connected to the network.

Most home and small office networks have a combination router/modem at their hub, which not only connects the network devices together but also handles communication with the outside world. Most ISPs will assign modems coming in to their network a unique IP address via DHCP. Any computer connected to that router/modem will, in turn, be assigned a different set of IP addresses by the router's DHCP system.

This is a good thing, too, because there is a physical limit as to how many IP addresses there can be on the Internet. If every computer in the world were to have its own IP, we would quickly run out of addresses. The solution is, every router connecting to the Internet gets its own IP address, while computers and other devices using that router get similar sets of numbers.

For instance, your modem's IP address might be 64.123.45.1, and your neighbor's modem might be 64.123.45.2. But on your network, your computer may be 198.162.2.1, and on his network, his computer might have the same exact IP address. But, there's no conflict, because as far as the Internet is concerned, it only cares about the routers' addresses.

Many routers sold for home use today also have firewall capabilities. A firewall is the metaphorical representation for the very real function a router/modem often has: to keep bad traffic out of its network.

Understanding this is important, because sometimes things don't always work the first time with network connections, and this basic knowledge of networking will help you apply quick fixes to your connection setup if the need arises.

Let's start with a look at how things normally work. These steps will apply to any Ethernet connection, and they assume that DHCP is enabled on your network.

1. Click System | Administration | Network. You will be asked to provide your administrative password.

2. Enter your password. The Network Settings dialog box will open.

3. Click Wired Connection; then click the Properties button. The Settings for Interface eth0 dialog box will open, as shown in Figure 5.7.

4. Confirm that the Configuration field's value is set to Automatic Configuration (DHCP).

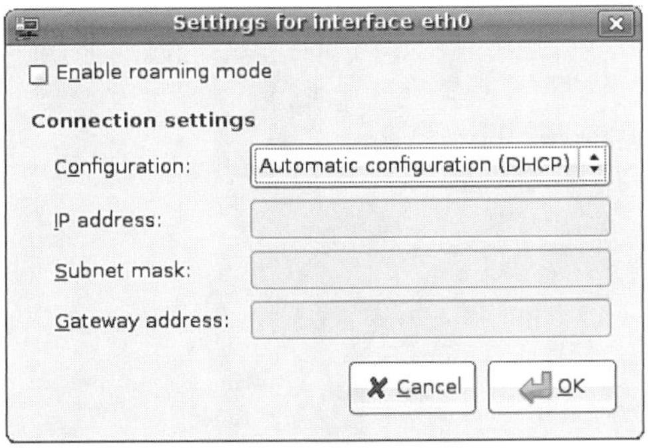

Figure 5.7
Configuring an Ethernet connection.

Setting the IP Address

If your network, for some reason, is set up so that individual devices use specific IP addresses, set your configuration to Static IP address. See your network administrator to get the necessary values for the IP Address, Subnet Mask, and Gateway Address fields.

5. Click OK. The Settings for Interface eth0 dialog box will close.

6. Click Close. The Network Settings dialog box will close.

Now all you need to do is plug in your Ethernet cable to your PC's NIC port. The Network Manager icon in the upper panel will display a swirling animation and notify you of a successful connection, as shown in Figure 5.8.

Now you can access the Internet or other computers and printers on your network.

WiFi

WiFi is one of the real success stories of Ubuntu. There used to be a time not too long ago when wireless network connectivity on Ubuntu, or indeed any Linux distribution, was a sketchy thing at best. Those times are past, and most wireless solutions work very well with Ubuntu.

Almost all new laptops have wireless built in, which is why most mobile users are interested in this section. But even in a home or office PC, wireless can be a good option, because it saves you the time, materials, and hassle in setting up a wired network.

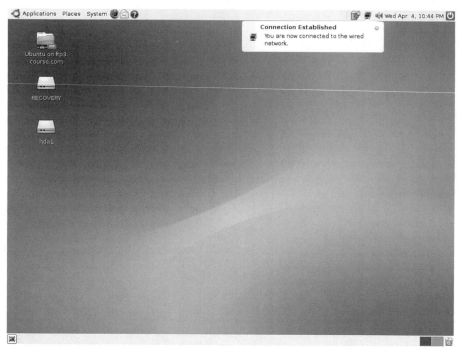

Figure 5.8
Successfully connected by wire.

Info on Wireless Cards

If you are adding wireless functionality to your computer, check out http://help.ubuntu.com/ community/WifiDocs/WirelessCardsSupported for information on the wireless cards that work best with Ubuntu.

Configuring wireless is, on one level, exactly like configuring wired network access. You still need to connect to a router, and you still need a unique IP address for that router to recognize your machine. And, like an Ethernet connection, DHCP is the best way to have that IP address automatically assigned to your PC.

Wireless requires an additional level of configuration. Think of your wireless card as a radio (which it is) that needs to tune into a specific radio station (that's your router). You have to tell your WiFi card exactly which radio station to look for. Or, if you move around with a laptop, it needs to be able to seek out all wireless routers within its range and give you the choice of which router to connect to.

After the whole radio/radio station connection is worked, you will have to tell your WiFi card how to actually talk to the router. This is because most routers' signals are encrypted so that no unauthorized computers can jump on a network. This is usually done with an encryption protocol known as *WEP*.

Setting Up WEP

If WEP is not enabled on your wireless router, it should be. See your router's documentation on how to set this up.

Wireless connections have three levels of complexity to deal with: the network addressing, the wireless network signal acquisition, and the security. Fortunately, Ubuntu's Network Manager handles them all in one place.

1. Click System | Administration | Network. You will be asked to provide your administrative password.

2. Enter your password. The Network Settings dialog box will open.

3. Click Wireless Connection; then click the Properties button. The Settings for Interface dialog box will open, as shown in Figure 5.9.

4. Confirm that the Enable Roaming Mode check box is selected.

5. Click OK. The Settings for Interface dialog box will close.

6. Click Close. The Network Settings dialog box will close.

Figure 5.9
Configuring a wireless connection.

Figure 5.10
Activating a wireless interface.

"Roaming mode" is a new feature in Ubuntu that essentially lets your WiFi card seek out all in-range wireless routers and lets you choose the one to which you connect. It makes using wireless almost ridiculously easy.

1. Right-click the Network Manager applet. A context menu will appear (see Figure 5.10).

2. Confirm that the Enable Wireless setting is checked. If not, select it.

3. Click the Network Manager applet. The control menu will appear (see Figure 5.11).

4. Click the desired wireless network. The Network Manager will display a swirling animation. If the network has no WEP security, or you have connected to it before and the security settings are recalled, the wireless connection will be made.

5. If WEP is enabled, select the appropriate WEP protocol and type in the passphrase for the network.

Figure 5.11
Choose a wireless network.

6. Click Connect to Network. The Network Manager will display a swirling animation, and the wireless connection will be made.

Conclusion

In this chapter, you discovered how easy it is to connect to a network and the Internet with Ubuntu's Network Manager tool. There's not a great deal of mystery to this process, which is how it should be.

Every once in a while, however, things don't always go the way you plan. Because of a lack of hardware manufacturers' support for Linux, some networking devices don't always function. But there are a great many fixes out there, and in Chapter 7 you will learn how to use them.

Before that, however, you need to learn how to find, update, and install software on your Ubuntu PC. Chapter 6, "Installing and Updating Software," will show you all you need to know.

CHAPTER 6

INSTALLING AND UPDATING SOFTWARE

Saying "out of the box" about Ubuntu is really a metaphorical statement. After all, there's no real box from which you unpacked your software, unless you happened to use the ShipIt program to request your free copy of Ubuntu. Still, it's a phrase that gets used a lot in the software business to refer to features and applications that come with a given piece of software or operating system when you first install it on your computer.

One of the really interesting thing about Ubuntu, and Linux in general, is that it comes with a lot of software out of the box. If you recall from Chapter 1, "What is Linux?," by its very modular nature, Ubuntu essentially *is* a collection of separate software applications all coordinated to work together so that the operating system behaves like a single, functioning tool.

Philosophy aside, however, Ubuntu still has a lot of applications packaged for users, enough to get started right out of the box. That doesn't mean there aren't more applications out there ready for you to use.

In this chapter, you will learn:

- How Ubuntu handles software installation.

- About software repositories and how to manage them.

- How to use Update Manager and Synaptic Package Manager.

- How to use the command line to install software.

How Ubuntu Installs Software

In the Windows world, there is usually one way to install software: clicking an installation application that starts up and runs the whole setup for you from start to finish.

In Ubuntu, like most Linux distributions, there are three methods of software installation. Admittedly, one way to install sure sounds attractive and less confusing, but the one-size-fits-all installation service comes with a potentially bad price: Windows installation routines can often overwrite important underpinnings in the operating system for the sake of the application that's currently being installed. This is good for your installed application, but potentially very bad for any pre-existing application on your system that was using that same section of Windows' code.

In Ubuntu, all of the three installation methods take great pains to install applications using only what's already in Ubuntu. If what the application needs is not installed in Ubuntu already, it has what is known as a *dependency*. The installing user (that would be you) will be told about any dependencies and asked how to proceed.

A description of the three installation methods is easy to provide:

- **Self-Contained Installation Program**. This methodology is very much like the method used by Windows. A special installation application is run that *automagically* handles the application's set up on your PC. This type of installation is not common on Ubuntu machines, though some of the larger consumer applications (OpenOffice.org or Firefox) can be installed in this manner. There is one important difference from Windows: No existing software is changed by the installation application. Dependencies are usually handled well, but it's not foolproof; sometimes existing files are overwritten.

- **Compiled from Source.** Remember how any user can get to the source code of any free software application? Well, once you have that code, you can perform what's known as a compilation to turn that code (which humans, at least the smart ones, can read) into something the PC can read and work with. Software compilation isn't hard, but it is time consuming at times, and dependencies are not automatically handled.

- **Package Management.** This method is unique to UNIX-based systems. All of the files and settings needed to install and run an application are either included in one package or listed in the package so a package management application will know what other applications are needed. Ubuntu uses Debian-based, or .deb, packages. (Other Linux distributions, such as Red Hat or SUSE, use Red Hat-based, or .rpm, packages.)

As you may have guessed, package management is the preferred method of software installation in Ubuntu. Package installation is actually performed by an application known as a *package manager*. It helps keep track of all of the applications that are already installed on your PC and also helps keep track of those dependencies mentioned previously. If you install a package that needs some additional software tools to operate properly on your Ubuntu system, it's the package manager that will figure out what other packages you need.

In Ubuntu, there are actually three package managers that will assist you in your installation needs:

- **Synaptic Package Manager.** This robust graphical package manager lists every package available for Ubuntu, which lets you shop for software applications from a very big list. Applications are categorized by type, status on your system (installed or not), or origin. System updates can be managed from Synaptic as well.

- **Update Manager.** Another graphical tool, this application has one job to do: keep your system as up-to-date as possible. If there's a new version of any of your installed applications out there, Update Manager will know about it and flag it for you to download and install.

- **Install and Remove Applications.** This application works directly with the Synaptic Package Manager. It provides an easy-to-use interface for Synaptic, similar to the Windows installation tool.

- **Apt-get.** The original package manager for Debian, this command line application makes getting new packages as easy as typing one line of text and pressing the Enter key.

Each of these four application is configured to find all of the packages from Ubuntu's package repositories. In the next section, we'll walk through repositories and how they work.

Understanding Software Repositories

One of the brilliant features of Ubuntu is that it only comes on one CD-ROM disc. Not every operating system can brag about that. Indeed, many Linux distributions are delivered to users through multiple disks.

Formerly, the strategy in delivering a Linux distribution to your home or office was not very complex: All of the applications a user needed or would ever need in the future would be delivered on one complete set of CD-ROMs (or, later, one or two DVDs). The advantage here was that once you downloaded and burned all of those CDs, you would be all set to run that distribution, without having to download additional software later. But the average CD image download, discussed in Chapter 2, "Before You Install Ubuntu," is nearly 700 MB. That's a lot of data, even for today's broadband connections. Having to do this for three, five, or even seven CDs is a very time-consuming undertaking for most users, unless they were willing to pay to have those same CDs delivered by mail.

Ubuntu flips the model around a bit. Working with the knowledge that a majority of Internet users now have broadband access, Canonical has decided to just send out the absolutely necessary Ubuntu applications on one CD and leave the rest on online servers scattered around the world for users to download as needed. These collections of applications are called *repositories*.

This may seem inefficient, since you must have Internet access of some kind to make this work. But consider this: Most operating systems update themselves via the Internet anyway, so in order to keep Ubuntu up to date, online access was needed anyway. And downloading and burning only one CD is a lot faster than CDs plural. Delivering a "core" distribution also gives the user much greater flexibility in picking and choosing what software applications he wants on his system. It also means his hard drives won't be loaded with stuff he doesn't need.

To give you an idea of just how much more software is available, consider these numbers: A standard installation of Ubuntu has around 1,100 packages. Currently, there are over 21,000 total application packages available.

Ubuntu, like its predecessor Debian GNU/Linux, organizes its software in repositories—those collections of applications mentioned earlier. There are four primary repositories for Ubuntu, each holding a specific class of software. Let's walk through them now.

Touring the Repositories

The four official Ubuntu repositories are named like something out of a science-fiction novel, but once you know what each repository holds, the labels make more sense.

- **Main.** This repository holds all of Ubuntu's officially supported software. Everything that Ubuntu must have to actually run is in here, and all of the software is under a free software license. Additional applications in this repository include AbiWord, Evolution, Firefox, Gaim, OpenOffice.org, and Thunderbird.

- **Restricted.** Ubuntu supports the apps in this small repository, but they do not come with a totally free license. Curiously, the Linux kernel is found here (because some of the drivers that plug into the kernel are not free). Other applications include drivers for proprietary hardware and kernel modules for VMWare.

- **Universe.** These software applications are free but are supported by their developers (the community), not by Canonical. Applications such as Apache, Eclipse, Firebird, PHP, and Python are included here, as well as many games and small utilities.

- **Multiverse.** Also community supported, the applications in this group are not under a totally free license. The Flash player, Java plug-ins, and Mplayer are found in this repository.

Adding Repositories

These are not the only repositories that Ubuntu can use. There are many community-run repositories on the Internet for Ubuntu, each holding specialized software that Canonical does not want to host. And because of licensing issues, even Canonical hosts another repository that it does not include in its set of four primary repositories.

There are many software applications out there that can run on Linux, but because their licenses are completely proprietary, some Linux distributions won't touch them with a 10-foot pole. Debian GNU/Linux is particularly strict about this kind of thing (which is why they have nonfree repositories set up). By virtue of its Debian origins, Ubuntu's makers feel obligated to abide by this philosophy, keeping totally commercial packages away from Ubuntu.

But there is an important distinction here. While Canonical does not release commercial software with Ubuntu, that does not preclude letting users have access to a commercial repository after they have downloaded and installed Ubuntu. A fine distinction, to be sure, but it gives users the advantage of making their own choices about what software they want to use.

All of the package managers in Ubuntu work off a master list of repositories stored on your PC. From this file, known as sources.list, the managers know which repositories to check for new software and whether there are any updates available for software installed on your system. If you want these managers to peruse another repository, you will need to modify sources.list with the new information. The good news? Ubuntu has a new tool that lets you do it in just a few steps.

1. Click the System | Administration | Software Sources menu command. You will be asked for your administrative password.

2. Enter your password and click OK. The Software Sources dialog box will appear, as shown in Figure 6.1.

3. Click the Third-Party Software tab. The Third-Party Software page will appear (see Figure 6.2).

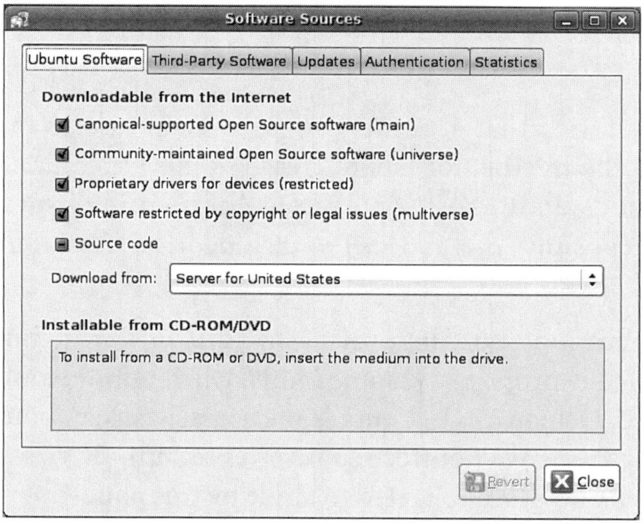

Figure 6.1
Updating Software Sources.

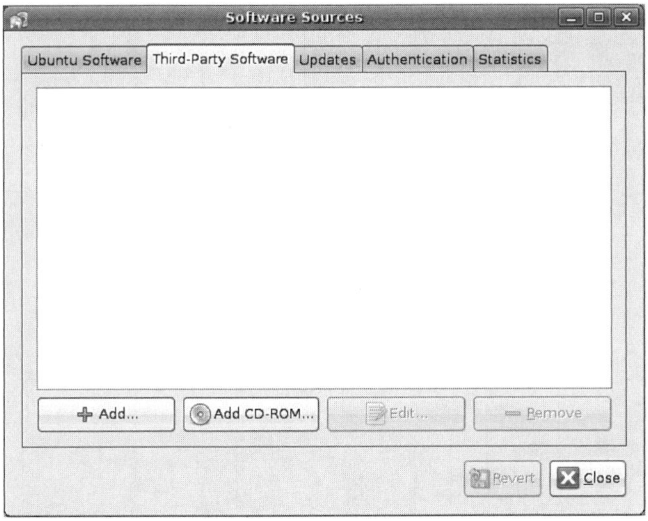

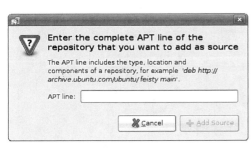

Figure 6.2
Adding new repositories.

Figure 6.3
Asking for the repository's address.

4. Click the Add button. A dialog box will appear asking for the complete APT line for the new source repository, shown in Figure 6.3.

Explaining Repository Commands

A repository is referred to in sources.list by a very specific line of text that defines not only where the repository is located on the Internet, but also what repository is specifically being connected. An example would be:

```
deb http://archive.ubuntu.com/ubuntu feisty main
```

Where deb is the type of package (Debian) you want to look for, http://archive.ubuntu.com/ubuntu is the Internet address of the server and directory where the repository is located, feisty is the version of Ubuntu you are using, and main is the name of the specific repository.

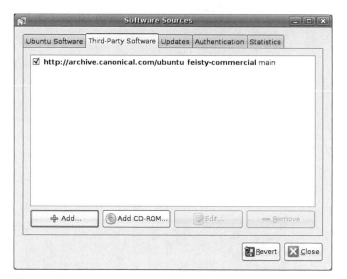

Figure 6.4
A new repository.

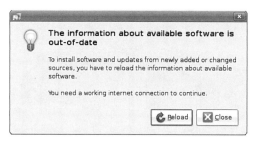

Figure 6.5
Package managers must be informed about new repositories.

5. Type **deb http://archive.canonical.com/ubuntu feisty-commercial main** in the APT Line field.

6. Click Add Source. The dialog box will close, and the new repository will appear in the list of repositories (see Figure 6.4).

7. Click Close. A warning dialog will appear (see Figure 6.5).

8. Click Reload. The Downloading Package Information message box will open, displaying the progress of the refreshing of the package lists. It will close automatically when complete, as will the Software Sources dialog box.

Now, the next time you run any of Ubuntu's package managers, it will be aware of the new repository and let you view and install software from it. This will include any commercial software that Canonical has been licensed to distribute.

Using Update Manager

Of all the Ubuntu package managers, you will likely use the Update Manager the most. This is because it's the one that constantly runs in the background to see what, if any, updates are available for software you have installed on your PC. This is nice because it has a set-it-and-forget-it quality that means you don't have to worry about whether you might have an older, buggy version of your software.

Updating Current Software

By default, the Update Manager is configured to notify you when software updates are available—something it checks on a daily basis when your PC is connected to the Internet. When updates for your installed software are found, an orange starburst icon will appear in the upper panel, along with an initial pop-up message, as shown in Figure 6.6.

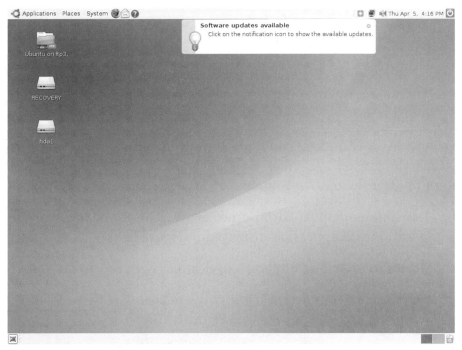

Figure 6.6
A heads-up about new updates.

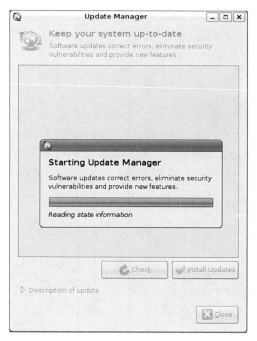

Figure 6.7
Starting Update Manager.

The message will close itself after a few seconds, but the notification icon will remain until Update Manager is actually run.

1. Start Update Manager by clicking the notification icon. The Update Manager window will open, and the start process will immediately begin, as shown in Figure 6.7.

2. When the process is complete, you'll see a list of updates Ubuntu suggests you install (see Figure 6.8). Click on an application to update to see a short description of what the update contains.

3. Click the Description of Update drop-down arrow. A list of changes for the selected application will appear, as displayed in Figure 6.9.

4. If you choose not to update an application, clear its check box to deselect it.

5. When your choices are complete, click Install Updates. The Downloading Package Files dialog box will appear (see Figure 6.10).

6. If you want to see more detail on the download, click the Show Progress of Single Files arrow, which will display a list similar to the one in Figure 6.11.

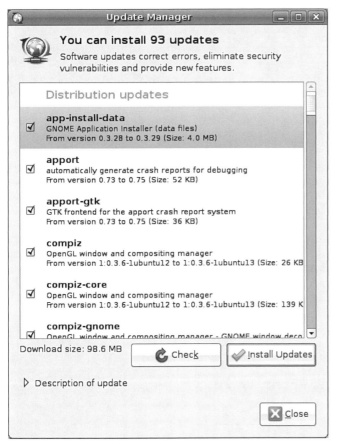

Figure 6.8
The update list.

7. Once the download is complete, the packages will be installed, as shown in Figure 6.12. Figure 6.13 shows the result of clicking the Details drop-down arrow to see how the process is coming along.

8. When finished, the Changes Applied message box will appear (see Figure 6.14).

9. Click Close to shut down the message box. The Update Manager will reflect Ubuntu's updated status (shown in Figure 6.15).

10. Click Close. The Update Manager will close.

Occasionally, you may be required to restart your Ubuntu system after an update. This is not very common, because the modular nature of Ubuntu means

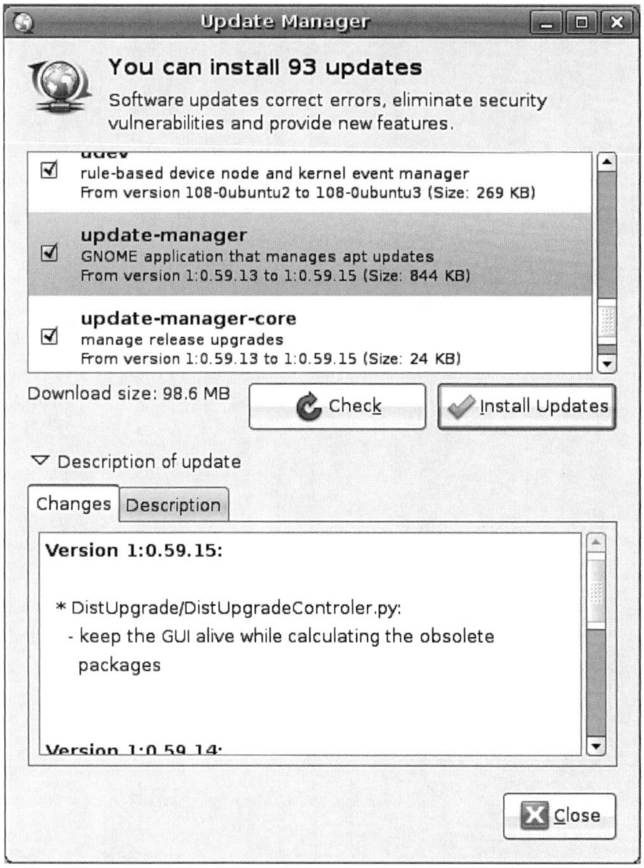

Figure 6.9
You can read about the whys of an update.

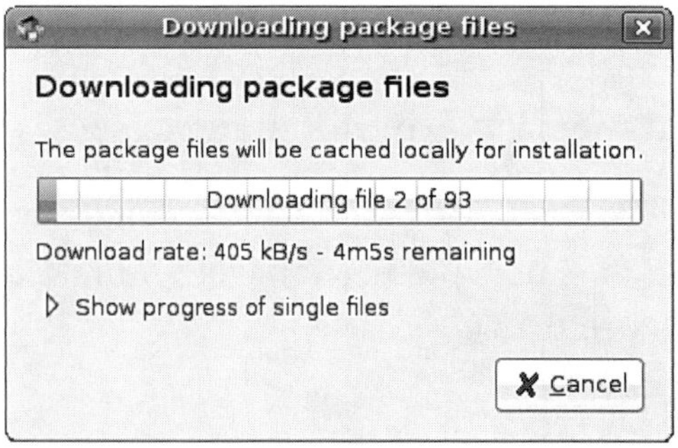

Figure 6.10
The update process begins.

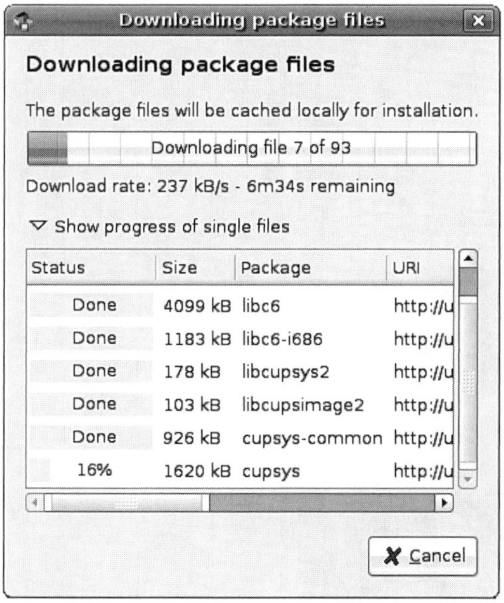

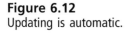

Figure 6.11
Monitoring individual file downloads.

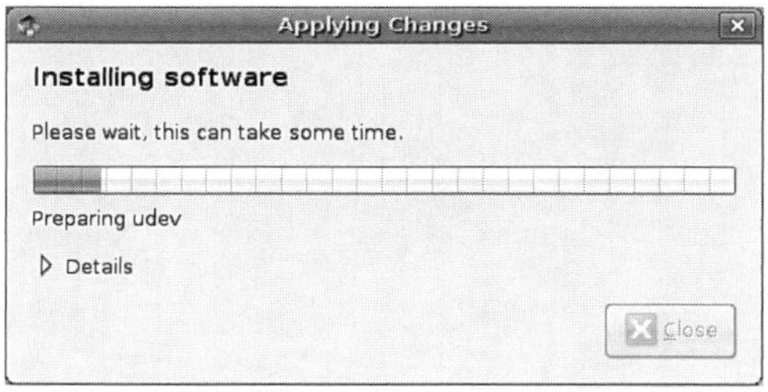

Figure 6.12
Updating is automatic.

that typically changes to one application won't affect others. But some updates, such as a newer version of the Linux kernel, do require a system restart for the changes to kick in. If that is the case, a message box like the one in Figure 6.16 will appear when you close the Update Manager.

Choose the option you want. It is recommended that you restart as soon as you can, but if you have other work to do, you can wait by clicking Restart Later. (A system shutdown at the end of the day will count as a restart.)

Figure 6.13
Monitoring individual file updates.

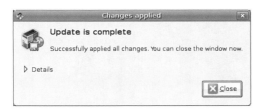

Figure 6.14
A completed update.

Tip
_____

One thing that's important to remember is that you can only run one update or package management session at a time. Otherwise, the package managers will confuse each other.
_____

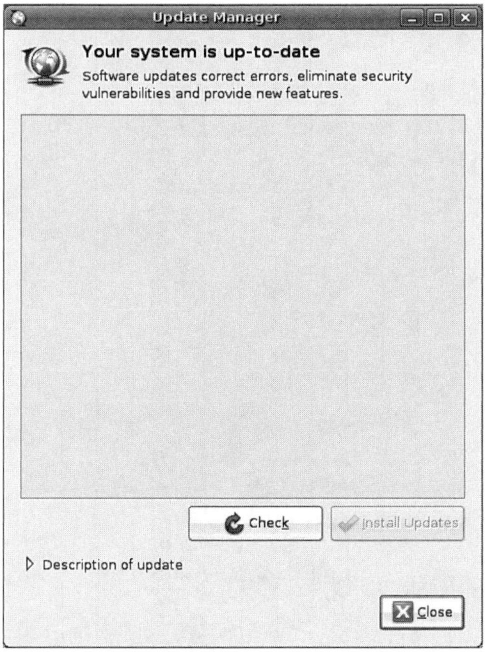

Figure 6.15
Ubuntu is up to date.

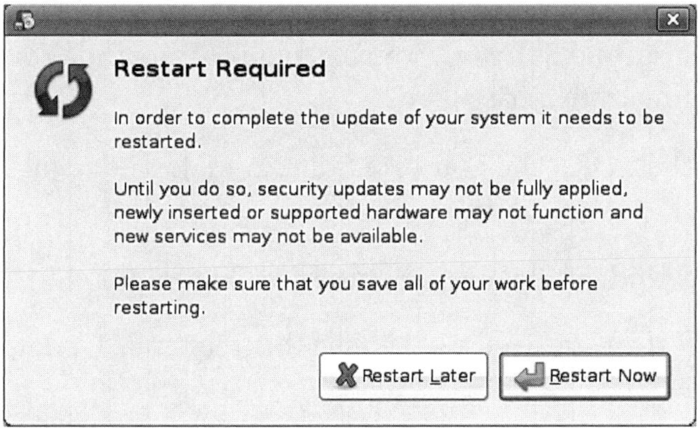

Figure 6.16
Some updates require restart.

Configuring Updates

At the beginning of the discussion of Update Manager, it was mentioned that this application checked for updates daily and notified you when updates were available. But what if you want to do more than that? You can configure Update Manager to reflect your needs very simply.

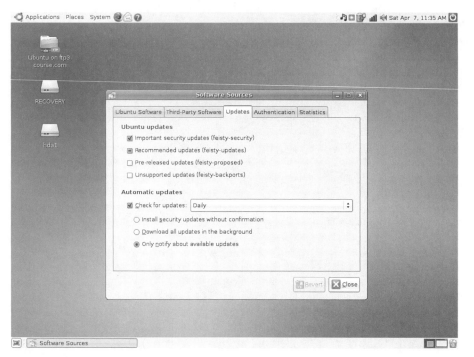

Figure 6.17
Configuring automatic updates.

1. Click the System | Administration | Software Sources menu command. You will be asked for your administrative password.

2. Enter your password and click OK. The Software Sources dialog box will appear.

3. Click the Updates tab. The Updates page will appear (see Figure 6.17).

4. Click the Check for Updates drop-down list to change the frequency Update Manager checks for updates.

5. For maximum security protection, click the Install Security Updates Without Confirmation radio button.

6. If you change your mind, click the Revert button.

7. Click Close. If any changes were made, a warning dialog will appear.

8. Click Reload. The Downloading package information message box will open, displaying the progress of the refreshing of the package lists. It will close automatically when complete, as will the Software Sources dialog box.

Using Synaptic Package Manager

As useful as the Update Manager is, it doesn't compare to the full-featured nature of the Synaptic Package Manager, Ubuntu's killer tool. This package manager is one of the tools unique to Ubuntu, and is probably a big contributor to Ubuntu's popularity.

It's just that good.

Unlike Update Manager, which just updates existing packages, Synaptic can update, install, and uninstall applications with just a few clicks.

Navigating Synaptic is easy. You can start the application by clicking the System | Administration | Synaptic Package Manager menu command, which (after you enter your administrative password) brings up the Synaptic window, as shown in Figure 6.18.

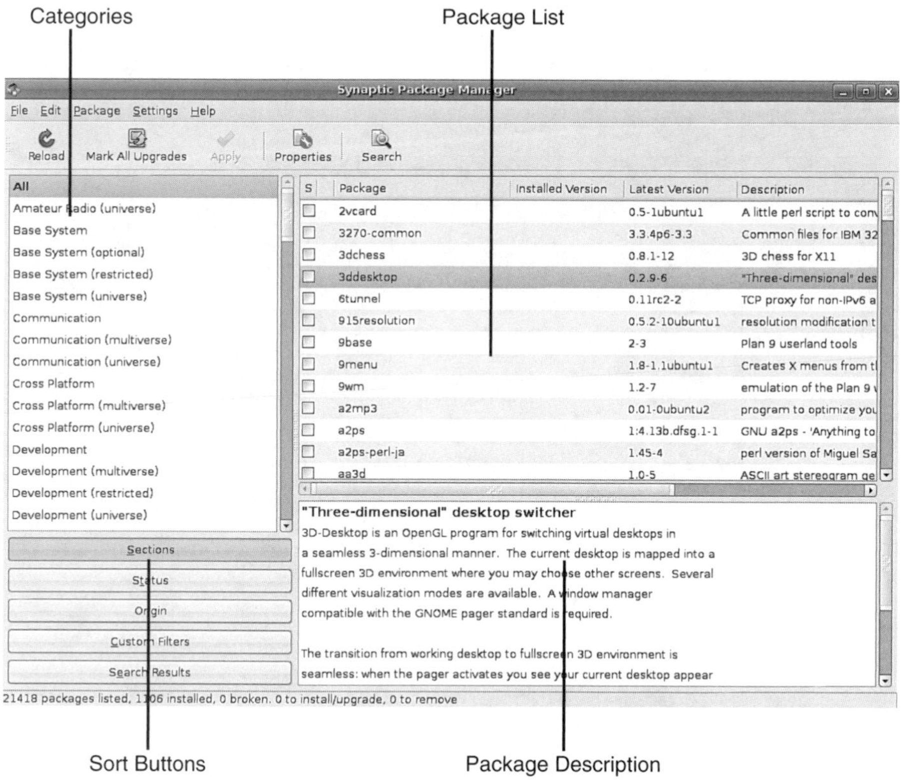

Figure 6.18
Synaptic Package Manager.

- **Categories.** Applications are sorted into various categories, which are listed in this pane. The categories are dictated by the sort buttons and can display package type, status of package (installed or not), or repository of origin.

- **Sort Buttons.** These buttons control the values listed in the Categories pane.

- **Package List.** When a category is selected, all of the packages it contains are listed in this pane.

- **Package Description.** Clicking a package will display a concise description of the application here.

Updating Current Software

Updating software in Synaptic is not a background operation as it is with the Update Manager, but it is still very straightforward.

1. Click the Status button. A list of Status categories will appear in the Category pane.

2. If available, click Installed (Upgradeable). A list of packages that need to be upgraded will appear in the Package List pane (see Figure 6.19).

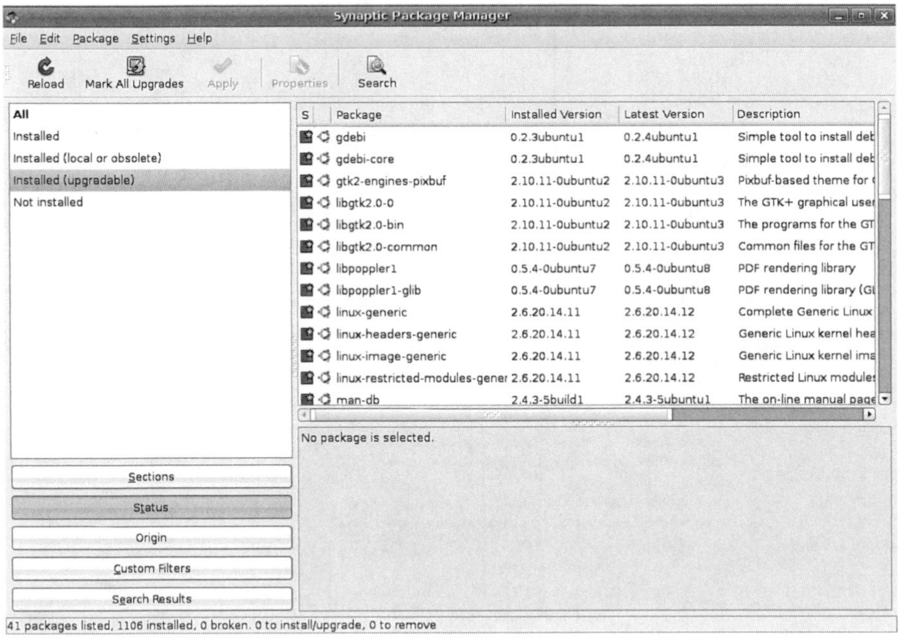

Figure 6.19
A list of updates.

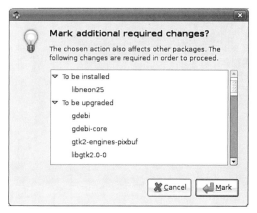

Figure 6.20
Confirm the upgrade choices.

3. Confirm that this list is the most current by clicking the Reload button. The Downloading Package Information message box will briefly appear as Synaptic checks the known repositories for current information.

4. Click the Mark All Upgrades button. A confirmation dialog will appear (see Figure 6.20).

Getting More than You Asked For

You may note in your upgrade activity that Synaptic is requesting to install new software. This does happen occasionally, as an updated application needs to access more software tools based on its dependencies as its capabilities expand.

5. Click Mark. The packages will now be marked for upgrade.

6. Click Apply. The Summary dialog box will appear, asking you once again to confirm your choices, as seen in Figure 6.21.

7. Click Apply. The update process will begin.

8. When the Changes Applied dialog box appears, click the Close button.

Installing New Software

While using Synaptic for updates is all well and good, where the application really shines is in package installation. Repository-based package installation is a powerful way of installing software. Not only is it easy, but also, once Synaptic

Figure 6.21
Confirm the upgrade choices again.

installs it, you can be sure that any future updates of the application will be tracked.

Looking for the Right Package

For any package installation or uninstallation, you can use the Search function in Synaptic to find any given package that Synaptic is aware of.

1. Explore Synaptic until you locate a package you want to install and select it. The description of the package will appear in the Description pane.

2. Click a package's Selection check box. A context menu will appear (see Figure 6.22).

3. Click the Mark for Installation menu command. If any additional packages are needed, a warning dialog will appear. Otherwise, proceed to Step 5.

Co-Dependencies

When you install new software, Synaptic may request to install other software. These are dependencies for the application you wanted to install in the first place. You must install them if you want your desired package to install.

4. Click Mark to Install Any Additional Packages. The warning dialog will close, and the appropriate packages will be marked for installation.

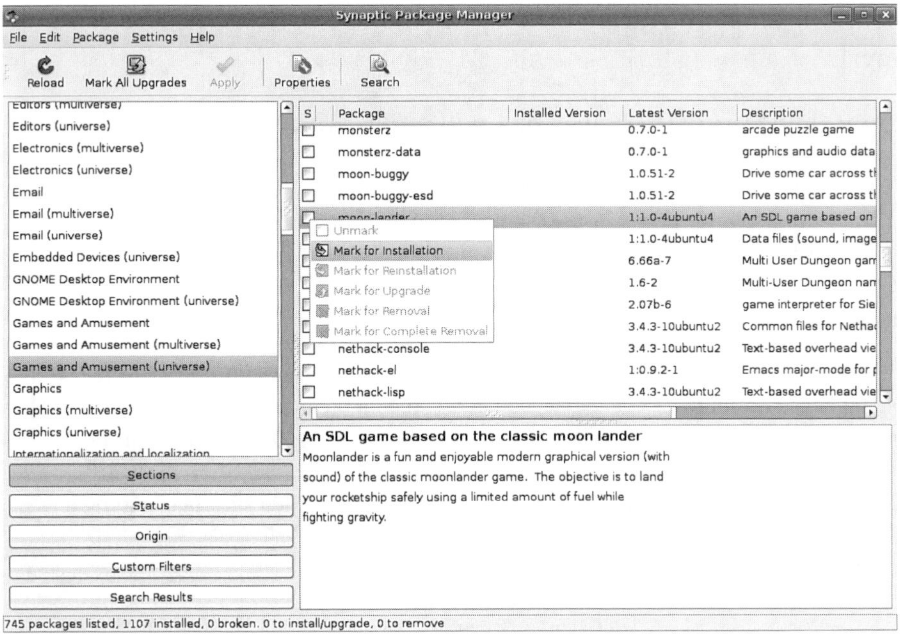

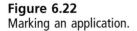

Figure 6.22
Marking an application.

5. Click Apply. The Summary dialog box will appear to confirm your changes.

6. Click Apply. The installation process will begin.

7. When the Changes Applied dialog box appears, click the Close button.

Uninstalling Software

Sometimes—not often—you will run into a situation where you need to remove an application from your Ubuntu system. I say "not often," because Ubuntu only installs what you really need, and anything else is software that you probably added in the first place.

Still, just in case the need arises, here is how to uninstall any application with Synaptic.

1. Explore Synaptic until you locate a package you want to uninstall and select it. The description of the package will appear in the Description pane.

2. Click a package's Selection check box. A context menu will appear.

3. Click the Mark for Removal menu command. The package will be marked for removal.

4. Click Apply. The Summary dialog box will appear to confirm your changes.

5. Click Apply. The installation process will begin.

6. When the Changes Applied dialog box appears, click the Close button.

How Far to Remove

If an application uses unique configuration settings (such as how individual users prefer to use the application), then you should mark the package for complete removal. This will uninstall the application and all of its configuration files. If "Installed (residual config)" appears in the Status Category pane, this is a sign that there are some configuration files left over from a Removal operation, which you can save if you think you will ever need to install that package again.

Managing Software with Install and Remove Applications

Synaptic is an excellent application to use for installation and upgrading of software, and you really can't go wrong using it. But sometimes using such a powerful tool is a bit of overkill for some users, particularly those coming from a Windows or Mac background.

To help with this, Ubuntu includes an application called *Install and Remove Applications,* which is very similar to Windows' installation application. While not a catchy name, it still uses the Synaptic program to do the work, and the interface is much simpler and—ideally—easier to manage.

1. Select the Applications | Add/Remove menu command. The Add/Remove Applications window will open (see Figure 6.23).

2. Change the value of the Show field's drop-down list to All Available Applications. The list of applications will change to include anything not installed on your machine.

3. Click Games. The Games packages will be displayed in the Applications pane (see Figure 6.24).

4. Click the Hearts check box. The Community Install message box will appear, asking you to confirm the installation choice (see Figure 6.25).

Figure 6.23
The Install and Remove Applications tool.

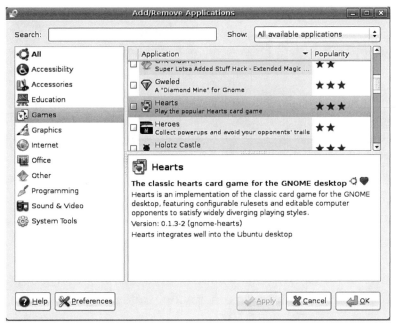

Figure 6.24
All work and no play.

Figure 6.25
Confirm your installation selection.

5. Click Install. The message box will close.

6. Click OK. An Apply dialog box will appear.

7. Click Apply. You will be asked for your administrative password.

8. Type your password and click OK. The Synaptic Package Manager will open
   and automatically install the software.

9. Click Close to close the Changes Applied dialog box and the Add/Remove
   window.

Removing an application using this simple interface is just as simple.

1. Select the Applications | Add/Remove menu command. The Add/Remove
   Applications window will open.

2. Change the value of the Show field's drop-down list to Installed Applications. The list of applications will change to include anything installed on
   your machine.

3. Click Games. The Games packages will be displayed in the Applications pane.

4. Click the Mahjongg check box. The Remove Installed Application message
   box will appear, asking you to confirm the removal choice (see Figure 6.26).

5. Click Remove or Remove All. The message box will close.

6. Click OK. An Apply dialog box will appear.

7. Click Apply. You will be asked for your administrative password.

8. Type your password and click OK. The Synaptic Package Manager will open
   and automatically remove the software and any dependent applications.

9. Click Close to close the Changes Applied dialog box and the Add/Remove
   window.

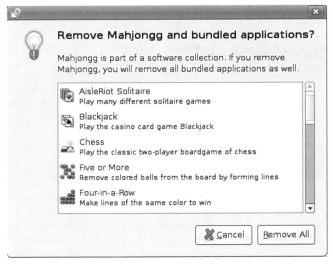

Figure 6.26
Confirm your removal selection.

Managing Software with Apt-get

Unlike the other two package managers in Ubuntu, apt-get is what is known as a command-line application. Much of what users see in any Linux distribution is driven by these command-line programs. In fact, both Synaptic and Update Manager use apt-get at their cores to do much of their work. Synaptic and Update Manager serve as easier-to-use graphical interfaces for apt-get.

"Apt" is shorthand for Advanced Packaging Tool and is common to all Debian-based Linux distributions. It is a very powerful manager, and because it doesn't have to take up system resources creating neat-looking interfaces, it's pretty fast, too.

Command-line applications are always run in a Terminal window, one of the plainest and most versatile tools found in Ubuntu. To start Terminal, click the Applications | Accessories | Terminal menu command (see Figure 6.27).

Entering commands in Terminal is just a matter of typing the command and pressing the Enter key. To see a list of all of the files in the current directory, type **ls** and then press Enter.

There are lots of very cool command-line tools to use, but for now, let's stay with apt-get and examine other tools later in the book. One thing that must be noted is

Username   Computer   Command
            (Host) Name   Prompt

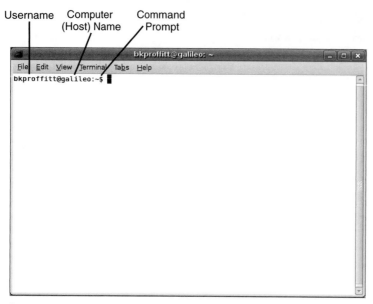

Figure 6.27
The Ubuntu Terminal.

that apt-get is an application that needs administrative permissions to run (just like Update Manager and Synaptic). To do this on the command line, type the command `sudo` before your `apt-get` commands. The first time you do this, you will be asked for your administrative password. But after that, just `sudo` will do.

The first thing you should do, particularly if you have made any changes to your repositories list, is make sure apt-get knows about it. To do this, type

`sudo apt-get update`

A long list of repositories will appear. When the screen reads Done and the command prompt reappears, it is finished. Once you do this, you have complete access to the latest repository lists. You can also use the `apt-cache` command to search for applications in the repositories. To find a game called moon-lander, for example, type

`sudo apt-cache search moon-lander`

This will return information on two packages:

```
moon-lander - An SDL game based on the classic moon lander
moon-lander-data - Data files (sound, images) for moon lander
```

If a package is listed, then installing it is as simple as running:

```
sudo apt-get install moon-lander
```

This will get you this result:

```
Reading package lists... Done
Building dependency tree
Reading state information... Done
The following extra packages will be installed:
  moon-lander-data
The following NEW packages will be installed:
  moon-lander moon-lander-data
0 upgraded, 2 newly installed, 0 to remove and 0 not upgraded.
Need to get 0B/1354kB of archives.
After unpacking 2060kB of additional disk space will be used.
Do you want to continue [Y/n]?
```

Type **Y** or just press Enter. The installation process will quickly finish.

Removing a package is just as easy. Type:

```
sudo apt-get remove moon-lander
```

This will display this output:

```
Reading package lists... Done
Building dependency tree
Reading state information... Done
The following packages were automatically installed and are no longer required:
  libsdl-mixer1.2 moon-lander-data libsdl-image1.2 libsmpeg0
Use 'apt-get autoremove' to remove them.
The following packages will be REMOVED:
  moon-lander
0 upgraded, 0 newly installed, 1 to remove and 0 not upgraded.
Need to get 0B of archives.
After unpacking 127kB disk space will be freed.
Do you want to continue [Y/n]?
```

Type **Y** or just press Enter. The uninstall process will finish quickly. You may have noticed in this example that apt-get informed you of additional packages that were added when you first installed this application using Synaptic earlier in the chapter. If you wanted to remove them as well, you could have typed **n** and then typed:

```
sudo apt-get autoremove moon-lander
```
which would have removed all of the associated applications.

If you want to have apt-get download the latest versions of your installed applications, type:

```
sudo apt-get upgrade
```

This will perform the same function as the Update Manager.

Conclusion

By now you know the three ways you can use package management to update, install, or uninstall software in Ubuntu. And you have much more ability to play and work in Ubuntu.

These functions will also help you get things to work in Ubuntu. As mentioned in earlier chapters, sometimes things in Ubuntu don't work as smoothly as they should. Fixes abound in the Ubuntu community, and now that you know how to install software, you can easily apply any needed fixes to your Ubuntu PC. You'll learn how in the next chapter, "Making Things Work."

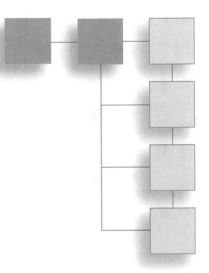

CHAPTER 7

MAKING THINGS WORK

Ubuntu is not perfect.

It will come as a surprise to some reading an Ubuntu book when this passage is found, but the truth must be told. Installing any operating system on an untried computer is a bit of a risk to begin with because unforeseen hardware conflicts can trip up any operating system installation. (Just ask recent Vista users who are finding some hardware and software compatibility problems with their new purchase.)

If you installed Ubuntu on a desktop PC, then you may not have had any problems or concerns show up thus far. And that's great, because eventually almost all of the trouble spots Ubuntu has now won't be affecting users in the future. And, of course, if you have purchased a Dell computer with Ubuntu pre-installed, then none of the concerns highlighted in this chapter will apply to you.

Even if you are not having difficulties making something work, this chapter will still be useful to you. There's still some unfinished business for most users to contend with:

- Creating and managing additional user accounts.

- Setting up a printer.

- Using USB storage.

- Working with digital cameras.

- Troubleshooting some hardware concerns.

Setting Up User Accounts

When you first installed Ubuntu, two user accounts were created: root and your own. Root is the name of Ubuntu's "super" account. Like all Linux distributions, the root user account is the most powerful—and the most dangerous. That's because root can literally do anything possible on an Ubuntu machine. This is very, very helpful if you are trying to accomplish a lot of admin tasks quickly and don't want to keep typing in the administrative password. But it's very, very bad if you make a mistake and accidentally end up deleting every file on your system.

This is not to mention what could happen if you walked away from a machine logged in as root and someone happened to walk by and play with your computer. Or hack into it from the outside, no matter where you are.

Important Safety Tip

Don't log in as root. Ever.

Your account will have some administrative capabilities, by virtue of the fact that the original, installing user of a system is going to be the one administering it. This is not always true, and your PC may need to have multiple user accounts on it so each user can have his own workspace.

To set up a new account, follow these steps.

1. Click the System | Administration | User and Groups menu command. The Users Settings dialog box will open, as shown in Figure 7.1.

2. Click the Add User button. The New User Account dialog box will open (see Figure 7.2).

Figure 7.1
Users and Group control.

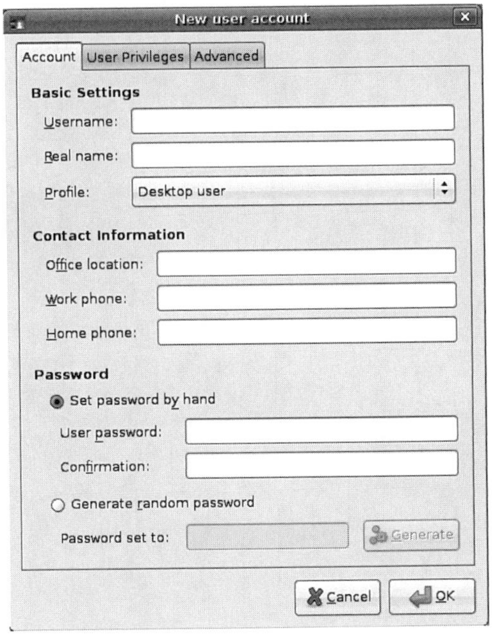

Figure 7.2
Basic user account information.

3. Using the user's information, fill in the information in the first two sections of the Account page. Set the Profile as Desktop User.

- **Administrative User.** This user has the rights and privileges to perform many tasks on this Ubuntu PC, provided he knows his administrative password.

- **Desktop User.** The regular user. He can see and use most of the applications on the PC, but he can't change system settings.

- **Unprivileged User.** A guest user who has very little access to a computer's applications and files, only enough to do assigned tasks.

4. Click the Generate Random Password radio button. A randomly generated strong password will appear in the Password Set To field.

Weak versus Strong

Ubuntu-generated passwords are very strong, which means they are more difficult for password cracking programs to figure out. Many users have weak passwords, like names, numbers, or words that they can easily remember. The problem is, the more English-like a password, the easier it is for a cracking program to guess that password.

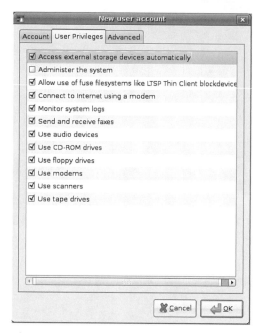

Figure 7.3
Basic user privilege information.

5. Click the User Privileges tab. The User Privileges page will appear (see Figure 7.3).

6. Confirm the privilege settings, unchecking any that you don't want this user to have.

7. Click the Advanced tab. The Advanced page will appear (see Figure 7.4).

8. Set the Main Group value to Users.

9. Click OK. The New User Account dialog box will close, and the new user will be added to the list of accounts.

10. Click Close. The User Settings dialog box will close.

After any user is created, you can modify his account if need be.

1. Click the System | Administration | User and Groups menu command. The Users Settings dialog box will open.

2. Click a user to select the account.

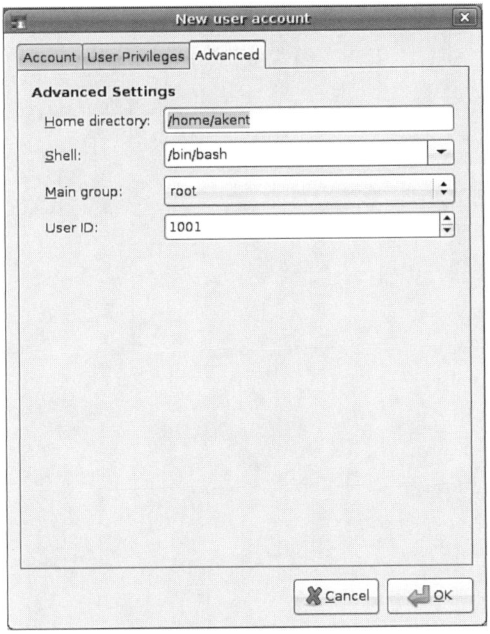

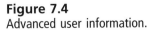

Figure 7.4
Advanced user information.

3. Click the Properties button. The Account '[user]' Properties dialog box will open (see Figure 7.5).

4. Make the changes you need in any of the three pages.

5. Click OK. The Account '[user]' Properties dialog box will close.

6. Click Close. The User Settings dialog box will close.

If a user will no longer be using this computer, such as when an employee leaves a company, it's a good idea to remove the user's account.

1. Click the System | Administration | User and Groups menu command. The User Settings dialog box will open.

2. Click a user to select the account.

3. Click the Delete button. A warning dialog box will appear (see Figure 7.6).

4. Click Delete. The user account will be removed from the list of accounts.

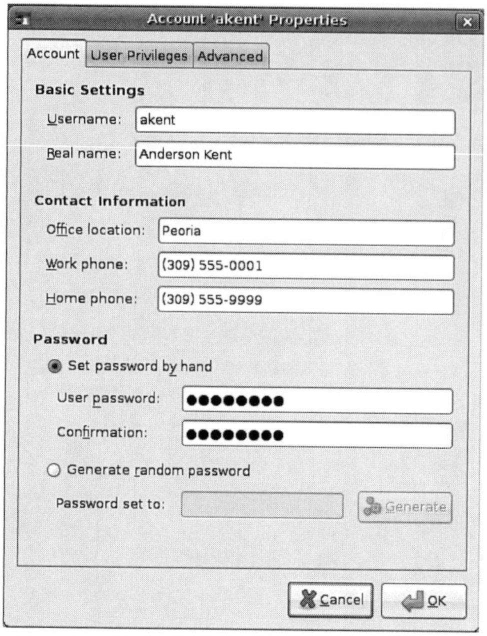

Figure 7.5
Editing user information.

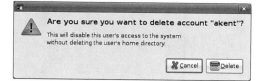

Figure 7.6
Make sure you want to delete a user account.

Really Gone?

When an account is deleted, the user's data is still intact. But only an administrator can get to it if need be.

5. Click Close. The Users Settings dialog box will close.

Using Printers

Early computers did not communicate well. The first digital calculating device that could safely be called a computer was the Harvard Mark I, a five-ton, 750,000-component device that read its programming code from paper tape and its data from punch cards. Data was output on a similar medium.

Multimedia was a bit of a wash as well. The only sound the Mark I generated was the internal clicking of its components, which sounded a bit like a "roomful of ladies knitting." Hardly multimedia.

For those of you old enough to remember the Apple I and II microcomputers released in 1973, you'll recall that they weren't big on multimedia either. Little beeps and clicks were about all the sound they emitted. Printing was coming along, though, as dot-matrix printers wound out reams of perforated paper.

Today, the number of communication devices that can be connected to PCs is phenomenal. Printers, speakers, television tuners, cameras, alarm systems... even cars.

In the meantime, you can focus on more immediate concerns, such as getting your own peripheral communication devices hooked up to your Ubuntu PC—namely, a printer.

Setting Up a Local Printer

There are two ways of connecting a printer to your Ubuntu PC. The first is locally, by plugging your printer in via your computer's parallel or, more frequently these days, USB port.

Once your printer is physically connected to your system and is powered on, follow these steps to get your printer working.

1. Click the System | Administration | Printing menu command. The Printers window will open (see Figure 7.7).

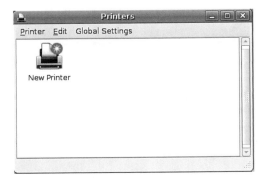

Figure 7.7
The Printers window.

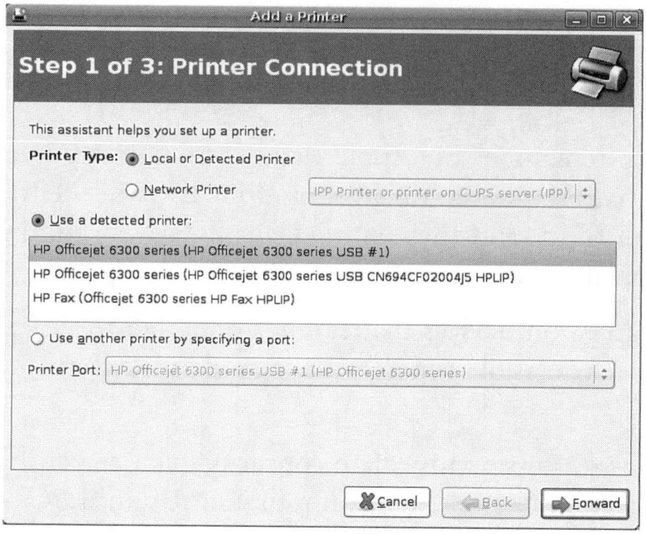

Figure 7.8
Starting the Add a Printer wizard.

2. Double-click the New Printer icon. The gnome-cups-add message box will appear, and your system will begin to search for a connected printer. When found, the Add a Printer wizard will appear (see Figure 7.8).

3. Confirm the Printer Type setting is Local or Detected Printer.

4. Confirm the correct printer is selected in the Detected Printer field.

One Printer or Many?

Sometimes, a single printer will show up as a multiple listing, as in the example in Figure 7.8. This is because some printers (particularly newer ones) have a separate on board memory card, which the CUPS database in Ubuntu reads as a separate device. Pick the listing with the most information and proceed. If this does not work, you can always come back and connect to the other option.

Ubuntu Loves HP

HP has done some excellent work making its printer drivers available for Linux users. If you have an HP printer, and an HPLIP option is available, definitely choose that one. HPLIP is an HP-developed control application for HP devices.

5. Click the Forward button. The Printer Driver page will appear (see Figure 7.9).

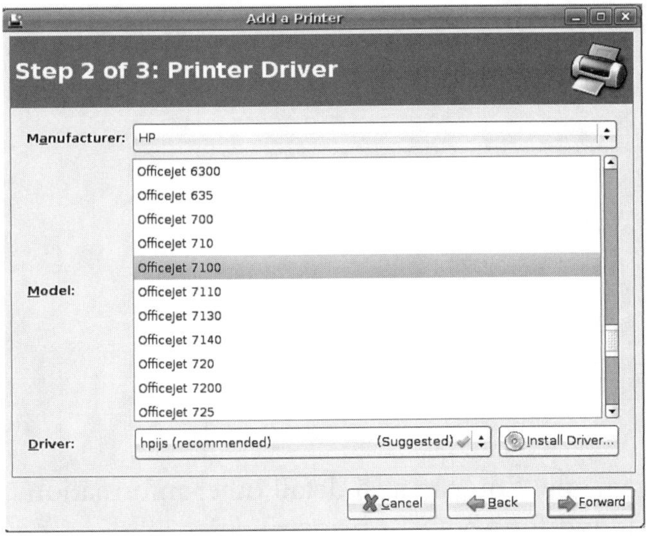

Figure 7.9
Confirm your printer driver.

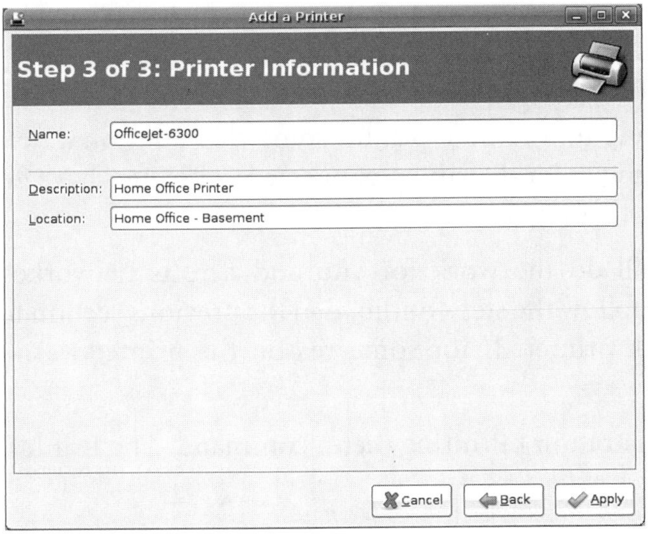

Figure 7.10
Enter information about your printer.

6. Confirm that the correct and recommended driver is selected for your printer.

7. Click the Forward button. The Printer Information page will appear (see Figure 7.10).

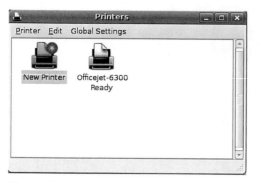

Figure 7.11
A ready printer.

8. Give your printer a unique name. You can also detail other information, such as where the printer is and for what it is primarily used.

9. Click Apply. The new printer will appear in the Printers window, as shown in Figure 7.11.

Setting Up a Network Printer

The steps involved in connecting to a remote printer somewhere out on a network are very similar to getting a local printer connected. You just have to identify where on the network that printer is.

Most of the time, Ubuntu will do the work for you and detects networked printers. If that's the case, then follow the steps outlined in the previous section to connect to a detected network printer. If for some reason the printer wasn't found, follow these steps:

1. Click the System | Administration | Printing menu command. The Printers window will open.

2. Double-click the New Printer icon. The gnome-cups-add message box will appear, and your system will begin to search for a connected printer. When found, the Add a Printer wizard will appear.

3. If the network printer you want isn't found, confirm the Printer Type setting is Network Printer.

4. Choose the type of connection.

- IPP Printer or Printer on CUPS (IPP). These printers are tracked by a CUPS-enabled server. If your network uses CUPS as a printer management tool, your network administrator will inform you of the proper configuration settings.

- Windows Printer (SMB). Like folders, printers connected to Windows machines can be shared. If there are shared printers on your network, a tool called *Samba* will let you find and connect to them.

- UNIX Printer (LPD). Printers connected to UNIX servers in your network can be found and plugged into.

- TCP/Socket, HP JetDirect, Raw connection. Printers directly connected to an Ethernet network should use this setting.

5. Enter the correct location of your printer on the network. (For example, a TCP/Socket connection will ask for Host and Port information, as shown in Figure 7.12. *Host*, in this instance, would be the IP address of your printer on your network. *Port* is usually 9100, so leave this value as is.)

6. Click the Forward button. The Printer Driver page will appear.

7. Confirm that the correct and recommended driver is selected for your printer.

8. Click the Forward button. The Printer Information page will appear.

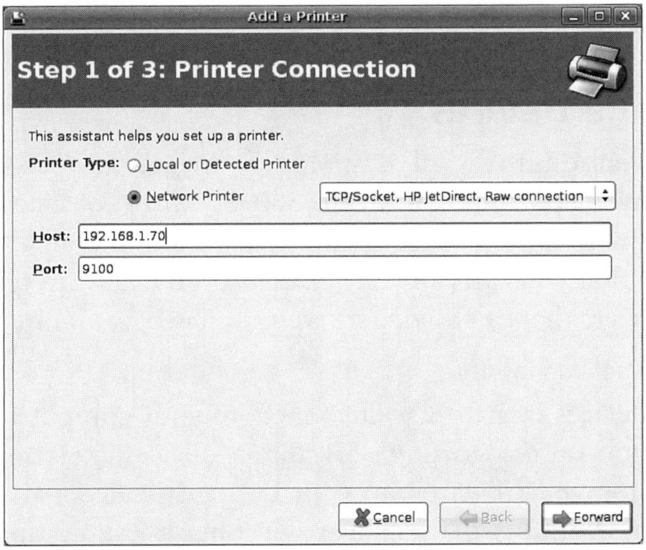

Figure 7.12
Addressing a printer.

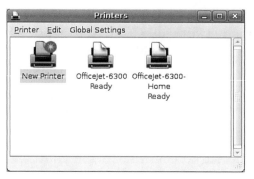

Figure 7.13
Another ready printer.

9. Give your printer a unique name. You can also detail other information, such as where the printer is and for what it is primarily used.

10. Click Apply. The new printer will appear in the Printers window, as shown in Figure 7.13.

Where's My Printer?

If, for some reason, your exact printer model isn't listed, try a listed device that has a similar model number. Many printers share drivers, especially ones made by the same company. If your printer isn't listed and there's nothing close, it may be time to get on the Internet and search for answers in the various Ubuntu forums. This is a very rare occurrence, as the CUPS database is constantly expanded.

Using USB Mass Storage Devices

One of the latest and greatest inventions in digital technology is the portable mass storage device that can hold anywhere from 256 MB to 300 GB worth of data. These portable devices come in a variety of configurations, from the small memory sticks or thumb drives that you carry in your pocket or on a lanyard to the big portable external hard drives that can hold, dare we say, massive amounts of data.

The common feature to these devices is that they all connect to your computer via a USB port. Ubuntu is very good at recognizing USB storage devices; literally, all you have to do is plug the storage hardware into your PC. A drive icon will appear on the desktop, and the Nautilus file manager will open to show the contents of the device, as displayed in Figure 7.14.

Drive
Icon

Figure 7.14
Transparent USB drive support.

Removing the drive just has one extra step. You could just pull the physical connection, and likely that would be okay. But to keep Ubuntu from being confused about where a drive went, you can use Ubuntu to remove its own awareness of the device. Then you can physically remove it.

Right-click a USB drive's icon. In the context menu that appears, select the Eject command. The icon will disappear from the desktop, and the device can be safely removed.

Setting Up a Digital Camera

Digital cameras are very commonplace these days, and being able to move your photos to your computer is a necessity, since that's where any editing and long-term storage of your snapshots are going to take place.

Ubuntu handles digital cameras in one of two ways. If it does not recognize the specific camera model, it will treat a connected digital camera like a USB storage device. When this happens, you can simply use the file manager to transfer photos from your camera's drive to your hard drive.

If Ubuntu does recognize your camera, then you will have access to some nifty tools that will speed your digital camera work right along.

1. Connect your camera to your computer and turn on the camera's power. If properly detected, the Camera Import dialog box (shown in Figure 7.15) will open.

2. Click Import Photos. A new Import Photos dialog box will open (see Figure 7.16).

3. Wait for a moment as the application reviews the contents of your camera. The contents will be displayed in the dialog box (see Figure 7.17).

4. Select a Destination directory for the photos.

5. Click Import. The photos will be downloaded onto your Ubuntu PC (see Figure 7.18).

Figure 7.15
The camera was detected.

Figure 7.16
The initial Import Photos dialog box.

Figure 7.17
The final Import Photos dialog box.

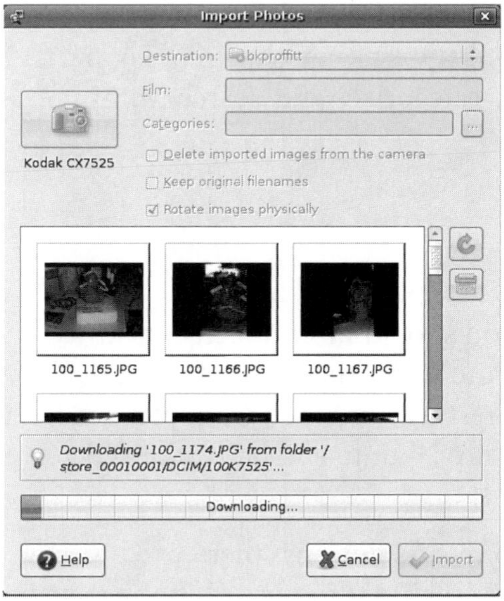

Figure 7.18
Downloading photos.

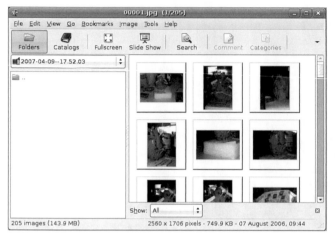

Figure 7.19
Your photo collection in gThumb.

Classified Photos

If you want, you can add Film and Categories information to your imported photos as you pull them in from your camera. Film is just a fancy label for directory name. Categories are customizable tags that you can assign to photos so you can easily find them later.

When the download is complete, the gThumb application, shown in Figure 7.19, will open. gThumb enables users to sort, categorize, and search within your photo collection.

Special Hardware Concerns

After the normal hardware needs are set, you should be completely ready to go. Alas, not every installation goes smoothly, and some known hardware bugaboos can creep in and make things more . . . interesting. In this section, you will learn about the most prevalent issues that occur with Ubuntu and hardware and get on track to fix them.

This is by no means a comprehensive group of solutions; there are too many different kinds of hardware out there to try such a thing in this book. But the most common problems should be addressed.

Wi-Fi Cards

Wireless interfaces are essential for mobile and desktop PCs because they offer freedom and mobility to connect to networks and the Internet in a much larger variety of locations. For the most part, Ubuntu's support of wireless (or Wi-Fi) cards is pretty good. But there's one brand of Wi-Fi card that used to be like Kryptonite for Linux users: the Broadcom cards.

Broadcom is a manufacturer that has steadfastly refused to create Linux drivers for their Wi-Fi hardware. This is very unfortunate, because a great many laptops' internal wireless interfaces are, in fact, Broadcom devices.

Recently, a solution was created, and the ability to run Broadcom devices has been built into the main Linux kernel. But to run Broadcom devices, the kernel needs access to a very specific set of files, known as the interface's firmware. Windows includes this firmware, and so do some Linux distributions (Macs use Motorola devices). But Ubuntu, true to its Debian roots, does not, because the firmware is commercial, and Canonical does not have permission to redistribute it.

Running a Broadcom Wi-Fi card in Ubuntu is possible; you just need to get the right software.

Here's the fastest way to get the firmware you need.

1. Click the Applications | Accessories | Terminal menu command. The Terminal window will open.

2. In Terminal, type:

   `lspci | grep Broadcom\ Corporation`

   If your system has a Broadcom device installed, the results will resemble this output:

   `00:0e.0 Network controller: Broadcom Corporation BCM4318 [AirForce One 54g] 802.11 Wireless LAN Controller (rev 02)`

3. Now type:

   `wget -c http://ubuntu.cafuego.net/pool/feisty-cafuego/bcm43xx/bcm43xx-firmware_1.3-1_2_all.deb`

   This will download the firmware as a DEB package to your home directory.

4. To install the firmware package, type:

   `sudo dpkg -i bcm43xx-firmware_1.3-1ubuntu2_all.deb`

Your wireless card should now be activated and functional.

Modems

Unlike Wi-Fi cards, which only have one real trouble spot as far as certain brands go, nearly every internal modem in a PC is going to have problems running in Linux. That's because these devices, referred to by class as *winmodems,* have drivers written only for the Windows environment.

There are two ways around this problem, should you need a modem for your Ubuntu PC. One is, acquire an external modem. These modems, as a rule, do tend to work in Ubuntu, because the way they plug into a PC (through the serial or PCMCIA ports) allows Ubuntu to communicate more freely with them.

If you don't want to spend the money, you can try the solutions presented by the Linmodem Project (http://linmodems.technion.ac.il/Linmodem-howto. html), a community service designed to get those winmodems running on Linux PCs.

Basically, there are two big steps to getting a winmodem to run on Ubuntu. First, you need to run an application called *scanModem* to determine exactly what kind of internal modem your system has (unless the modem is an ISA-type device, in which case no solution will help). Second, you need to apply specific solutions based on the modem's manufacturer.

To download and run scanModem, follow these steps:

1. In Terminal, type

   `wget -c http://132.68.73.235/linmodems/packages/scanModem.gz`

   The package will be downloaded to your home directory.

2. To decompress the compressed .gz file, enter:

   `gunzip scanModem.gz`

3. Now type:

   `chmod +x scanModem`

4. To run scanModem, enter:

   `sudo ./scanModem`

Several new folders will be created in the home directory.

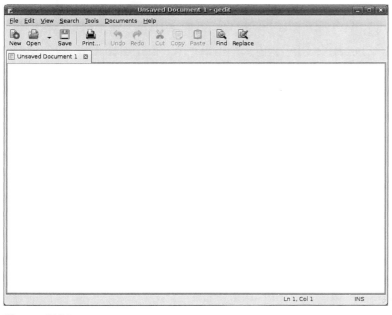

Figure 7.20
The Gedit application.

5. Click the Applications | Accessories | Text Editor menu command. The Gedit application will open (see Figure 7.20).

6. Click the Open button. The Open dialog box will open.

7. Navigate to the Modems folder in your home directory.

8. Select 1stRead.txt and ModemData.txt and click Open. The files will be opened in Gedit.

9. Read the files to determine what type of modem you have.

Once you have the modem type discovered, you should visit the Ubuntu Community Documentation site for winmodems at https://help.ubuntu.com/community/DialupModemHowto. There, you will find manufacturer-specific solutions for most modem brands.

Video Cards/Monitors

In the Olde Times of Linux (say, five whole years ago), monitor configuration was a crapshoot. That's because the layer of Linux that handled the actual graphical environment was not configured to run on a lot of monitors and video cards. Trust me when I say that it was often not pretty—literally.

In the present day, Ubuntu and its companion distributions are much more likely to be properly configured upon installation. Every once in a while, a certain monitor or video card may fake Ubuntu out and leave you with a screen that looks stretched or squished. At that point, you need to rerun the configuration script for the `xorg` graphical environment.

1. In Terminal, type:

   `sudo dpkg-reconfigure xserver-xorg`

   The Package Configuration application will start running in the Terminal, as demonstrated in Figure 7.21.

2. Using the arrow keys, highlight the X server driver that matches your video card. Typically this is already detected and selected for you.

3. Press the Tab key until OK is highlighted and press Enter. The next page will appear.

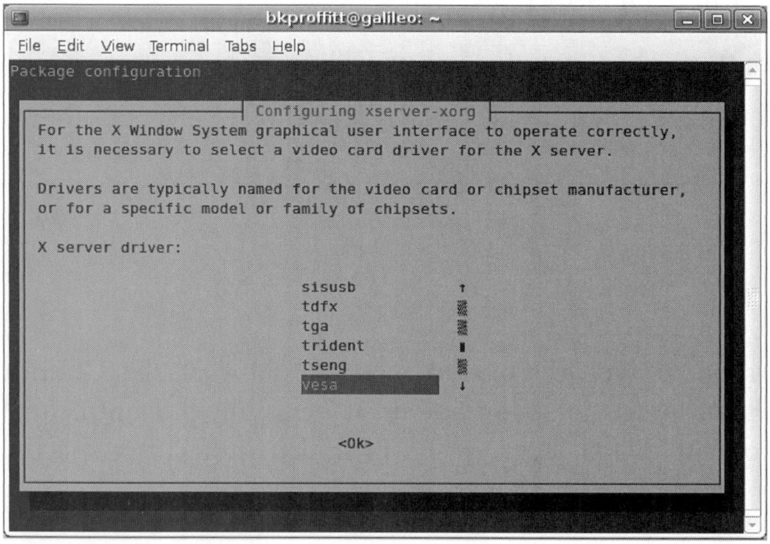

Figure 7.21
The text-only reconfiguration for xorg.

4. Continue through the application, entering values as applicable. When completed, the application will end, and the Terminal will report the creation of a new xorg.conf file.

Detected Settings

Don't worry if you don't know what some of the values are. The configuration program has detected most of your hardware's settings. Pages to pay particular attention to include the video mode page, where you can set the resolutions available to your monitor, and the color depth page, where the number of colors for your monitor can be selected.

Sound Cards

Sound is another concern that shows up in some Ubuntu installations. Curiously, though, Ubuntu (and Linux) pretty much has sound card compatibility licked. Yet, there is this one strange problem that consistently crops up: The sound card is properly detected, and yet there is no sound. This happens quite a bit with cards running the VIA driver and is actually a GNOME problem, not one that belongs to Ubuntu specifically. Fortunately, it's an easy fix.

Try this if you don't have sound, and you know the VIA-based sound card was detected.

1. Double-click the Volume icon in the upper panel. The Volume Control window will open (see Figure 7.22).

2. Click the Edit | Preferences menu command. The Volume Control Preferences dialog box will open.

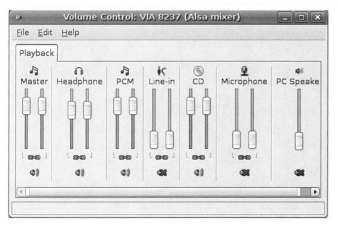

Figure 7.22
Ubuntu's volume control.

3. Click the External Amplifier check box to select it. A new Switches tab will appear in the Volume Control window.

4. Click Close. The Volume Control Preferences dialog box will close.

5. Click the Switches tab. The Switches page will open.

6. Click the External Amplifier check box.

7. Click the File | Quit menu command. The Volume Control window will close.

There are other sound concerns that do appear, and there are many resources on the Web that deal with manufacturer-specific problems. This one, however, seems to come up a great deal, and it would be remiss to not mention the easy solution.

Conclusion

In this chapter, you learned how to complete hardware installation on your Ubuntu PC. You also learned to navigate some of the trickier spots in Ubuntu/ hardware compatibility.

This chapter brings us to the end of Part I, "Installing and Configuring Ubuntu." In Part II, "Using Ubuntu," we'll do exactly that: explore the Ubuntu operating system and see what kind of tools it has to make your home or office experience a great one.

PART II

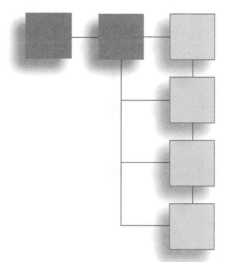

USING UBUNTU

CHAPTER 8

TAKING THE GRAND TOUR

It's installed, it's running smoothly, and now you have a whole Ubuntu operating system to play with. After all of this configuring and customizing, you're probably wondering: Does Ubuntu actually *do* anything?

Indeed it does. For instance, when you hear people comparing Linux to Windows, one of the big gripes you will hear is the perceived lack of available Linux applications. At the moment, Windows has some 100,000-plus applications available. While there are not quite that many Linux applications, the number of available applications is greater than many realize.

Because Ubuntu applications typically are not commercially advertised, they are far less well known than their Windows counterparts. Word, PowerPoint, and Excel—most people have heard of these applications. But how many have heard of Writer, Impress, and Calc? Not many, although that's changing rapidly. Those who have heard of them know that these applications are part of a very robust office suite, fully comparable *and* compatible with Microsoft Office.

The GIMP (GNU Image Manipulation System) is another prime example of an application that is just as feature rich as its Windows counterpart, Adobe PhotoShop. But, since the GIMP, like most of its Linux brethren, is not on the public radar, it is treated as nonexistent—at least for the time being.

In this chapter, you will visit some of the essential tools packaged with Ubuntu, including the following:

- Firefox, a popular browser on any platform.

- Evolution, a powerful Outlook-like e-mail application.

- OpenOffice.org, the fastest-growing office suite in the world.

- Additional Ubuntu applications that you will find many uses for.

Introducing Firefox

In the olden days of the Internet (all of 15 years ago), life was uncomplicated. The simple concept of hyperlinks on a text page was just emerging. Some links went to other pages; others went to files to be downloaded—perhaps a picture or two. Browsers such as Lynx only had to contend with text—life was good.

In 1993, everything changed forever. The National Center for Supercomputing Applications (NCSA) at the University of Illinois created Mosaic, which was a browser capable of displaying text and pictures. Suddenly, users could see illustrated Web pages, which facilitated the flow of information. A year later, one of the Mosaic developers left NCSA and launched his own browser—Netscape Navigator 1.1.

Since then, the capability of browsers has grown even more in response to more complex content. Need to hear a sound file? The browser will take care of it. Need to view a Flash animation? Not only will a browser display it for you, but the browser also can automatically go get the required viewer if you don't already have it.

These sophisticated features are a long way from the early Internet days, that's for sure.

One of the direct descendants of that early Netscape browser is Firefox, a cross-platform open source browser that has taken the desktop world by storm, no matter what the platform. Even on Windows, traditionally the bailiwick of Internet Explorer, Firefox has a 10+ percent browser share, which may not seem like a lot, except when you consider that it's only been around for a couple of years.

What makes Firefox special is its speed, stability, and security. Unlike Internet Explorer, which is closely tied to the Windows operating system on a code level,

Firefox is a separate application. So even if someone can figure out how to hack Firefox maliciously, he won't damage anything beyond the browser. When Internet Explorer is hacked, all of Windows can be made vulnerable.

Another unique feature of Firefox is its available extensions. Because Firefox is open, developers can create small add-on programs that can handle a variety of tasks, like displaying newsfeeds, synchronizing a user's settings with any Firefox browser he uses, blocking advertising … it's a long list.

Finally, something that Firefox has had for quite some time, before Internet Explorer just recently picked it up, is a tabbed interface (see Figure 8.1). Tabs let you display multiple pages in a single window, a very useful feature for power surfers.

In Chapter 10, "Surfing the Web," you will take a closer look at Firefox, as well as some of the other browsers available in Ubuntu. For now, let's take a quick look at Ubuntu's flagship e-mail client, Evolution.

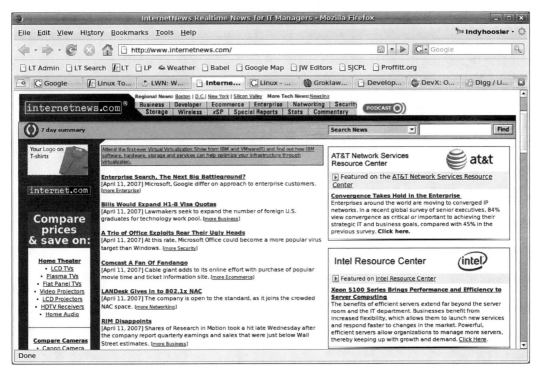

Figure 8.1
The tabbed Firefox interface.

Introducing Evolution

In 1999, GNOME founder Miguel de Icaza made mention of the Camel mail code-set, which was the very beginning of the Evolution e-mail client. Originally called *Helix Code,* de Icaza's company would start working on what would become one of the most popular mail clients on Ubuntu or any other Linux operating system.

Though the GNOME interface already has plenty of mail clients, calendars, and address books, a certain level of integration was missing. Few of the mail clients, for instance, take advantage of the address book or features in Microsoft's Exchange server. None of the programs available offer the sort of all-in-one convenience of a Groupwise or Outlook. Evolution was designed to change this (see Figure 8.2).

The application has seen a lot in its day: a name change of its originating company to Ximian, and then Ximian's later purchase by the large IT company, Novell. But through it all, Evolution has remained closely tied to its GNOME origins, and since Ubuntu is primarily a GNOME distribution of Linux, it makes sense that it would be featured so prominently in Ubuntu.

Chapter 11, "Mail Call," will demonstrate how to use Evolution. Now let's turn our attention to OpenOffice.org.

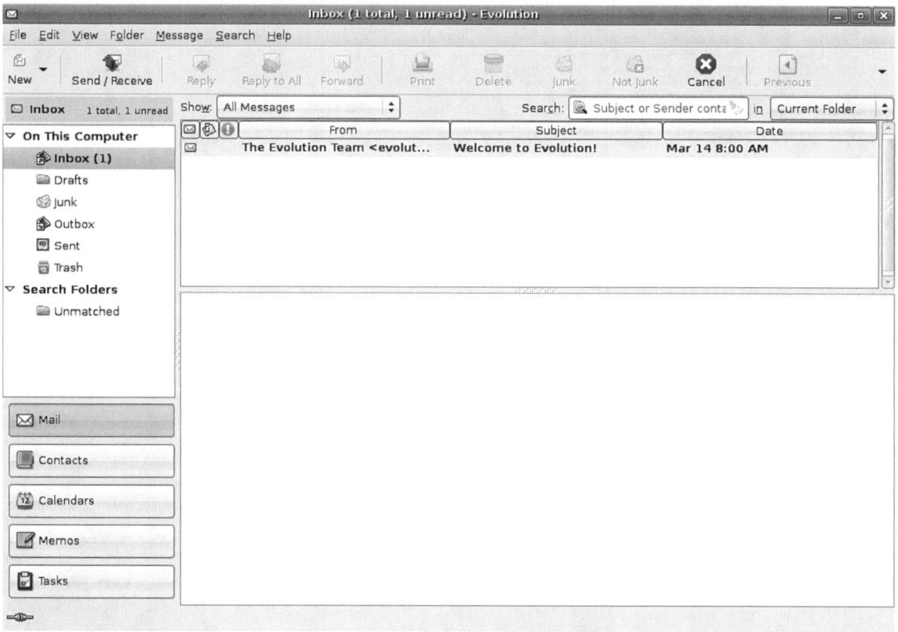

Figure 8.2
The Evolution application.

Introducing OpenOffice.org

OpenOffice.org is a product to which you should definitely pay attention. Is OpenOffice.org the *Greatest Office Suite Ever Made*? No. Everything can be improved upon, and not everyone will like using OpenOffice.org. But OpenOffice.org does offer something other office suites do not: a unique, totally integrated interface that seamlessly blends its different components.

It's time to start it up and see for yourself how this powerful office suite is put together.

Writer

The written word is still a major component of our daily lives. Newspapers, Web pages, and books—the written word comprises them all. Even our audio and visual media stem from written scripts and news copy.

Writer was the first product developed by the original Star Division for the old StarOffice suite and is therefore the most complete. You can see its robust nature in Figure 8.3, which shows a typical Writer window. You can see that Writer offers a number of familiar tools.

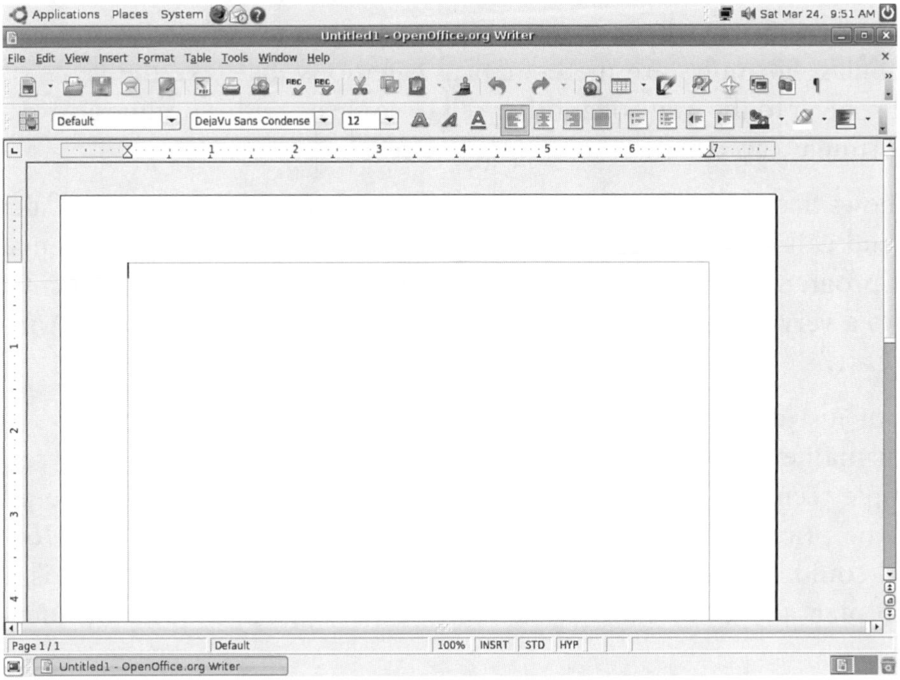

Figure 8.3
The key elements of Writer.

The uses for Writer are as boundless as your imagination. These uses will be examined in Chapter 15, "Documenting with Writer." You can create any form of written document and use elements from any other part of OpenOffice.org to suit your needs.

Calc

Spreadsheets get their name from the old-fashioned ledger sheets used by desk-bound accountants. In their work, they would lay out numbers on what were at times huge sheets of grid-lined paper. Sometimes these sheets would be yards long, and if a mistake were made in just one cell . . . well, let's just say the mistake would be rather tedious to find and fix.

The concept of these paper sheets has been carried over to electronic form. It made sense to keep data in this familiar tabular format. Thus, the first spreadsheet program, VisiCalc, was born. Though no relation to Calc, a lot of the concepts introduced in VisiCalc provide the basis for Calc's design.

Cells are the heart of a spreadsheet. They contain the data. The data values can be numbers, letters, words—whatever you want to keep track of. Cells can also contain formulas. Formulas are mathematical equations that take the value of one cell and relate it to the value of another cell to come up with a unique answer. If needed, formulas can equate whole ranges of cells.

Figure 8.4 shows that the basic elements common to all spreadsheets are in Calc: cells, rows, and columns. You can't have a spreadsheet without these elements. Spreadsheet programs differ in the way they present and utilize these elements, but Calc uses a very intuitive interface, as you will learn in Chapter 16, "Analyzing with Calc."

Calc does not just display data in neat little columns and rows. Nor does it just perform mathematical functions, though it does so rather well. You can create multiple scenarios with your data. What would happen to my overall revenues if the price of asparagus rocketed to a new high this season? How much profit could I make if asparagus stayed at its current level? Calc is a great way to plan ahead for mortgages, loans, asparagus, and other business concerns.

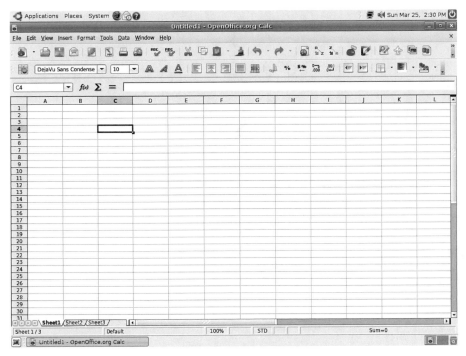

Figure 8.4
The Calc interface.

Impress

There was a time in the business world when average workers were not expected to share their knowledge with the rest of the workplace all at once—for one thing, they lacked the tools to do so. But in these days of open communication, there are more and more opportunities to do what most people hate to do: public speaking.

OpenOffice.org has a component that helps relieve some of that anxiety. Impress is a robust presentation tool designed to show your ideas to the world. Figure 8.5 shows a sample Impress presentation.

Impress can let you create a presentation from scratch or build one from an existing outline. You can use the Presentation wizard to add templates, backgrounds, and even additional slides all in one easy process, as will be demonstrated in Chapter 17, "Presenting with Impress."

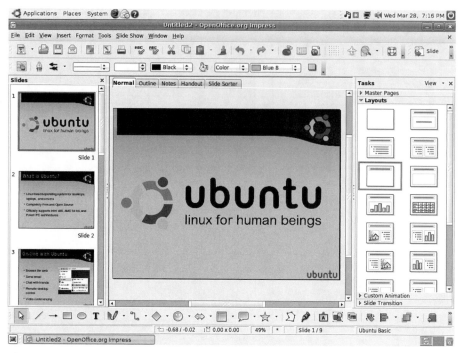

Figure 8.5
Beginning an Impress presentation.

Perhaps best of all is that any presentation created in Impress not only can be used in a standard slide show but also can be converted for use on the World Wide Web, giving you a chance to create flashy Web pages in a snap.

Base: Track Your Data

Databases are scary. There, it's said, out in the open.

Many people often think of databases as dark, shadowy beasts that lurk in their PCs, chewing up and spitting out data and reports only if coaxed out with strange and cryptic queries.

Not necessarily. In recent years, personal databases have become more friendly and intuitive. Base is no exception.

Of all the OpenOffice.org components, Base needs the most input from the user before creating a database. As simplified as databases have become, you still can't snap one together with a single command. You need to know what tables will hold what data, what the data entry form will look like, and what reports the database will need to generate.

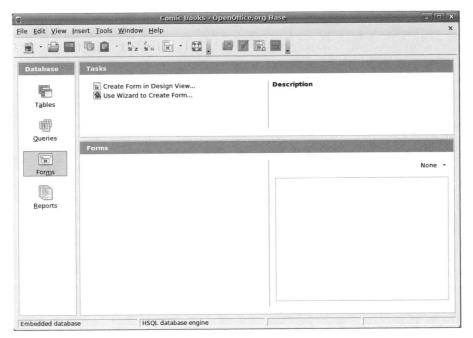

Figure 8.6
The Base interface.

Sounds scary again, doesn't it? It's really not, and to demonstrate this, take a look at Figure 8.6, which displays the Base application.

In Chapter 18, "Organizing with Base," you will learn more about this so-called shadowy beast and learn to tame it.

Other Nifty Ubuntu Tools

It's not all about work and productivity tools, mind you. Ubuntu has other applications designed to put you in touch with others and tap into your creativity.

Gaim

Gaim is the primary instant messaging client for Ubuntu. Developed by a team of former America Online developers to be compatible with that Internet provider's messaging system, known as *AIM,* Gaim is now compatible with a whole host of other messaging systems, including MSN, Yahoo!, Jabber, ICQ, IRC, SILC, SIP/ SIMPLE, Novell GroupWise, Lotus Sametime, Bonjour, Zephyr, Gadu-Gadu, and QQ.

Figure 8.7
The Gaim application.

All at the same time.

If you have a messaging account on any of these services, and your friends and colleagues do, you can use a single Gaim client to talk to any of them when you need to.

Figure 8.7 shows the Buddy List for Gaim, where all of the online contacts are stored. In Chapter 12, "Messaging Tools," you'll delve more into Gaim.

The GIMP

If you thought Ubuntu had a weird name, then the GIMP application may set you back a bit. The GIMP (short for GNU Image Manipulation Program) is a free-of-charge app often compared to Adobe Photoshop because it has many of the same capabilities.

The GIMP has some special features that make it necessary for you to perform a secondary installation when you first start the application. When the GIMP Installation dialog box appears, click Install. When the installation is successfully completed, a message box will appear, informing you of the completed installation. Click Continue to open the GIMP interface, shown in Figure 8.8.

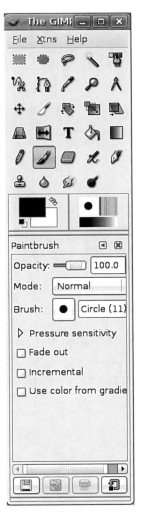

Figure 8.8
The unusual GIMP interface.

The GIMP interface is sort of odd, in that there is no "canvas" screen immediately visible—just a toolbar and (if your options are set for it) a Tip of the Day
message box. But once you begin working with the program, you will find its
capabilities amazing.

Ekiga Softphone

Imagine the capability to make a call to anyone on the planet—for free. That's
what Ekiga Softphone will allow you to do, using a networking system known as
Voice over IP (VoIP). Instead of data packets carrying data, VoIP clients break

Figure 8.9
The Ekiga Softphone.

down auditory signals into digital data, package that into IP data packets, and send them on their way out into the Internet. That's the very simple explanation of VoIP. We'll cover it in more detail in Chapter 12 as well as go over the interface shown in Figure 8.9.

Totem Movie Player

Movies in Linux have been another long-standing sore spot for users. Not that Linux was technically incapable of displaying movies, but rather that the software makers who created movie formats like AVI, WMA, or DVD were unwilling to let Linux players use their formats without paying very large fees.

Some Linux players eventually reverse-engineered these formats to the point they could be displayed. One of the best of these is the Totem Movie Player (see Figure 8.10), and it is included in Ubuntu.

In Chapter 13, "Multimedia Tools," you will learn how to use the Totem Movie Player, as well as other audio/visual applications.

Rhythmbox

A very important expectation for any computer these days is the capability to play music. Whether it is MP3 files or CDs from your collection, you will expect Ubuntu to have something to handle this important task.

Figure 8.10
The Totem Movie Player.

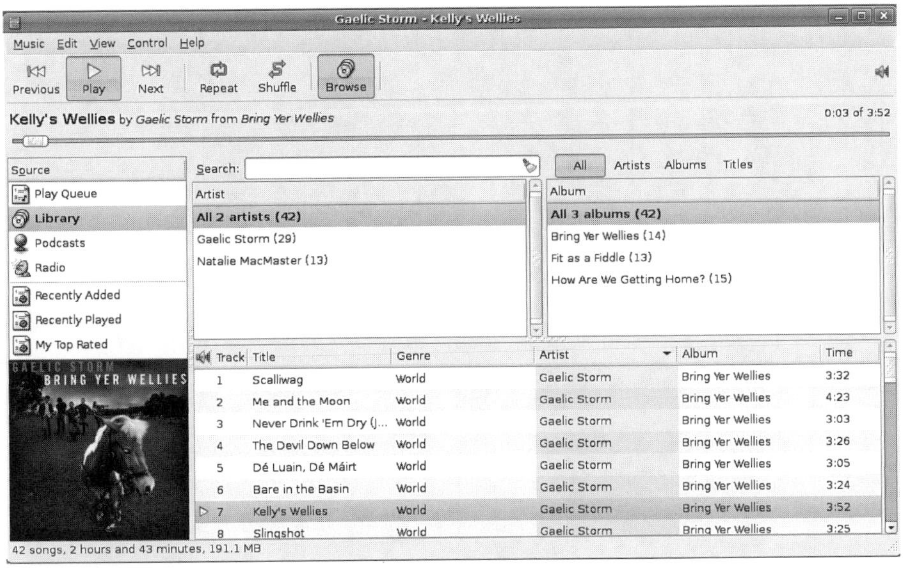

Figure 8.11
The Rhythmbox interface.

As a matter of fact, the application for this task is Rhythmbox, a sophisticated audio player that can handle standard audio files, CDs, podcasts, and streaming Internet radio (see Figure 8.11). Rhythmbox will be examined more closely in Chapter 13.

Conclusion

This chapter hasn't been very big on detail, but it gives you an important preview of the rest of the book. In the rest of Part II, "Using Ubuntu," we will tour the most important Ubuntu applications. In Part III, "Using OpenOffice.org," Chapters 15–18 will explore the powerful home and office tool included free of charge in Ubuntu.

CHAPTER 9

BASIC FILE MANAGEMENT

Before you start exploring the Ubuntu applications, it is important for you to take a look at where and how your personal data files are stored.

"Personal data files" refers to any file that you can access within Ubuntu, such as an OpenOffice.org document, a music file, or an application file you've downloaded. The reason why the "personal" definition is applied is because, unlike the Windows operating system, there are many, many files that you don't have permission to access.

In fact, if you recall the directory structure of Ubuntu from the "Partitions Ubuntu Will Need" section of Chapter 3, "Installing Ubuntu," the only Ubuntu directory you will have ready access to is the /home directory—and even then, just the one that belongs to your user account.

Still, there are going to be times when you will need to perform some file management duties. In Ubuntu, there are two good ways to accomplish this. In this chapter, you will learn:

- How to use the Nautilus file manager to manage files.

- How to use the command line to perform the same functions, and more.

Using Nautilus

Nautilus is the name given to the default file manager in GNOME, the Ubuntu desktop environment. When you look at Nautilus for the first time (see Figure 9.1), you will see a lot of things that will look rather familiar to a Windows user.

There are actually two modes to view Nautilus: the Browser mode, which is in Figure 9.1, and the Spatial mode, which has fewer navigation tools and instead displays the contents of each directory as a separate window (see Figure 9.2). This may seem awkward, but anyone coming to Ubuntu from a Mac background will recognize the same functionality in the Mac OS Finder application.

We will examine how to switch modes in the "Configuring Nautilus" section later in this chapter. For now, we will stay in the Browser mode to demonstrate basic file management tasks.

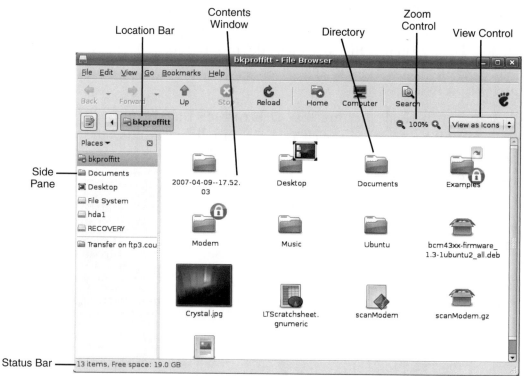

Figure 9.1
The Nautilus interface (Browser mode).

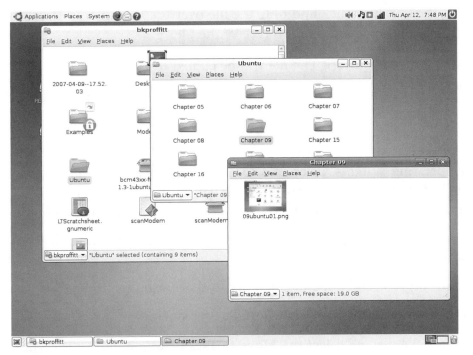

Figure 9.2
The Nautilus interface (Spatial mode).

Moving and Copying Files

Moving and copying files with a graphical file browser is a simple process: You pick up the file or directory you want to move or copy and drag and drop it into its new location. But there are some details that will help.

1. Click the Places | Home Folder menu command. The Nautilus file manager will open.

2. Double-click the Documents directory. The contents will be displayed.

3. Click and drag a file to your /home directory in the side pane.

4. Release the mouse button. The file will be moved to the /home directory.

5. Click your /home directory in the Location Bar. The window will display the contents of your /home directory.

6. Locate the file you moved to this directory.

7. Holding the Ctrl key, click and drag the file over the Documents directory icon. The folder icon will open to receive the file.

8. Release the mouse button. The file will be copied to the Documents directory.

Deleting Files

Like other operating systems, deleting a file or a directory in Ubuntu doesn't really delete it. Instead, the file is moved to the Trash directory, where it will sit until you decide to delete the contents of the Trash directory permanently.

This eliminates most worries about accidentally erasing something that you don't want to disappear.

There are two ways to send a file or directory to the Trash directory.

- Click the file and press the Delete key.

- Right-click the file and select the Move to Trash command on the context menu.

If you decide to remove the files from the Trash directory permanently, follow these quick steps:

1. Click the Trash icon in the lower panel. Nautilus will open, displaying the contents of the Trash directory (see Figure 9.3).

2. Review the contents of the directory. Be sure that everything is safe to delete.

3. Move any files you need out of the Trash directory.

4. When ready, click Empty Trash. A warning dialog box will appear (see Figure 9.4).

5. Click Empty Trash. The files will be permanently deleted.

Finding Files

When you get a lot of files and directories, it will become increasingly difficult to remember where everything is. And why should you? Storing and remembering things is what we have built computers for!

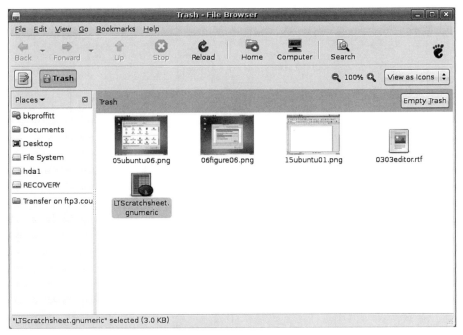

Figure 9.3
The Trash directory.

Figure 9.4
Confirming final deletion.

Nautilus has an easy-to-use tool to locate files.

1. Click the Search button. The Location Bar will change to a Search tool (see Figure 9.5).

2. Type in a search term and press the Enter key. The results will be displayed, as shown in Figure 9.6.

3. You can add additional search parameters. Click the Plus icon. A new filter will be added to the Search Results section of the screen (see Figure 9.7).

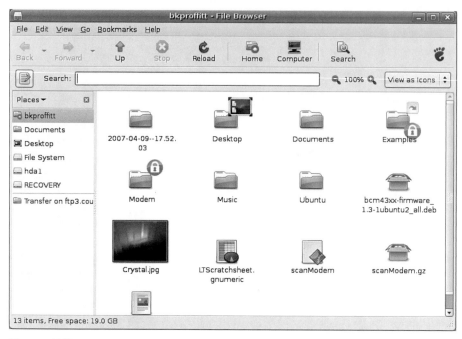

Figure 9.5
Searching for answers.

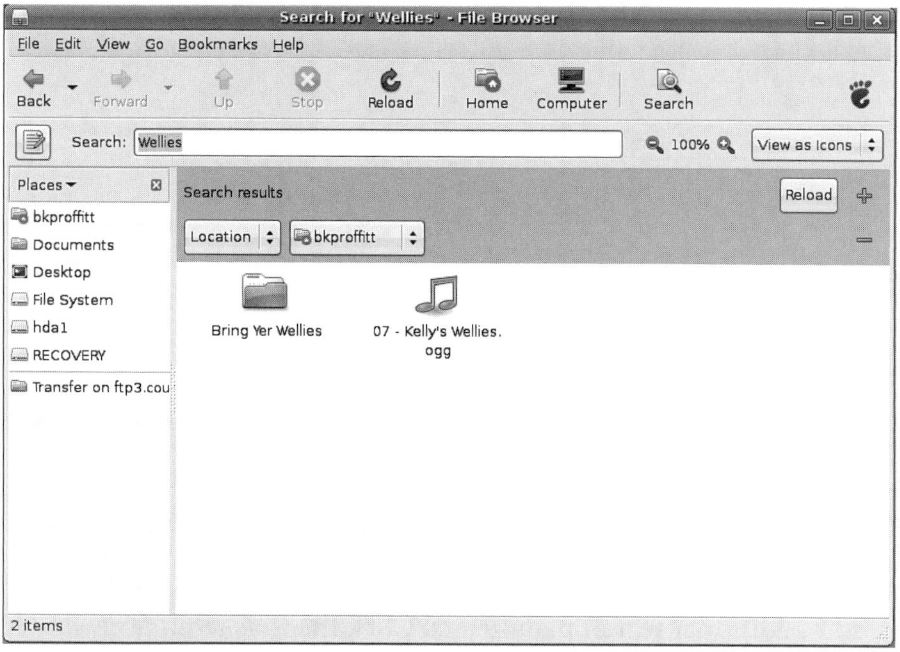

Figure 9.6
Finding some wellies.

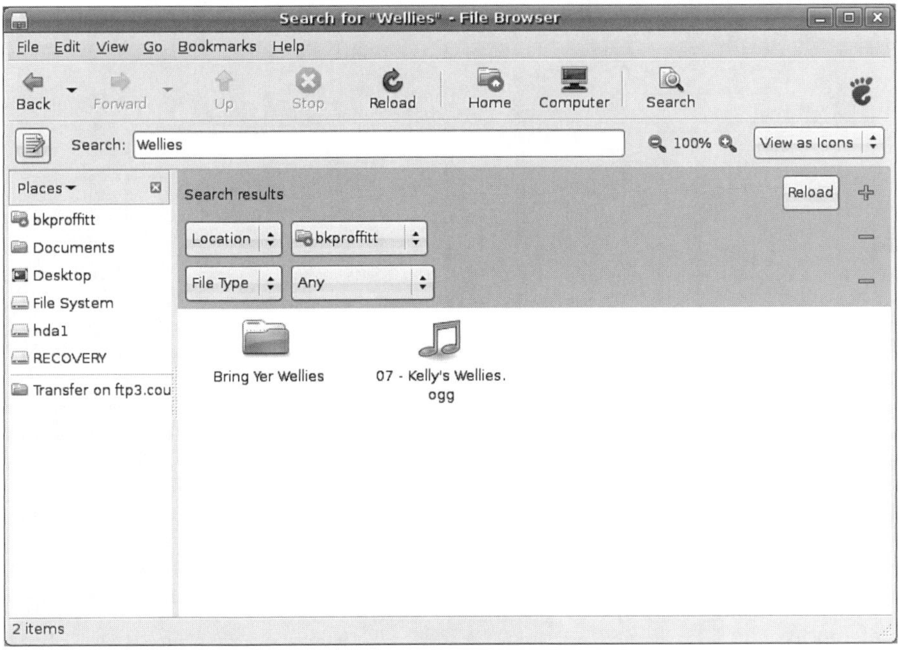

Figure 9.7
Narrowing the search.

4. Click the criterion lists to add additional parameters.

5. Click Reload. The new results will be displayed.

6. To leave the Search screen, click the Back button.

Configuring Nautilus

As mentioned earlier, Nautilus has two distinct modes: Browser and Spatial. Thus far, we have been working in the Browser mode, but if you want to use Nautilus in Spatial mode, here's how to do it.

1. In Nautilus, click the Edit | Preferences menu command. The File Management Preferences dialog box will open (see Figure 9.8).

2. Click the Behavior tab. The Behavior page will open (see Figure 9.9).

3. Click the Always Open in Browser Windows check box. The option will be deselected.

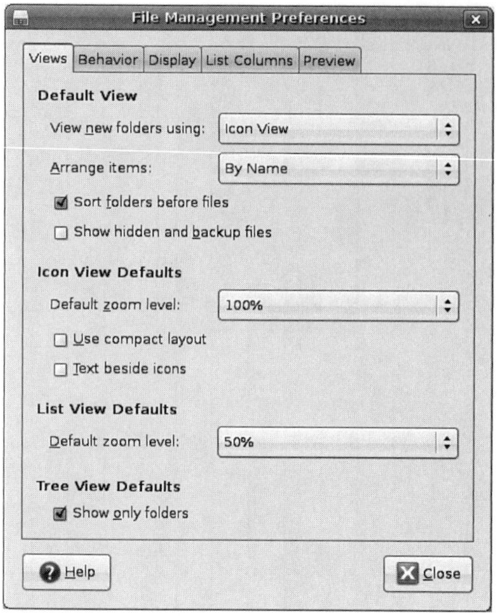

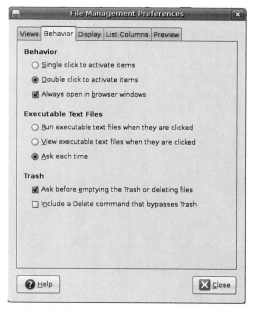

Figure 9.8
Defining your preferences.

Figure 9.9
Changing modes.

4. Click Close. The File Management Preferences dialog box will close.

5. Restart Nautilus. It will now be in Spatial mode.

In the Browser mode, you can tweak your settings quite a bit. Try these actions to experiment on the presentation of Nautilus.

- Click the Side Pane drop-down list and select one of the options.

- Test the Zoom control settings.

- Change the View control value from View as Icons to View as List.

After playing around with the settings, you may find a configuration of Nautilus that you prefer. This can only help your efficiency and satisfaction with Ubuntu.

Command-Line File Management

Even if you plan to spend most of your time in GNOME or one of Ubuntu's other GUIs, you will find using these file management commands in Terminal very useful.

Copying Files: The `cp` Command

The `cp` command is similar to the MS-DOS command `copy`; it's used to copy files or directories from one place to another. You can copy one file to a new file, one file to another place, or a large number of files all at once to a new place. When you copy a file, you do not delete the original file by default. If you want to move a file rather than make a copy of it, use the `mv` command instead.

To use the `cp` command, type `cp`, followed by any options, and then type the directory or filename(s) you want to copy, followed by the destination. If you want to copy multiple files, you can use wildcards, or you can list multiple files separated by spaces.

Table 9.1 lists some of the available options for the `cp` command.

Let's say that you download a `.zip` file called `program.zip` into your `/home` directory, and you want to unzip it, but you don't want to do it in your `/home` directory. You can `cp` the file into the `/tmp` directory and work with it there. To do this, type in the following:

```
cp program.zip /tmp
```

Table 9.1 cp Command Options

Option	Name	Description
-f	Force	Removes any existing files of the same name.
-i	Interactive	Prompts the user if there is an existing file of the same name in the destination directory.
-p	Preserve	Tells the cp command to preserve the original file's permission, ownership, and timestamp data, if possible.
-R, -r	Recursive	Copies directories located under the starting directory. The default is not to copy subdirectories.

Note that you do not get an error message if the file already exists unless you use the Interactive option. If the file exists, you are asked whether you want to overwrite the file or not, like this:

```
cp -i program.zip /tmp
cp: overwrite /tmp/program.zip'?
```

If you answer **y**, the file is overwritten; if **n**, the file is not overwritten.

If you have a group of files you want to move into another directory without having to type each filename individually, you can use wildcards. If you want to copy all files in the current directory to another directory, type:

```
cp * /tmp
```

This copies all files in the directory to the /tmp directory; however, it does not copy directories unless specifically told to. To copy files and directories, use the Recursive option.

```
cp -R * /tmp
```

If you'd like to copy all files with a specific extension to another directory, you can use wildcards to copy groups of files selectively, like this:

```
cp *.jpg *.gif images
```

This copies all JPEG and GIF files to the images directory without copying any other files with them. You can also use the question mark character (?) to match a single character rather than a group of characters.

Moving Files: The mv Command

The mv command can be used to move a file or files to another directory or to rename a file or files. The mv command is similar to the move command under MS-DOS, but the mv command is much more powerful than its MS-DOS equivalent. The mv command does delete the original file that is being moved, so be sure to use the command carefully. The mv command is also used to rename files in Ubuntu, so it also takes the place of the REN command under MS-DOS.

To move a file, type mv, followed by any options, then the name of the file(s) or directories to be moved, and then the destination to which you want the file(s) moved. As with the cp command, you can use wildcards to move multiple files rather than typing individual filenames.

Table 9.2 lists some of the available options for the mv command.

To move the file index.html to another directory without making a backup or being prompted in the event of an overwrite, use the mv command, followed by the name of the file and its destination:

```
mv index.html /home/bkproffitt/backup/
```

If you're not certain whether a file of the same name already exists, use the Interactive mode of mv. If the file already exists, your output looks like this:

```
mv -i index.html /home/bkproffitt/backup/
```

```
mv: replace /home/bkproffitt/backup/index.html'?
```

Table 9.2 mv Command Options

Option	Name	Description
-b	Backup	Creates a backup file of any files that would be overwritten by moving a file. By default, backup files have a tilde character (~) extension.
-f	Force	Removes any files of the same name when trying to move a file without prompting the user.
-i	Interactive	Prompts the user if moving the current file will overwrite another file. If there are no conflicting files, mv simply moves the file with no complaint.
-S	Suffix	Appends a suffix to any backup files. By default, the tilde suffix is applied, but you can specify any type of suffix, such as .bak or .tmp.

You can use wildcards to move more than one file to another directory. Be careful! The mv command can move directories as well as regular files. Be sure you actually want to move everything under a directory before using the wildcard (*).

If you want to move all of the .html files in the current directory to the /home/httpd/ directory, you use this command:

```
mv *.html /home/httpd/
```

The *.html specifies that you want to move all files that end in .html to another directory. If you want to move all files in the current directory to the /home/httpd/ directory, you type

```
mv * /home/httpd/
```

Ubuntu does not have a separate rename command, so the mv command is used to rename files. If you want to rename index.html to index.html.old, for instance, you use the mv command like this:

```
mv index.html index.html.old
```

As far as Ubuntu is concerned, moving a file and renaming it are the same thing.

Creating Directories: The mkdir Command

The mkdir command is pretty straightforward. It behaves the same way that the MS-DOS command MKDIR works. The Ubuntu command does have some additional functionality—you can set the permissions of the directory when it is created.

To create a new directory, simply type **mkdir** and any options and then the name of the directory you want to create.

Table 9.3 lists some of the options for the mkdir command.

Table 9.3 mkdir Command Options

Option	Name	Description
-m	Mode	Creates a directory with specified permissions.
-p	Parents	Creates parent direcrtories as needed.
-v	Verbose	Gives a written report for each directory created.

To create a new directory called html under the current directory, use the mkdir command followed by the name of the new directory:

```
mkdir html
```

If you want to create a new directory called download under the /tmp directory:

```
mkdir /tmp/download
```

This creates a directory named /download under the /tmp directory. You do not need to be in the /tmp directory to create a subdirectory for it. If a file or directory named /download already exists in the /tmp directory, you'll receive the following error message:

```
mkdir /tmp/download
mkdir: cannot make directory download': File exists
```

Listing and Finding Files: The ls Command

The ls command lists the contents of a directory. This command is similar to the MS-DOS command DIR. In fact, typing dir in Ubuntu is the same as typing ls -c. The ls command is one of the commands you use the most in the Ubuntu Terminal. You can also use the ls command to get information about a specific file in a directory.

To use the ls command, you simply type the command, followed by any options you want to invoke and any filenames (including wildcards) that you want to specify.

Table 9.4 lists some of the available options for the ls command.

You probably want to know what files are in your /home directory from time to time, so it's a good idea to know how to check. To list the files in your /home directory, type the following command:

```
ls ~
```

That's all you need to type. The ~ character is a shortcut that refers to your /home directory.

If you decide you want to edit configuration files, you probably have to look for hidden files—files that do not show up in a standard listing. To list all files in a directory, type in the following:

```
ls -a
```

Table 9.4 ls Command Options

Option	Name	Description
-a	All	Using the -a option lists all files in a directory, including hidden files.
-A	Almost all	Lists all files in a directory, except for . and . . . .
-i	Inode	Prints inode number of each file.
-l	Long	In addition to the filenames, lists the file type, permissions, owner name, size of the file, and the last time the file was modified. Also known as the *verbose mode*.
-r	Reverse	Lists the directory contents in reverse order.
-sk	Kilobytes	Lists file sizes in kilobytes. The s specifies that, yes, you want to see the sizes.
-X	Extension	Sorts files by their extension; files with no extension will be sorted first.

When listing all of the files in your /home directory, you find that there are quite a few more files than you might have thought.

If you want to see all of the files in a directory and their attributes, combine the -a and -l options, as follows:

```
ls -al
```

You'll see a listing of all files in the directory, as well as their permissions, modification dates, whom they belong to, and the size of the files. The first letter indicates whether it is a file, directory, link, or other. A file is a dash (-), a directory is d, a symbolic link is l, and a hard link is represented as a regular file. Other characters indicate it is a special type of file. After that letter, the permissions come. There are three groups of three letters. The first set is the permissions given to the owner of the file. The next set of three is for the group of the file, and then finally the permissions for everyone else. Then you'll see the owner of the file, followed by the group to which the file belongs. By default, the size of each file is displayed in bytes. Next in the listing you'll see the last time the file was modified, or touched, and then the name of the file itself, as shown in this excerpt:

```
total 15244

drwxr-xr-x      43      bproffitt users     4096 2007-05-03 19:03 .
drwxr-xr-x      4       root      root      4096 2007-01-20 22:15 ..
-rw-r--r--      1       bproffitt users   656308 2007-02-21 18:09 13969-crystal-1.0.2.tar.bz2
-rw-r--r--      1       bproffitt users   526684 2007-02-21 10:11 42804-domino-0.4.tar.bz2
-rw-r--r--      1       bproffitt users   603993 2007-02-21 18:20 51302-Dark Plastic 2.tar.gz
-rw-------      1       bproffitt users     1358 2007-04-19 21:43 .bash_history
-rw-r--r--      1       bproffitt users     1177 2007-01-20 22:15 .bashrc
drwx------      7       bproffitt users     4096 2007-05-03 19:04 .beagle
drwxr-xr-x      2       bproffitt users     4096 2007-01-20 22:15 bin
-rw-r--r--      1       bproffitt users   132063 2007-01-20 23:40 bookmarks.html
drwxr-xr-x      6       bproffitt users     4096 2007-04-27 09:42 Books
-rw-r--r--      1       bproffitt users    62048 2007-02-26 07:12 BProffitt.pdf
```

Touchy Files

The expression *touch* is not one I coined. In UNIX-style operating systems, like Ubuntu, a file is said to be touched when it is modified or viewed by a user in some way. A file is not touched when you just list the contents of a directory the file is in or view the contents of the file.

Moving Around the Filesystem: The cd Command

The cd command changes your working directory to another directory that you specify. This command is used to navigate the directory structure in Linux. Typing only cd returns you to your /home directory. The cd command works similarly to the CD command under DOS. However, the cd command is a little more flexible in that it allows for shortcuts to change between your /home directory and the previous working directory.

Use the cd command to change directories. Specifying no directory returns you to your /home directory.

The parent directory is denoted by .. (two periods). To go up one level in the directory structure, simply type the following:

cd ..

Clear Typing

You must have a space between the .. and cd. If you type cd.. with no space, you'll get an error message telling you that the command cd.. is not found.

If you want to go up several levels in the directory structure, you can do so by typing this:

`cd ../../`

This moves you up two levels from your current directory.

To change to a specific directory, issue the `cd` command and then type the name of the desired directory. If you're working in your /home directory and decide to switch to the /tmp directory, you use this command:

`cd /tmp`

Directory Structure

It is important to note that /tmp and tmp are not the same in this instance. The /tmp tells the shell you want to go to the tmp under the / (root) directory and not a tmp directory under the present working directory.

To get to your /home directory quickly, simply use the `cd` command with no arguments, like this:

`cd`

If you do not specify a directory, the bash shell assumes you want to go back to your /home directory. You can also use the tilde (~) symbol to specify your /home directory, as in the following example:

`cd ~`

If you want to jump quickly back to the directory you were last in, without typing the full pathname of that directory, type this shortcut:

`cd -`

After you get the hang of the `cd` command and Ubuntu's directory structure, you may find that using the command-line interface is not as unfriendly as you might have thought when you first started.

Where the Heck Am I?: The pwd Command

The command `pwd` is simple; it's a one-trick pony. If you have lost track of where you are in the directory structure, you simply use `pwd` to get the shell to print out the present working directory.

At the command shell, type in

`pwd`

The output is the current working directory. The `pwd` command does not take any options or arguments.

Conclusion

In this chapter, you learned how to manage files and directories both in the Nautilus file manager and on the command line. As you have seen, it is very similar to any operating system you've used in the past, so the transition to Ubuntu should be that much easier.

In Chapter 10, "Surfing the Web," you'll start looking beyond your Ubuntu desktop and find out about one of the best ways to browse the Internet: Firefox.

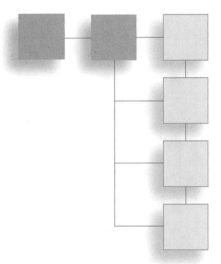

CHAPTER 10

SURFING THE WEB

Browsers have actually been around for a long time, but they were never really called browsers. Instead, they were called *text readers* or *read-only applications,* because what these programs did was open simple files of text and let someone read them—like a book. These programs were on computers called *dumb terminals.*

It seems odd to call a computer dumb, but compared to the computers used today, these computers weren't very smart. All they did was display information from big, monster servers called mainframes that were the size of an average living room. These servers weren't all that smart, either, but they were good enough to take a lot of information and help businesspeople and scientists make sense of it.

The problem was that all these dumb terminals could only talk to the servers they were connected to. There was an Internet back then, but there was no World Wide Web; Internet traffic was mainly limited to messaging and file transfers, using tools such as Usenet, Archie, or Gopher.

Then, in 1990, a scientist in Switzerland, Sir Tim Berners-Lee, got a brilliant idea. What if you could read files on any computer connected to the Internet any time you wanted? You could put those files on a special server that had one job—showing those files to anyone who asked for them. Sir Tim Berners-Lee, who was knighted for his work at the CERN institute, knew this idea would only work if all of these files were made readable by any computer. File compatibility was (and still can be) a huge obstacle for users to overcome.

So, Sir Berners-Lee suggested that people use Hypertext Markup Language (HTML) files. Because they are essentially ASCII text files, HTML files could be read by any computer, would let people create any content they wanted, and would have hyperlinks—something that would revolutionize the way people absorbed material.

Browsers came about as instruments to read all of these new HTML files. As with the dumb terminals, Sir Berners-Lee just wanted people to read information quickly in files—not change their content. So he and his colleagues figured out a way to make a program that did nothing but read and display HTML. Other people got involved and made the application read more complicated HTML code.

People began calling the information on the Web page and the process of reading those pages *browsing*—and that's where the browser name come from. Later, when the general public started using the Web, the verb *browsing* got morphed into *surfing*. The name *browser* stuck, though, because it still more accurately describes what this type of application does. You can call any program like this a browser, of course. A program that does nothing but show pictures could be a picture browser. But these days the name is more synonymous with Web browsers, such as the most famous open source browser today: Firefox.

In this chapter, you will learn about:

- The origins of Firefox.

- Basic browsing tools.

- Using tabs and live bookmarks.

- Adding extensions and themes.

Using Firefox

If you missed the infamous Browser Wars or have blocked it out of your mind along with the rest of the nineties, here's a quick summary.

In 1994, a young programmer named Marc Andressen left the National Center for Supercomputing Applications (NCSA), the academic home for the first graphical browser for the Web, called *NCSA Mosaic*.

Andressen founded Netscape Communications, and the company's first browser, Netscape Navigator 1.1, surpassed Mosaic in many important ways—not the least of which was added HTML extensions that only Netscape would support, such as tables, colors, text size, and (Lord help us all) blinking text. None of these functions were included in the original HTML specifications; Netscape added them because they looked good. And they did look good (except for the blinking) and eventually led to the adoption of these extensions by early Web developers, who in turn encouraged visitors to their sites to download and install Netscape to see their cool new Web site. This viral marketing had its effect—soon, Navigator controlled more than 90 percent of the browser market.

Around this time, Microsoft realized that this Internet thing was a good idea, and they were clearly missing the boat. To lure people away from the Web itself, the company started the Microsoft Network. MSN 1.0 was a flop, however, which prompted Microsoft to go head-to-head against Netscape.

Meanwhile, fearful of a complete lack of standards for this rapidly growing facet of the Internet, the World Wide Web Consortium (W3C) was established to implement standards for HTML, the basis of all of the Web sites in that day. The W3C took too few innovative steps while working on the HTML 3.0 specifications in 1995, because right at the beginning of 1996, Navigator 2.0 was released, supporting just a few of the HTML 3.0 specs and quite a few of its own. In as pure a case of market-driven events as you will ever see, the W3C threw up its collective hands and released HTML 3.0 soon after, which many of the Netscape extensions included.

One of these new extensions was the support of the new programming language JavaScript, which along with the related Java language offered Netscape users a platform-independent way of accessing innovative tools on any Web page.

Soon after this, Microsoft released Internet Explorer (IE) 2.0, which was very similar to Navigator 1.1 and contained some of its own extensions, such as background music and scrolling text. As far as releases go, it would have been no big deal—save for the fact that IE 2.0 was released free of charge. Then, to make it worse for Netscape, Microsoft announced that it would only implement support for "true" standardized HTML from that point on. In the first half of 1996, Web designers started to make sites that were "optimized for Netscape" or "optimized for MSIE."

The Browser Wars had begun.

Critics of IE (and there were plenty) knew that the only way Microsoft would ever be on equal footing with Netscape would be if IE supported something similar to

JavaScript. In August 1996, the critics got what they wanted, when Navigator and IE 3.0 were each released within a single week, with IE 3.0 including a new technology called *ActiveX*. ActiveX went beyond the simple scripting model of JavaScript and the plug-in methodology of Navigator. Now, IE users could pick up the tools they needed to read any special Web media automatically—they didn't need to find and install any helper apps like Navigator did.

No one would be laughing at Netscape anymore.

The next targeted release of the Big Two browsers would be 4.0, and each company had its own plan for changing the face of the desktop itself. IE would become integrated directly into the Windows desktop (a decision that has since come back to bite them), while Navigator would become more powerful and versatile, so it would essentially become the platform upon which every application a user needed would run. The desktop would become the Internet, it was announced at a Netscape conference in 1997. But it was too late: Netscape's market share was dropping like a rock. By the end of that same year, Navigator held anywhere from 10 to 20 percent of the overall browser market share.

By the turn of the century, IE's market share was consistently 95 percent or higher.

There was no clear end to the Browser Wars, though many believe it came to a halt in December 1997, when the U.S. government levied charges of unfair competitive practices against Microsoft because of its decision to integrate IE into the then-upcoming Windows 98.

But what may have seemed like the end for Netscape may have actually turned into the beginning of the end for IE. In 1998, Andressen announced the release of the Netscape Communicator 5.0 application suite, which contained the Navigator browser and Messenger e-mail client, as well as a calendaring function under the open source Mozilla Public License. "Mozilla," once the name of Netscape's lizard mascot, would now become the name of the project created to manage the now-free Netscape code.

The Netscape Communicator suite would eventually be known as the *Mozilla Application Suite,* and many spin-offs would be created from this rich repository of source code, including several browsers for Linux, such as Galeon, Epiphany, and K-Melon. The Mozilla Foundation, the organization charged with maintaining the Mozilla code, continued to work on the entire suite, but some application developers felt that the suite itself (codenamed *SeaMonkey*) was just too big to be fast and effective. Even the Mozilla browser (or its commercial offspring, Navigator, which was still being produced by Netscape's new parent company, America Online), was considered by many to be rather slow and cumbersome.

In 2002, two developers, Blake Ross and Dave Hyatt, started working on a new kind of browser, a stripped-down, lean and mean bit of code that was called *Phoenix*. And even though the name didn't stick, it would prove to be prophetic.

Two years and two name changes later (Phoenix was already taken, and so was the next chosen name, *Firebird*), Firefox 1.0 was released for Windows, Mac OS X, and Linux. It was very fast and minimalistic: Early versions had just a Back button and a Location Bar. Everything else was just frills. What kept people flocking to this sleek little browser were two things: tabbed browsing, where one browser window could have many open Web pages, and the capability to add extensions to Firefox. These were not like the HTML extensions of the prior century: These extensions were actually small applets that worked in much the same way as the old Netscape plug-ins. Need to view a certain type of media on a Web page? Download and install an extension. But unlike plug-ins, extensions were easily installed and managed in a uniform way, while Netscape plug-ins were sometimes inconsistent with regard to these features.

Slowly, but surely, it became apparent that Firefox was rising quickly to become a serious challenger to IE's dominance. IE's own nearly constant security failings didn't help: because of that fateful decision to integrate IE into Windows—a decision that started the whole trouble with the Justice Department—crackers could more easily use IE's vulnerabilities to break into Windows. Firefox, a completely separate application, had no such problems in Windows (and certainly not in Ubuntu).

The Browser Wars, it seems, are back. Only this time, the battle is being fought over features, not the shifting sands of HTML standardization.

Browsing

Browsing is more than just clicking through a collection of hyperlinked files. What really makes the whole thing work is the uniform resource locator (URL). URLs are pseudo-English labels that make it possible to find and retrieve resources across the Internet in a consistent, predictable, well-defined manner.

Every Web server has an IP address, but URLs make it easy for regular folk to type an address into the Location Bar of Firefox and bring up a page.

Of course, when you look at URLs such as `http://www.llanfairpwllgwyngyllgo gerychwyrndrobwllllantysiliogogogoch.co.uk/`, using the IP address might actually be a blessing, but for the most part, URLs are easier.

We Can't Make This Stuff Up

Llanfairpwllgwyngyllgogerychwyrndrobwllllantysiliogogogoch is a village on the Isle of Anglesey in North Wales that currently holds the Guinness record for the longest English place name. The village's Web site holds the record for the longest valid URL.

You can begin browsing with Firefox as soon as you start the application. If you are not connected to the Internet yet, starting Firefox will prompt your computer to start making that connection, especially if you are on dial-up access.

1. Click Applications | Internet | Firefox Web Browser. The Firefox application will start (as shown in Figure 10.1).

Figure 10.1
Firefox 2.0 in Ubuntu.

Starting Firefox

You can also start Firefox by clicking its launcher icon in the upper panel.

2. Double-click the Location Bar so the URL in the field is highlighted.

3. Type the URL for the Web site you want to visit in the Location Bar.

A Helping URL Hand

You do not have to type the URL identifier http:// before the Web site address. Firefox will fill it in for you.

4. Press Enter or click the Go button to go to the new page.

5. Place the mouse cursor over a highlighted or underlined hyperlink. The link will change color, and the full URL for the link will appear in the Status Bar at the bottom of the window.

6. Click the hyperlink to go to the new page.

You don't have to type in the full address every time you visit a Web site, thanks to the Autofill feature in the Location Bar. Just start typing the URL, and Firefox will display a list of similar URLs for you to choose from.

After you have been browsing for a while, you may need to go back to a Web page you visited earlier in your current browser session. Two controls on the Navigation toolbar, the Back and Forward buttons, will enable you to navigate through the pages you have visited.

Note, however, that navigation through Web pages is not tracked for *every* Web page you visit during a session. Firefox uses a sequential navigation method that tracks only the pages along a particular path. For instance, assume you were browsing Page A, then Pages B, C, and D. On Page D, you found a hyperlink back to Page B and clicked it to visit that page. Now, from Page B again, assume you went off and visited Pages E and F. If you were to use the Back button in this session, the order of pages that would appear for each click of the Back button would be F to E to B to A. Pages C and D, because they were on another "track" of browsing, would no longer be a part of the browser's navigation—even if you were to cycle forward through the same pages again using the Forward button.

Of course, you can do more with the Back and Forward buttons than just cycle through Web pages one at a time.

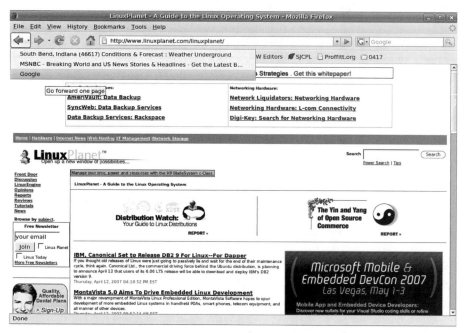

Figure 10.2
Stepping back through a browsing session.

1. After navigating to a few Web pages, click the drop-down list control for the Back button. A list of recently visited pages will appear (see Figure 10.2).

2. Click one of the options. That page will appear in the browser window.

3. Click the drop-down list control for the Back button. A list of recently visited pages will appear.

4. Click one of the options. That page will appear in the browser window.

One of the nicer features of Ubuntu is its capability to call up the default Web browser whenever any hyperlink or Web page shortcut is clicked—in any application. That capability is particularly handy in e-mail clients, such as Thunderbird or Evolution, where you often receive URLs from friends or colleagues.

Tabs

Tabs are not unique to Firefox; they were a feature in other browsers before it came along. But Firefox can certainly get some credit for popularizing this feature.

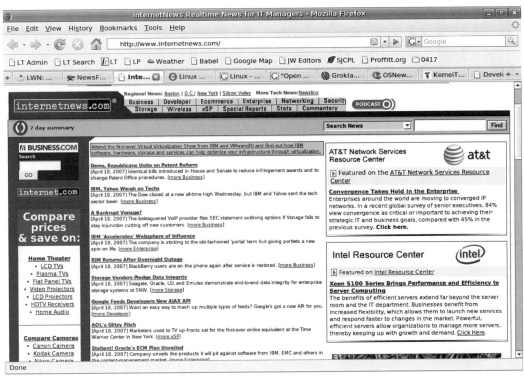

Figure 10.3
Tabs in action.

Tabs allow you to visit many pages and give each one its own window within the Firefox browser. A visual example of this can be seen in Figure 10.3.

As you can see, each tab holds its own Web page. More than that, tabs are really independent browser sessions, all in one window. So if you were to navigate through a series of pages, you could use the Back and Forward buttons just as described in the previous section. If you switch to another tab, however, the navigation rules will change to sites visited in the new tab.

To open a new tab, select the File | New Tab menu command. You can also press Ctrl+T on your keyboard. Once a new, blank tab is opened (see Figure 10.4), you can type in a URL in the Location Bar or use a bookmark to navigate to a new page.

Another way to open a tab is to right-click a hyperlink. In the context menu that appears, click the Open Link in New Tab menu command. The linked page will open in a new tab. A shortcut to this action is to press the Ctrl key and click a hyperlink. The page will open in a new tab.

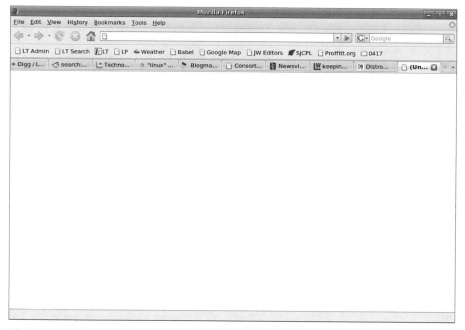

Figure 10.4
A blank tab.

Tabs can also be moved around and put in whatever order you prefer. Simply click a tab and drag and drop the tab in the new position, which will be indicated by a small arrow in the Tab bar as you move the mouse pointer (see Figure 10.5).

More Tab Tricks

If you want to view another tab, just click it with the mouse pointer. If you want to cycle through the tabs in order, press Ctrl+Tab on the keyboard. This will take you to the right along the Tab bar. Pressing Shift+Ctrl+Tab will cycle through tabs to the left.

When you are finished with the contents of a tab, you might want to close it. This is not just for aesthetics; having a lot of tabs open can put a strain on any computer, even your Ubuntu machine. So once you are ready to close a tab, simply click the red Close icon on the tab you want to shut down. The tab and its contents will disappear.

If you made a mistake and closed the wrong tab, don't worry about it. You can get it back by right-clicking the Tab bar. In the context menu that appears, click the Undo Close Tab menu command. The last closed tab will reappear.

Tab Arrow

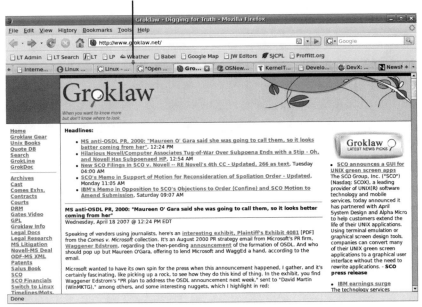

Figure 10.5
The tab's new position is marked by an arrow.

Undoing Closed Tabs

If you have closed the last tab in the browser, the Undo Close Tab command will not work unless you have the Tab bar always enabled.

If you really want to clean up fast and reduce all of the tabs down to one, click the tab you want to keep. Then right-click that tab and select the Close Other Tabs menu command. Every tab but the one you selected will close.

Bookmarks

Human beings are creatures of habit, and often we find ourselves clinging to the familiar as we move through our busy lives. Firefox accommodates this trait with its Bookmarks feature. Bookmarks are markers that, when selected in a menu or clicked in the Bookmark toolbar, will take you directly to the Web page you want—without typing the URL address.

You can create a bookmark for one page or many, utilizing the tab feature in Firefox. Then, when you need to, you can open up one or multiple pages with just a click.

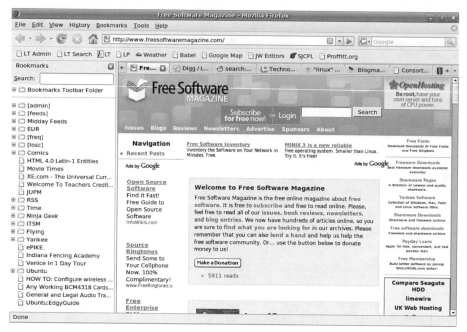

Figure 10.6
The Bookmarks sidebar.

To open a bookmark, click the Bookmark menu and select the bookmark you want. If there is a bookmark in the Bookmark toolbar, all you need to do is click it. Finally, if the sidebar is open in Firefox, you can access bookmarks from there.

You can open the Bookmarks sidebar by selecting the View | Sidebar | Bookmarks menu command (see Figure 10.6).

Opening the Sidebar

Pressing Ctrl+B will also open the Bookmarks sidebar.

When you find a page you want to save, you can bookmark it and add it to your bookmark collection.

1. From a page you want to save, select the Bookmarks | Bookmark This Page menu command. The Add Bookmark dialog box will open (see Figure 10.7).

Bookmarking Tabs

Pressing Ctrl+D will also bookmark the current tab's contents. If you have multiple tabs open, right-click the desired tab and select the Bookmark This Tab menu command on the context menu.

Figure 10.7
The Add Bookmark dialog box.

Figure 10.8
The Bookmark All Tabs dialog box.

2. Confirm or edit the name of the bookmark you want to use.

3. Click the Create In drop-down list if you want the bookmark to appear somewhere other than the main Bookmarks menu and select a new location.

4. Click Add. The bookmark will be added to the desired location, and the Add Bookmark dialog box will close.

You can also bookmark multiple tabs at the same time. This is very useful, since opening a group of pages all at once is a huge time saver.

1. From any page, select the Bookmarks | Bookmark All Tabs menu command. The Bookmark All Tabs dialog box will open (see Figure 10.8).

Tip

Right-click the Tab bar and select the Bookmark All Tabs menu command on the context menu to open the Bookmark All Tabs dialog box.

2. Enter the name of the bookmarks folder you want to use.

3. Click the Create In drop-down list if you want the bookmark folder to appear somewhere other than the main Bookmarks menu and select a new location.

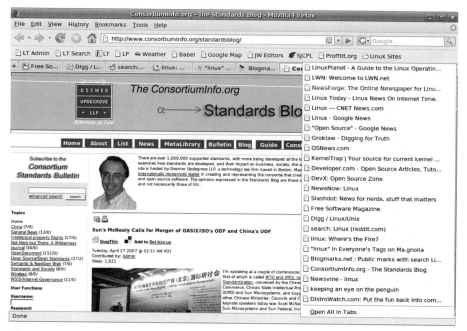

Figure 10.9
Listing a bookmark folder.

4. Click Add. The bookmarks folder will be added to the desired location, and the Bookmark All Tabs dialog box will close.

If you put a bookmarks folder in the Bookmarks toolbar, clicking the folder will open a menu that displays all of the contents of the folder (see Figure 10.9). You can click the pages one at a time to open them individually or select the Open All in Tabs to open every page in a separate tab.

Caution

Opening many tabs at once can slow your system down, particularly if the pages have a lot of graphics or animated ads. If you notice this on your system, consider making smaller bookmark folders. Or don't open all your bookmarks at the same time.

As time goes on, you will find your collection of bookmarks has grown quite a bit. Firefox includes a solid tool to organize bookmarks in a way that makes the best sense for you.

1. From any page, select Bookmarks | Organize Bookmarks. The Bookmarks Manager window will open (see Figure 10.10).

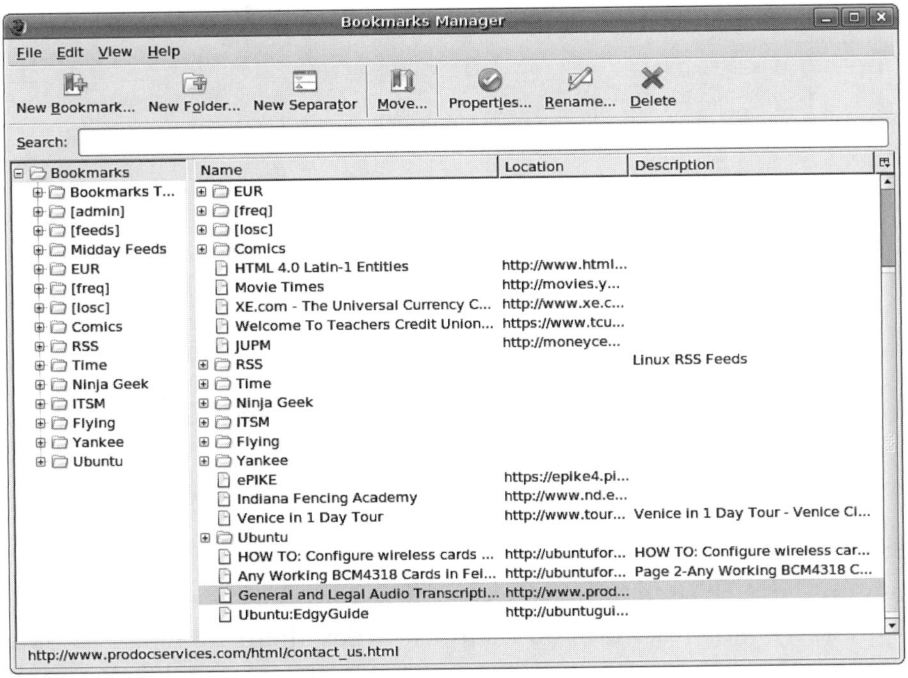

Figure 10.10
The Bookmarks Manager.

2. Click any folder's expansion icon. The contents of the folder will be displayed.

3. Click and drag any item up or down the list of bookmarks. A placeholder line will appear to mark the bookmark's position.

4. Release the mouse button. The bookmark will be moved to the new location.

5. Click the New Folder button. The Properties for New Folder dialog box will open (see Figure 10.11).

6. Enter the name of the bookmark folder in the Name field.

7. Click OK. The folder will be added to the Folder and the Bookmark panes.

8. Click and drag a bookmark to a position over one of the folders in the Folder pane.

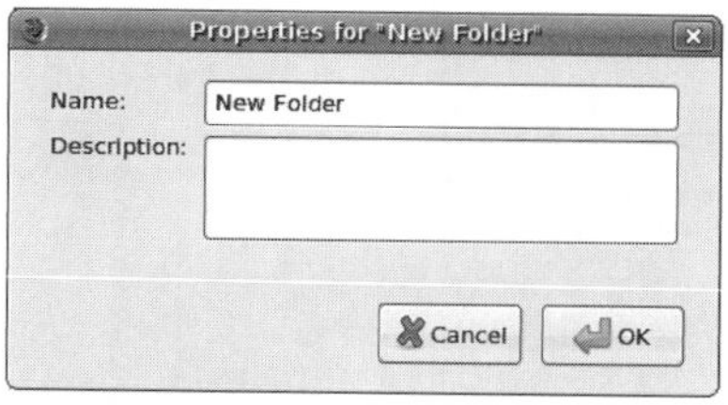

Figure 10.11
Manually creating a new bookmark folder.

9. Release the mouse button. The bookmark will be placed in the folder.

10. Click a bookmark or folder to remove it and click the Delete button. The bookmark will be removed.

Search Engines

Finding things on the Web used to be very easy; with only 500 or so Web sites in existence in the early nineties, you could almost index them by hand. Today, there are billions of Web pages, and finding useful things can be daunting sometimes. Firefox has a search tool that not only uses the most powerful search tools around but also allows you to choose the search engines you prefer.

Using the Search bar is easy: just type in what you are looking for and press Enter. By default, the Search bar connects to the Google search engine, and it will display the results of your search in a new tab.

Suggestive Searches

The latest version of Firefox will suggest search terms similar to what you type, in an effort to save you time. If you see the term you were looking for, select it and press Enter to start the actual search.

To change search engines, click the Search bar's drop-down list and select the engine you want to use instead, as shown in Figure 10.12.

Follow these steps to add or remove a search engine.

1. Click the Search bar drop-down list and select the Manage Search Engines option. The Manage Search Engine List dialog box will open (see Figure 10.13).

2. To remove a search engine, click the engine to select it.

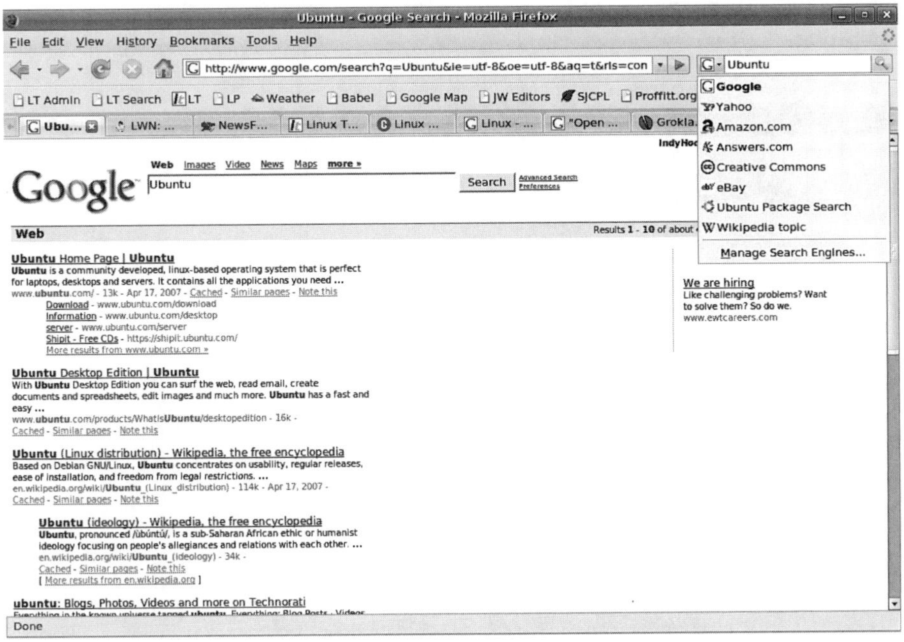

Figure 10.12
Initially available search engines.

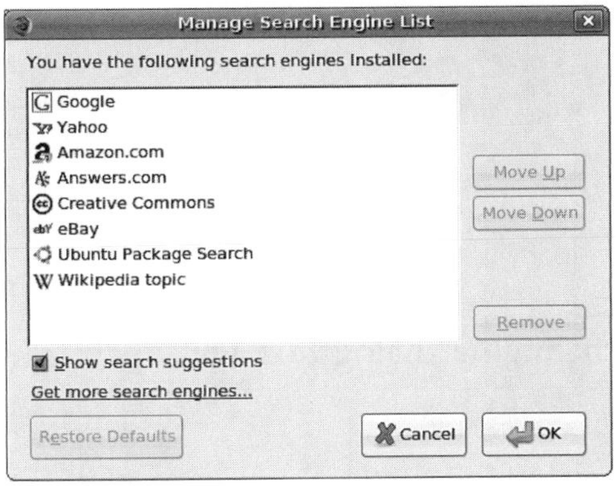

Figure 10.13
Managing search engines.

3. Click Remove. The search engine will be removed from the installed list.

4. Click the Get More Search Engines hyperlink. The Manage Search Engine List dialog box will close, and a new Firefox window will appear, displaying the Search Engines page on the Firefox Add-Ons site (see Figure 10.14).

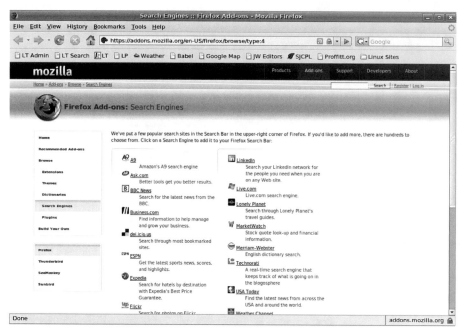

Figure 10.14
Adding search engines.

Figure 10.15
You can use a new search engine right away.

5. Click a search engine. The Add Search Engine dialog box will open (see Figure 10.15).

6. Click Add. The new search engine will be added to the Search bar list.

Live Bookmarks

A relatively new phenomenon on the Web is the presence of Really Simple Syndication (RSS) feeds, or *feeds* for short. An RSS feed is typically a very brief synopsis of the contents of a Web site. Users can "subscribe" to a site's feed and be able to see just by looking at the brief synopsis if the site's content has been updated. Clicking a link in the RSS feed will take the user right to the content on the feed's site.

Many Web sites use RSS feeds to syndicate content from other sites. If you have a site about Ubuntu, for instance, you might want to display the headlines from various Linux sites, such as Linux Today, Linux Weekly News, or LXer.

Firefox has a feature that's very useful for those of us who don't have a Web site to add RSS feeds to—live bookmarks, which automatically update their content and display the source sites' content automatically.

Identifying sites that can have a live bookmark is easy. Any site that has an available RSS feed will be noted by an orange RSS icon in the far right of the Location Bar. If you find such a site and want to subscribe to its feed, then just follow these steps.

1. From a site with an available feed, click the RSS icon in the Location Bar. The site's feed page will appear, with a subscription prompt at the top of the page (see Figure 10.16).

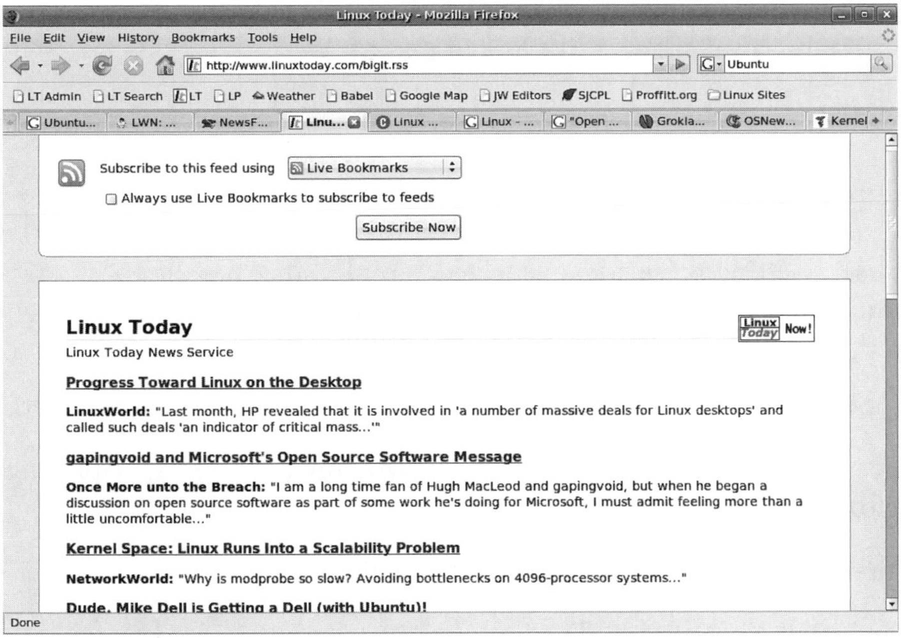

Figure 10.16
Subscribing to an RSS feed.

Figure 10.17
Live bookmarks are added like regular bookmarks.

2. Click the Subscribe Now button. The Add Live Bookmark dialog box will open (see Figure 10.17).

3. Enter the name of the live bookmark you want to use.

4. Click the Create In drop-down list if you want the live bookmark to appear somewhere other than the Bookmarks toolbar and select a new location.

5. Click Add. The live bookmark will be added to the desired location, and the Add Live Bookmark dialog box will close.

Once a live bookmark is in place, it will periodically update itself and display the contents of the subscribed site just like a bookmark folder.

Add-ons

Another feature unique to Firefox over other browsers is the ability to add add-ons, such as extensions to enhance your browser experience, or themes to dress up your browser. Getting these add-ons is very simple, since for the most part, they are all found in one place: the Firefox Add-ons Web site. But you don't need a URL to go there; Firefox's Add-ons tool will take care of everything.

1. Click Tools | Add-ons. The Add-ons window will appear (see Figure 10.18).

2. Click the Get Extensions link. A new Firefox window will appear, displaying the Firefox Add-ons site (see Figure 10.19).

3. Navigate the site to find an extension you would like to install.

4. Click the Install Now button. The Software Installation dialog box will appear (see Figure 10.20).

Figure 10.18
Managing Add-ons.

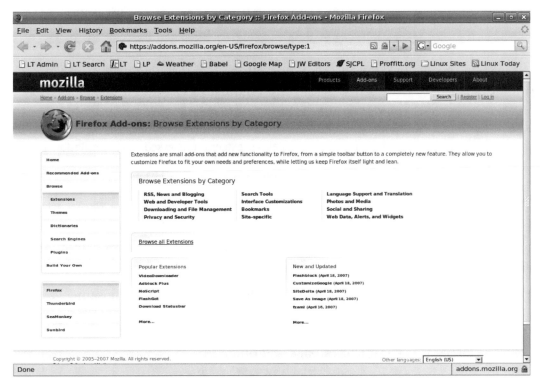

Figure 10.19
The Firefox Add-ons site.

Figure 10.20
The Software Installation dialog box.

Confirm Compatibility

Please note the Works With column's information to be sure an extension will function with the version of Firefox you are currently using.

5. When ready, click the Install Now button. The installed extension will appear in the Add-ons window (see Figure 10.21).

Extension Tricks

You may need to restart Firefox to fully install an extension. If asked, click the Restart Firefox button. You may need to re-open the Add-ons window if this occurs.

The Add-on tool does more than add extensions. It also handles access to each extension's preferences commands, as well as uninstall them when the time comes. Clicking the Find Updates button will immediately begin a search for the latest versions of all of your extension software.

Finding and managing browser themes is done in very much the same way.

1. Click Tools I Add-ons. The Add-ons window will appear.

2. Click Themes. The Themes page will open.

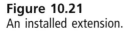

Figure 10.21
An installed extension.

3. Click the Get Themes link. A new Firefox window will appear, displaying the Firefox Add-Ons Themes site.

4. Navigate the site to find a theme you would like to install.

5. Click the Install Now button. The Software Installation dialog box will appear.

6. When ready, click the Install Now button. The installed extension will appear in the Add-ons window.

Theme Installation

You may need to restart Firefox to fully install a theme. If asked, click the Restart Firefox button. You may need to re-open the Add-ons window if this occurs.

7. Click the new theme in the Themes page. Information about the theme will appear in the Add-ons window (see Figure 10.22).

8. Click the Use Theme button. The theme will be activated.

9. Restart Firefox if necessary.

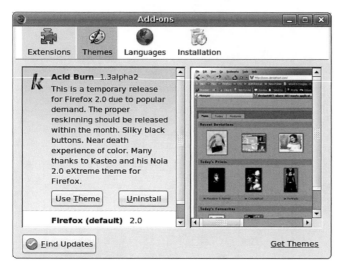

Figure 10.22
An installed theme.

Conclusion

In this chapter, you learned some of the finer points of operating the Firefox browser. With the multitude of extensions, it is a very realistic statement to say that this tool will be the most powerful application in the Ubuntu toolset.

In Chapter 11, "Mail Call," we will examine how to use the other most-used aspect of the Internet—e-mail—and how Ubuntu's e-mail clients handle this important job.

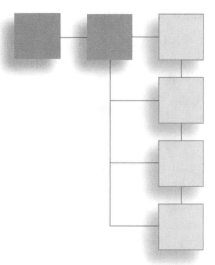

CHAPTER 11

MAIL CALL

In a brand-new building in Austin, Minnesota, sits the Spam Museum, a shrine completely dedicated to a processed meat product that has earned itself a unique place in American culture. Here, at least, Spam is a good thing.

Everywhere else and apart from culinary discussions, the term *spam* has decidedly less appeal. Unsolicited e-mail messages comprise a very large majority of all e-mail traffic in the world. Most of it, fortunately, we never see, as our Internet providers' and employers' mail servers clean most of it out. The part that does get through, though, is still unwanted. You need a good e-mail client that will help you slog through spam, as well as organize all of the good e-mails that you want to receive.

Ubuntu, like most Linux distributions, is endowed with a very robust and capable e-mail client: Evolution. But there is another application that's very popular among Ubuntu users that you might also want to try: Thunderbird. Rather than recommend which one to use, it is left to the reader to compare and choose based on personal preferences. After all, they both have similar features, are easy to use, and are non-commercial applications. In this chapter, for both applications, you will learn how to do the following:

- Create an e-mail account.

- Download your messages.

- Organize your e-mail.

- Filter spam away forever.

Using Evolution

Evolution is the GNOME environment's personal information manager and workgroup application. It hasn't been around long, since September 2004, when it was released as part of GNOME 2.8. Since Ubuntu is primarily a GNOME-using distribution, it makes sense that it would be included in Ubuntu as the default e-mail application.

If you've used Microsoft Outlook, there's a lot about Evolution that you are going to recognize: e-mail, calendar, address book, and task list functions are part of its feature set. If you are in an office that uses Microsoft Exchange Server, Evolution is one of the non-Microsoft clients that can fully connect to Exchange and utilize it. You can also sync your Palm Pilot and Windows Mobile device with your Evolution data.

This chapter will focus mostly on the e-mail capabilities of Evolution.

Setting Up an Account

Getting an e-mail account these days is a pretty simple thing. Most employers have them for their employees, universities have them for students and staff, and private Internet service providers often provide multiple e-mail accounts per Internet connection: one for each member of the family, if you want.

Most e-mails (especially away from internal business accounts) are delivered over the Internet via the Post Office Protocol (POP) or Internet Mail Access Protocol (IMAP). A POP or IMAP account works something like this: Someone sends you an e-mail. The Internet's control servers route that message to your e-mail server, which can be located anywhere in the world. There, your message will sit until you come along and download it (and any other messages) into your e-mail client. Unless you have an e-mail server in your home or cubicle, e-mails never come directly to you. This is actually good, because this two-step process gives your mail server and your client (such as Evolution) a chance to clean out spam and junk mail.

Outbound mail is a little different. You type a message, address it, and hit Send. The message is immediately sent out to the destination server via a Simple Mail Transfer Protocol (SMTP) server. It doesn't stay there long; the SMTP server has one job to do, and it does it very quickly. It checks the address in your message and makes sure there's actually a mail server ready to receive messages at the other end. If there is, boom! Off your message goes. If there isn't, the SMTP server will immediately bounce your message back to your client and tell you what went wrong.

Return to Sender

Note that the SMTP server on your end only checks for valid mail servers. If the username in the address is incorrect, or that user no longer has an account, it's the job of the receiving POP server to figure that out and send you the bounce message. It's a fine line, but if you get a bounce message, knowing from where it was sent will help you figure out what went wrong.

Whenever you set up a new e-mail account, your Internet service provider will provide you with some important information that you need to memorize or store in a safe place somewhere. Specifically, you need:

- Your new e-mail address.

- Your username for the POP server.

- Your password for the POP server.

- The Internet address of the POP server.

- The Internet address of the SMTP server.

When you first start Evolution, you will immediately be given the opportunity to set up an e-mail account. You can set up as many accounts as you would like, but you should have the complete set of information for at least one of your accounts before working on these steps when you start Evolution for the first time.

1. Click the Applications | Internet | Evolution Mail menu command. The Evolution Setup Assistant dialog box will open (see Figure 11.1).

Opening Evolution

The Applications | Office | Evolution menu command will also open Evolution, as will clicking the Evolution launcher icon in the upper panel. Clicking any e-mail link in a Web browser will also start Evolution.

2. Click Forward. The Identity page will open, as shown in Figure 11.2.

3. Type the appropriate information in the fields. It is important that you put information in the required fields.

4. Click Forward. The Receiving Email page will open (see Figure 11.3).

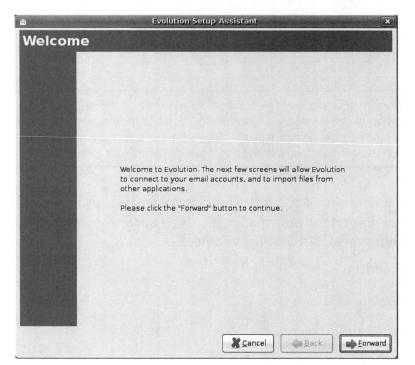

Figure 11.1
The Evolution Setup Assistant.

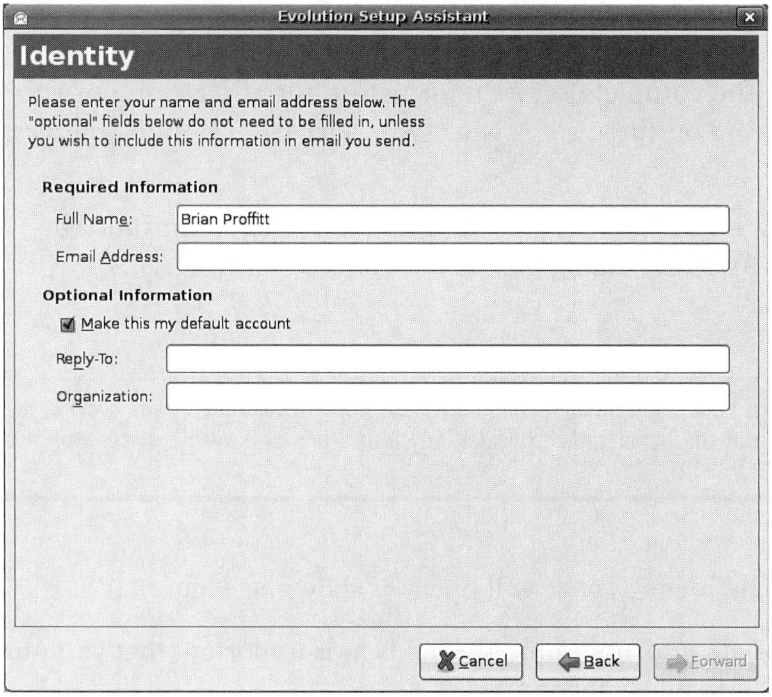

Figure 11.2
Declare your identity.

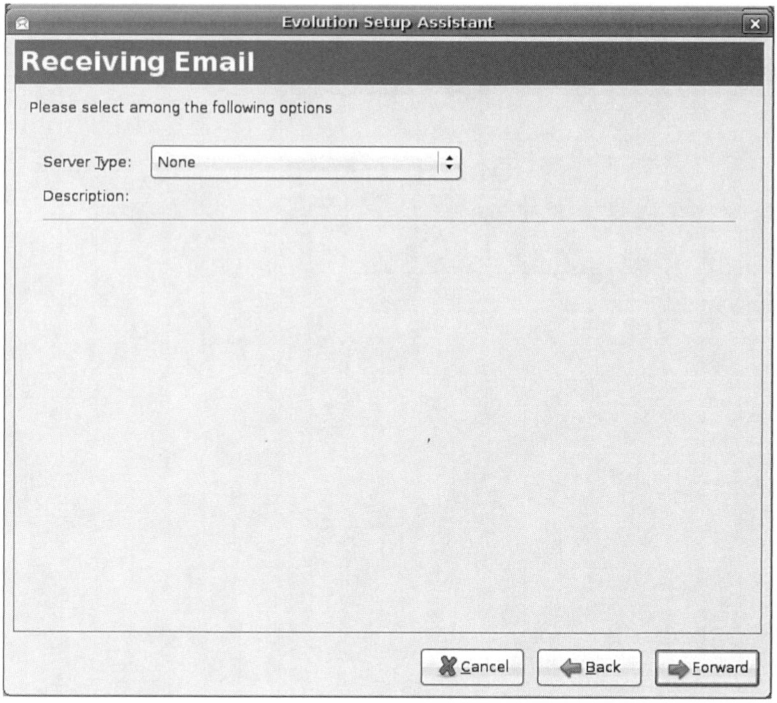

Figure 11.3
Specify the server type.

5. Select POP from the Server Type drop-down list. The appropriate config-uration fields will appear on the bottom section of the dialog box, as displayed in Figure 11.4.

Non-POP Accounts

If you are using something other than a POP-type account, contact your system administrator and obtain the necessary information.

6. Type the address of your POP server in the Server field.

7. Confirm your username in the Username field.

8. If your mail server uses encryption, select the appropriate value in the Use Secure Connection field.

9. Most POP servers use a password for authentication. If you are not sure, click the Check for Supported Types button. The POP server will be queried, and the correct authentication value should be inserted.

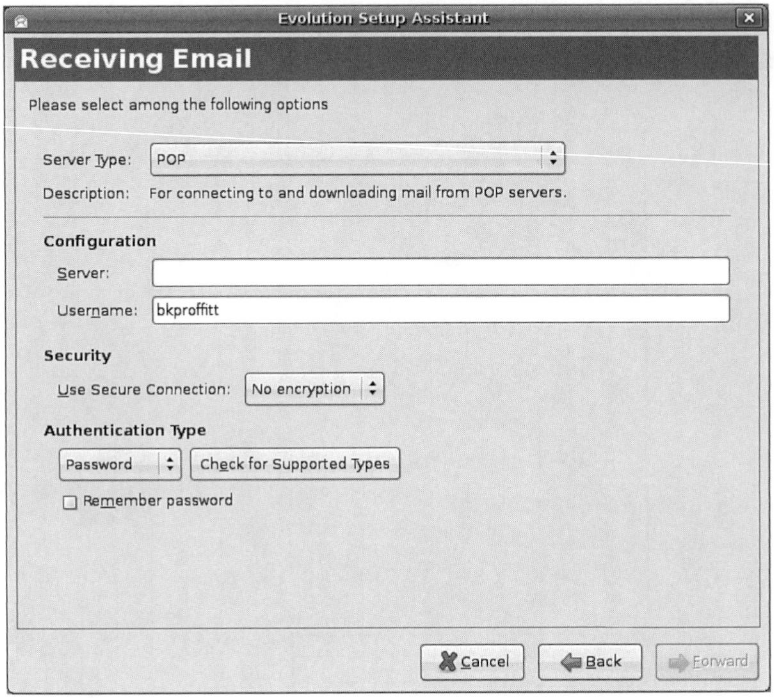

Figure 11.4
Specify the POP settings.

10. Click the Remember Password check box if you want Evolution to pick up mail without asking you for a password every time (though this could be a potential security risk).

11. Click Forward. The Receiving Options page will open (see Figure 11.5).

12. Check the appropriate check boxes to get the settings you want.

Many Clients, One POP Server

If this Ubuntu PC will be the primary place you will want your messages stored, don't check the Leave Messages on Server option. Leaving it unselected will mean that once downloaded, your messages will no longer take up space on the server. If this PC is a secondary computer (such as a laptop on the road), check this option, so when you get back home to your main PC, everything that came to you while you were away will be downloaded to one place.

You can set Evolution to download e-mail automatically at a certain interval—no less than 10 minutes, so you don't overload your POP server. That's a good idea for those of you with an always-on Internet account. If you are using dial-up, consider leaving this option off. If you can control the timing of e-mail downloads, you can manage the flow of traffic through your narrowband connection.

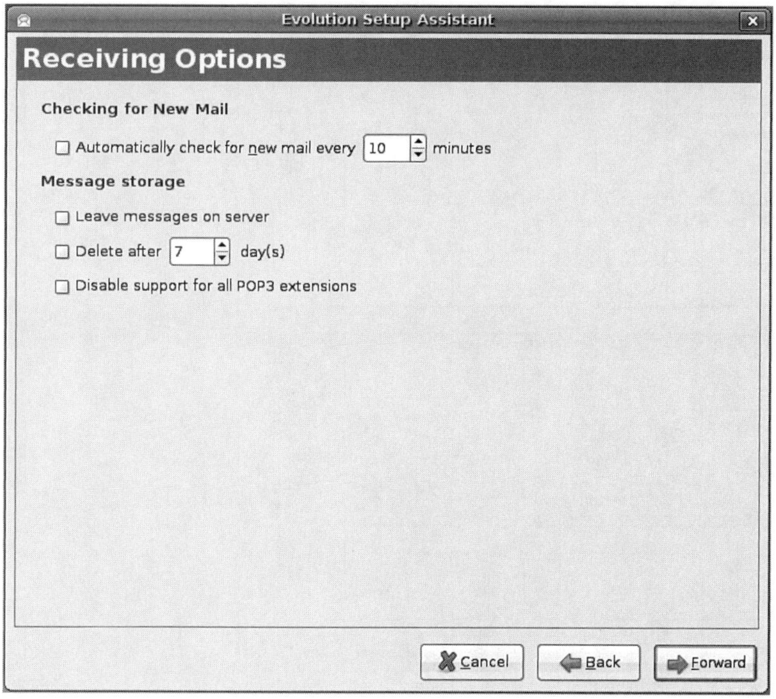

Figure 11.5
Detail your reception preferences.

13. Click Forward. The Sending Email page will open (see Figure 11.6).

14. Type the address of your SMTP server in the Server field.

15. If your SMTP server uses encryption, select the appropriate value in the Use Secure Connection field.

16. Some SMTP servers use a password for authentication. If you are not sure, click the Check for Supported Types button. The SMTP server will be queried, and the correct authentication value will be inserted.

17. Confirm your username in the Username field.

18. Click the Remember Password check box if you want Evolution to send mail without asking you for a password every time.

19. Click Forward. The Account Management page will open (see Figure 11.7).

20. Name the account and click Forward. The Timezone page will appear (see Figure 11.8).

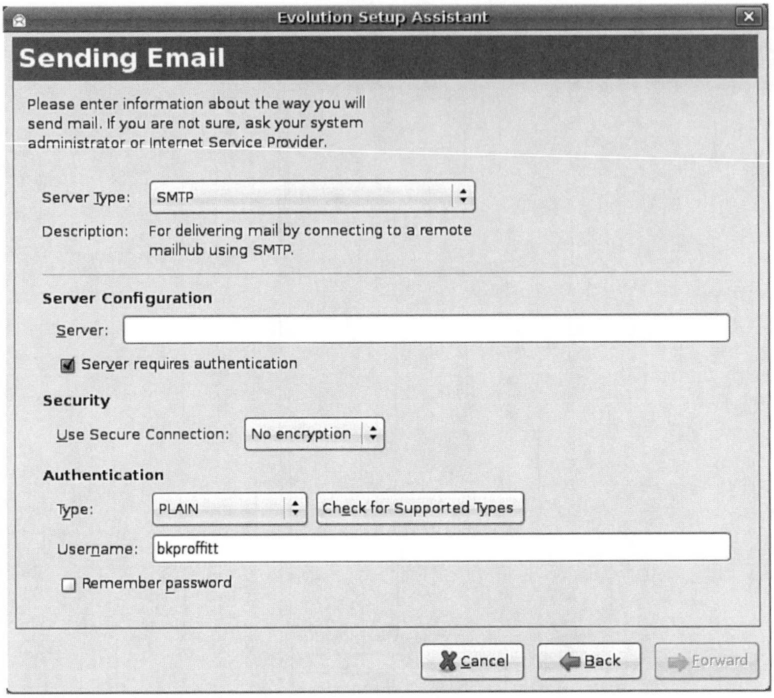

Figure 11.6
Specify the SMTP settings.

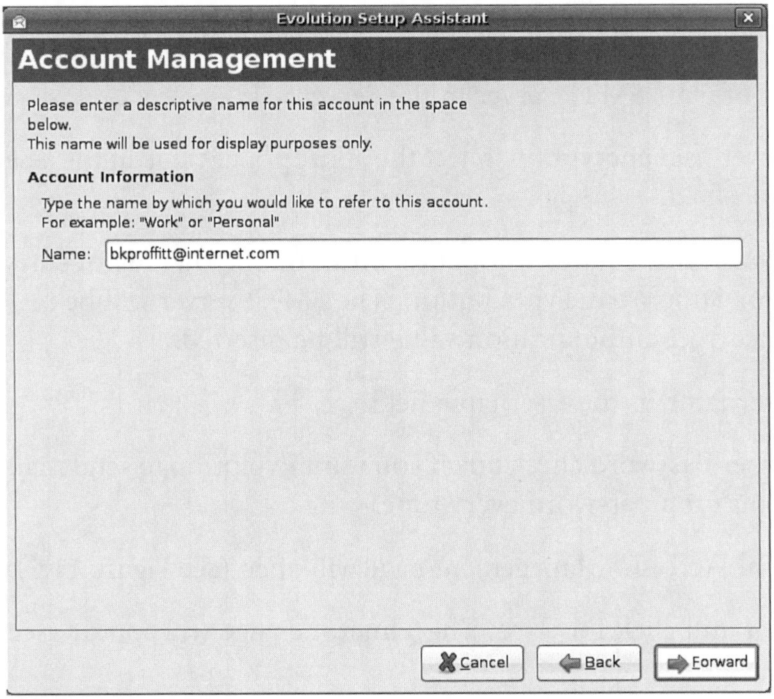

Figure 11.7
Name the account.

Figure 11.8
Set your timezone.

21. Set your timezone using the map of the Selection drop-down list.

22. Click Forward. The Done page will appear (see Figure 11.9).

23. Click Apply. The Evolution Setup Assistant dialog box will close, and
    Evolution will open.

If you set your account to automatically check for mail, as soon as Evolution opens,
the Enter Password for <Your Account Name> dialog box will open. Type in the
password and click OK. The dialog box will close, and your mail will be downloaded.

If you want to add another e-mail account to Evolution, you will need to use the
Evolution Account Assistant, which is identical to the Setup Assistant. To access
it, follow these few steps in Evolution.

1. Click the Edit | Preferences menu command. The Evolution Preferences
   window will open (see Figure 11.10).

2. Confirm the Mail Accounts option is selected and click the Add button. The
   Evolution Account Assistant dialog box will open, as shown in Figure 11.11.

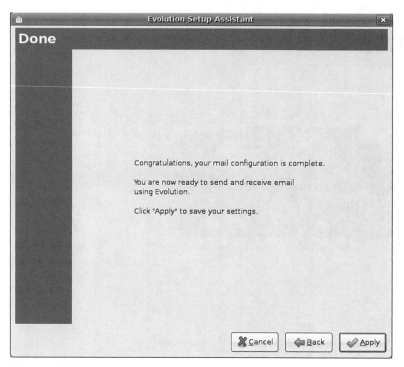

Figure 11.9
Finished and ready to go.

Figure 11.10
Evolution preferences.

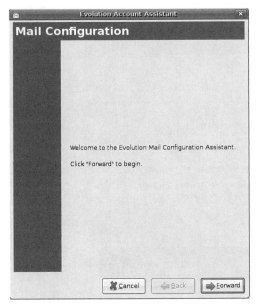

Figure 11.11
The Evolution Account Assistant.

3. Follow the steps you used for the Evolution Setup Assistant to complete the task.

Receiving and Sending Mail

Once you have one account set up in Evolution, you are free to send and receive e-mail as long as you are connected to the Internet.

If you did not set Evolution to download messages automatically (or just want to see what's out there before the next scheduled download occurs), click the Send/Receive button (or press F9 on the keyboard). Your messages will be downloaded.

As you can see in Figure 11.12, the Evolution window is very similar to Microsoft Outlook.

Reading a message is simple: Just click a message in the Message list, and its contents will be displayed in the Preview window. Double-clicking a message will open the message in its own message window (see Figure 11.13), complete with a set of tools to use on the message.

After you have read an e-mail, you will note that it is no longer bold in the Message list, and its envelope icon will be open.

Folders   Message List

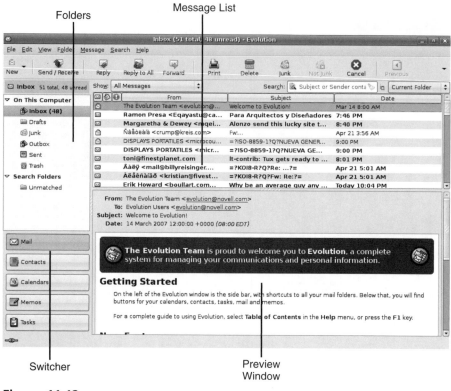

Switcher   Preview
               Window

Figure 11.12
The Evolution window.

You can do more with an e-mail than just read it. In fact, more often than not, a message will warrant a reply. To reply to the *send* of the message only:

1. Select a message to which to reply. The message will be displayed in the Preview window.

2. Click Reply. A preaddressed Re: message window will open.

3. Type your reply in the body of the message.

4. Click Send. The message window will close, and the message will appear in the Outbox until it is sent to the SMTP server.

If the message was sent to you and other people, you can send a reply to all the recipients and the sender.

1. Select a message to reply to all recipients. The message will be displayed in the Preview window.

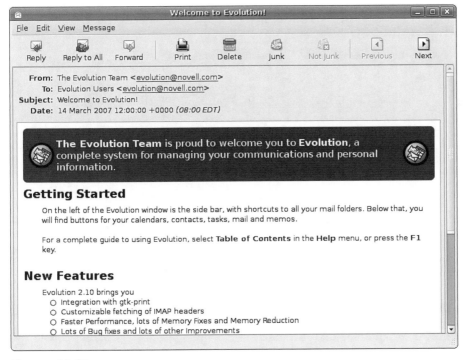

Figure 11.13
A message window.

2. Click Reply to All. A preaddressed Re: message window will open.

3. Type your reply in the body of the message.

4. Click Send. The message window will close, and the message will appear in the Outbox until it is sent to the SMTP server.

If you want to forward a message to someone else, it's just as easy.

1. Select a message to forward. The message will be displayed in the Preview window.

2. Click Forward. A preaddressed Fwd: message window will open.

3. Type an additional message in the body of the message.

4. Click Send. The message window will close, and the message will appear in the Outbox until it is sent to the SMTP server.

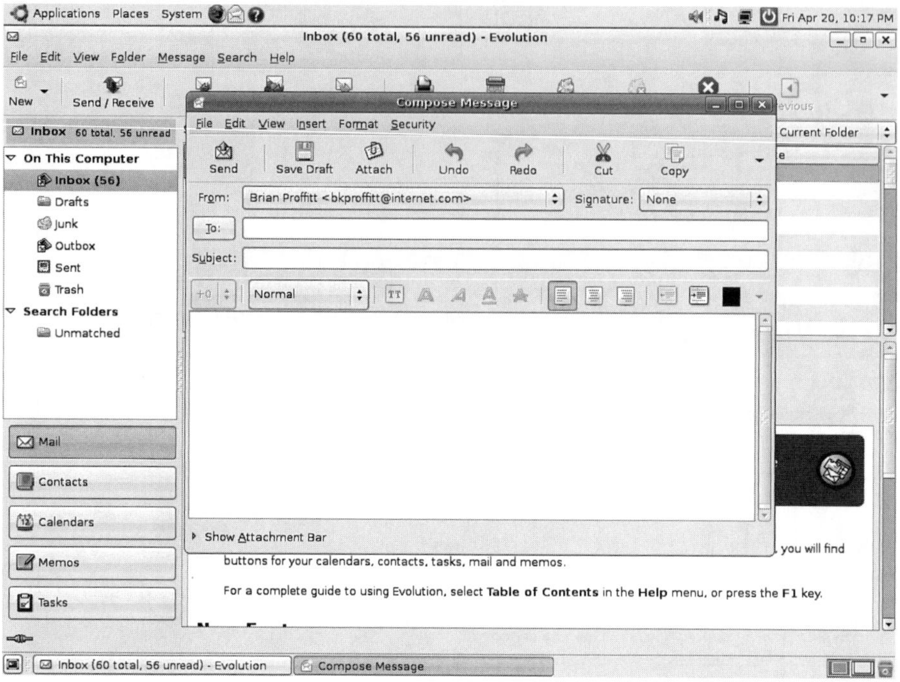

Figure 11.14
A new message window.

If you want to send a new message to a single or multiple recipients, here's how.

1. Click New. A Compose Message window will open (see Figure 11.14).

2. Type an e-mail address in the To field.

Contact Connection

If you use the Contacts tool in Evolution, you can create a database of names and e-mail addresses. Then you can click the To button and open the Select Contacts from Address Book dialog box and quickly choose the addresses you need without typing a single ampersand.

3. If you need to carbon copy a recipient, select the View | Cc Field menu command in the message window and type the address in.

4. Type a subject.

5. Type a message in the body.

6. Click Send. The message window will close, and the message will appear in the Outbox until it is sent to the SMTP server.

Organizing Mail

After you have read your messages and sent your replies, what next? You don't want to leave your Inbox cluttered, and unless it's junk mail, you don't want to delete everything, either.

Evolution is very good about handling lots of e-mail at once. Let's take some steps to organize the Inbox first.

If you click the Show drop-down list, you will see a list of categories to filter the Message list. Click these, as you desire, to see the results on your Inbox.

You can also sort messages based on the criteria of the columns in the Message list. If you want to sort by date, click the Date column header. A down arrow will appear in the header button, and the messages will be listed from earliest to most recent down the screen. Clicking the Date header again will change the sort order from most recent to earliest. You can do this for any column header.

The folders are a really useful tool in Evolution for organizing your information. Using folders, you can essentially treat messages as files (which, you should know, they are) that can be organized just like files in the Nautilus file manager, which you learned about in Chapter 9, "Basic File Management."

Creating a folder is very quick.

1. Right-click the Inbox folder. A context menu will appear.

2. Select the New Folder menu command. The Create Folder dialog box will open (see Figure 11.15).

3. Type a folder name.

Figure 11.15
Making a new folder.

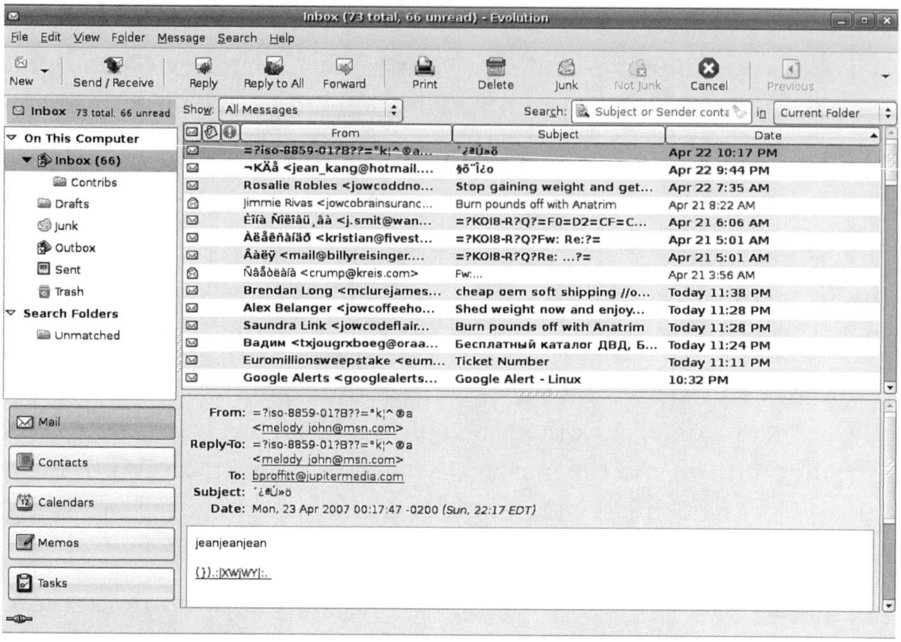

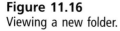

Figure 11.16
Viewing a new folder.

4. Click Create. The Create Folder dialog box will close, and the new folder will
   be added to the Inbox.

5. To view the new folder, click the expansion icon next to the Inbox folder (see
   Figure 11.16).

After you have folders created, you can set up rules in Evolution that will examine
incoming messages and automatically move certain messages into those folders.
If you have a project you are working on, you can create a rule that will move any
message containing a reference to that project into a folder you've created.

Evolution helps with this process by letting you choose a representative message
and build the rule from that point.

1. Right-click the example message. A context menu will appear.

2. Select the Create Rule from Message menu command; then select one of the
   Filter On options (Subject, Sender, or Recipients). The Add Filter Rule
   dialog box will appear (see Figure 11.17).

3. Confirm or edit the Search name rule.

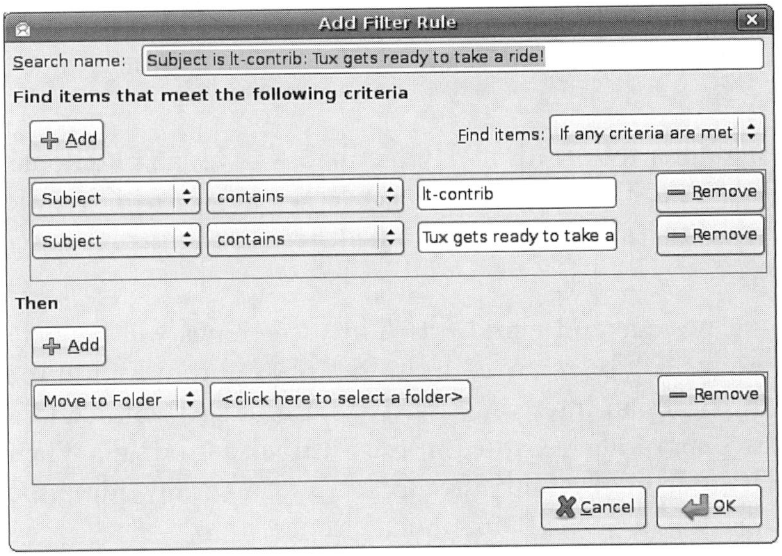

Figure 11.17
Creating a new rule.

4. Confirm or edit the Subject criteria. If one of the criteria isn't needed, click its Remove button.

5. Confirm that the Move to Folder option is selected.

6. Click the Select a Folder field. The Select Folder dialog box will open.

7. Select the desired folder and click OK. The Select Folder dialog box will close.

8. Click OK. The Add Filter Rule dialog box will close.

To run the filter on your existing Inbox messages, select the Message | Apply Filters menu command.

Protecting Your Inbox

If you've been paying attention, you may have noticed quite a lot of spam in the Inbox shown in the previous figures. The sad truth is, no one is ever immune to spam, or junk mail, as Evolution refers to it. There are ways to minimize it, the most important method being to keep your e-mail address close to the vest. Sometimes that's not possible, especially with work accounts. But if you have a personal e-mail address, just give it to family and friends and never post it on the Web.

When, not if, you start getting junk mail, Evolution initially will let it roll right into your Inbox, leaving you wondering where all this vaunted protection is. Don't worry, it's there.

Evolution uses a Bayesian filter to sort through junk mail. A Bayesian filter looks at messages and decides if it's spam or not based on criteria it has learned over the course of time. But in order to learn, it has to be trained, and that's where the user comes in.

When you select a junk message and mark it as *Junk,* two things will happen: First, the offending message will be removed from the Inbox and moved to the Junk folder. Second, the Bayesian filter will "learn" that messages with certain words and characteristics should be regarded in the future as junk mail. When more messages like that come in, the Junk filter should automatically dump the spam into the Junk filter, leaving your Inbox much cleaner.

There are a few things to remember when working with Evolution's Junk filter. To begin with, it takes a while to learn what's really junk or not, so for the first few sessions it may not seem like it's doing its job. Eventually, less spam will slip though as the learning process continues.

Another important point: The Junk filter is not infallible, especially early in its learning process. Not only will spam go unmarked, but genuine e-mails may get treated as spam by mistake. Therefore, it's very important that you periodically scan the contents of your Junk folder to look for real messages. If you do find any, be sure to click on the Not Junk button when the message is selected. This will help Evolution's Junk filter learn faster.

Using Thunderbird

As you learned in Chapter 10, "Surfing the Web," the Mozilla Application Suite is the source for the open source Firefox browser. The Mozilla Foundation, the organization charged with maintaining the Mozilla code, still works on the entire suite, but some application developers feel that the suite itself (codenamed *SeaMonkey*) was just too big to be fast and effective.

Just as a development team spun off a light and fast Web browser from Sea-Monkey, another team took the code for SeaMonkey's e-mail and contact manager and created the Thunderbird application.

Compared to Evolution, Thunderbird is lighter on features. If you are looking for an all-in-one personal information manager application like Outlook,

Thunderbird may not be the best choice. But if you don't need all of those tools and just want a fast e-mail client, Thunderbird will definitely fit the bill.

Unlike Evolution, Thunderbird is not included in the default installation of Ubuntu. So you will need to install it if you want to use it. Start the Synaptic Package Manager as demonstrated in Chapter 6, "Installing and Upgrading Software," and search for the Thunderbird package. Once found, mark it for installation, and allow the dependent packages to be installed as well.

Setting Up an Account

When you first start Thunderbird, you will immediately be given the opportunity to set up an e-mail account. Remember, you will need all of your account information to get things set up.

1. Click the Applications | Internet | Thunderbird Mail menu command. The Account Wizard dialog box will open (see Figure 11.18).

2. Confirm that the Email Account radio button is selected and click Next. The Identity page will open, as shown in Figure 11.19.

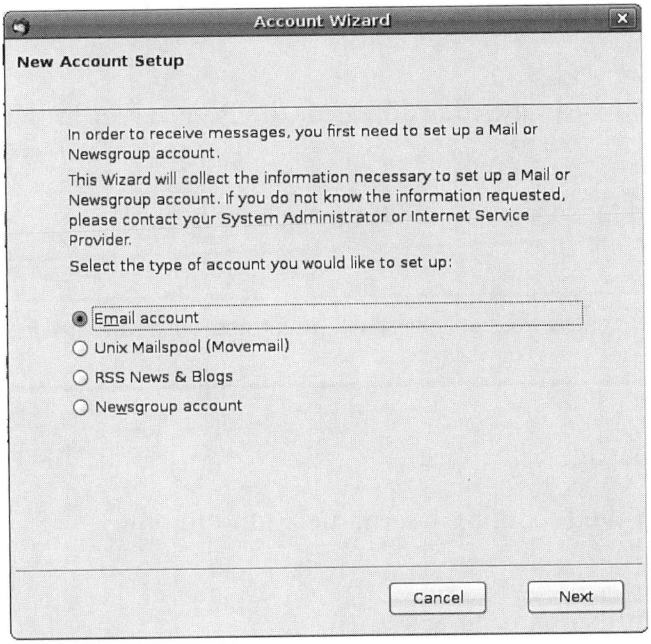

Figure 11.18
The Account wizard.

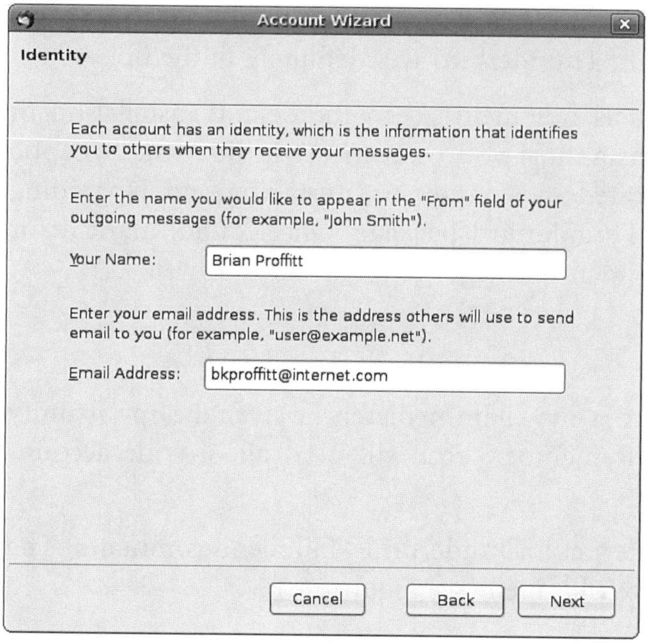

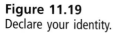

Figure 11.19
Declare your identity.

3. Type the appropriate information in the fields and click Next. The Server Information page will open.

4. Select the POP radio button and type the address of the POP server in the Incoming Server field.

5. Type the address of the SMTP server in the Outgoing Server field.

IMAP Users

If you are using an IMAP account, contact your system administrator and obtain the needed information.

6. Click Next. The Usernames page will appear.

7. Confirm your username in the Incoming Username and Outgoing Username fields.

8. Click Forward. The Account Name page will open.

9. Name the account and click Next. The Congratulations page will appear (see Figure 11.20).

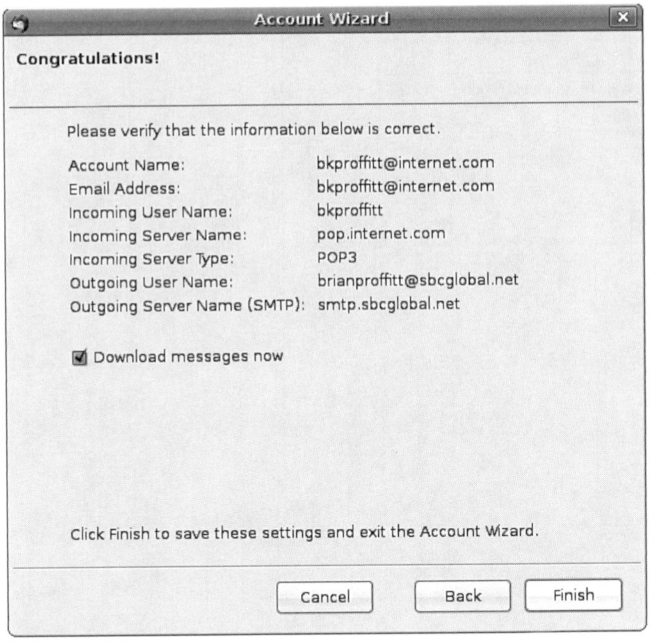

Figure 11.20
Confirm your account settings.

10. Confirm your settings and that the Download Messages Now check box is selected.

11. Click Finish. The Account Wizard dialog box will close, and Thunderbird will open.

As soon as Thunderbird opens, you will be asked for the POP server's password. Type in the password and click OK. The dialog box will close, and your mail will be downloaded.

If you want to add another e-mail account to Thunderbird, you will need to use the Account wizard again. To access it, follow these few steps in Thunderbird.

1. Click the Edit | Account Settings menu command. The Account Settings dialog box will open (see Figure 11.21).

2. Click Add Account. The Account wizard dialog box will open.

3. Follow the steps you used for the Account wizard to complete the task.

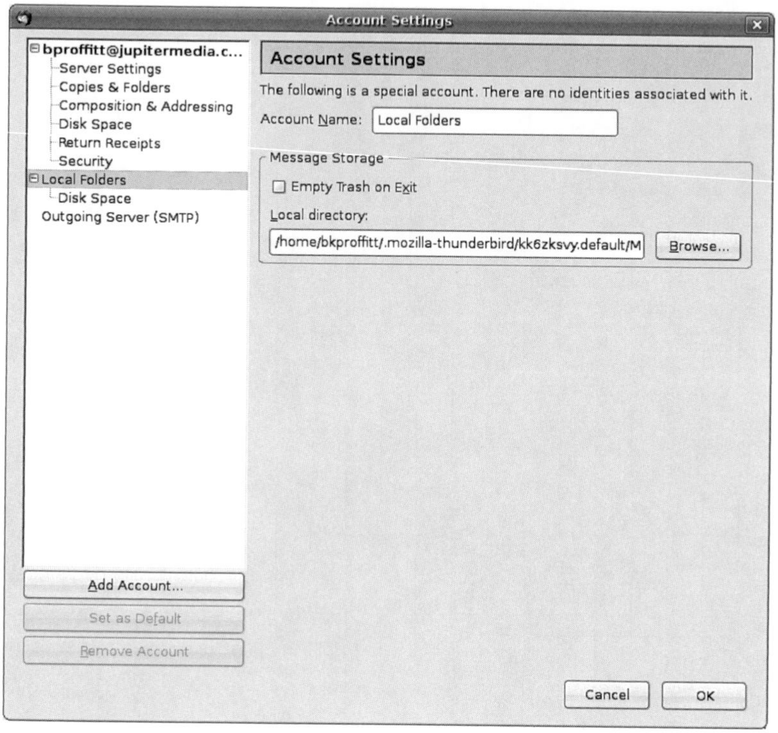

Figure 11.21
Thunderbird account settings.

Receiving and Sending Mail

When you have one account set up in Thunderbird, you are free to send and receive e-mail as long as you are connected to the Internet.

To download messages, click the Get Mail button (or press Ctrl+Shift+T on the keyboard). Your new messages will be downloaded.

As you can see in Figure 11.22, Thunderbird is very streamlined.

To read a message, click a message in the Message list, and its contents will be displayed in the Message pane below. Double-clicking a message will open the message in its own message window (see Figure 11.23), complete with a set of tools to use on the message.

After you have read an e-mail, you will note that it is no longer bold in the Message list, and its envelope icon will be open.

Folders   Message List

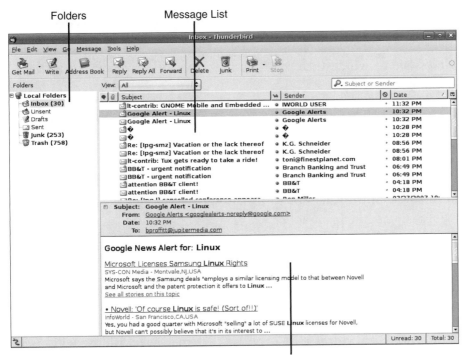

Message Pane

Figure 11.22
The Thunderbird window.

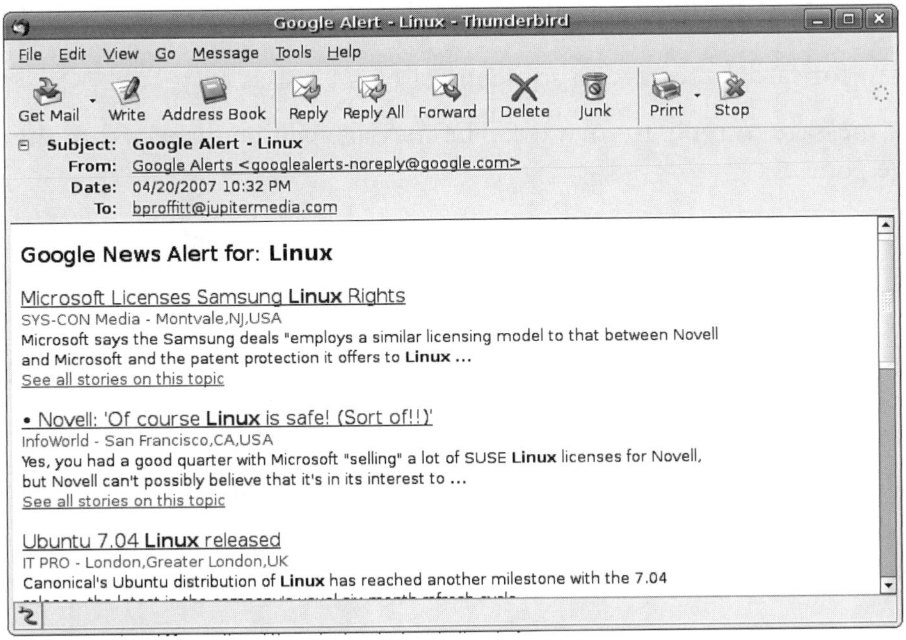

Figure 11.23
A message window in Thunderbird.

To act on a message, you can reply, reply all, or forward it. To reply to the *sender* of the message only:

1. Select a message to which to reply. The message will be displayed in the Message pane.

2. Click Reply. A preaddressed Compose: Re: message window will open.

3. Type your reply in the body of the message.

4. Click Send. The message window will close, and the message will appear in the Unsent folder until it is sent to the SMTP server.

If the message was sent to you and other people, you can send a reply to all the recipients and the sender.

1. Select a message to reply to all recipients. The message will be displayed in the Message pane.

2. Click Reply All. A preaddressed Compose: Re: message window will open.

3. Type your reply in the body of the message.

4. Click Send. The message window will close, and the message will appear in the Unsent folder until it is sent to the SMTP server.

If you want to forward a message to someone else, it's just as easy.

1. Select a message to reply to forward. The message will be displayed in the Message pane.

2. Click Forward. A preaddressed Compose: Fwd: message window will open.

3. Type an additional message in the body of the message.

4. Click Send. The message window will close, and the message will appear in the Unsent folder until it is sent to the SMTP server.

If you want to send a new message to a single or multiple recipients, follow these steps.

1. Click Write. A Compose window will open (see Figure 11.24).

2. Type an e-mail address in the To field.

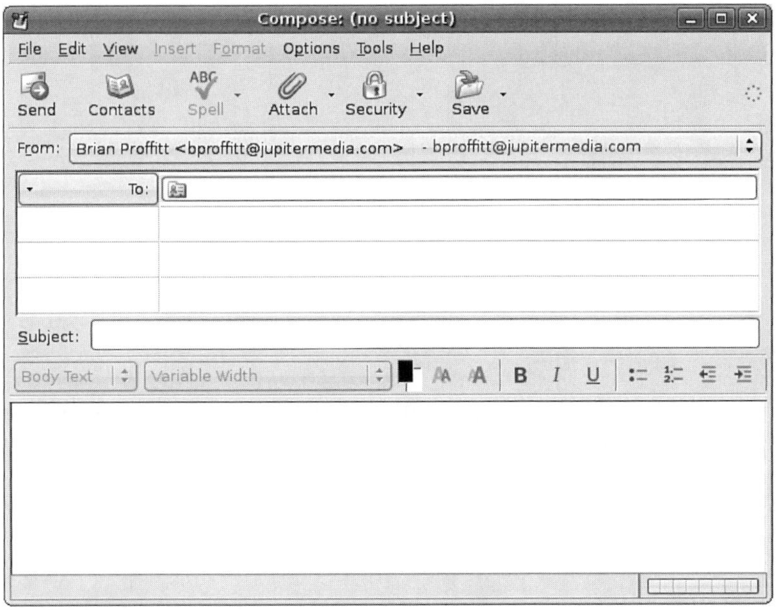

Figure 11.24
A new Compose window.

3. If you need to enter another recipient, click another address field and type the address in.

4. Select the Address type (To, Cc, Bcc, etc.) for the additional address.

5. Type a subject.

6. Type a message in the body.

7. Click Send. The message window will close, and the message will appear in the Unsent folder until it is sent to the SMTP server.

Organizing Mail

Like any e-mail client, it is very easy to get your Inbox full of lots of stuff you may not want to keep around. Let's take a quick tour of some organizational methods.

If you click the View drop-down list, you will see a list of categories to filter the Message list. Click those as you desire to see the results in your Inbox.

You can also sort messages based on the criteria of the columns in the Message list. If you want to sort by date, click the Date column header. A down arrow will

Figure 11.25
Making a new folder.

appear in the header button, and the messages will be listed from earliest to most recent down the screen. Clicking the Date header again will change the sort order from most recent to earliest. You can do this for any column header.

Folders are also a really useful tool in Thunderbird, just as with Evolution.

Creating a folder is easy.

1. Right-click the Inbox folder. A context menu will appear.

2. Select the New Folder menu command. The New Folder dialog box will open (see Figure 11.25).

3. Type a Folder Name.

4. Click OK. The New Folder dialog box will close, and the new folder will be added to the Inbox.

Once you have folders created, you can set up filters in Thunderbird, too. And you can also choose a representative message and build the filter from that point.

1. Click the example message.

2. Select the Message | Create Filter from Message menu command. The Filter Rules dialog box will appear (see Figure 11.26).

3. Confirm or edit the filter name.

4. Confirm or edit the selection criteria.

5. Confirm that the Move Message To option is selected.

6. Click the Local Folders drop-down list and select the desired folder.

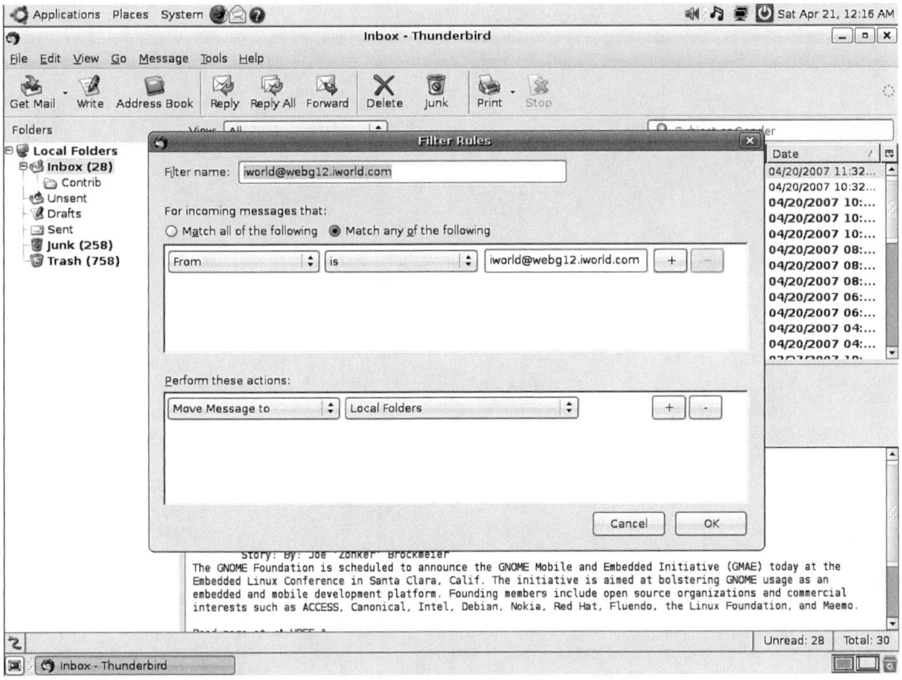

Figure 11.26
Creating a new filter rule.

7. Click OK. The Filter Rules dialog box will close, and the Message Filters dialog box will appear (see Figure 11.27).

You can go ahead and close this dialog box. To run the filter on your existing Inbox messages, select the Tools | Run Filters on Folder menu command.

Protecting Your Inbox

Like Evolution, Thunderbird uses an adaptive Bayesian filter to sort through junk mail. But, unlike Evolution, you have more control over the junk mail controls.

If you select the Tools | Junk Mail Controls menu command, the Junk Mail Control dialog box will open (see Figure 11.28).

The only tab you need to worry about is the one selected: Settings. On this page, you can determine what constitutes junk mail a little better and also determine what to do with junk mail you've marked yourself.

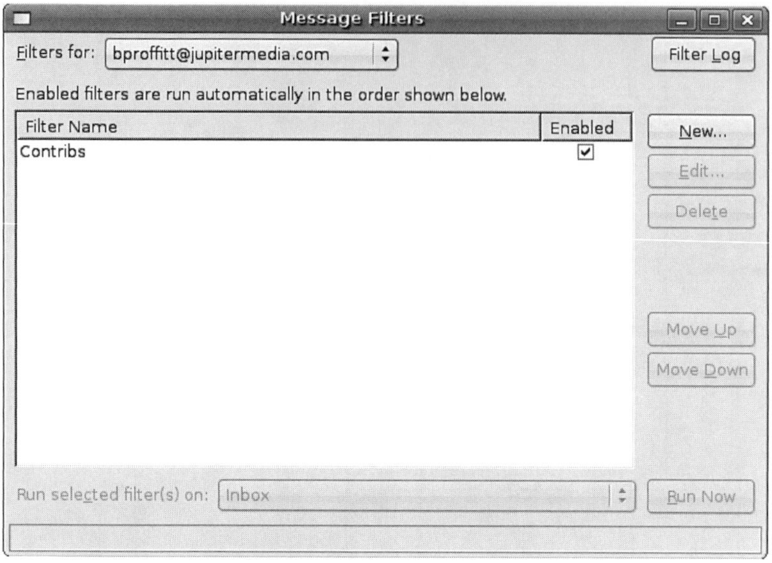

Figure 11.27
Message filters.

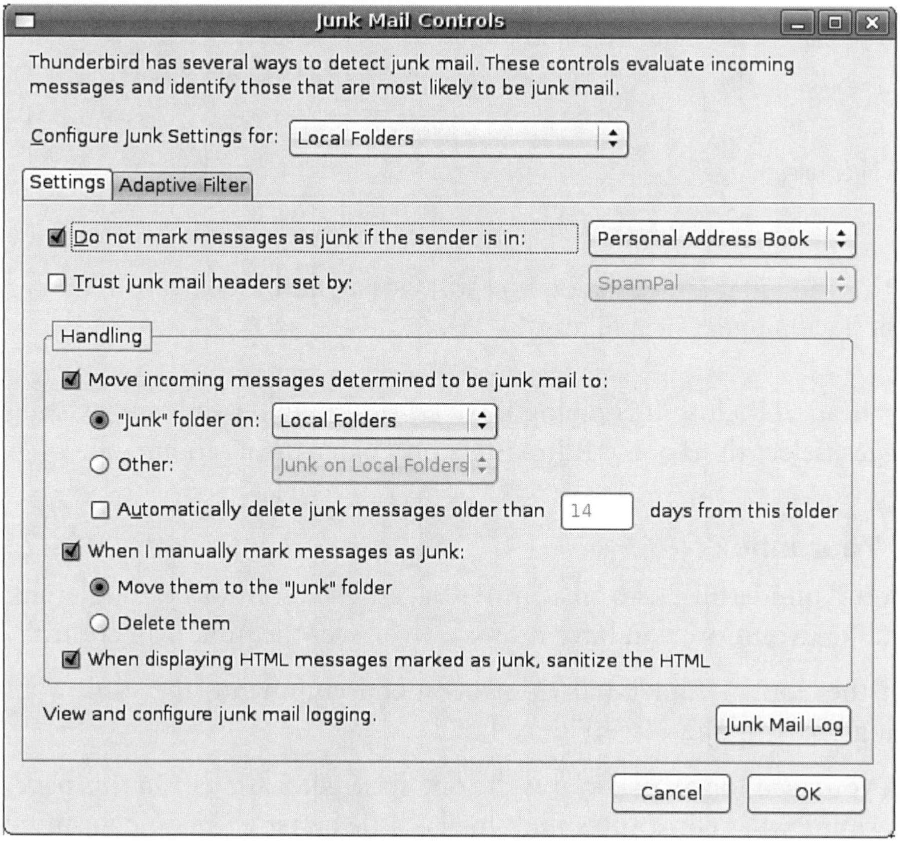

Figure 11.28
The Junk Mail Controls dialog box.

Remember, no filter is foolproof, and you need to check the Junk folder periodically to make sure nothing genuine has gotten tagged as spam.

Conclusion

There is a lot more to e-mail these days than just reading and writing. With this medium becoming so integral in our daily lives, it's good to see that there are excellent tools in Ubuntu that can make e-mail use easy.

In Chapter 12, "Messaging Tools," you will learn about an even newer form of communication available in Ubuntu: instant messaging and Internet phone calls.

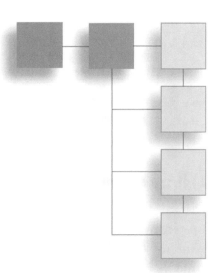

CHAPTER 12

MESSAGING TOOLS

When you come right down to it, the invention of the Internet was really meant as a way for scientists in academic and government environments to communicate vast swathes of data with each other in a very quick and reliable manner. The military saw uses for this kind of global network, too, which is why the U.S. Department of Defense sponsored the early DARPAnet infrastructure that would eventually become the Internet.

The kind of data they needed to transfer was voluminous and needed to be moved back and forth securely in a hurry, something that the phone system could not provide. So it comes with some irony that, after all is said and done, companies are turning the Internet into another global voice network, just like the phone system.

Instantaneous communication is a really wonderful thing, which most of us take for granted. Imagine, you can pick up a cell phone, conduct an instant messaging (IM) session or (more recently) use Voice over IP (VoIP) technology and communicate with someone thousands of miles away. To people living just 50 years ago, this would border on magic. Our children have all grown up with such advances, and we've adapted fairly well, so it's hard to step back and appreciate how cool this really is.

In this chapter, you will find out how Ubuntu provides the tools to conduct IM and VoIP conversations via the Internet, specifically learning how to:

- Obtain your own IM account.

- Use Gaim to conduct an IM session.

- Call anyone in the world with the Ekiga Softphone.

Using Gaim (Pidgin)

Instant messaging, as we know it today, is actually a conglomeration of a variety of technologies. First, there was Internet Relay Chat (IRC), the stream-of-consciousness chat sessions in which many users could participate at the same time. A little bit later, as private networking providers like America Online or Prodigy grew into popularity, they featured their own versions of chat sessions, although these chat sessions were between just two users at a time: A private chat session that was dubbed by these network providers as *instant messaging*.

Today, almost all of these types of instant text communications, whether in IRC, in an IM session, or through text messaging on cell phones, are given the moniker "instant messaging."

Gaim is a software client that started as a free alternative to the America Online Instant Messaging (AIM) service. AIM is free for anyone to use and is no longer restricted to just AOL members. But initially, there were only Windows or Mac clients for AIM, and Linux users wanted a piece of the action. Thus, the GTK+ AOL Instant Messenger (Gaim) client was born.

AOL bucked a bit at this intrusion on their networks and took some steps to lock out incoming Gaim users. They also didn't like the name, since AOL was trade-marked. The developers responded by changing the acronym to just the Gaim proper name, which worked well for a while. Eventually, AOL learned to embrace Linux users, even to the point of using the Gaim source code to develop their own AIM for Linux client. But the name thing still stuck in AOL's craw. They decided to trademark the term "AIM" and demanded that Gaim change its name. After lengthy discussions about a settlement, the Gaim developers decided that they could change the name.

In Feisty Fawn, Gaim is still going by its original name, but when the client is next released, it will be called Pidgin. This concession to AOL is actually something that reflects the reality of Gaim's new capabilities. No longer is this client limited to just the AIM network. Now users can chat with these other networks, too:

- AIM

- Gadu-Gadu

- Jabber

- Internet Relay Chat

- MSN

- Novell GroupWise

- Rendezvous

- SILC

- Yahoo! Messenger

- Zephyr

As you can see, that's a lot of flexibility, far beyond just the AIM network, so there is a certain sense to the name Pidgin, which means a simple language used between multiple language users who do not share a common tongue.

There are two steps that have to occur before you can conduct an IM or chat session on any of these networks. You need to get yourself an account on one of these networks (if you don't have one already), and you need to configure that account in Gaim.

The really great thing is that you can set up multiple accounts in Gaim and have them running all at once. If you are so inclined, you can hold many conversations with different friends and colleagues at the same time.

Getting an IM Account

With all of the protocols listed in the previous section, it's a good chance that you will already have an account on one of these private networks. If you do, gather your login information and skip head to the next section, "Signing On," to begin your Gaim session.

Figure 12.1
The AIM home page.

For those users who have not acquired an account on one of these networks, it is recommended that you sign up for an AIM account. Because AIM is free to any Internet user who signs up, and Gaim was initially designed for AIM conversations and therefore is more robust in this network, it makes good sense.

First, connect to the Internet and open up Firefox. Then follow these steps:

1. Type **www.aim.com** in the Location Bar and press Enter. The AIM home page will appear (see Figure 12.1).

2. Click the Get a Screen Name link near the top of the page. The Screen Name page will appear (see Figure 12.2).

3. Confirm that the Create a Screen Name radio button is selected and click Continue. The Screen Name information screen will appear (see Figure 12.3).

4. Fill in the information in the required fields.

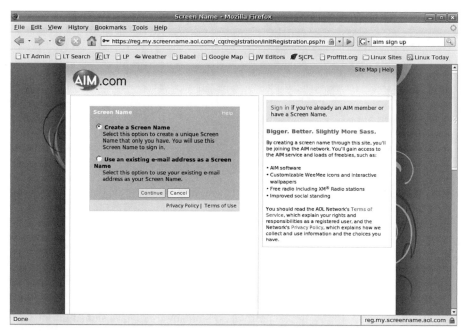

Figure 12.2
Starting the creation process.

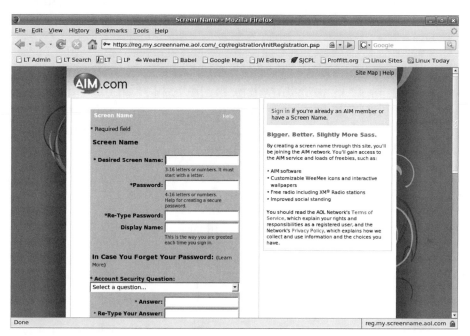

Figure 12.3
The AIM account information.

Figure 12.4
Entering Accounts in Gaim.

Name Flexibility

Try to be flexible with your desired screen name choices. So many users have signed up for AIM, it's sometimes hard to get your first choice of a screen name.

5. Click Submit. If all the fields were filled in correctly, and the screen name is available, you will see a congratulations message with your new screen name.

Signing On

The first time you sign on to Gaim, you will be prompted to add information for at least one account before the application will start. Using the information from a pre-existing account or from the steps you took in the previous section, signing up is fast and painless.

1. Select the Applications | Internet | Gaim Instant Messenger menu command. The Accounts dialog box will open (see Figure 12.4).

2. Click Add. The Add Account dialog box will open (see Figure 12.5).

3. Fill in the Screen Name and Password fields. You can optionally fill in the Local Alias field, which displays the alias you prefer when you are having conversations.

4. Click Save. The Add Account dialog box will close, and the new account will appear in the Accounts dialog box (see Figure 12.6).

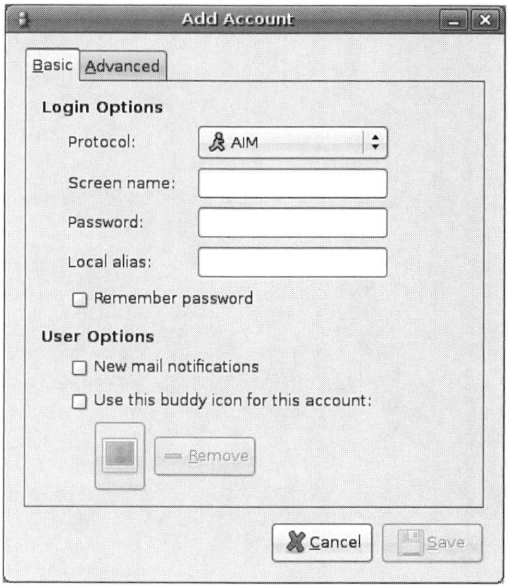

Figure 12.5
Account configuration in Gaim.

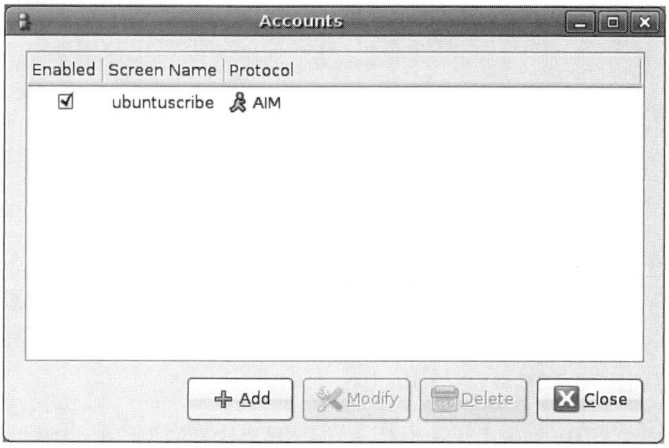

Figure 12.6
The initial Gaim account.

5. Click Close. The Accounts dialog box will close, and the Gaim notification icon will appear in the upper panel on the Ubuntu desktop.

6. Click the Gaim icon. The Buddy List window will open, as shown in Figure 12.7.

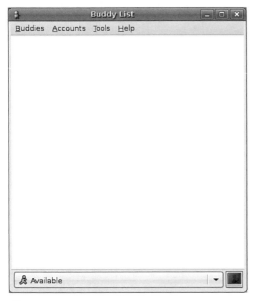

Figure 12.7
No buddies . . . yet.

Instant Messaging with Gaim

When you first create an account, you will be confronted with a temporary but unpleasant thought: You have no buddies.

A buddy is Gaim-speak for the online personas of your friends or associates. Gaim doesn't let you just IM anyone. You have to specify the person you want to IM first. Once you are mutual buddies, Gaim's Buddy List will display each other and specify which buddies are online and available for you.

Adding a buddy is the first step. Many people with AIM or other IM accounts send their contact information out via e-mail or post it on their Web sites.

1. Select the Buddies | Add Buddy menu command. The Add Buddy dialog box will open (see Figure 12.8).

2. Type the screen name for the person you want to connect with. You can add an alias if you want.

3. Click Add. The Add Buddy dialog box will close, and the new buddy will be added to your Buddy List, as displayed in Figure 12.9.

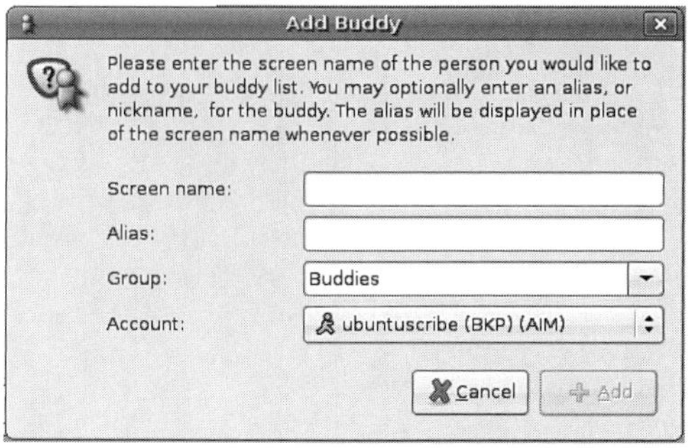

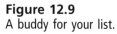

Figure 12.8
Add a buddy.

Figure 12.9
A buddy for your list.

The buddy *Kent* displayed in Figure 12.9 is actually available, as the default AIM icon is bright yellow, and there is no "away notification" attached to the Kent icon. If Kent were online but not available to IM, an away message similar to the one shown in Figure 12.10 would be present.

If the buddy were not connected to the AIM (or another network), the icon would display an Offline status, as shown in Figure 12.11. Once completely signed off, the buddy will disappear from the Buddy List altogether.

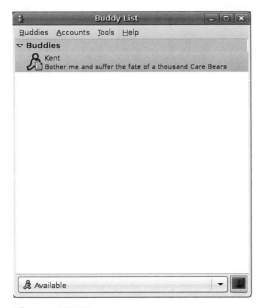

Figure 12.10
Sometimes buddies are cranky.

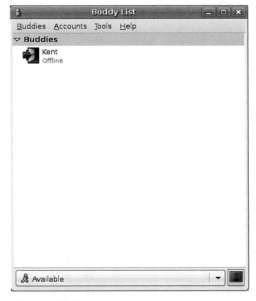

Figure 12.11
Other times, buddies are leaving.

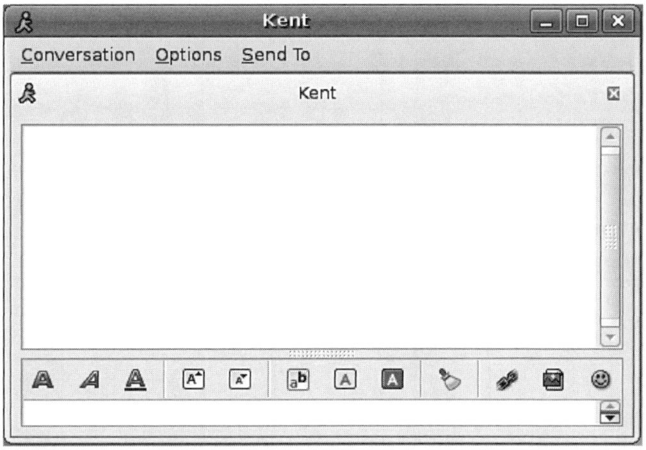

Figure 12.12
Starting an IM conversation.

If you want to IM with a new buddy, follow this set of steps.

1. Double-click a buddy you want to IM. The conversation window for that buddy will open (see Figure 12.12).

2. In the input line at the bottom of the conversation window, type a message to the buddy and press Enter.

3. Depending on your buddy, the reply could come back very quickly or in a few minutes and will be displayed in the IM window (see Figure 12.13).

4. If in the course of a conversation, you would like to send a file to your buddy, click the Conversation | Send File menu command. The Open File dialog box will open.

5. Navigate to the file you want to send and click Open. The File Transfers dialog box will open (see Figure 12.14).

6. The recipient of the file will be directed to choose whether to accept this transfer. If he does accept, the transfer process will complete automatically, and the File Transfers dialog box will close (see Figure 12.15).

7. If someone wants to send a file to you, a notification dialog box will open (see Figure 12.16).

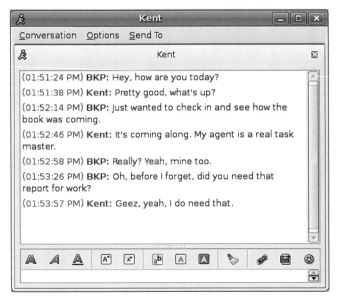

Figure 12.13
An IM conversation in progress.

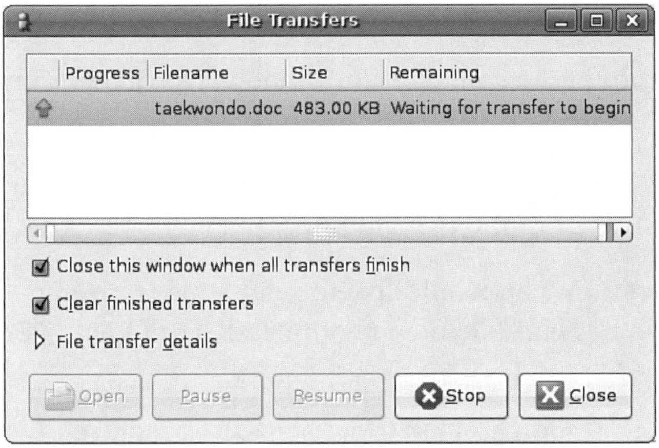

Figure 12.14
Sending a file.

AIM Security

Always make sure you know who you're talking to and what file he is supposed to be sending. Never accept files from anyone you don't know or that you were not expecting.

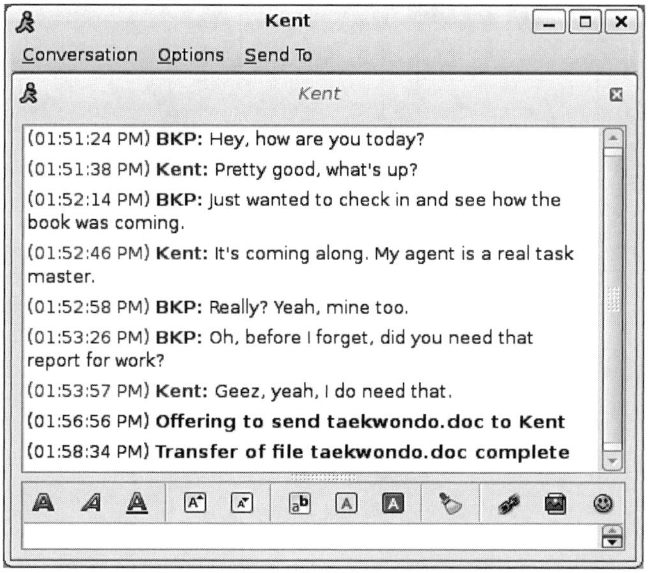

Figure 12.15
A successful transfer.

Figure 12.16
An incoming file.

8. Click Accept if you were expecting this file. The Save File dialog box will open.

9. Save the file where you want it and click Save.

10. To end the conversation, simply send your goodbyes and close the conversation window.

If you want to set yourself as away (unavailable), click the Status drop-down list at the bottom of the Buddy List window and select the Away option.

Figure 12.17
Another incoming file.

To create a custom away message, click the New option in the Status drop-down list and fill in the fields in the Status dialog box, shown in Figure 12.17. Click Save or Save & Use when the message is ready.

Using Ekiga Softphone

Formerly known as *GnomeMeeting*, the Ekiga Softphone is an application that enables VoIP communication, as well as video conferencing, if you have a webcam for your Ubuntu PC.

Using Ekiga, you can talk or video conference to anyone in the world who is using a Session Initiation Protocol (SIP) service, such as Ekiga. For a subscription fee, you can also dial up any regular phone, as well.

At a minimum, to really get the benefit of this application, your Ubuntu PC will need a functioning sound card, with speakers, as well as a working microphone. This will get you voice communication capability, which will be very useful.

There are a lot of acronyms and technical terms associated with getting Ekiga up and running. The developers of this application have made it easier by putting together a 10-step Configuration Assistant, which will be examined in the next section.

Configuring Ekiga

The first thing you will need to do when configuring Ekiga is to get an SIP-service account. If you are an experienced softphone ("software phone") user already, you probably already have a SIP account, with either ekiga.net or one of the other SIP services.

If you've never tried a SIP service before, you can sign up for ekiga.net's basic free service as you step through the Configuration Assistant.

1. Select the Applications | Internet | Ekiga Softphone menu command. The First Time Configuration Assistant dialog box will open (see Figure 12.18).

2. Click Forward. The Personal Information page will appear.

3. Confirm your given name and click Forward. The ekiga.net Account page will appear (see Figure 12.19).

4a. If you have already registered with ekiga.net, enter your username and password, click Forward, and proceed to Step 10.

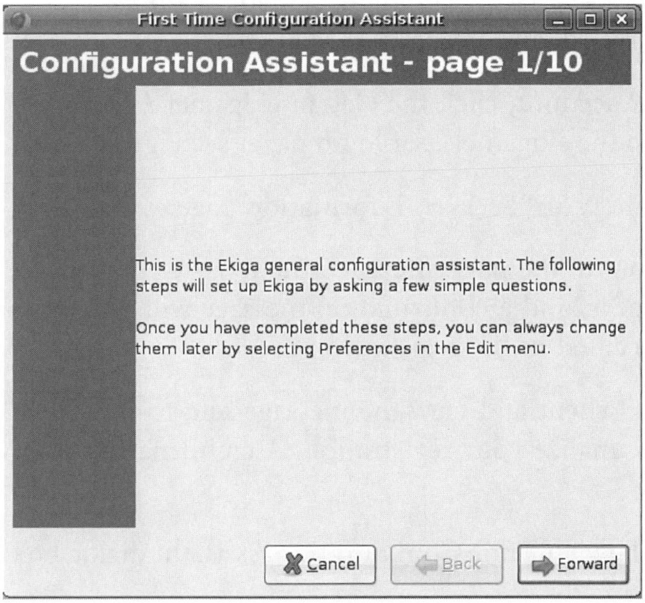

Figure 12.18
The Ekiga Configuration Assistant.

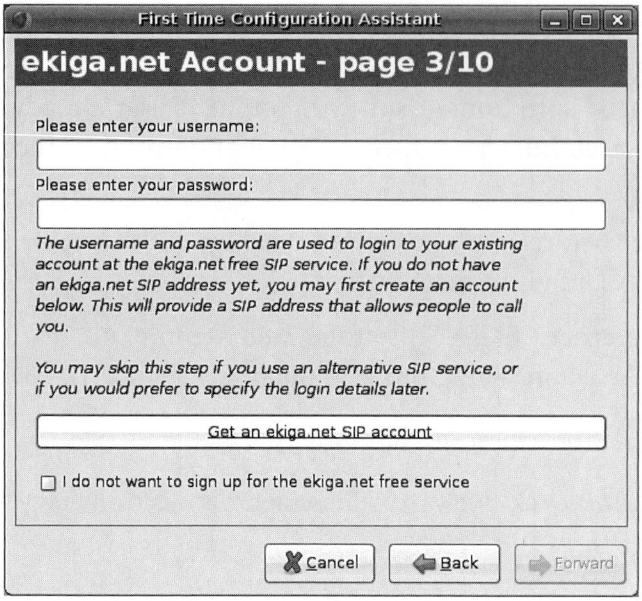

Figure 12.19
A SIP account is needed.

4b. If you already use another SIP service, click the I Do Not Want to Sign Up ... check box, click Forward, and proceed to Step 10.

4c. If you do not have any SIP account, click the Get an ekiga.net Account button. Firefox will open to the ekiga.net user login page (see Figure 12.20).

5. Click the Subscribe link. The VoIP SerWeb information page will appear.

6. Fill in all of the information on the page and click the Register button. A confirmation page will appear, and a confirmation message will be sent to the e-mail account you specified in the registration process.

7. Open your preferred e-mail client and view the message sent to you from ekiga.net. Click the link to finalize your registration. A confirmation page will appear in Firefox.

8. Close Firefox to return to the First Time Configuration Assistant dialog box.

9. Type your username and password in the appropriate fields and click Forward. The Connection Type page will appear.

Figure 12.20
The ekiga.net login page.

10. Select your connection type from the drop-down list and click Forward. The NAT Type page will appear and will immediately begin to detect your Internet connection's router settings (see Figure 12.21).

11. If your router does not support SIP or H.323 protocols, you may be asked to enable STUN support. That is usually the best option, so click Yes.

Ekiga and Firewalls

If you get stuck, http://wiki.ekiga.org/index.php/Ekiga_behind_a_NAT_router is a relatively easy-to-follow page on the various messages that might show up after a NAT detection. See this page if an error message comes up.

12. Click Forward. The Audio Manager page will appear.

13. Confirm your audio manager and click Forward. The Audio Devices page will appear (see Figure 12.22).

14. Confirm your audio output and input devices and click Test Settings. The Audio Test Running dialog box will appear (see Figure 12.23).

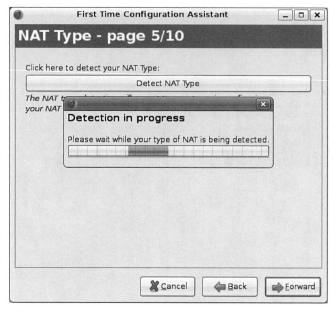

Figure 12.21
Detecting NAT type on your Internet router.

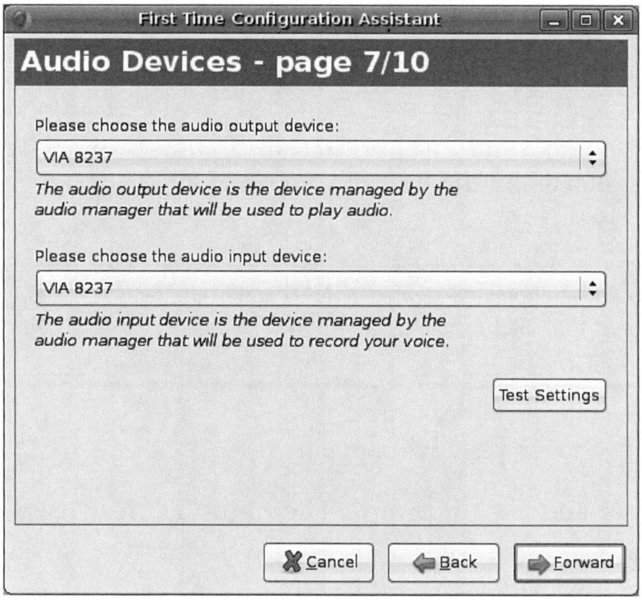

Figure 12.22
Detecting audio devices.

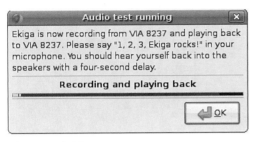

Figure 12.23
Testing audio devices.

15. Speak into the microphone and hear yourself four seconds later. Click OK to close the Audio Test Running dialog box.

16. Click Forward. The Video Manager page will appear.

17. Confirm the V4L setting for the video manager and click Forward. The Video Devices page will appear.

18. Confirm your video input device and click Test Settings. The Video Test Running dialog box will appear.

19. Watch yourself in the monitor. Click OK to close the Video Test Running dialog box.

20. Click Forward. The Configuration Complete page will appear.

21. Click Apply. The First Time Configuration Assistant dialog box will close, and the Ekiga window will open (see Figure 12.24).

Reaching Out and Touching Someone

There are two ways of using Ekiga to make a voice-over Internet call. The first is to call a fellow SIP service user on either ekiga.net or another SIP service. All you need is the intended receiver's SIP address.

1. Type the address of the call recipient in the URL field.

2. Click the Dial button to start the call.

3. When the call is connected, talk through your PC's microphone and listen via speakers.

Figure 12.24
The main Ekiga window.

4. When the call is completed, click the Hang Up button. The call will be disconnected.

The second type of call is from your Ubuntu PC to a regular phone anywhere in the world. This is a commercial service, but it is still cheaper to use than many traditional phone services. In order to use PC-to-Phone functionality, you need to set up an account and pay for the time you will use.

1. Click the Tools | PC-to-Phone Account menu command. The PC-to-Phone Settings dialog box will open (see Figure 12.25).

2. Click the Get an Ekiga PC-to-Phone Account hyperlink. Firefox will open to the Diamondcard.us Web site.

3. Click the payment option you want to use. The Sign Up page will appear.

4. Enter all of the relevant payment information and click Submit. An account information page will appear.

5. Fill in the Username and Password fields, confirming the rest of the information.

6. Click Submit. A Congratulations page will appear, and a confirmation e-mail will be sent to your specified e-mail account.

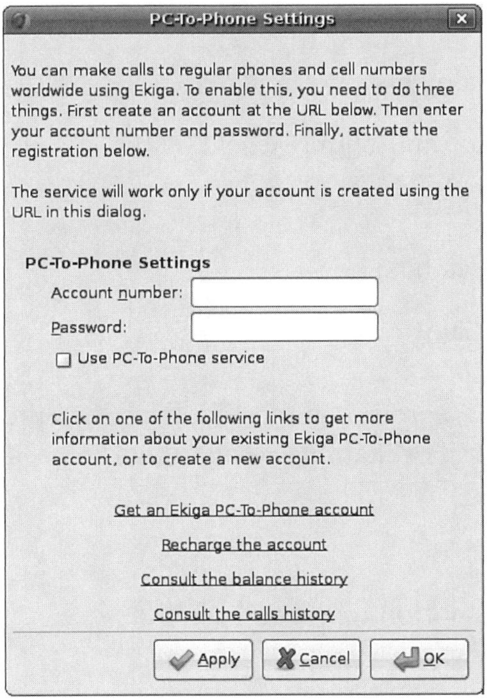

Figure 12.25
Setting up a paid account.

7. Open your preferred e-mail client and view the "Credit Card order" message sent to you from Diamondcard.us. Click the link to start the payment verification process. A verification process screen will open in Firefox. Click Submit.

Note:

The payment verification process can take a while (perhaps a couple of business days) for first-time users, and you will have to wait until the payment is completely verified before you can use the Diamondcard.us telephony service.

8. Return to your e-mail client to view the "Diamond Worldwide Communication Service Signup Confirmation" message. Within it, you will find a login URL to the Diamondcard.us service. Click the link to open the Diamondcard.us login page.

9. Log in to the Diamondcard.us account page using the username and password created during the purchase process.

10. Note the Account ID and PIN code numbers on your account page.

11. Return to the PC-to-Phone Settings dialog box.

12. Type the Account ID number in the Account Number field.

13. Type the PIN code into the Password field.

14. Click the Use PC-to-Phone Service check box.

15. Click OK. The PC-to-Phone Settings dialog box will close.

To make a call to a phone, type **00** after the `sip:` prompt in the URL field, then the country code, followed by the phone number. For example, a call to a girl named Jenny might be:

`sip:0015558675309`

Once the number is typed in, click the Dial button to begin the call.

Conclusion

Now you are ready to communicate instantly with a whole new host of people using your Ubuntu PC. The advantages for business of such communications is enormous, and it is well worth your time to learn.

But the PC is not all about work, especially an Ubuntu PC with its advanced multimedia capabilities. In Chapter 13, "Multimedia Tools," you will learn how to enjoy your favorite multimedia presentations, whether it is music or movies. Get ready to rock the Ubuntu way.

CHAPTER 13

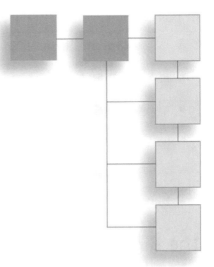

MULTIMEDIA TOOLS

Computers were never really designed to handle audio and video. This capability was more of an afterthought that occurred when computer processors got really fast and video monitors came into existence. At this point, more users began noticing the similarities between computers and televisions.

If a computer has a screen and a television has a screen, folks wondered, why couldn't they both display pictures? Never mind the fact that computers and televisions were about as technologically alike as an elephant and a rhododendron. The new monitors represented a challenge to programmers: how to bring animation and video to these new devices.

Was all this multimedia? In the strictest sense, yes. Machines designed to create one form of media were being used to create another form. More than one medium on one device certainly qualifies as multimedia. Of course, what we think of as multimedia is full-motion video with stereo sound blasting out of our speakers.

Sights and sounds on your computer are very necessary things, even though your boss might not always agree. The ability to play music and video files on a PC seems, at first, an indulgence. More and more, however, business workers are asked to put together multimedia presentations and interactive Web sites for their employers. It makes increasing sense to have that functionality built into modern operating systems.

And it doesn't hurt to be able to play some tunes while typing that quarterly report for the boss, either.

In this chapter, you will review:

- Why some multimedia is not ready to play out of the box.

- How to play CDs.

- Playing MP3 files, including podcasts.

- Getting tuned into Internet radio.

- Burning CDs.

- Playing video files.

The Big Deal: Formats and Codecs

One of the biggest problems with running Linux in general is coming up against an incompatible file format. Many people who encounter this problem often blame the software developers for not being able to put together a decent program. In reality, it's not the developers' fault. It is actually not that hard to put together an application that will run MP3s or Windows Media files. The problem lies in the licenses that these formats often carry.

If you recall from Chapter 1, "What Is Ubuntu?," there was a discussion on the nature of Ubuntu's free and open source software licenses and a comparison with how they worked versus proprietary licenses. When software companies use a proprietary license, they want to get paid when someone uses their software. There is nothing inherently bad about this; everyone's got to eat. But there is often conflict about this between the free and proprietary software worlds, and unfortunately it's the user who gets caught in the middle.

The conflict centers on the way developers in both camps want to get paid (because open source software developers have to eat, too). Proprietary vendors have the revenue model that says "when people use our software, they need to pay us for using it, because we invented it." The open source revenue model flips that around: When people use our software, we'll let them have it for free and make money providing support for our software.

The open source people would gladly pay the proprietary developers to use their software, but since they don't charge license fees for their open software, there's nothing to actually give to the proprietary vendors. There's the revenue generated from support, of course, but the profit margin is so tight for the pay for support and updates business model, there is still very little to send to the proprietary vendors.

The problem is exacerbated by what proprietary vendors have identified as theirs. It's not just the software application that's copyrighted; sometimes, it's the actual format of the file that's protected by an individual or company. The popular MP3 format is one example. Thomson Consumer Electronics has made several legal claims that it owns the patent for the code to play the MP3 file format (known as a *codec*, which stands for enCOder/DECoder) and has vigorously pursued software developers who make MP3 players and don't pay Thomson a fee for those applications.

Some software developers have just avoided the legal issues and moved to another format. Linux developers, for instance, prefer the open source Ogg Vorbis audio format. And some developers, like Apple, have gone ahead and settled in some manner with Thomson.

But there's still a lot of MP3 files out there, and as PC users, we want to be able to listen to them. Ubuntu does not officially support any software that plays MP3s, because of these ongoing legal pursuits, but there are ways to obtain software "patches" to run MP3 files in some of the included audio software.

Some of you may be wondering at this point if this is illegal. While there is still ongoing patent litigation, there are no injunctions for MP3 player inventors to stop what they are doing, and users are not going to be penalized for installing code on their systems.

Unfortunately, this is not the case with the codecs used to play DVDs on a PC. The Motion Picture Association of America has pushed through litigation in Congress that makes it illegal for anyone in the U.S. to use unlicensed software to play DVD movies. Note, that's *use* the software, not just *make*. So if you are residing in the U.S., you cannot legally use software in Linux to watch DVDs, even though there's perfectly good software to do it. But since that DVD-on-Linux player software is given away, its makers are unable to afford a license to use the DVD codecs. Also, the very act of watching a DVD means you have to decrypt the content, which is illegal to do in the U.S.

It seems kind of strange, because all Ubuntu users want to do is watch a movie from a DVD they bought and paid for. But while the MPAA is hell-bent on battling movie piracy, which is a laudable goal, innocent users, like those who run Linux systems, will get caught in the crossfire.

Audio on Ubuntu

There's something nice about being able to stick a CD into your computer and listen to it, with no muss or fuss. But it's not just CDs that get music to your PC these days: There are plenty of Internet sites out there that will let you purchase MP3 versions of your favorite tunes, as well as streaming Internet "radio stations." Podcasts are the biggest fad right now: MP3 files put together by news organizations or bloggers, which can be played on computer or portable MP3 players.

Let's start listening.

Playing CDs

Audio CDs, fortunately, are encoded with an Advanced Audio Coding format (AAC) that is a very open standard, so Ubuntu (and other Linux distributions) has no legal issues about playing them. Even better, AAC files are higher quality than MP3s, and Ubuntu includes some robust applications to actually enhance your music collecting experience.

There are two applications in Ubuntu that will play CDs: Sound Juicer and Rhythmbox. Sound Juicer is a music player and extractor, and it is the default application that will open when you first insert a CD into the CD-ROM drive on your computer.

Rhythmbox is a full-featured media application, analogous to Apple's iTunes or Real's RealPlayer. It will also play CDs for you, although not by default. It is designed for handling and organizing music files stored on your system or out on the Internet.

What many Ubuntu users usually do is use both applications in tandem. Sound Juicer is used to copy files from audio CDs and store them in a format that takes up less space on your hard drive. Rhythmbox can then be used to organize your music into playlists for your listening pleasure.

Of course, how you use these applications is up to you. Some users will just want to listen to music on one CD at a time—maybe their hard drive is nearly full with other files. In that case, the simple interface of Sound Juicer is perfect.

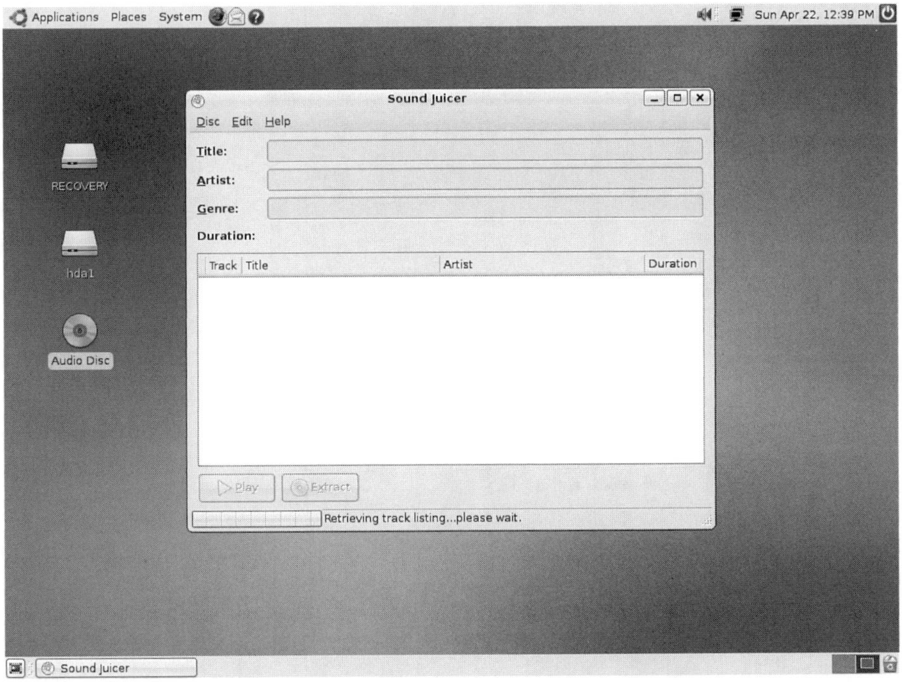

Figure 13.1
Getting track information for an audio CD.

1. Insert an audio CD into your CD-ROM drive. The Audio Disc icon will appear on your desktop.

2. Double-click the Audio Disc icon. The Sound Juicer window will open and query the MusicBrainz Web site for playlist and title information for this CD (see Figure 13.1).

The Brainz of the Outfit

MusicBrainz is a community music site that attempts to create a comprehensive music information database. Albums, artists, tracks, and a whole host of information are collected there by volunteers.

3. Click Play. The CD will begin to play (see Figure 13.2).

4. To move to another track, select the Disc menu and then the appropriate command. You can also double-click the desired track name to move right to that section of the CD.

5. Click Pause. The playback will stop.

Figure 13.2
Playing audio CD music.

If playing a CD straight is all you want to do, then at this point you're all set. But if you have room on your hard drive and a little extra time, why not protect your CD from wear and tear and save the files to your PC? This will also give you the advantage of being able to play your music if the CDs aren't handy.

To accomplish this, simply click the Extract button. The extraction process will begin, with a status report displayed on the bottom of the Sound Juicer window (see Figure 13.3). After a few minutes, the CD's contents will be extracted.

Changing File Locations

Sound Juicer extracts CD files into your home director, in artist/album directories. If you want to change where extracted files are stored, select the Edit | Preferences menu command and change the Music Folder setting.

After extraction, the ripped files are now stored on your hard drive, initially in Ogg Vorbis format. If you have no more CDs to play or extract, you can close the Sound Juicer application and remove any CD from your CD-ROM drive.

If you have a collection of music files on your Ubuntu PC, then Rhythmbox is the application to use.

Figure 13.3
Extracting audio CD music.

Opening Rhythmbox

> The first time you start Rhythmbox, you will see a wizard that asks if you want to import any music files on your computer into a centralized music library. If you have music on your computer, follow the instructions in the series of wizard dialogs to import the files into your library for the first time.

You can start by importing the music files you just extracted with Sound Juicer into Rhythmbox's library of music.

1. Select the Applications | Sound & Video | Rhythmbox Music Player menu command. The Rhythmbox window will open (see Figure 13.4).

2. Select the Music | Import Folder menu command. The Import Folder into Library dialog box will open, as shown in Figure 13.5.

3. Navigate to the artist's folder for the extracted music and click Open. The music will be loaded into Rhythmbox's library.

To play a song or album or even all the songs by a particular artist, you can use the default Browse mode in Rhythmbox to narrow down the songs you want to

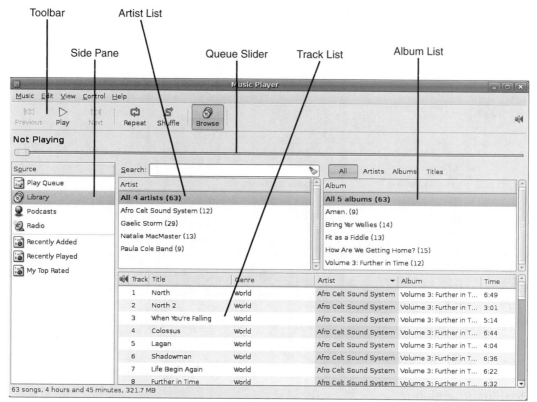

Figure 13.4
Getting into the Rhythmbox.

play. At any time, just click Play, and the first song in the track list will be displayed.

- Click the artist you have interest in listening to. All the tracks for the artist will be displayed in the track list.

- Click the album you want to hear. All the tracks for the album will be displayed in the track list.

- Double-click any individual track. The song will begin to play (see Figure 13.6).

If you prefer to hear only certain songs, in a certain order, you can create a playlist in Rhythmbox. Playlists are not only good for organizing music, but they also need to be created so you can burn an audio CD.

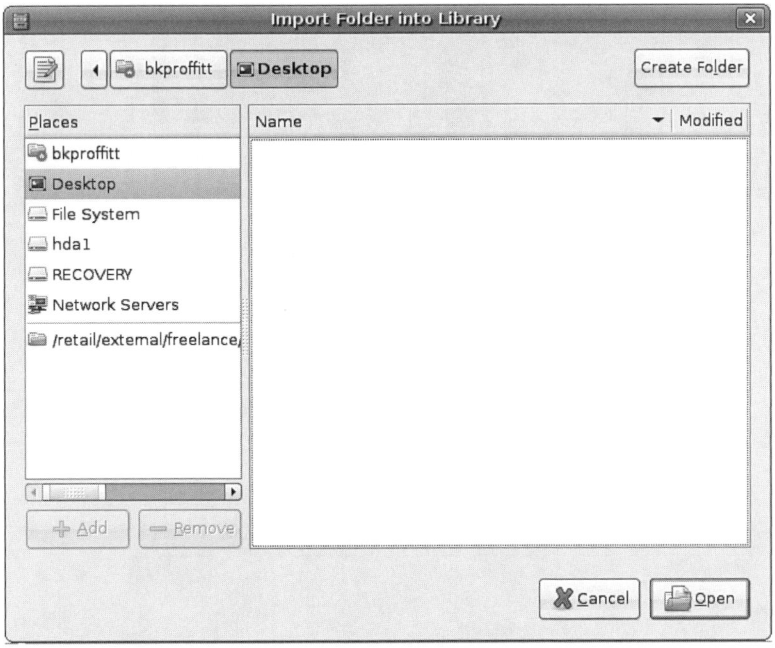

Figure 13.5
Importing music files.

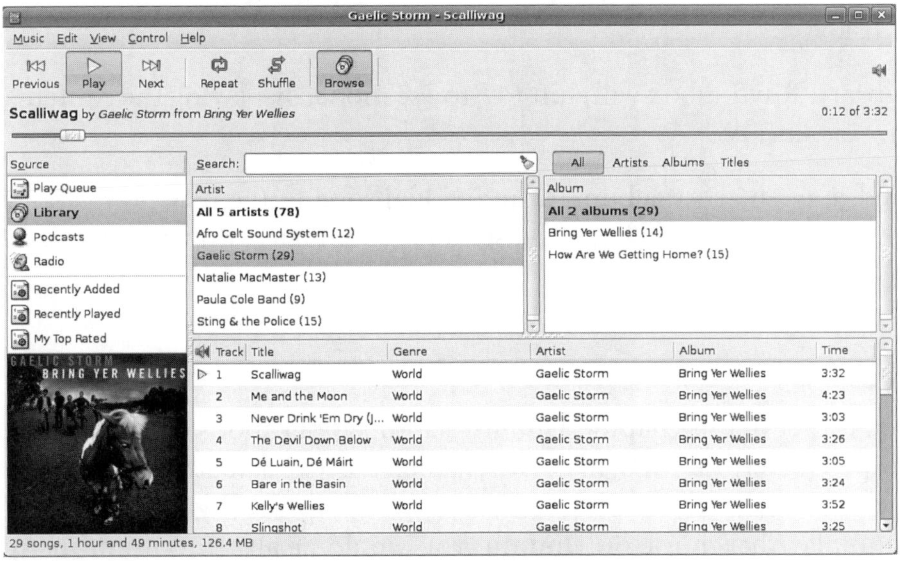

Figure 13.6
Playing music in Rhythmbox.

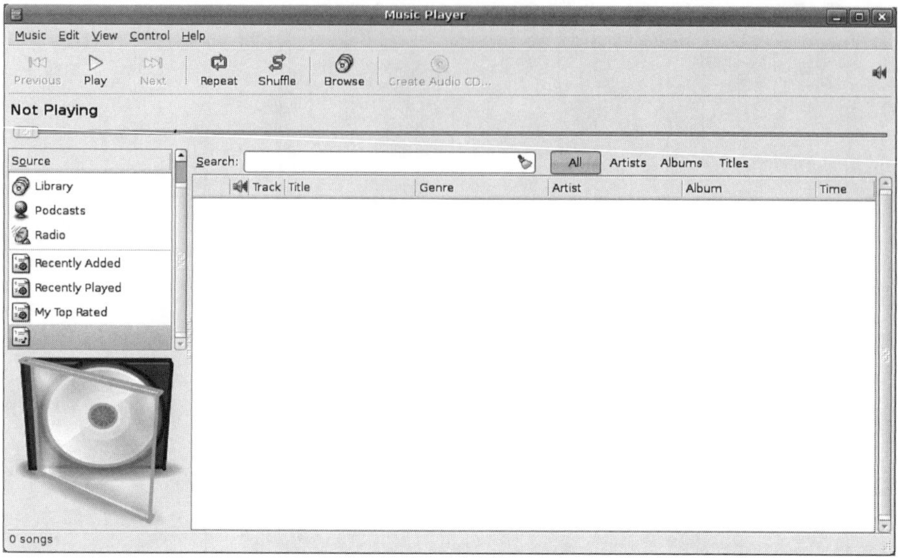

Figure 13.7
Beginning the playlist creation.

1. Select the Music | Playlist | New Playlist menu command. Rhythmbox will be configured to the playlist window (see Figure 13.7).

2. Type a name for your playlist and press Enter. The name will appear in the playlist list.

3. Click Library. Rhythmbox will shift to Browse mode, displaying the contents of the music library.

4. Click and drag an artist, album, or individual song to the new playlist and release the mouse button. The playlist will be populated with the selected songs.

Playing MP3s

As mentioned earlier in this chapter, Ubuntu's audio applications don't have the capability to play or create MP3 files. When music is extracted from CDs, for example, Sound Juicer saves the files in the Ogg Vorbis format by default. If you only wanted to play that music on Ubuntu, you would be all set. But not many portable music players can handle Ogg files; they need MP3. Plus, many podcasts are stored as MP3 files.

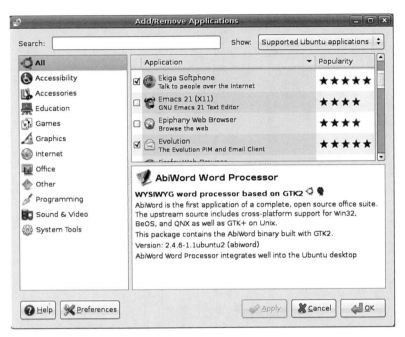

Figure 13.8
Application installation.

Clearly, it's in your best interest to make sure your applications can deal with MP3 files. Here's how to do that.

1. Select the Applications | Add/Remove menu command. The Add/Remove Applications window will open (see Figure 13.8).

2. Change the value of the Show field's drop-down list to All Available Applications. The list of applications will change to include applications installed on your Ubuntu PC.

3. Type **gstreamer** in the Search field. The results will be displayed (see Figure 13.9).

4. Click the GStreamer Extra Plugins option. The Restricted Software message box will appear, reiterating the potential legal effects of running this software.

5. If you understand the associated legal issues, click OK. The Restricted Software message box will close.

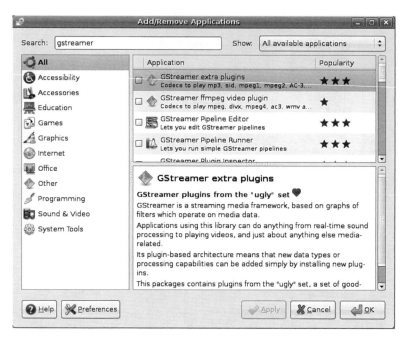

Figure 13.9
Narrowing down the list.

6. Click OK. An Apply message box will appear.

7. Click Apply. You will be asked for your administrative password.

8. Type your password and click OK. The Synaptic Package Manager will open and automatically install the software.

9. Click Close to close the Changes Applied dialog box and the Add/Remove window.

The previous steps will enable Rhythmbox to play MP3 files. Now you need to configure Sound Juicer to create MP3 files when it extracts music from CDs.

1. Select the System | Administration | Synaptic Package Manager menu command. The Synaptic Package Manager window will open.

2. Click the Search button. The Find dialog box will open.

3. Type **gstreamer0.8** and click Search. The Find dialog box will close, and the results will be displayed in Synaptic (see Figure 13.10).

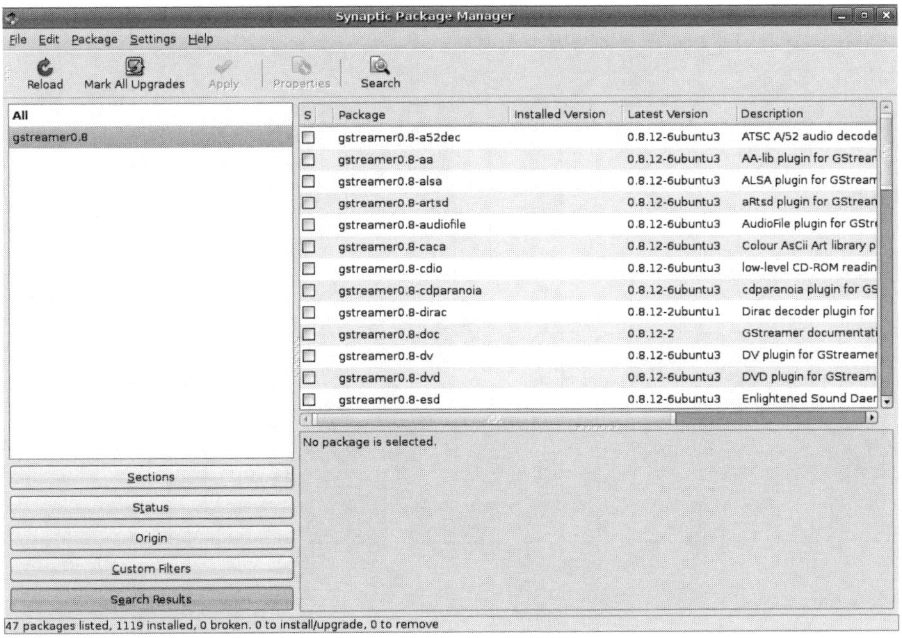

Figure 13.10
More GStreamer plug-ins.

4. Locate the `gstreamer0.8-lame` package and click its check box to Mark for Installation. A Mark Additional Required Changes message box will appear.

5. Click Mark. The message box will close.

6. Click the Apply button. The Summary dialog box will open.

7. Confirm the files you need (`gstreamer0.8-lame` and `liblame0`) are set for installation and click Apply. The Summary dialog box will close, and the packages will be installed.

8. Click Close to close the Changes Applied dialog box.

Now you are set to extract CDs into MP3 files, which you can play on any MP3 player. First, you need to specify this output format in Sound Juicer.

1. In Sound Juicer, select the Edit | Preferences menu command. The Preferences dialog box will open, as shown in Figure 13.11.

2. Click the Edit Profiles button in the Format section. The Edit GNOME Audio Profiles dialog box will open (see Figure 13.12).

Figure 13.11
Sound Juicer preferences.

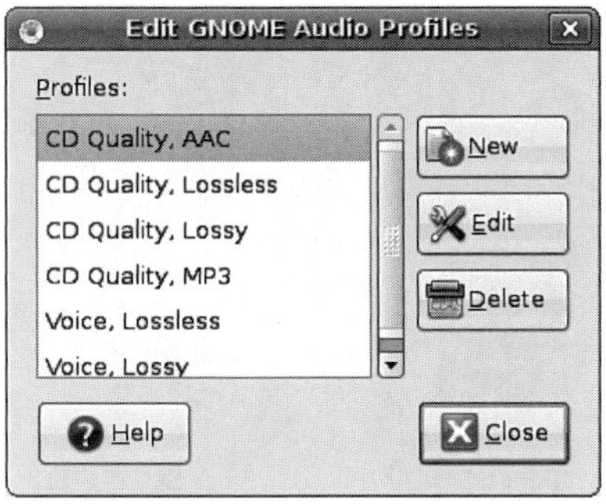

Figure 13.12
GNOME Audio Profiles.

3. Click New. The New Profile dialog box will open.

4. Type MP3 and click Create. The New Profile dialog box will close, and the MP3 profile will appear in the list of GNOME audio profiles.

Bug Alert

There was, at the time of publication, a bug that would not allow the editing of profiles in Sound Juicer. Presumably it has been fixed, but you should note that it could block these final steps in setting up Sound Juicer.

5. Click MP3 and click Edit. The Editing Profile dialog box will open.

6. Type the following command into the GSteamer Pipeline field.

```
audio/x-raw-int,rate=44100,channels=2 ! lame name=enc vbr=0 bitrate=192 ! id3v2mux
```

7. Type **mp3** in the File Extension field.

8. Click the Active check box and click Close. The Editing Profile dialog box will close.

9. Close all dialog boxes and restart Sound Juicer. The MP3 option should now appear in the Output Format field.

Playing Podcasts

Here's a secret: Podcasts aren't anything you haven't seen before on the Internet. It's just that some technologies have been combined in new and interesting ways.

There are two things that make up a podcast: First is the audio file, usually in MP3 format. Second is the podcast's feed, which is essentially no different from the Web feeds discussed in Chapter 10, "Surfing the Web." A *feed* is a special Web page that lists new files on a periodic basis, allowing feed clients (such as Firefox's Live Bookmarks feature) to come along and check for new files.

Rhythmbox has its own feed reader, only it monitors feeds of podcasts. All you need to do is point Rhythmbox to the right place to pick up the feed, and it will do the rest.

Finding Podcasts

Finding podcasts on any subject matter that interests you is almost too easy. Visit Google.com and run a search on any subject that interests you and add "podcast" to the search terms. It should not take you long.

After you have found a podcast feed to link to, you will need to add the URL of the feed to Rhythmbox. Here's a way to do it with minimal typing.

1. In Firefox, find a page with a podcast link.

Recognizing Podcast Addresses

In case you aren't sure which URL to use, podcast feed URLs almost always end with an .xml extension.

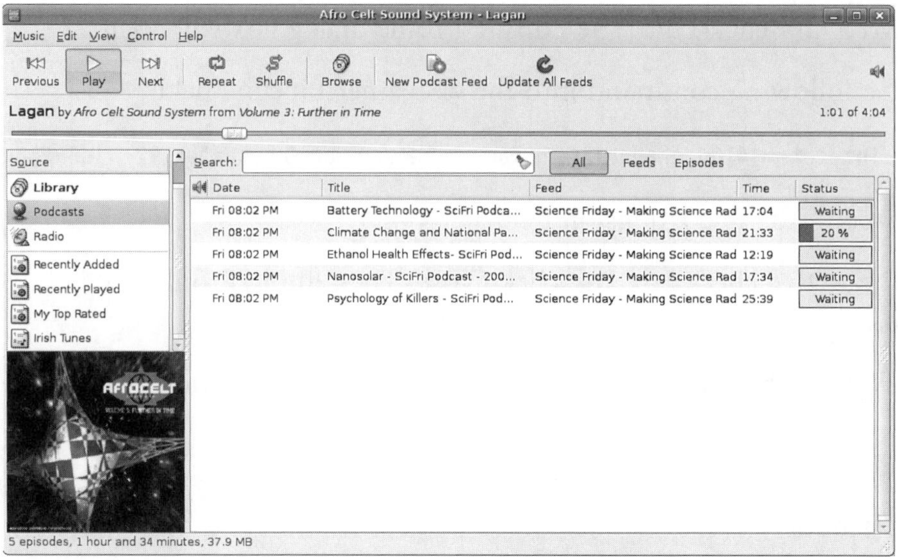

Figure 13.13
Downloading podcasts.

2. Right-click the link and select Copy Link Location on the context menu that appears.

3. In Rhythmbox, click Podcasts in the Source list.

4. Click the New Podcast Feed button. The New Podcast Feed dialog box will open.

5. Press Ctrl+V to paste the copied URL from Firefox in the URL of Podcast Feed field and click Add. The podcast will begin to load the most recent files (see Figure 13.13).

6. After a podcast is downloaded, click the appropriate podcast and click Play. The podcast will begin playback.

When you want to get the latest podcasts, click the Update All Feeds button.

Tuning into Internet Radio

Streaming media is a fancy term for online multimedia content that is downloaded to your Ubuntu PC but not stored there. It is the primary delivery method used by Internet radio to deliver content.

This method offers two big advantages. The first advantage is for the end user. As streaming media is sent to the client machine, it is processed immediately by the streaming media application, which gives the end user instant playback without having to wait for the entire file to download. After the file is played, the data is deleted, thus saving on precious hard drive space.

The second advantage to this approach is for the producer of the content. Because streaming media cannot be saved by the client, live events such as concerts can be broadcast without the fear of an unscrupulous end user bootlegging the material. Streaming media can also be sent out to many users simultaneously, which makes the broadcast of on-demand events and music possible.

One of the most popular applications of streaming audio is the live broadcast of radio station content on the Internet. Both standard and Internet-only radio stations are widely available on the Internet, many of which are suitable to listen to even on 56K dial-up connections. The sound quality of these radio broadcasts is not exceptionally sharp, but it's no worse than listening to a local station on a small radio. And if you're listening to a station in Kenya from Wausau, you're doing pretty well already.

Rhythmbox (again) is the tool to use for playing Internet radio stations. It won't find them for you, but that can be handled in Firefox. It should be noted that there is a much more diverse range of formats than Internet radio can broadcast. Be sure, when you are looking, to find streams that Rhythmbox can use, such as Ogg Vorbis and (if you followed the steps in the previous section) MP3. Real Audio and Windows Media streams will not be able to play in Rhythmbox.

Bug Alert

Although Rhythmbox is built to handle Ogg Vorbis files, at the time of the Ubuntu Feisty release, there were problems with streaming Ogg files, which sometimes cause Rhythmbox to freeze or the broadcast to stop. It is recommended that you use MP3 streams until a fix can be downloaded.

1. In Firefox, find a page with an Internet radio link.

2. Right-click the link and select Copy Link Location on the context menu that appears.

3. In Rhythmbox, click Radio in the Source list.

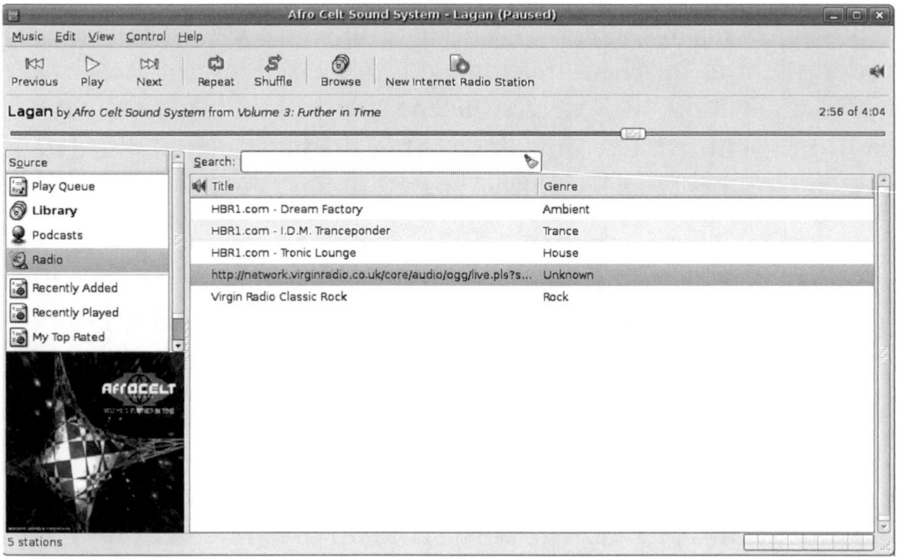

Figure 13.14
A new radio station.

4. Click the New Internet Radio Station button. The New Internet Radio Station dialog box will open.

5. Press Ctrl+V to paste the copied URL from Firefox in the URL of Podcast Feed field and click Add. The station will be added to the list of radio stations (see Figure 13.14).

6. Click the station and click Play. The steaming broadcast will begin.

Formatting Station Names

When a station is added, its title appears as the actual URL, which is a bit cumbersome. To edit the entry, right-click the station entry and select Properties from the context menu. In the Properties dialog box that opens, edit the Title and Genre fields to something more manageable.

Backing Up CDs

If you want to protect your collection of original CDs, you can burn a copy onto another CD and use that instead. Rhythmbox can handle this, but it only burns playlists that you have already created. If you just want to burn a copy of an album, creating a playlist and then starting the copy process is a little roundabout.

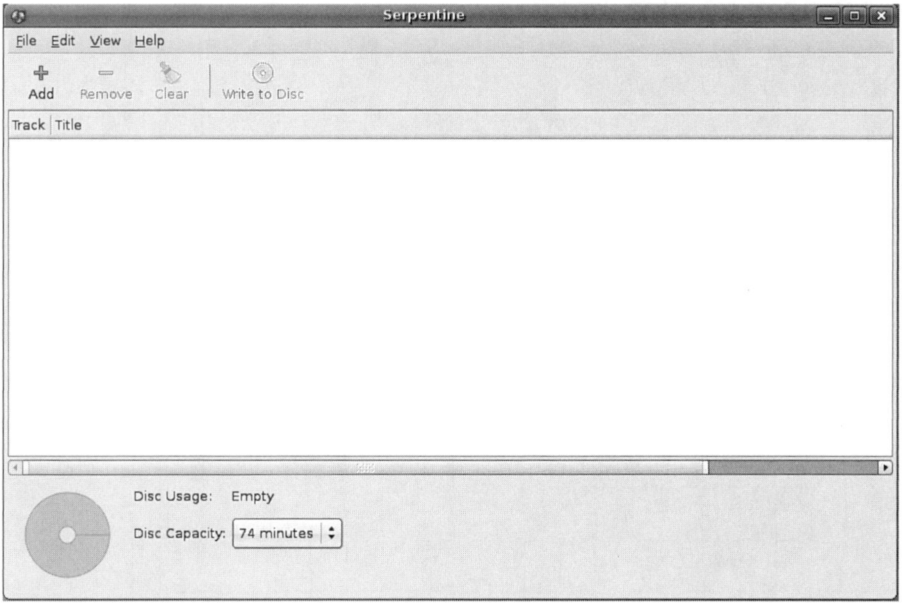

Figure 13.15
The Serpentine application.

Instead, you can use Serpentine to handle your CD burning chores.

1. Insert a blank CD-R or CD-RW into your CD-ROM drive. The Blank CD Disc icon will appear on the desktop.

2. Select the Applications | Sound & Video | Serpentine Audio CD Creator menu command. The Serpentine window will open (see Figure 13.15).

3. Click the Add button. An Open dialog box will appear.

4. Navigate to the folder containing the music files you want to burn and click Open. The files will be listed.

5. Click the files to select them, using the Ctrl key to select individual files or the Shift key to select a range.

6. Click Open again. The files will be loaded into the Serpentine file list (see Figure 13.16).

7. Click the Write to Disc button. A confirmation message box will appear.

8. Click Write to Disc. The Writing Audio Disc dialog box will appear, detailing the progress of the task (see Figure 13.17).

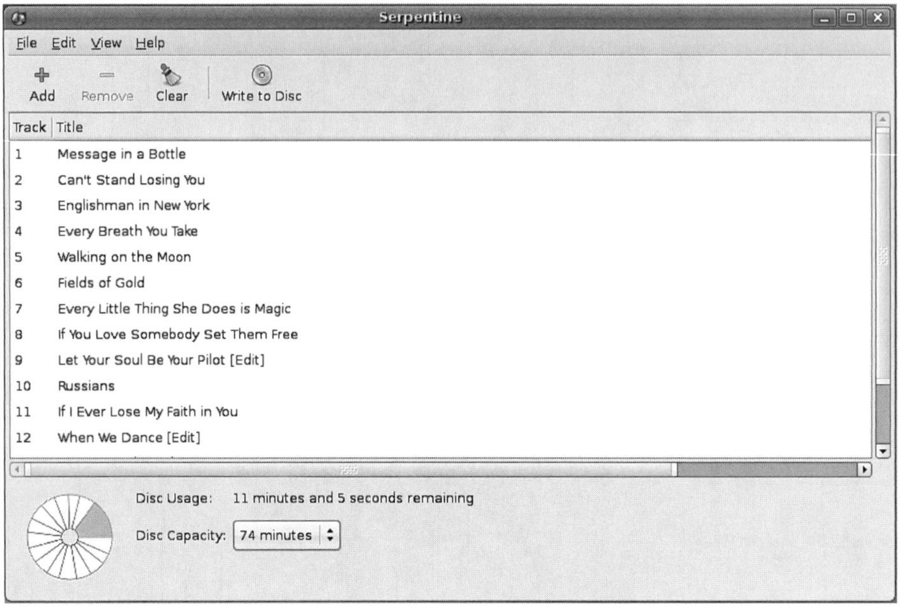

Figure 13.16
Getting the list of music ready.

Figure 13.17
Writing an audio disc.

Cancel Is Bad

Do not click Cancel in the middle of the disc-writing process. Your disc will be rendered unusable if the writing is interrupted.

9. When complete, the disc will be ejected from your drive. Click Close in the final message box to complete the process and close all dialog boxes.

Video on Ubuntu

Music is not the only thing you can find for entertainment on the Internet. You can find movie files in many places as well.

Many of these files may be clips or previews of other, longer events. But a surprising number of video files are short or full-length movies—many of which are created and distributed by independent filmmakers who might otherwise not be able to let the public see their work.

If Rhythmbox is the nerve center for audio files, then the Totem Movie Player is the center for video files. It can handle many video formats, and what it can't handle, it will proactively seek out and install the right codecs to play the file.

1. Select the Applications | Sound & Video | Movie Player menu command. The Totem Movie Player window will open (see Figure 13.18).

2. Select the Movie | Open menu command. The Select Movies or Playlists dialog box will open.

3. Navigate to the file you want to open and click Add. The dialog box will close, and the file will open in the movie player and begin to play (see Figure 13.19).

Figure 13.18
The Totem Movie Player.

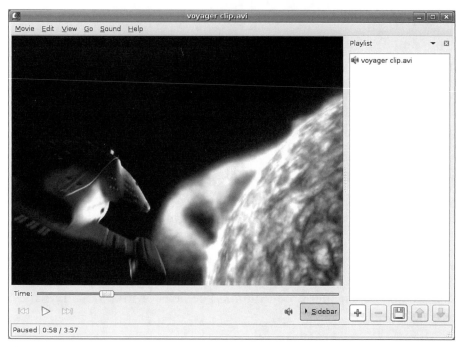

Figure 13.19
Get the popcorn!

Figure 13.20
A new codec is needed.

Occasionally, when you open a video file in Totem, it will be a file format that won't be recognized by the movie player. At this point, you will see a message box like the one in Figure 13.20, asking if you want to try to find the right codec to play the file.

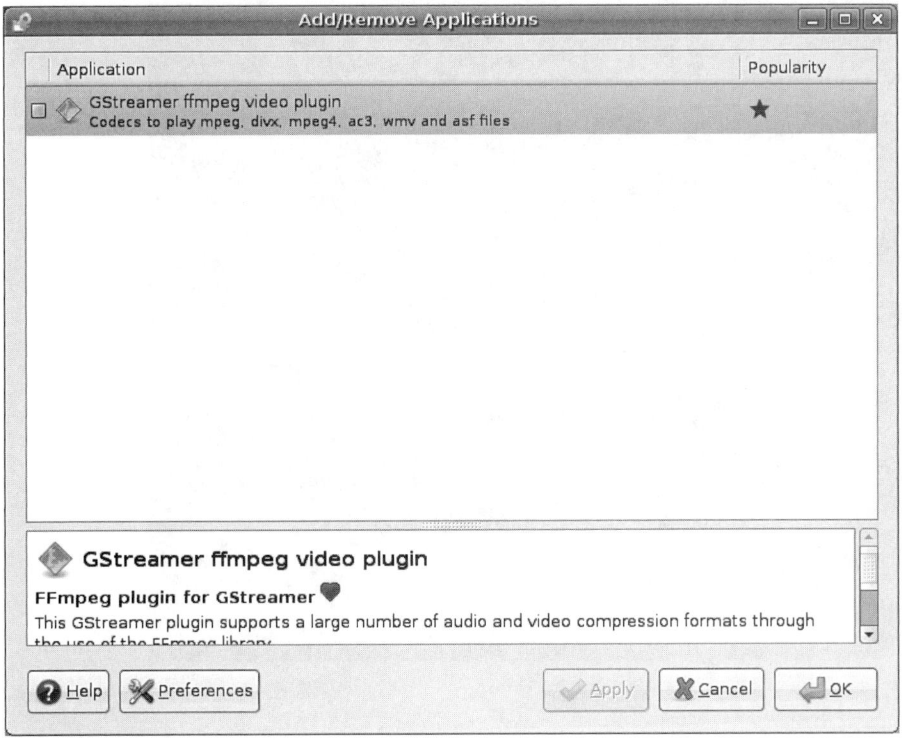

Figure 13.21
A successful codec search.

1. In the Search for Suitable Codec? dialog box, click Yes. The search will begin, and if something is found that will work, the Add/Remove Applications window will appear (see Figure 13.21).

2. Click the suggested application's check box and click OK. The Restricted Software message box will appear, reiterating the potential legal effects of running this software.

3. If you understand the associated legal issues, click OK. The Restricted Software message box will close.

4. Click OK. An Apply dialog box will appear.

5. Click Apply. You will be asked for your administrative password.

6. Type your password and click OK. The Synaptic Package Manager will open and automatically install the software.

Figure 13.22
Where Ubuntu users have gone before.

7. Click Close to close the Changes Applied dialog box and the Add/Remove Applications window.

8. The movie will open in Totem and begin to play.

The movie will play within the Totem window, with all the expected play, rewind, and fast forward controls you might expect. You can skip around the movie using the slider below the view screen.

For a much better viewing experience, press the F key. If the video is detailed enough, it will expand to fill the screen, as is nicely shown in Figure 13.22.

One thing to keep in mind: Not only are many videos protected by a strange format, but there are also added protections enabled to keep the files from being viewed by any application other than the intended one. One example of this is any video (or audio) file purchased and downloaded from the iTunes Music Store. These files are essentially MP4 files, which Ubuntu could play, save for the added copy-protection on the files that lets them be played only on iTunes.

Conclusion

In this chapter, you learned how to use audio and video tools to play most of your favorite multimedia files.

But what about the files you can't play, like the example at the end of the previous section? And it sure would be nice to play DVDs on Ubuntu. And what if there's this one application on Windows that you just can't bear to part with? Do you have to keep a Windows partition sitting on your machine, taking up hard drive space?

Answers to these questions can be found in the next chapter, "Getting All the Goodies," where we'll examine an interesting add-on to Ubuntu called *Automatix*. If Ubuntu is the tasty Cracker Jack, then Automatix is the surprise in the box.

CHAPTER 14

Getting All the Goodies

Ubuntu, in case you hadn't noticed, is a really great operating system. Linux users love it because, well, it's Linux, and they like pretty much anything with a penguin on it (the penguin is the official mascot of Linux). Windows and Mac users like it because it's familiar and offers a feature set very close to what they're used to for a much lower cost.

But you may have noted the use of the term "very close." Because, as much as this book can and will tout Ubuntu, there are some feature limitations in the operating system that have appeared because of licensing and copyright issues that Canonical has chosen to abide by.

This is a common theme for some of the applications that work on Ubuntu, as discussed in Chapter 13, "Multimedia Tools." It's not that Ubuntu can't run this software; it's just that Canonical is not licensed to distribute it with the rest of its software. The good news, for the most part, is that there's nothing wrong with users going out and getting this "missing" software for themselves. For instance, Real, the makers of RealPlayer, a popular media software applications, isn't included in Ubuntu because it's completely commercial, even the Linux version. But Real welcomes users to come and download the free-of-charge application.

The same situation applies to popular applications, such as Adobe Flash Player, Adobe Acrobat Reader, or Google Earth. There's even one application suite, known as CrossOver Office, that will let you run some Windows applications right on your Linux desktop. All of them are excellent applications that run on Linux, but they are too proprietary for Canonical to include.

And then there are the very few applications that Canonical can't include because their presence would constitute using unlicensed software, which would be bad for Canonical and (in one case) potentially bad for users.

You can, if you want, go out and without too much difficulty find all of these applications (and more) to make your Ubuntu PC a complete Windows or Mac replacement. All it takes is some time and a little patience. But if you're one of those people who doesn't have a lot of either, there's a third-party application that will help you download and install these programs. It's called Automatix.

In this chapter, you will discover how to for the following:

- Install and use Automatix2.

- Install and run CrossOver Office to run Windows applications.

- Play (if you are legally able) DVD movies on your Ubuntu PC.

Installing Automatix2

Along with the package managers that come with Ubuntu, there is a third-party package manager out there that, when installed on your Ubuntu PC, will make your computer much more powerful.

Automatix2, which is the current version of Automatix, has one job, and one job only: to install specialized applications for Debian GNU/Linux-based systems. That includes any member of the Ubuntu family of distributions. When you install Automatix2, you will have the option to install any of 94 applications from these categories:

- **CD/DVD Burning and Ripping.** Tools for copying and burning optical media on your system.

- **Chat.** The latest (beta) version of Gaim and other communication apps, including the Skype free VoIP client.

- **Codecs.** Multimedia codecs to play many more audio and video formats than provided in Feisty.

- **Drivers.** Drivers for Broadcom WiFi cards and NVIDIA video cards are included.

- **E-mail.** Thunderbird and Google Mail tools.

- **File Sharing.** Peer-to-peer clients, including Azureus.

- **Media Players.** RealPlayer, Totem-xine, and Audacity are a few of the powerful multimedia tools in this category.

- **Miscellaneous.** Fonts, menu configuration, and file reading utilities.

- **Office.** Productivity tools like GnuCash, Adobe Acrobat, and Google Earth.

- **Programming.** Java, C#, and other development environments can be found here.

- **Utilities.** Internet tools, such as FTP clients and dial-up tools.

- **Virtualization.** Operating system emulation is easy with these tools.

- **Windows Emulators.** CrossOver Office, a commercial Windows emulator, lets you run Windows apps on Ubuntu.

- **Web Browser.** Extra browsers, such as Opera and Swiftfox.

After you install Automatix2, you will be able to pick and choose the applications you want from the Automatix2 interface, so you will be able to make an informed choice on what software you want to run.

Before beginning, there are some important things to consider. The first and most important is that many of these applications that Automatix2 will install for you are configured and maintained by Automatix2's developers or some other third-party vendor. If you need to get some support for any of these applications, Canonical and the rest of the Ubuntu support sites will *not* be able to help you, even if it was an application that came with the original Ubuntu 7.04 release. Sometimes Automatix2 will install its own custom version of an application that differs from the one you got from Ubuntu, which will preclude the Canonical folks from being able to help you.

Also, when you install Automatix2, many new repositories are added to your sources.list. This could have the effect of mixing up dependencies for existing packages. This is rare, but it does happen.

Also, one of the packages that can be installed is the AUD-DVD codecs, which will enable an Ubuntu PC to play back DVD movies. But, and this is a big exception, as mentioned in Chapter 13, the use of these codecs is currently illegal in the United States.

The Law in Question

This restriction on unlicensed DVD players is in place because of the 1998 Digital Millennium Copyright Act (DCMA). The DCMA forbids the sale of any unlicensed encryption technology. However, in order to even watch a DVD movie, you need to decrypt its copy protection protocols. In fact, the Motion Picture Association of America (MPAA), which lobbied for this section of the law to try to stop global media piracy, even filed criminal charges in the Norwegian courts against young Norwegian programmer Jon Johansen, who first discovered how to decrypt commercial DVDs. (The prosecution, much to the MPAA's dismay, lost.) The DCMA, however, still exists. So most DVD software for Linux is illegal in the U.S. because most of that software is not using the *licensed* codecs and decryption technology.

If this seems silly to you, you're not alone. But that's the way the law currently stands.

Now, if any of these cautionary notes concern you in any way, you may want to forego many of the installation steps in this chapter and just acquire the individual applications you want without the use of Automatix2. (This will be detailed in the "Working with Windows" and "Traveling the Globe" sections.) If the whole DVD thing sounds too risky, take heart and skip ahead to the "Looking Forward" section—there's a legal, easy-to-use solution coming in the near future for Ubuntu users.

To begin, let's start the process of installation for Automatix2. Since Canonical does not support or distribute this application, you won't be able to use either the Synaptic Package Manager or the Install and Remove Applications application used in Chapter 13 to acquire the Automatix2 package. Not to worry, it's a simple process. Be sure you are connected to the Internet and follow these steps.

1. In Firefox, navigate to www.getautomatix.com. The Automatix home page will appear (see Figure 14.1).

2. Click the Installation link. The Installation page will appear.

3. Click the Easy Direct Installation link in the Contents section. The page will jump down to the Easy Direct Installation section.

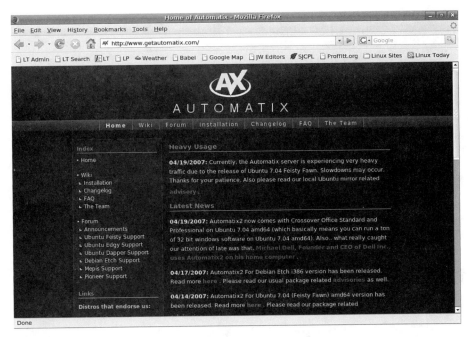

Figure 14.1
The Automatix home page.

4. Click on the link for the Ubuntu 7.04 heading for your type of system. The Opening Automatix2 dialog box will open (see Figure 14.2).

5. Click the Save to Disk radio button; then click OK. The Opening Automatix2 dialog box will close, and the Downloads message box will appear, detailing the status of your download.

6. Close Firefox.

The package will be saved to whatever location you have specified Firefox to save downloaded files (typically your desktop). Instead of starting the Synaptic Package Manager to install this package, you can start the process from the package itself.

1. Double-click the saved Automatix2 package. The gdebi Package Installer window will open, as shown in Figure 14.3.

2. Click Install Package. You will be asked for your administrative password.

3. Type in your administrative password and click OK. The installation process will begin, including the download and installation of any dependency packages.

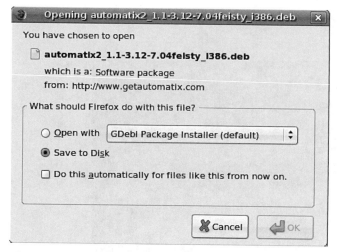

Figure 14.2
Downloading the Automatix2 package.

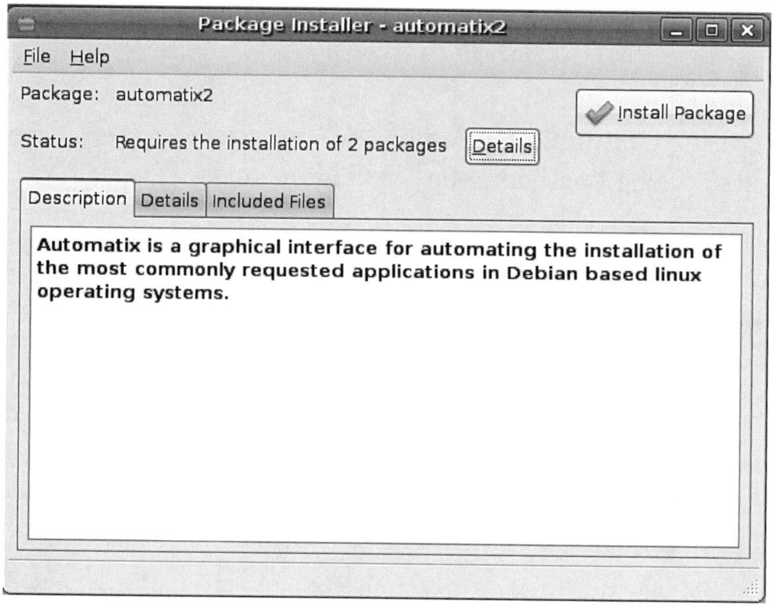

Figure 14.3
Installing with the gdebi Package Installer.

4. When the Installation Finished message box appears, click Close.

5. Select the File | Exit menu command, and gdebi Package Installer will close.

Using Automatix2

To start Automatix2, select the Applications | System Tools | Automatix menu command.

Run One Update at a Time

Before you run Automatix2, be sure that Synaptic Package Manager and the Update Manager are *not* running.

The first time you start Automatix2, a legal warning dialog box will appear (see Figure 14.4).

If you understand the message and will comply, click Yes. Automatix2 will immediately update the list of repositories in Ubuntu used to update and install software to its own specifications (see Figure 14.5). When that operation is complete, the Automatix2 splash box will appear. Click OK to close it.

These messages and warnings will only appear the first time you run Automatix2; after that, starting Automatix2 will take you directly to the main Automatix2 window, shown in Figure 14.6.

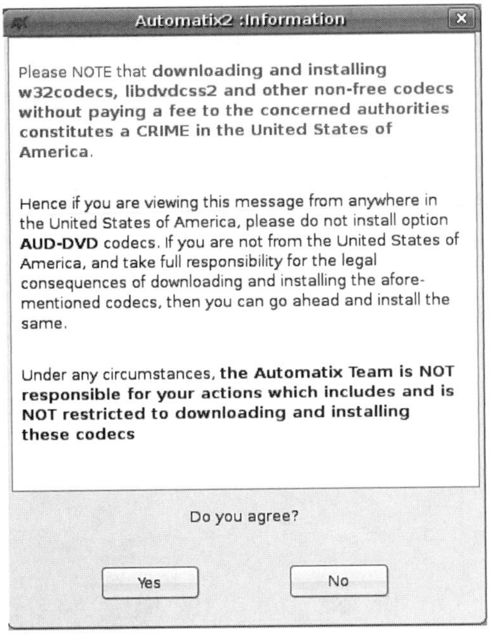

Figure 14.4
Consider yourself very warned.

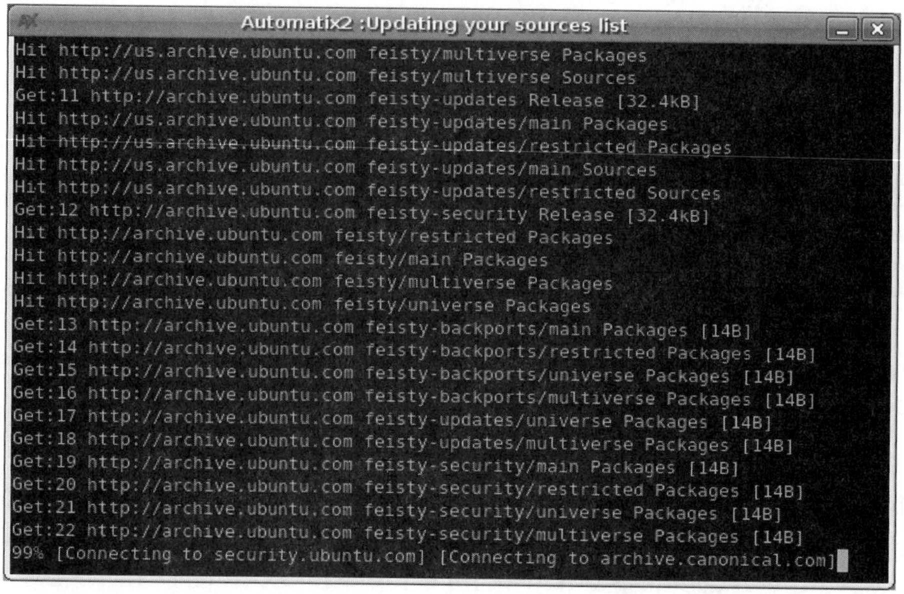

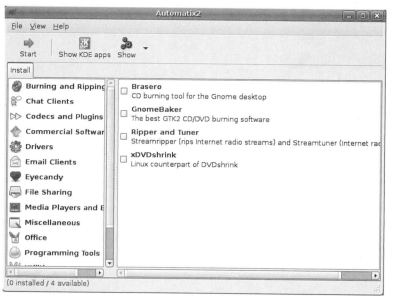

Figure 14.5
Updating repositories.

Figure 14.6
The Automatix2 window.

The interface for Automatix2 is very simple. On the left side of the window are the categories of applications. Clicking any of these categories reveals the applications for that set in the application list on the right.

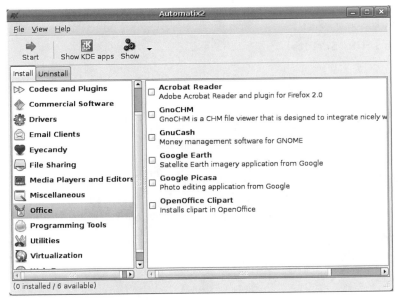

Figure 14.7
The Office applications.

Installing an application is very easy, demonstrated in this example.

1. Click the Office category. Its applications will be displayed (see Figure 14.7).

2. Click the Acrobat Reader check box. The option is selected.

3. Click Start. Automatix2 will automatically download and install the Adobe Acrobat packages (see Figure 14.8).

4. To start Adobe Acrobat, click the Applications | Office | Adobe Reader menu command.

To uninstall applications installed with Automatix2, the steps are simple.

1. Click the Uninstall tab. Only applications installed by Automatix2 will be displayed.

2. Click an application's check box. The option is selected.

3. Click Start. Automatix2 will automatically uninstall the application packages.

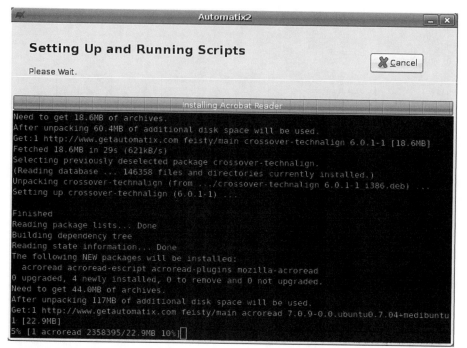

Figure 14.8
Auto-installing packages.

The fastest way of uninstalling Automatix2 is to open the Terminal and type this command:

```
sudo apt-get remove automatix2
```

Working with Windows

One of the biggest fears for anyone moving to a new operating system is "will my applications work?" For a long time, Windows users could sit back with a certain smugness and deride Linux as a platform that couldn't run the simplest Windows application. Those days are long gone, as many superior applications are natively available for Linux (OpenOffice.org, Firefox, and Evolution to name a few).

But let's be fair—sometimes. there's just that one application that you really have to have that has no Linux equivalent, or the Linux equivalent is something you just don't like.

That's when an emulator comes in to play. In software terms, an emulator is an application that mimics another software environment so that certain apps can run on it. Emulators act as self-contained simulators of another operating system, and these days they run pretty well. However, there are some drawbacks. No emulator is perfect, and most do better with applications that they are prepared for rather than just any old application that comes along. For example, an emulator application called Cedega runs Windows games and works best with games it specifically supports.

Also, emulators tend to run other OS' applications more slowly, since the PC has to handle the demands of the emulator and the application that's running on top of it.

In Ubuntu, the best-known Windows emulator is WINE, which stands for "WINE Is Not an Emulator." Even though many people consider it an emulator, it is actually a native environment upon which Windows applications in Linux can be run. The only hitch, and it's a big one, is that WINE is hard to configure, even for advanced users. Fortunately, a company called CodeWeavers has put together an application that makes WINE configuration a breeze: CrossOver Office.

Installing CrossOver is almost like installing any other application in Automatix2.

1. Click the Commercial Software category. Its applications will be displayed.

2. Click the Crossover Office Standard 6.0-1 check box. The option is selected.

3. Click Start. A dialog box will appear, emphasizing that CrossOver Office Standard is a 30-day demo application, and if you want to use it past that time, you will need to purchase a license from CodeWeavers.

4. Click Yes to continue. Automatix2 will automatically download and install the CrossOver Office packages.

5. Select the File | Exit menu command. Automatix2 will close.

Because CrossOver Office is a commercial application, it does not automatically show up in the Applications menu as some other installed programs do. To fix this, open up a Terminal window (Applications | Accessories | Terminal) and enter this command:

```
killall gnome-panel
```

This will refresh the main Ubuntu menus and insert a new CrossOver menu in the Applications menu.

Installing Windows Software

Installing Windows software on your Ubuntu PC is likely going to be a bit more time consuming than installing it on a native Windows PC. This is generally because CrossOver's installation procedure has to make sure everything is squared away perfectly with your application so it can run well.

CrossOver Compatibility

Before you begin, visit the CodeWeavers CrossOver Compatibility Center (C4) page for specific information about the application you want to install: www.codeweavers.com/compatibility/.

After you have checked compatibility, you can start the installation process. You can either install from a CD or use a downloaded executable (.exe) file.

1. Select the Applications | CrossOver | Install Windows Software menu command. The CrossOver Installation wizard will open (see Figure 14.9).

2. Click the application you want to install; then click Next. The installation source page will open (see Figure 14.10).

3. Click the Product Location option you want. Use the Browse buttons to find files if needed.

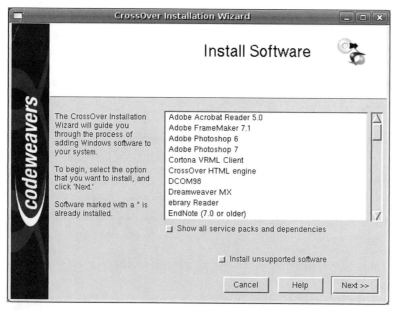

Figure 14.9
The CrossOver Installation wizard.

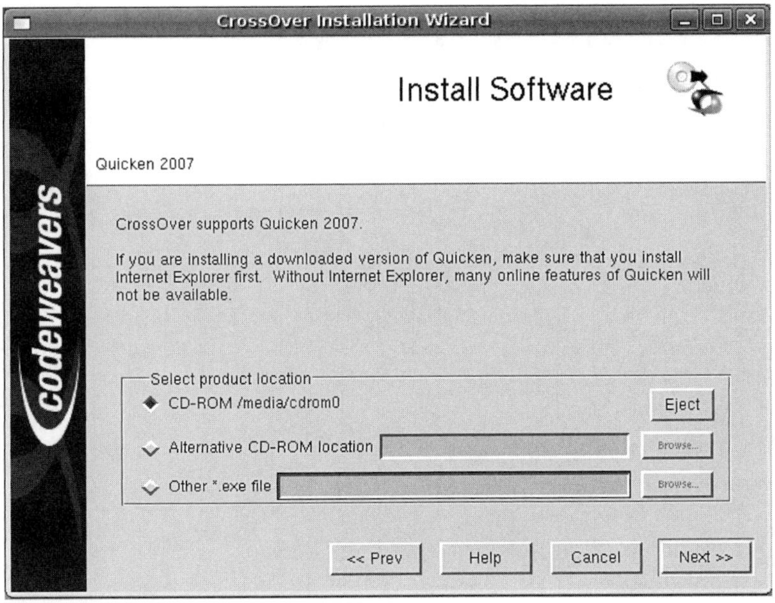

Figure 14.10
Specify the installation source.

4. Click Next. The bottle page will appear, as shown in Figure 14.11.

Bring Your Own Bottle

CrossOver Office keeps the specific configurations for applications separate from each other because some applications may function better in a Windows 98 simulation, while others perform well in a Windows 2000 environment. In keeping with the WINE engine at its core, the Code-Weavers developers have named these separate environments "bottles." It is recommended that you follow the bottle recommendations suggested by the CrossOver application.

5. Specify the appropriate bottle option and click Next. The bottle will be created, and the application's native installation routine will begin (see Figure 14.12).

Try Before You Buy

If you haven't chosen to purchase a CrossOver license yet, the CrossOver Demo dialog box will appear now. Click Register Later to continue.

6. Install the application just as you would in Windows. The process will proceed as if you were in Windows.

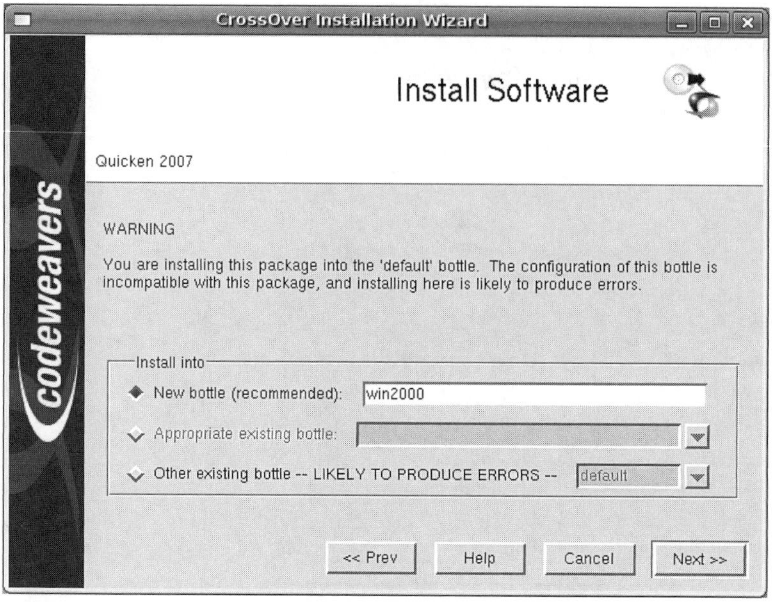

Figure 14.11
Specify the installation bottle.

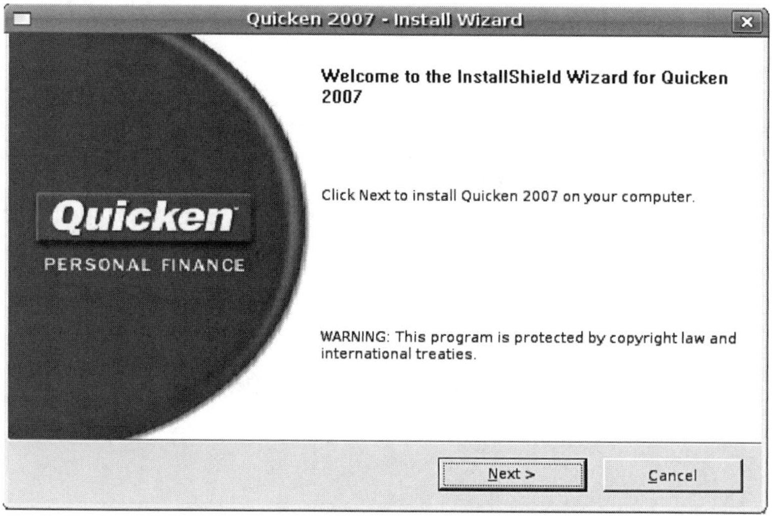

Figure 14.12
Now install the application as if you were in Windows.

7. When complete, the native Windows installation dialog box will close, and the final page of the CrossOver Installation wizard will appear. Click Finish.

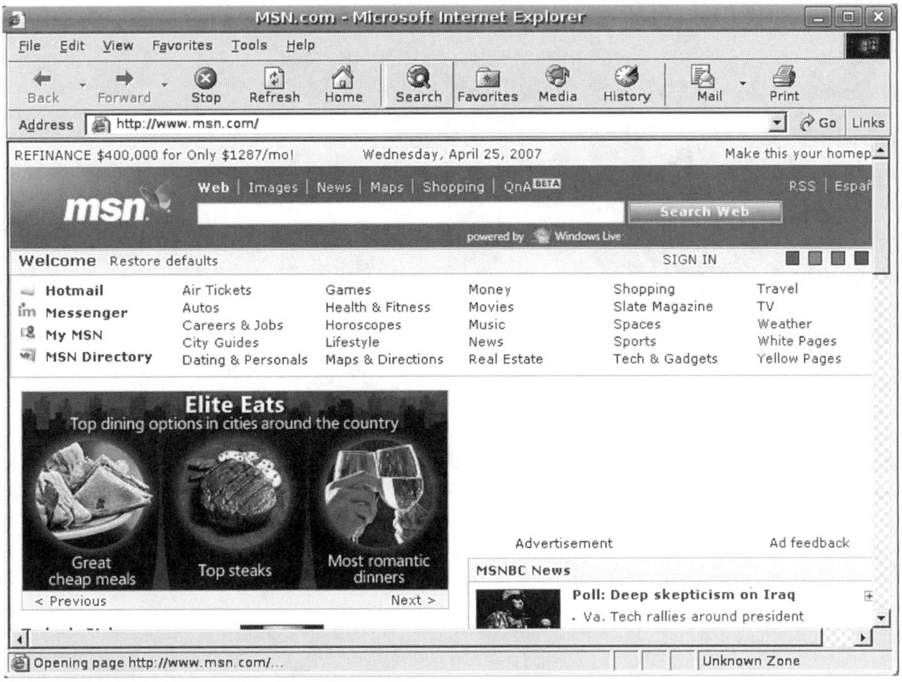

Figure 14.13
Internet Explorer on Ubuntu.

Running Windows Applications

After your application is installed, all you need to do to run it is double-click its icon on the desktop, if it's present. If not, select the Applications | Windows Applications | Programs menu command and then the desired application. Your Windows application will start and run just as it normally would (see Figure 14.13).

Playing DVDs

Another useful feature of Automatix2 is the convenient way it installs the software you need to play DVD movies. Unfortunately, as explained earlier in this chapter and in the online warnings, this option is not available to U.S. residents.

So if you're not living in the U.S. right now, feel free to follow these steps to get your Ubuntu system ready for playing DVDs. If you are residing in the U.S., stop and move on to the next section, "Looking Forward," for some encouraging news.

Figure 14.14
"Actually" watch movies in Ubuntu.

1. Click the Codec and Plugins category. Its applications will be displayed.

2. Click the AUD-DVD Codecs check box. The option is selected.

3. Only if you understand the legal ramifications, click Start. Automatix2 will automatically download and install the AUD-DVD packages. (It will take a while.)

4. Select the File | Exit menu command. Automatix2 will close.

Now all you need to do is insert a DVD into your PC's DVD drive. Totem Movie Player will automatically start, and you can watch any movie you'd like (see Figure 14.14).

Looking Forward

If you are a law-abiding U.S. resident, you are likely a bit frustrated that you can't enjoy the functionality demonstrated in the previous section. You won't have to be frustrated for long!

In early 2007, Canonical announced a partnership with another commercial Linux vendor, Linspire (www.linspire.com). Linspire has its own Linux distribution, cleverly named *Linspire,* and like Ubuntu, it is also based on the Debian GNU/Linux distribution. This shared ancestry made it easy for these two companies to form a technological partnership—the fruits of which Ubuntu users will soon enjoy.

Linspire's approach to applications is different from Canonical's, in that Linspire believes that any application users need, regardless of its proprietary status, should be provided to them. Thus, Linspire has much more licensed software than other Linux distributions, including Ubuntu—including, for example, a fully licensed, legal everywhere DVD player.

As a direct result of this partnership, Linspire will become based on Ubuntu, and Ubuntu will be able to use Linspire's unique software management and acquisition program, Click n' Run (CNR). When CNR is ready for Ubuntu in June 2007, Ubuntu users will be able to download and install a large range of software, free, open, or proprietary. Many of the concerns regarding patents, copyrights, and other laws will be rendered moot.

The CNR system will not be ready by the time this book goes to press, but thanks to the folks at Linspire, some early alpha screenshots of the system give some hints at what the functionality will look like.

Figure 14.15 shows an early (alpha) design for the CNR.com home page. All of the available software applications are organized into categories. When you click on a category, you'll see subcategories with the listing of programs.

CNR.com will also encourage user involvement by making the product pages "wiki-ized" and interactive so that users can get involved by providing content, screenshots, user reviews, and more information on each software program. Figures 14.16 and 14.17 display the preliminary designs for the Screenshot and Release Notes pages.

Not only will there be a Web site for Ubuntu users to download commercial applications, but there will also be an installable plug-in application for Ubuntu 7.04 that will act as a package manager for the CNR applications.

According to Linspire, the CNR plug-in is a software application browser-based plug-in that complements the tools and services available on the CNR.com Web site. The CNR plug-in auto-starts when Ubuntu boots and is always running in the background.

Figure 14.15
The CNR.com home page (alpha design).

To open the CNR plug-in, you can click the green running man icon in your lower panel. When the CNR plug-in opens you will see a multitabbed window appear that provides you with a number of features, as shown in Figure 14.18.

From the CNR plug-in, you can install, uninstall, and update software. You can also view a history of your installation, including a description, status (successful, failed, canceled, pending, processed), and completion time.

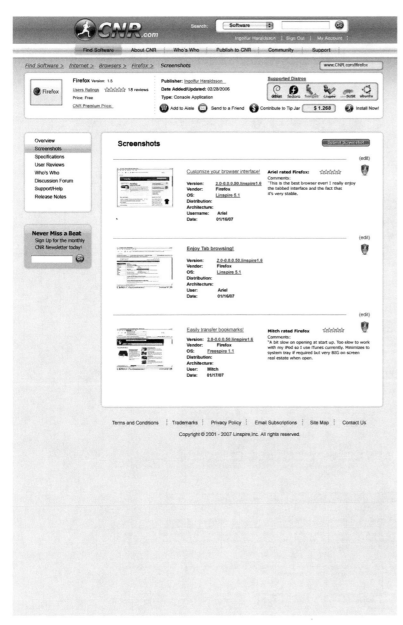

Figure 14.16
The CNR.com Screenshots page (alpha design).

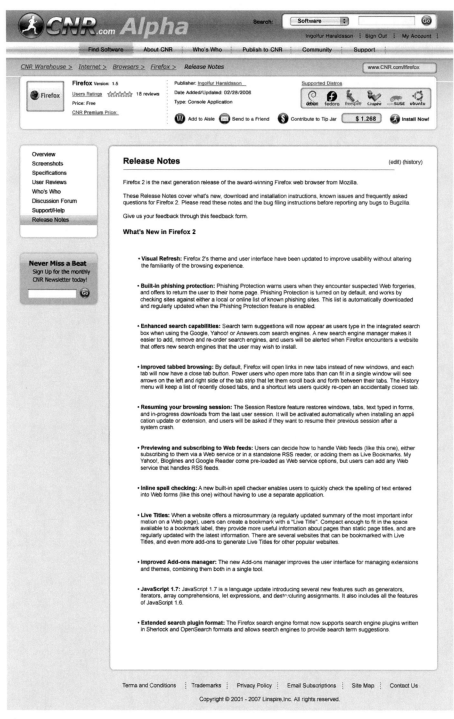

Figure 14.17
The CNR.com Release Notes page (alpha design).

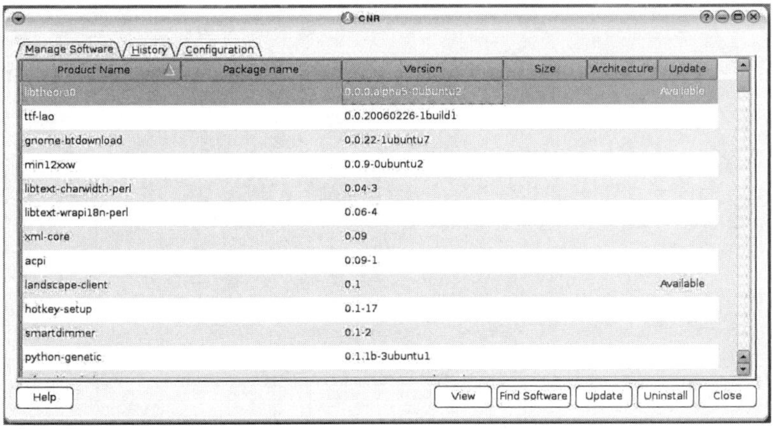

Figure 14.18
The CNR.com plug-in (alpha design).

Conclusion

In this chapter, you learned about Automatix2, third-party software designed to make Ubuntu as functional, if not more so, as any Windows computer. Along the way, you delved into CrossOver Office, a stable Windows emulator.

While hanging on to some Windows applications is all well and good, let's not forget, Ubuntu has some serious native tools of its own. In Part III, "Using OpenOffice.org," you'll get to dive into the major components of this powerful office suite to complete your journey into Ubuntu.

PART III

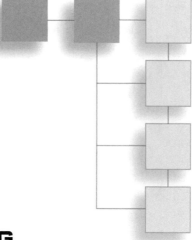

USING OPENOFFICE.ORG

CHAPTER 15

Documenting with Writer

It was a dark and stormy night . . .

The urge to put words on paper is very strong in most cultures. Paper and ink lend a sense of permanence that we don't seem to have in our own brains. Scientists speculate that we do indeed remember everything we have experienced, perhaps all the way back to Minute One. But until we can figure out how to *remember* all of that detail, we still need to write it down.

The written word has more uses than just archiving memories and events. It's still the most pervasive form of communication in the world. Every type of media uses writing as its basis, even television (though some writing there is a bit shaky). The Internet has been the fastest-growing medium in the world, and even with the advent of streaming audio and video, people mostly read the written works of others.

Clearly, this writing thing will be around for some time, and it's important that you have the right tools to put your words together so you can worry about what to write, as opposed to how to write it.

The Writer component of OpenOffice.org makes a great tool to get your words on paper or on computer screens around the planet. In this chapter, the basics of the Writer interface will be explored, as well as the steps used in creating special elements in a Writer document.

The Writer Interface

Contrary to what you might think, Writer is not a separate application in the OpenOffice.org suite. Think of it more as a set of clothes that OpenOffice.org puts on to go to work building a document. It's still OpenOffice.org and shares many of OpenOffice.org's functions, but with the new outfit on, it's Writer.

Part word processor, part desktop publisher, Writer is jammed with tools and functions to put a document together. This section will detail the tools found in the toolbars, menus, and shortcut keys that make up the Writer outfit.

Exploring the Toolbars

When Writer appears on the screen, you can get a good look at its interface and see how closely it resembles other word processing programs (see Figure 15.1). First, the Standard toolbar appears on the top of the window, and the Formatting toolbar adds even more functionality. Since the toolbars are a great resource while you work in Writer, let's examine them more completely.

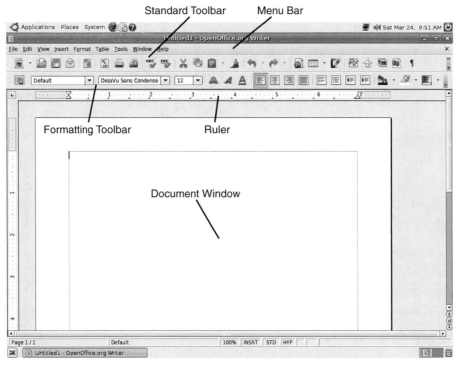

Figure 15.1
The Writer interface.

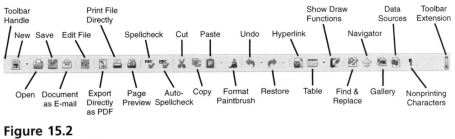

Figure 15.2
The Standard toolbar.

Standard Toolbar

The first set of tools to examine is the Standard toolbar, a toolset tightly configured for Writer. Typically, the Standard toolbar appears on the top of the screen, although it can be repositioned (see Figure 15.2).

In Table 15.1, the basic functions of each of these buttons are described.

Formatting Toolbar

As you would expect, the Writer version of the Formatting toolbar primarily focuses on the manipulation of text and paragraph styling (just as the Calc Formatting toolbar concerns itself with row and cell manipulation).

Figure 15.3 shows the Formatting toolbar for Writer. Table 15.2 describes the functions of the same set of tools.

Customizing Toolbars

The Standard and Formatting toolbars are not the only two sets of tools available in Writer, not by a long shot. In fact, as of OpenOffice.org 2.2, the version that ships with Ubuntu 7.04, there is a total of 23 available toolbars in Writer. Most of these toolbars will pop up as needed. For instance, when you begin to insert a table, the Table toolbar will appear as a floating window.

To make a toolbar visible at any time, a quick procedure is all you need.

1. Click the View | Toolbars menu. The Toolbars submenu will appear (see Figure 15.4).

Table 15.1 The Standard Toolbar Buttons

Name	Function
Toolbar Handle	A toolbar control that allows users to move any docked toolbar to any position within OpenOffice.org and undock a toolbar as well.
New	A single click opens a new Writer window and document. Clicking the drop-down control displays a list of OpenOffice.org documents that can be created.
Open	Opens the Open dialog box, where existing documents can be opened.
Save	Saves the current document.
Document as E-mail	Starts the default Ubuntu e-mail program (usually Evolution) and creates a new e-mail with the current document as an attachment.
Edit File	Turns the read-only status for the document on and off.
Export Directly as PDF	Opens the Export dialog box, set to convert the document to a PDF file.
Print File Directly	Prints the document to the default Ubuntu printer.
Page Preview	Toggles between Preview and Edit modes.
Spellcheck	Opens the Spellcheck dialog box and runs a spelling check on the document.
AutoSpellcheck	Toggles the "check as you go" status for the document on and off.
Cut	Cuts selected text from the document.
Copy	Copies selected text in the document.
Paste	Pastes cut or copied text into the document.
Format Paintbrush	Enables the application of a format to selected text.
Undo	Regresses the last editing change made to the document.
Restore	Returns any undone changes.
Hyperlink	Opens the Hyperlink dialog box, where you can insert an HTML hyperlink to selected text.
Table	Opens the Insert Table dialog box with a single-click. A click-and-hold action reveals the row-by-column table creator.
Show Draw Functions	Toggles the Drawing toolbar on and off.
Find & Replace	Opens the Find & Replace dialog box, which enables users to search for and replace text in a document.
Navigator	Opens the Navigator tool, which displays various elements of the document in one location, allowing users to view and navigate to different sections of the document.
Gallery	Opens the Gallery pane, which contains backgrounds, bullets, sounds, and other elements to insert in your document.
Data Sources	Opens the Data Sources pane, which allows users to create form letters from various sources.
Nonprinting Characters	Toggles nonprinting character visibility in the document.
Toolbar Extension	Allows users to see the rest of the toolbar's buttons if the OpenOffice.org window is not wide enough.

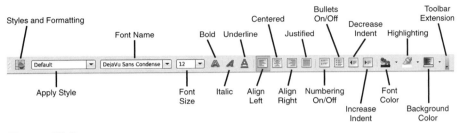

Figure 15.3
The Formatting toolbar.

Table 15.2 The Formatting Toolbar Buttons

Name	Function
Styles and Formatting	Toggles the Styles and Formatting window, which displays the styles and formats within an open document.
Apply Style	Applies the selected style to selected text.
Font Name	Changes the font of selected text.
Font Size	Changes the font size of selected text.
Bold	Applies the bold style to selected text.
Italic	Applies the italic style to selected text.
Underline	Underlines selected text.
Align Left	Aligns selected paragraphs to left margin.
Centered	Centers selected paragraphs on page.
Align Right	Aligns selected paragraphs to right margin.
Justified	Justifies selected paragraphs to fill all space between margins.
Numbering on/off	Changes selected paragraphs to a numbered list.
Bullets on/off	Changes selected paragraphs to a bulleted list.
Increase Indent	Indents selected paragraphs.
Decrease Indent	Shifts selected paragraphs towards left margin.
Font Color	Click applies displayed color to selected text. Click and hold reveals more colors to apply.
Highlighting	Click applies displayed highlight color (or fill) to selected text. Click and hold reveals more fills to apply and the capability to remove fills.
Background color	Applies background color (or fill) to document.
Toolbar Extension	If the OpenOffice.org window is not wide enough, clicking this extension allows users to see the rest of the toolbar's buttons.

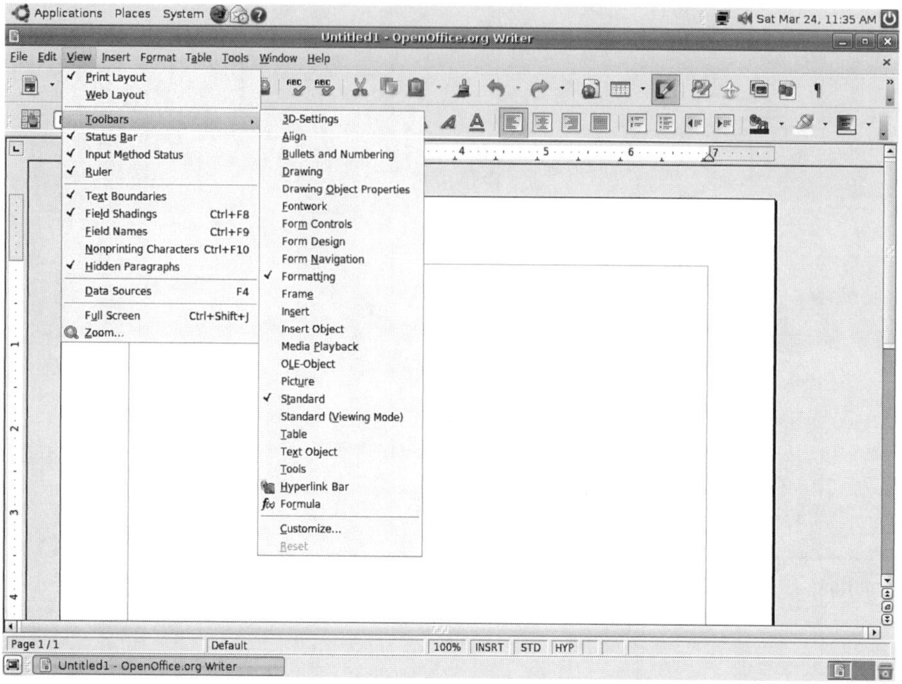

Figure 15.4
Your choice of toolbars.

2. Click Picture. The Picture toolbar will appear as a floating toolbar (see Figure 15.5).

3. To dock, or attach, a floating toolbar so that it no longer blocks the document window, carefully click and drag the toolbar's title bar toward the part of the window you want the toolbar to be docked. A gray outline will appear, marking the planned position of the toolbar. Use a light touch.

4. Release the mouse button. The toolbar will be dropped into the desired space on the border of the document window (see Figure 15.6).

5. To undock or move a toolbar to another position, click the toolbar handle (refer to Figure 15.2) and drag the cursor toward the part of the window you want the toolbar to be in. A gray outline will appear, marking the planned position of the toolbar.

6. Release the mouse button. The toolbar will be dropped into the desired space.

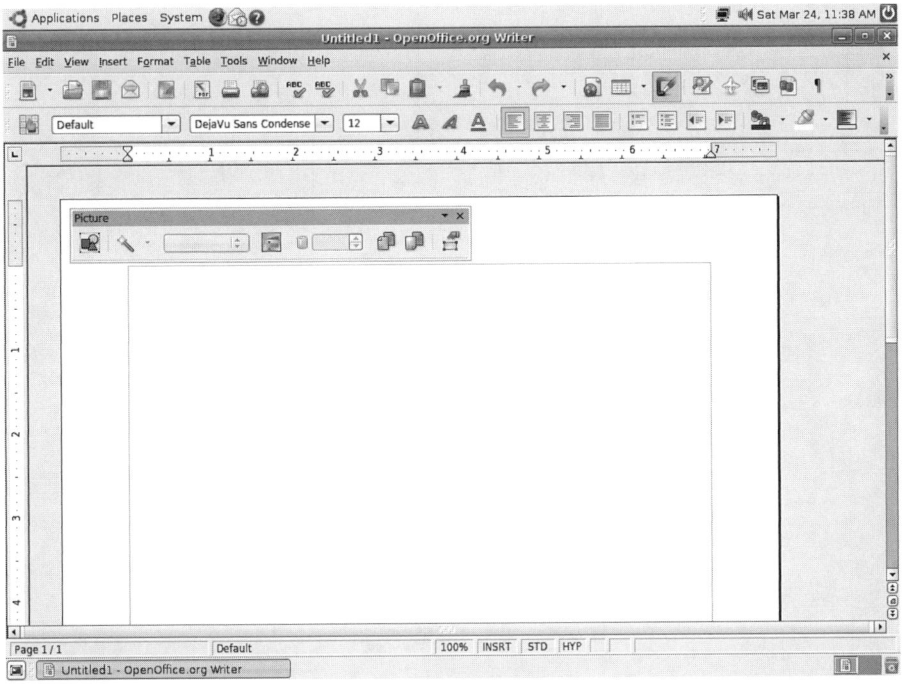

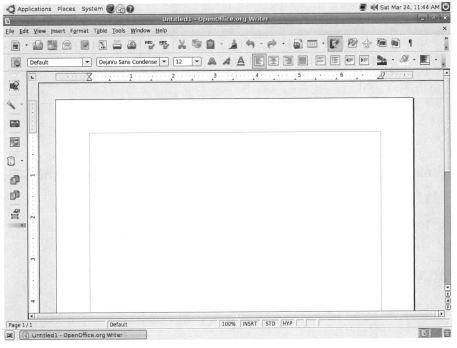

Figure 15.5
New toolbars float.

Figure 15.6
Docking toolbars is easy.

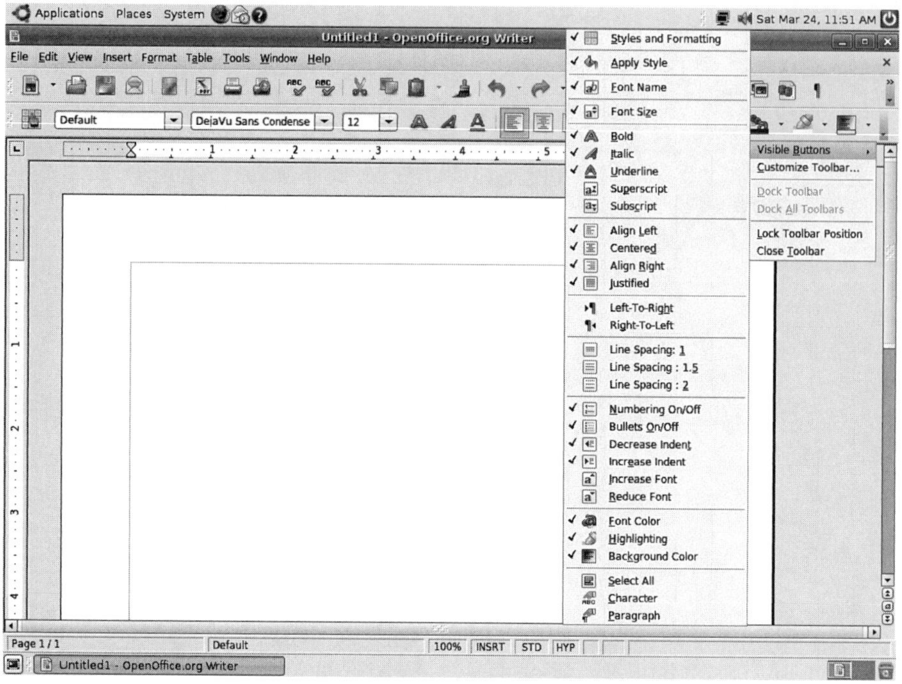

Figure 15.7
Choose which buttons to see and which to hide.

You can also make any button in a toolbar's toolset visible or hidden, as demonstrated in the following steps.

1. Click the toolbar extension button on the Formatting toolbar. The Extension menu will appear.

2. Select the Visible Buttons command. A submenu of the available buttons will appear (see Figure 15.7).

3. Checked menu commands represent visible buttons. Click any unchecked button. The selected icon appears in the Formatting toolbar.

4. Click the toolbar extension button on the Formatting toolbar again. The Extension menu will appear.

5. Select the Visible Buttons command.

6. Select a checked icon option. The selected icon disappears from the Formatting toolbar.

What Do All These Menus Mean?

The toolbars contain a voluminous number of functions to assist in the creation of documents. Yet they pale in comparison to the depth of the menu commands found in Writer. The menus represent every toolbar command, plus many additional commands. In theory, you could put every menu command on the toolbars, but that would add so much clutter to the screen that you'd only have a two-inch-tall space in which to type your document.

Because of the sheer number of menu commands, this section of the chapter will not detail every available command. Instead, the more commonly used menu commands will be explained.

Editing Your Document

Of all of the available menus in Writer, the Edit menu is perhaps the most useful. It contains the most pervasive commands in Writer, except for the Open and Save commands in the File menu.

In this menu, you'll find the ubiquitous Cut, Copy, and Paste functions, as well as the Undo, Redo, and Repeat commands. You can open the Search & Replace dialog box from here, as well as track changes to the document.

The examples in this section will highlight the most basic of these commands, starting with cutting and pasting any document object using the Edit menu commands.

1. In an open Writer document, select a passage of text, a graphic, or a form field.

Click Mania

You can select an entire paragraph of text by quadruple-clicking anywhere within the paragraph. Double-clicking selects a word. Triple-clicking selects an entire sentence in a paragraph.

2. From the Edit menu, click Cut.

3. Move the cursor to another area of the document.

4. Again from the Edit menu, click Paste. The cut text appears in the new spot.

You can create copies of document items such as text or graphics in just a few steps.

1. To copy an item, select the desired item.

2. From the Edit menu, click Copy.

3. Move the cursor to another area of the document.

4. From the Edit menu, click Paste. A copy of the text appears in the new spot.

Here is how the Undo, Redo, and Repeat functions of the Edit menu can help your work.

1. After performing any edit within a document, click Edit | Undo. The most recent change to the document vanishes.

Undo Actions

The Undo, Redo, and Repeat commands will always be followed by a one-word description of the action that will be performed.

2. Click Edit | Redo to put the change back on screen.

3. Click Edit | Repeat to repeat the most recent change.

Viewing Your Document

The way you look at things influences how you treat them. For example, look at a bug down on the ground, and you will likely feel indifferent. Look at the same bug through an electron microscope, and you may shudder in revulsion.

How you view a document is important to your work. When you have a document with a lot of graphics, seeing the whole page at once helps you balance the look of the page. Conversely, those with vision problems may want to make the print appear really big without increasing the font size. Follow these steps to change your outlook on your document.

1. In an open document, click View | Zoom. The Zoom dialog box appears (see Figure 15.8).

2. Select the option that matches your desired view choice.

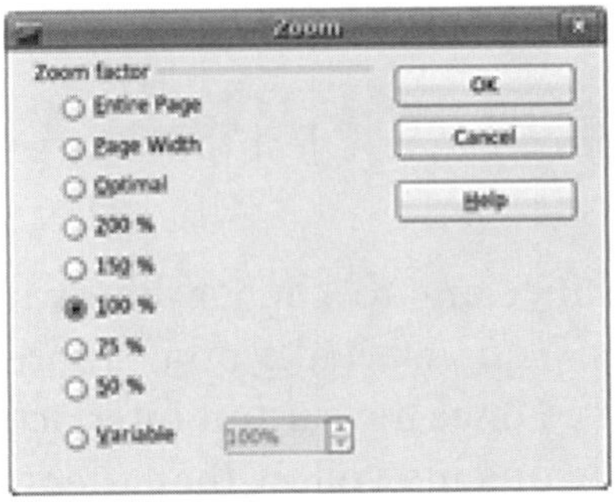

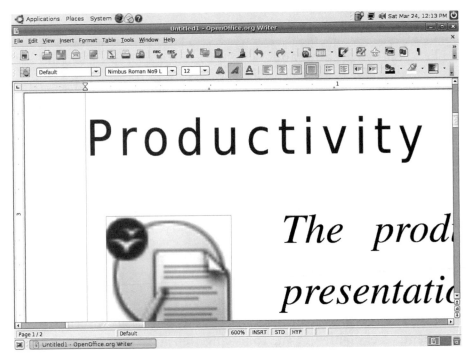

Figure 15.8
Decide how close up you want to see the document.

Figure 15.9
At 600%, things get really big.

- If you want a precise zoom percentage, click the Variable option and enter the numeric value (see Figure 15.9).

Zoom-a-zoom!

The minimum zoom percentage is 20%, and the maximum zoom percentage is 600%.

- To see an entire page, select the Entire Page option in the Zoom dialog box.
- For the best size for your current screen dimensions, select the Optimal option.

We've already discussed the capability of OpenOffice.org to change its own interface by moving toolbars and changing menus. You can make other more subtle interface changes that can be just as important. To see the various interface add-ons that can assist you in working with your documents, follow these steps.

1. In an open document, open the View menu.

2. Click the Text Boundaries command.

3. Click the Ruler command.

4. Click the Field Shadings command.

5. Click the Status Bar command. Note the screen changes after implementing all of these commands. You can experiment to decide which combination is most efficient for the way you work.

Inserting Cool Stuff

In the early days of electronic document creation, there was text. That was it. Things got rather exciting when italic text came on the scene. Underlining caused a huge ruckus. But then things sort of calmed down.

That lasted for a few years (eons in computer time), until someone got the idea to put real-time artwork in documents. Now, if you don't have graphics in your document, people look at you funny.

Writer's Insert menu contains the commands to quickly and easily insert artwork into your document, as explained in the following steps.

1. In an open Writer document, select Insert | Picture | From File. The Insert Picture dialog box appears (see Figure 15.10).

2. In the Insert Picture dialog box, navigate through the directories to select the desired image.

3. Check the Preview check box to see the graphic files as you select them in the file list.

4. When you have selected the image you want to insert, click the Open button.

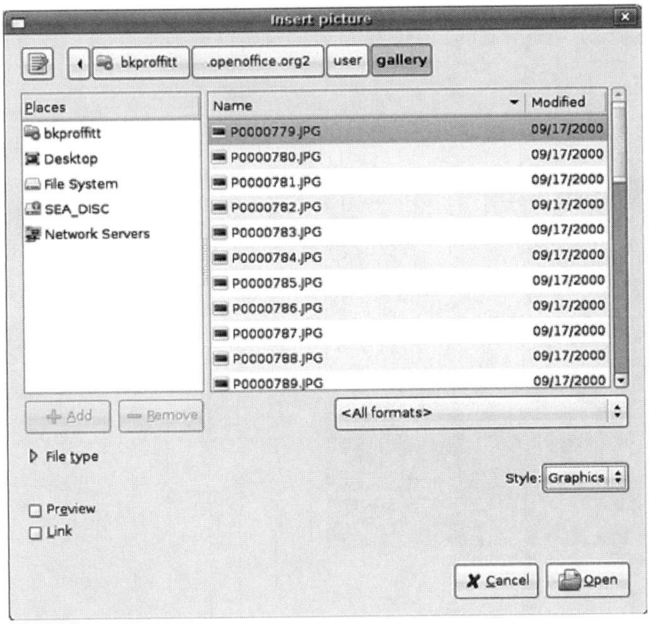

Figure 15.10
Preview the art you want to insert in the Insert Picture dialog box.

In the document, the graphic appears surrounded by a box comprised of green squares (see Figure 15.11). These are the graphic handles. The following steps show you how to size, move, and anchor the graphic in your document.

1. Place the pointer over the left-center handle. The pointer changes to a left-right arrow. Drag the handle to the left to stretch the graphic horizontally. You can repeat this action with any of the graphic handles.

Copying Graphics

Holding the Ctrl key while dragging any graphic handle immediately produces a copy of the graphic.

2. Place the pointer within the graphic and drag it across the screen. The graphic moves with the pointer.

3. To wrap text around the graphic, right-click the graphic. A context menu will appear.

4. Select Wrap | Optimal Page Wrap. The text of the document now wraps around the graphic (see Figure 15.12).

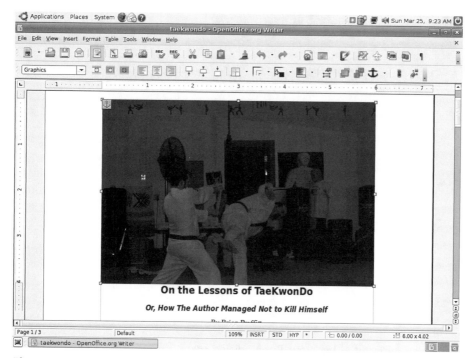

Figure 15.11
An inserted graphic, ready for placement.

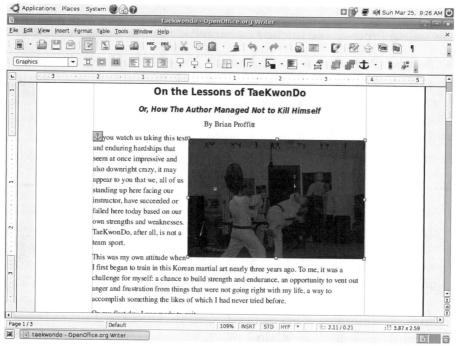

Figure 15.12
A neatly wrapped graphic in a document.

Cool Wraps

For a cool effect, choose Wrap | In Background from the context menu. Text flows *over* the graphic.

5. To keep graphics close to a particular section of the document, select the appropriate Anchor command from the context menu.

Absolute Positioning

For absolute positioning, choose the Anchor | As menu command from the image's context menu. The graphic remains exactly where placed in the document.

Umlauts, grave marks, Dingbats. Terms that sound like they belong in a dark, spooky cemetery. Believe it or not, these are descriptions of special characters that Writer can place in your document.

Because the standard 101- or 103-key U.S. PC keyboards have no room for them, OpenOffice.org has an easy-to-use dialog box to find and insert special characters.

1. Place the cursor at the spot in the document where you want the special character inserted.

2. In the Insert menu, click Special Character. The Special Characters dialog box opens (see Figure 15.13).

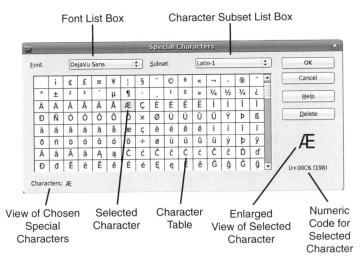

Figure 15.13
The Special Characters dialog box.

3. Select the Dingbats font in the Subset list box.

4. Select any desired character. The character will appear in the Characters field at the bottom of the dialog box.

5. Click OK. The character is placed within the document.

Key Combinations

Key combinations are the quickest way to execute commands. As fast as a mouse is, anytime you have to lift your fingers and grab a mouse, it slows your typing down.

Accelerator keys do a good job of emulating menu commands, but often key combinations are even shorter and therefore faster.

Table 15.3 lists the key combinations found in Writer's default menus. Though this is not all of the available key combinations, these tend to be used most often.

Table 15.3 Writer Key Combinations

Key Combination	Equivalent Menu Command
Ctrl+A	Edit | Select All
Ctrl+C	Edit | Copy
Ctrl+F	Edit | Search & Replace
Ctrl+N	File | New, From Template
Ctrl+O	File | Open
Ctrl+P	File | Print
Ctrl+Q	File | Exit
Ctrl+S	File | Save
Ctrl+V	Edit | Paste
Ctrl+X	Edit | Cut
Ctrl+Z	Edit | Undo
Ctrl+Shift+J	View | Full Screen
F4	View | Data Sources
F5	Edit | Navigator
F7	Tools | Spellcheck
F9	Tools | Update | Fields
F11	Format | Styles and Formatting
Ctrl+F2	Insert | Fields | Other
Ctrl+F3	Edit | AutoText
Ctrl+F7	Tools | Language | Thesaurus
Ctrl+F8	View | Field Shadings
Ctrl+F9	View | Field Names
Ctrl+F10	View | Nonprinting Characters
Ctrl+F12	Insert | Table

Key Listing

For a complete listing of all of the key combinations available in Writer, click any toolbar's extension control, choose Customize from the menu, then click the Keyboard tab in the Customize dialog box.

Creating Documents

Flight school offers two kinds of lessons: those on the ground and those in the air. In ground school, students learn how a plane flies and what all of the instruments do. In the airplane, student experience how everything works together to perform the miracle of flight.

The tools of Writer have been described with some detail in the previous sections of this chapter. Ground school is over. Now it is time to fly and experience how to use those tools to accomplish basic tasks for your document.

Formatting Text

Formatting a document is essential in today's world. No longer are readers content to see a page with plain-looking letters. Even a large fiction novel, which is nothing but words, has been formatted with the font that the publisher feels is most attractive and at the same time most legible.

Writer has three levels of formatting: characters, paragraphs, and pages. The Format menu holds the starting point for all of these levels.

When you format these items, you apply new fonts, change font sizes and colors, set tab stops, indent lengths, and set page margins—and that's just for starters.

The following two examples will guide you through the basics of formatting at the character and paragraph levels.

1. In an open Writer document, select a passage of text.

2. From the Format menu, click Character. The Character dialog box appears (see Figure 15.14).

3. In the Font list, choose a desired font.

4. In the Typeface list, select Bold Italic.

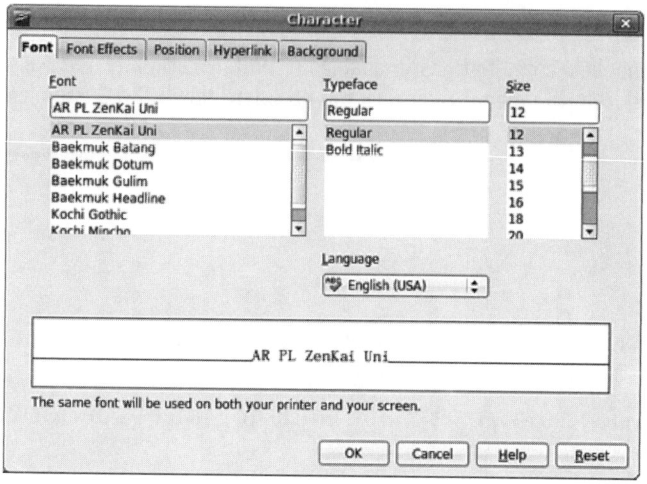

Figure 15.14
Format text with the Character dialog box.

5. In the Size list, select 14 pt.

6. Click the Font Effects tab. The Font Effects tab will open.

7. In the Effects area, select the Outline check box.

8. Choose a different color from the Font Color list.

9. Click OK to see the results of your setting changes (see Figure 15.15).

Not only can you alter the look of characters, but you can also make hyperlinks out of them.

1. With text selected, click Format | Character once more.

2. In the Character dialog box, select the Hyperlink tab.

3. In the URL field, type the Web address of the file you want to link to. (Use the Browse button to locate a file on your Ubuntu system.) Your selected text should be in the Text field.

4. Click the Background tab.

5. Select a color with which to highlight your text.

6. Click OK to check your work.

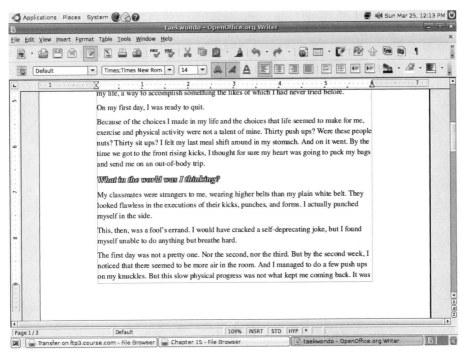

Figure 15.15
Altered text, courtesy of the Character dialog box.

1. With your cursor within any paragraph in the document, click Format | Paragraph. The Paragraph dialog box appears (see Figure 15.16).

2. Using the arrows, change the measurement in the Before text field to 1.00".

3. In the Line Spacing field, change to the Double option.

4. Click OK to see the results of the changes.

Paragraphs can be justified to fill the width of a page, as shown in the following steps.

1. With the cursor in another paragraph, click Format | Paragraph.

2. Click the Alignment tab.

3. Click the Justified radio button. Leave the other settings as is.

4. Click OK to see the results of the changes.

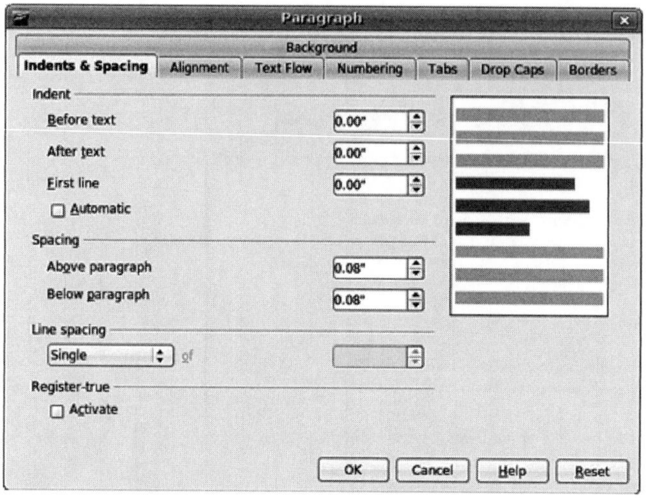

Figure 15.16
Use the Paragraph dialog box to format similar blocks of text.

The qualities of paragraphs can be changed in this dialog box, too.

1. With the cursor at the beginning of another paragraph, click Format I Paragraph again.

2. Click the Tabs tab.

3. In the Position field, change the 0.00" setting to 2.50".

4. In the Type section, select the Right radio button.

5. In the Fill Character section, select the . . . . radio button.

6. Click OK.

7. Press the Tab key to see the results of your settings.

You can even create a large drop cap at the beginning of your paragraph.

1. With the cursor in another paragraph, click Format I Paragraph again.

2. Select the Drop Caps tab.

3. Select the Display Drop Caps check box.

4. Select the Whole Word check box.

5. Click OK to see the results of your changes (see Figure 15.17).

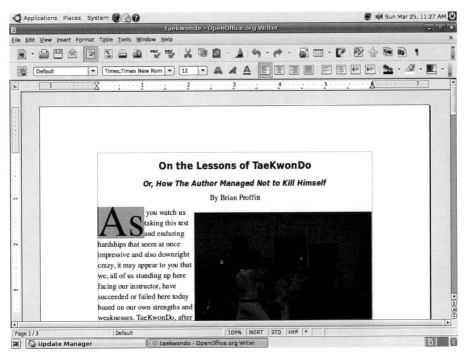

Figure 15.17
Drop caps lend a more literary look to your document.

Formatting Pages

Formatting a document can be tricky work. You have probably already noticed in your wanderings through the various tools that Writer has quite a few potential settings to tweak.

First, don't panic. Most likely you won't need to use many of these settings except in very specialized documents. They are just there when you need them.

You'll use some settings, though, more often than others. Perhaps not every day, but certainly every once in a while, particularly in a business setting that uses specialized stationery. These settings include page margins, headers and footers, and multiple columns. This section explains how to accomplish these tasks, starting with setting page margins.

1. Create a new text document in OpenOffice.org.

2. From the Format menu, click Page.

3. In the Page Style: Default dialog box (see Figure 15.18), click the Page tab.

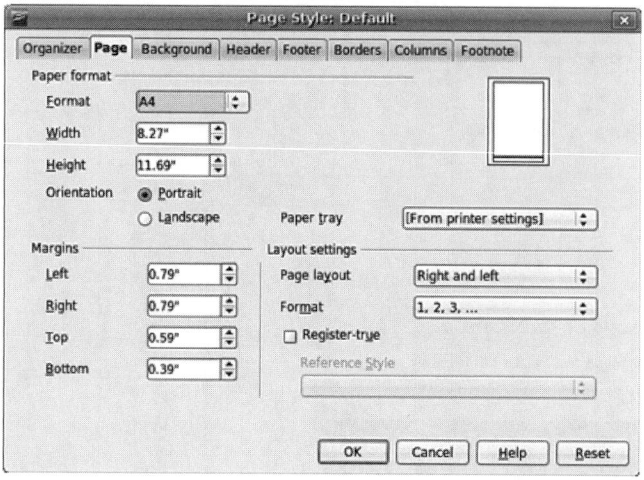

Figure 15.18
The Page tab contains the settings for page margins and size.

4. In the Format field, select the Legal option. Note the changes in the Preview area.

5. Try to even out the margins by changing the Left, Right, Top, and Bottom settings to 1.50".

6. Click OK to complete.

View Margins

To see the margins of the document on screen, click View | Text Boundaries.

Organizing Styles

In the Organizer tab of the Page Style dialog box, you can change the style of pages by selecting from preset categories.

This task shows how to add headers and footers to a document.

1. In the legal-size document, click Format | Page.

2. In the Page Style: Default dialog box, click the Header tab (see Figure 15.19).

3. Select the Header On check box to make the rest of the options on the tab available.

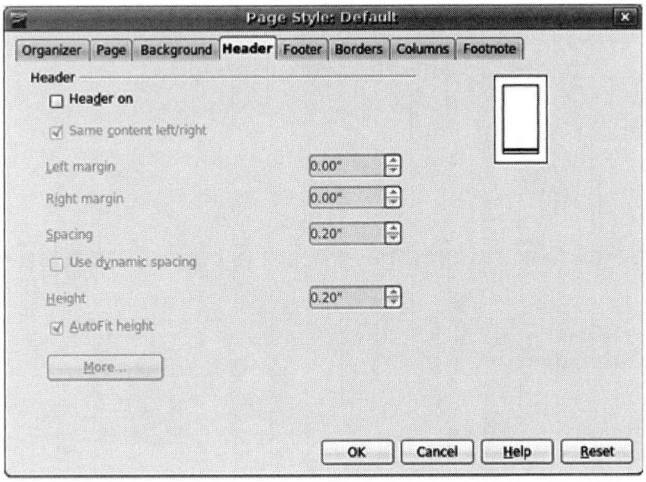

Figure 15.19
Build a header on this tab of the Page Style dialog box.

4. Increase the Spacing value (which is the space between the header and document) to 0.25".

5. Select the AutoFit Height check box.

6. Clear the Same Content Left/Right check box, which allows for different headers on facing pages.

7. Click the Footer tab.

8. Repeat the settings from the Header tab, except this time leave the Same Content Left/Right check box selected.

9. Click OK to close the dialog box.

Documents are made up of different kinds of pages. The first page is one such type and is generally configured differently, as seen in the following steps.

1. In the document, place the cursor in the header area of the first page.

2. Select the Insert | Fields | Page Number menu command.

3. Click the Align Right icon on the Formatting toolbar. (Odd-numbered pages are always right pages.)

4. Create enough dummy text to make the document at least four pages long.

5. Look at the header on Page 3. It has a right-aligned number 3.

6. Place your cursor in the header area of Page 2.

7. Choose Insert | Fields | Page Number.

8. Look at Page 4 to see that the even-numbered page headers now contain left-aligned numbers.

9. Place your cursor in any footer area.

10. Click Insert | Fields | Date.

11. Click the Centered icon on the Formatting toolbar.

12. All the footers in the document now contain the present date (see Figure 15.20).

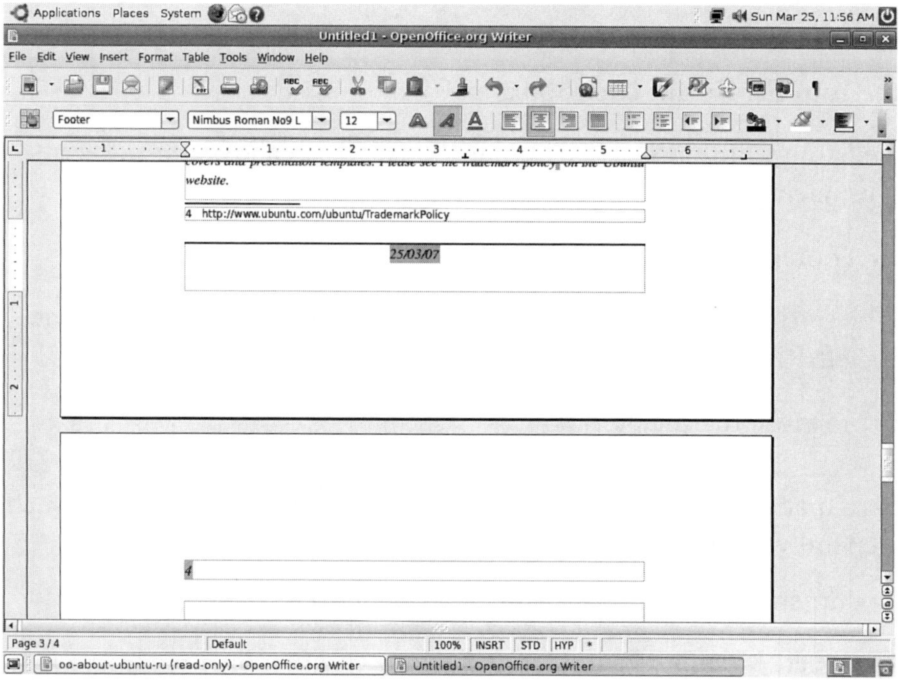

Figure 15.20
It's easy to create headers and footers.

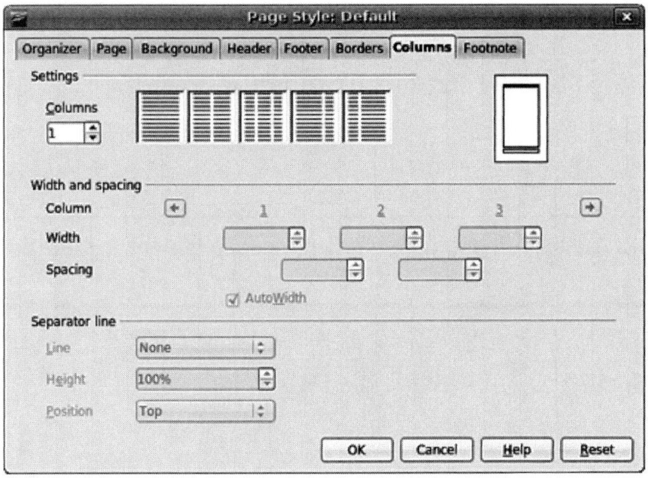

Figure 15.21
The Columns tab reveals a powerful Interface for column creation.

These steps highlight the method used to create columned text in Writer.

1. Create a new text document in OpenOffice.org.

2. From the Format menu, click Page.

3. Click the Columns tab in the Page Style: Default dialog box (see Figure 15.21).

4. If you want two or three equal-width columns, click the appropriate preset in the Columns area.

Off-Center Columns

The Columns area also presents two off-center column options. Use them if you want a one-third/two-thirds look to your page.

5. If you need more than three columns, select the desired value in the Columns field.

Limit Column Numbers

Unless you are creating an index-like document, it is recommended that you stay to four or fewer columns, as more columns make text harder to read.

6. If you need unequal columns, clear the AutoWidth check box.

7. Adjust the widths and spacings between columns to your specifications.

Viewing Off-Screen Columns

If you have more than three columns, use the left and right arrow navigation buttons to view the off-screen column settings.

8. Select a separator line width in the Line field, if desired.

9. Click OK.

Making Lists

If you want to remember something, write it down.

We all do it every day: create lists of things to do, groceries to buy, people to send cards to. Lists are a big part of our lives, if only because our brains are wired to think in sequential terms.

We like it when we can plan ahead, and since we perceive the world around us moment by moment, we tend to organize our thoughts sequentially, too. So we use lists to plan and to communicate.

Lists in documents are commonplace. Two major types of lists include numbered lists and bulleted lists. The following steps describe how to create numbered and bulleted lists in Writer.

1. Type a four- to five-item list, pressing Enter after each item.

2. Select the entire list.

3. From the Format menu, click Bullets and Numbering.

4. In the Bullets and Numbering dialog box, click the Numbering Type tab (see Figure 15.22).

5. Choose any of the eight options.

6. Click OK. Figure 15.23 shows a numbered list example.

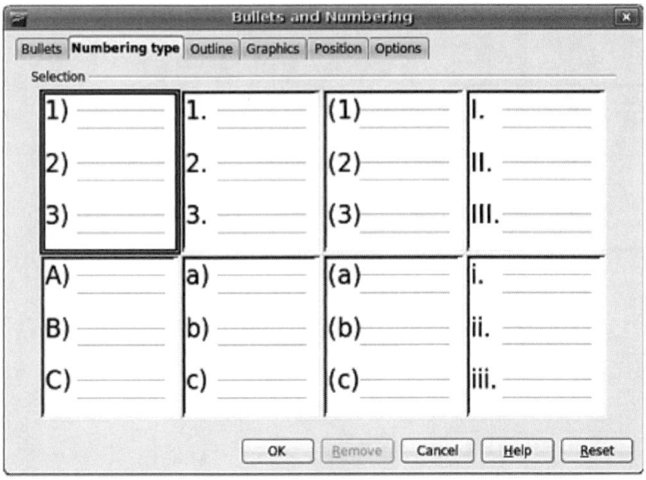

Figure 15.22
Select the style of numbering here.

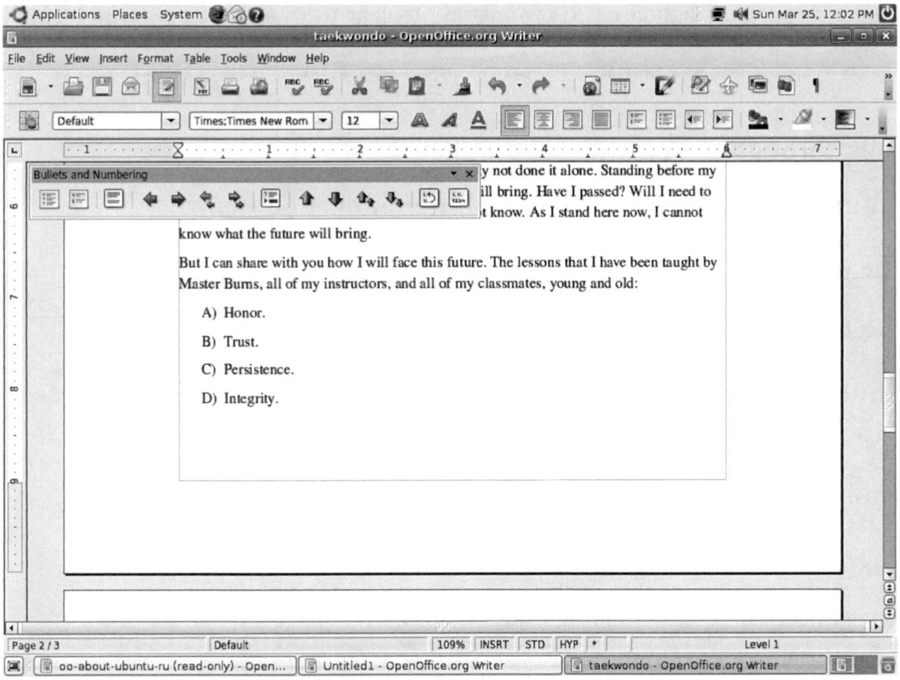

Figure 15.23
A sequential list should always be in the right order.

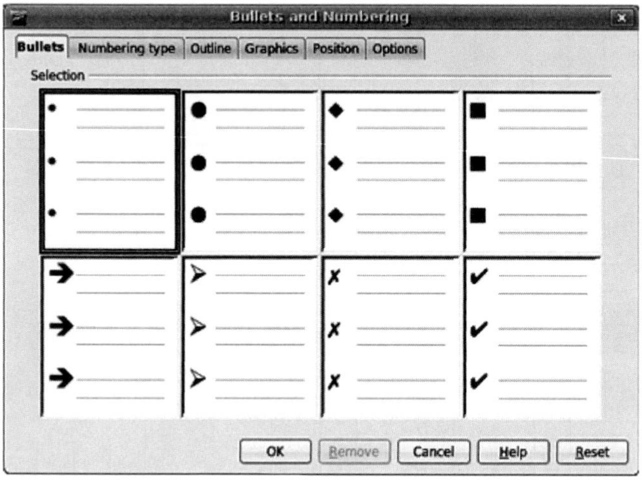

Figure 15.24
Select bullet styles in this tab.

Numbering Lists

Click the Numbering On/Off button on the Formatting toolbar to create a list with the default numbering style.

Now we'll walk through the creation of a bulleted list.

1. Type a four- to five-item list, pressing Enter after each item.

2. Select the entire list.

3. From the Format menu, click Bullets and Numbering.

4. In the Bullets and Numbering dialog box, click the Bullets tab (see Figure 15.24).

5. Choose any of the eight options.

Graphical Bullets

For more options, click the Pictures tab to choose from several graphics-based bullets.

6. Click OK. Figure 15.25 shows a bulleted list example.

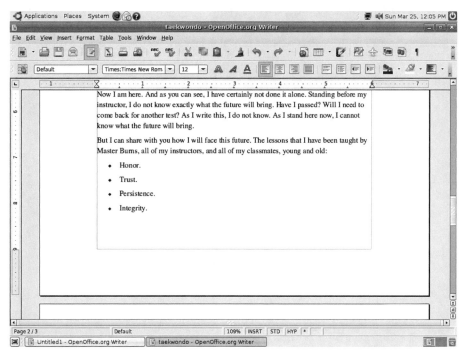

Figure 15.25
Bulleted lists present items in no particular order.

Bulleting Lists

Click the Bullets On/Off button on the Formatting toolbar to create a list with the default bullet style.

Building Tables

The final basic document element to be explored is the table. More complete than lists, tables provide a fast, compact way of getting information across to readers.

Creating a table in Writer is a fairly automated process, though it is not a full-fledged AutoPilot, as the following steps will show.

1. In an open Writer document, place the cursor at the point where you want to insert the table.

2. From the Insert menu, click Table.

3. In the Name field of the Insert Table dialog box, type a one-word name for the new table (see Figure 15.26).

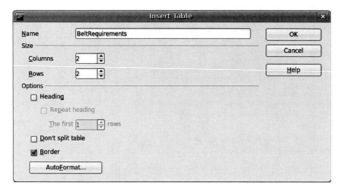

Figure 15.26
Begin building a table.

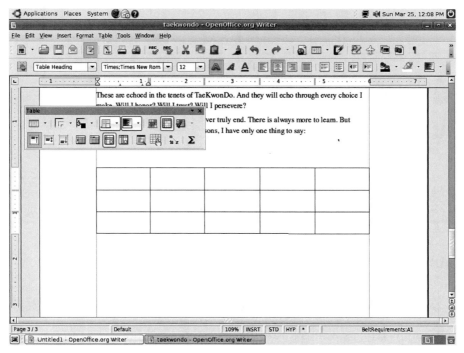

Figure 15.27
The newly designed table.

4. In the Size area, enter the number of rows and columns desired.

5. If the table needs a header, be sure to select the Heading check box. If the rows and columns should be outlined, select the Border check box.

Repeating Headings

If a table may lie on more than one page, select the Repeat Heading check box.

6. Click OK. Figure 15.27 shows a 5-column, 3-row table.

Conclusion

This introduction to Writer and its many tools covered a lot of material, but there is more to OpenOffice.org than just a word processor.

Chapter 16 will focus on the spreadsheet of OpenOffice.org, the venerable Calc application.

Analyzing with Calc

Accountants aren't the only ones using spreadsheets these days. With online banking, online trading, and online loan applications available to the average consumer, more and more people use spreadsheets to track their rapidly changing finances.

This new demand, coupled with the already present needs of the business world for clearer, faster reporting, requires a spreadsheet program that is pretty powerful. Calc delivers the spreadsheet power you need to your Ubuntu desktop. This component of OpenOffice.org delivers many of the same functions found in Microsoft Excel or Lotus 1-2-3 and maintains interoperability with these applications and the rest of OpenOffice.org.

This chapter will review some of the basics of spreadsheets and Calc in particular. In addition, value formats and data formatting will be explained.

A Spreadsheet Primer

You have likely used a spreadsheet before at one time or another. Many spreadsheet users, however, often do not create or modify the basic workings of the spreadsheets they use. They just plug in the numbers and print the assigned reports like they're supposed to.

There comes a time in computer users' lives when they need to create a spreadsheet for themselves. At that time, it's a good idea to know how these spreadsheet doodads work.

It all comes down, more or less, to cells. A familiar type of cell is the basic building block of your body. There are many different types of cells: muscle cells, skin cells, liver cells—the list goes on and on. But no matter what kind of cell you look at, they all have pretty much the same basic structure: nucleus, plasmalemma, cell wall, mitochondrions, and other hard-to-pronounce components. Even though they have the same overall structure, cells can have vastly different jobs because of the specialized way they have been put together.

The same theory applies to spreadsheet cells. They are all rectangular, and they all can contain data. But each cell in a spreadsheet can have a different task. One cell may sit empty, filled in with an attractive shade of purple. Another cell may contain the number 42. Still another may contain a formula that refers to the number 42 in another cell and displays something completely different.

Cells are all the same, but they can be used in many different ways.

Cells are typically positioned and referred to as rows and columns. By universal convention, spreadsheet rows are denoted with numbers, and columns are denoted with letters. Because spreadsheets sometimes need more than 26 columns, the columns after the letter Z move to a two-letter notation (AA, AB, AC, and so on). This lettering convention continues to column IV, which makes 256 the maximum number of columns a Calc spreadsheet can have. A spreadsheet can contain 65,536 rows, giving you the potential to fill 16,777,216 cells. With over 16 million cells to fill, you probably won't run out of space to perform the needed calculations unless maybe you work for NASA.

You identify cells by their row and column position in the spreadsheet. The cell that's four rows down and eight columns across is identified as cell H4. Find the cell reference by looking at the bold column and row headings or reading the coordinates (C4) from the Name Box field in the Formula Bar, as seen in Figure 16.1.

Multiple cells are called *ranges*. An inverted color fill denotes a selected range of cells. The coordinates of a range include the cell in the upper-left corner of the range and the cell in the lower-right corner of the range. Thus, you would reference the range selected in Figure 16.2 as D2:G14.

Now you've got the basics down. As you progress through the chapter, you will start to see how the cells of a spreadsheet fit together to make a body of data.

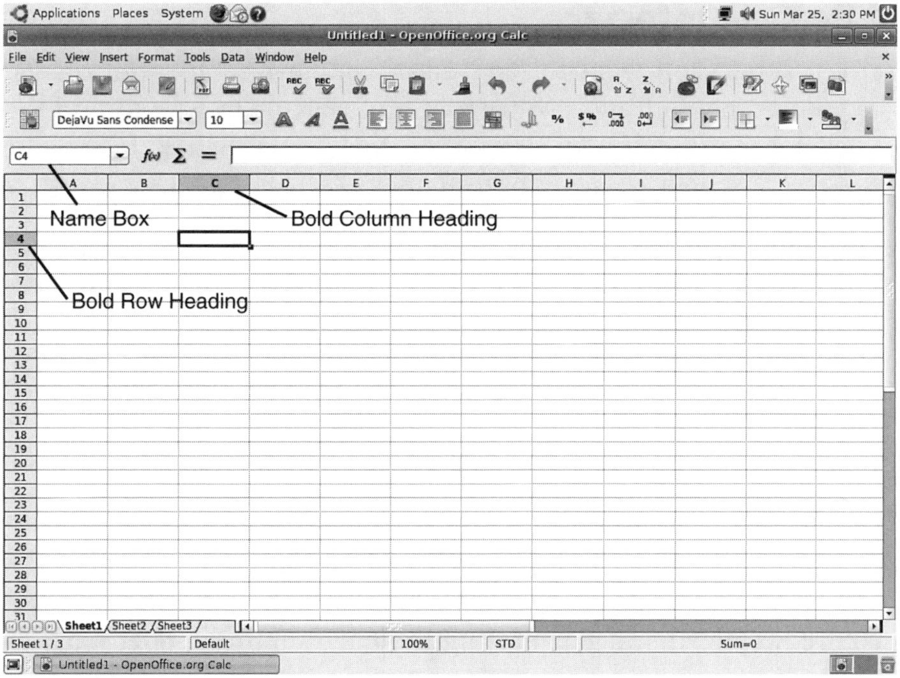

Figure 16.1
Reading a cell's coordinates.

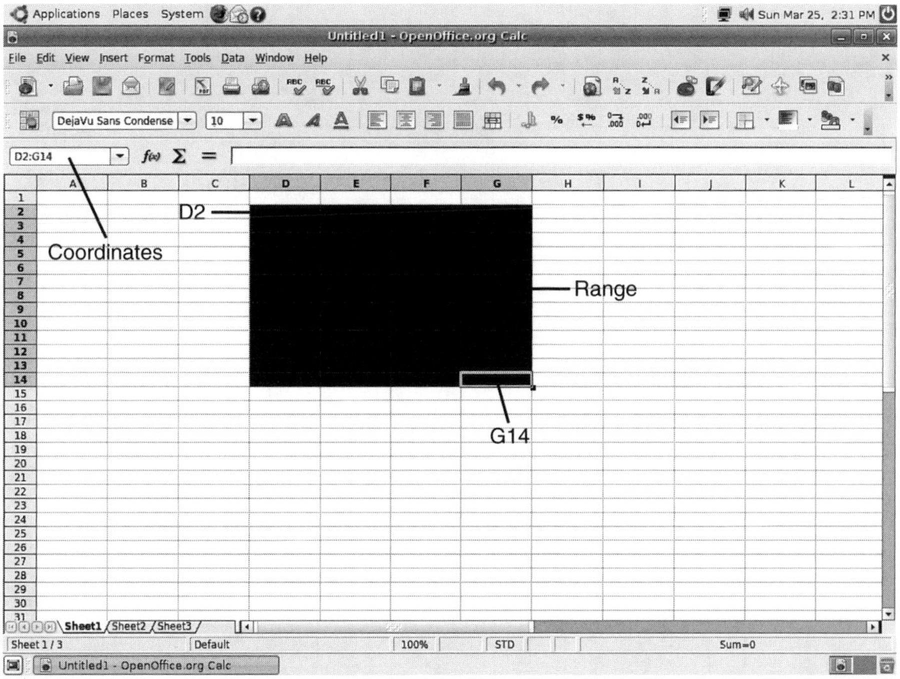

Figure 16.2
Reading a range's coordinates.

Learning the Calc Interface

When you start cooking, you want to have all of your ingredients out on the counter before you begin. Nothing is so frustrating as having to stop to find the jar of saffron when your hands are covered in flour. Even better, have your ingredients chopped, cut, and measured out before you begin for true speed.

The same concept applies when building a spreadsheet. You need to have all of your tools out before you begin. In this section, the Calc tools will be examined, with special emphasis on those tools unique to Calc.

Working with Calc Tools and Menus

You will have probably noticed that the Calc and Writer interfaces have many similarities (see Figure 16.3).

Calc, of course, makes use of the ubiquitous Standard toolbar. As in all of the OpenOffice.org components, its toolset remains mostly the same. If you need to review the core Standard and Formatting toolbar functions, refer back to

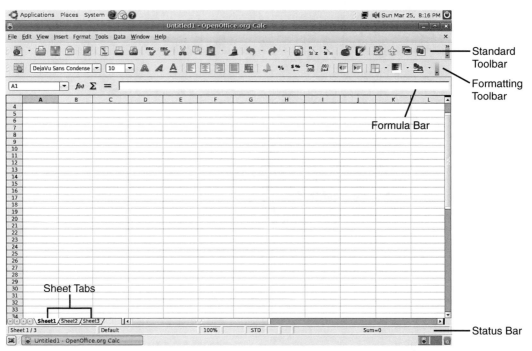

Figure 16.3
The primary toolsets of the Calc interface.

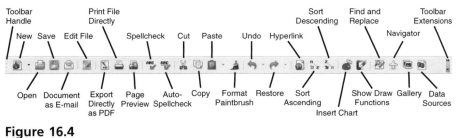

Figure 16.4
The Calc Standard toolbar.

Table 16.1 Calc-Specific Standard Toolbar Buttons

Name	Function
Sort Ascending	Allows users to move any docked toolbar to any position within OpenOffice.org.
Sort Descending	Opens a new Writer window with a single click. Clicking the drop-down control displays a list of OpenOffice.org documents that can be created.
Insert Chart	Opens the Open dialog box, where existing documents can be opened.

Chapter 15, "Documenting with Writer." For now, let's look at what's different for each of these toolsets.

Standard Toolbar

The Calc Standard toolbar deals mostly with file and data manipulation.

Figure 16.4 illustrates the Standard toolbar for Calc. Table 16.1 lists the functions of the new or changed buttons on the Standard toolbar.

Formatting Toolbar

The Calc Formatting toolbar primarily focuses on the manipulation of data values and their presentation.

Figure 16.5 illustrates the Formatting toolbar for Calc. As with the Standard toolbar, many of the functions in this Formatting toolbar duplicate the functions in Writer. Table 16.2 lists the functions of the new or changed buttons in the Formatting toolbar.

The use of these buttons will be explored in the section "Good-Looking Data," later in this chapter.

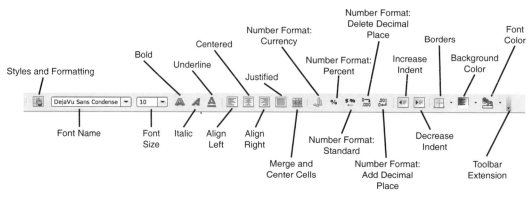

Figure 16.5
The Calc Formatting toolbar.

Table 16.2 Calc-Specific Formatting Toolbar Buttons

Name	Function
Merge and Center Cells	Centers data horizontally in selected cells.
Number Format: Currency	Applies currency format to numeric data in selected cells.
Number Format: Percent	Applies percentage format to numeric data in selected cells.
Number Format: Standard	Applies standard format to numeric data in selected cells.
Number Format: Add Decimal Place	Adds a decimal place to the significant value of data in selected cells.
Number Format: Delete Decimal Place	Removes a decimal place from the significant value of data in selected cells.
Decrease Indent	Decreases the amount of indent space for data in a specific cell.
Increase Indent	Increases the amount of indent space for data in a specific cell.
Borders	Applies borders to selected cells.

Formula Bar

The Formula Bar is a toolbar only found in Calc. It is small in terms of the number of functions it contains, but it is probably the most important toolbar in this component. Here is where you enter all of the functions and formulas used in your spreadsheet.

The Formula Bar has two distinct modes: the Cell Edit mode and the Data Input mode. The distinction may seem a bit too fine, but you'll pick up on it quickly.

In the Cell Edit mode, the Formula Bar's tools deal with the selected cell or cells as they relate to other cells. When in Data Input mode, the functions of the Formula Bar apply to data or formulas within *one* cell.

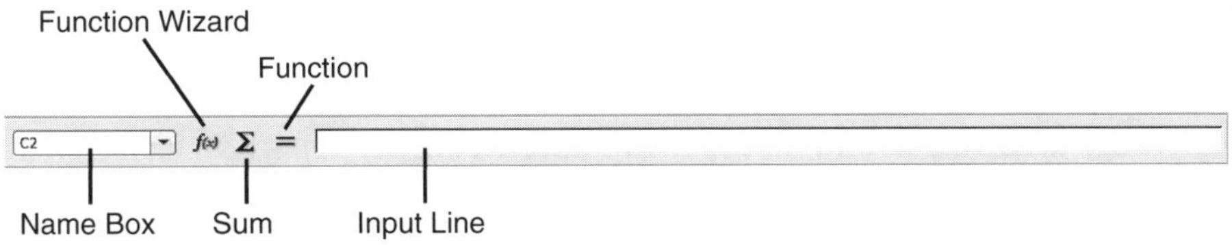

Figure 16.6
The Calc Formula Bar in the Cell Edit mode.

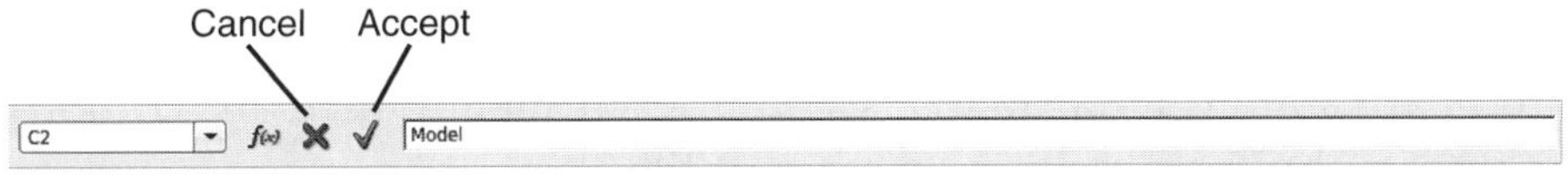

Figure 16.7
The Calc Formula Bar in the Data Input mode.

Figure 16.6 shows the Formula Bar in the Cell Edit mode, and Figure 16.7 shows the same bar in the Data Input mode.

Table 16.3 lists the functions of all of the buttons in either mode of the Formula Bar.

Table 16.3 Formula Bar Buttons

Name	Mode	Function
Name Box	Both	Displays coordinates of selected cell or cell range. Entering coordinates into this field and pressing Enter navigates the cursor to the input cell or cell range.
Function Wizard	Both	Opens the Function wizard.
Sum	Edit	Activates the SUM function, which adds the values of selected cells and displays the total in an adjacent cell.
Function	Edit	Activates the Data Input mode and begins the entry of a formula into the selected cell and its input line.
Cancel	Input	Removes input value and restores cell to last value.
Accept	Input	Copies value in input line to selected cell.
Input Line	Both	Displays or enables entry of data values and formulas into selected cell.

Putting Styles and Formatting and Navigator Tools to Work

The Styles and Formatting toolbar is an underrated tool in OpenOffice.org. In Writer, it hardly seems necessary, given the presence of the Apply Styles field in the Formatting toolbar.

In Calc, the Formatting toolbar doesn't contain such a field, so the Styles and Formatting toolbar becomes more important.

While the appearance of the Styles and Formatting toolbar varies between OpenOffice.org components, its functionality remains the same. The Styles and Formatting toolbar catalogs all available styles in each OpenOffice.org component and lets you apply those styles in the active file.

Figure 16.8 displays the Styles and Formatting toolbar in its Calc incarnation.

The Styles and Formatting toolbar has two sections: a style section on the left and a tool section on the right. The contents of the style section vary in different OpenOffice.org components. In Calc, for instance, there are only two style buttons, where Writer has five buttons. These style buttons control the contents of the Style list in terms of the object type to which the styles apply. This differs

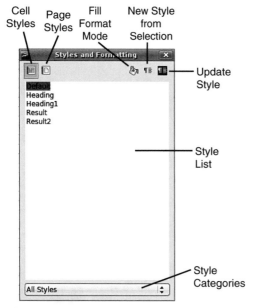

Figure 16.8
The Calc Styles and Formatting toolbar.

Table 16.4 The Calc Styles and Formatting Toolbar Buttons

Name	Function
Cell Styles	Changes the Style List display to available cell styles.
Page Styles	Changes the Style List display to available page (or sheet) styles.
Fill Format Mode	Changes cursor to Fill mode. Clicking a cell or page applies the selected style to that object.
New Style by Example	Records the style of the current cell or page and activates the Create Style dialog box to name the new style.
Update Style	If you change an existing style, updates all instances of that style in the document.

from the Style Category list at the bottom of the Styles and Formatting toolbar window. This list controls the Style list as well by further categorizing the available styles. Table 16.4 details the functions of the buttons within the Calc Styles and Formatting toolbar.

The best way to understand how the Styles and Formatting toolbar works is to see it in action.

1. In an open Calc spreadsheet, open the Styles and Formatting toolbar window by clicking the Styles and Formatting toolbar button on the Formatting toolbar.

2. Select any cell with data in the spreadsheet.

3. Double-click the Heading style in the Styles and Formatting toolbar. The Heading style formats the cell.

4. Click the Fill Format Mode button in the Styles and Formatting toolbar.

5. Select the Default style in the Styles and Formatting toolbar.

6. With the cursor now appearing as a paint can, click the cell with Heading style. The style of the cell changes to Default.

Default Style Differences

Notice in Figure 16.9 that the Default style may not conform to the default text style your spreadsheet already possesses.

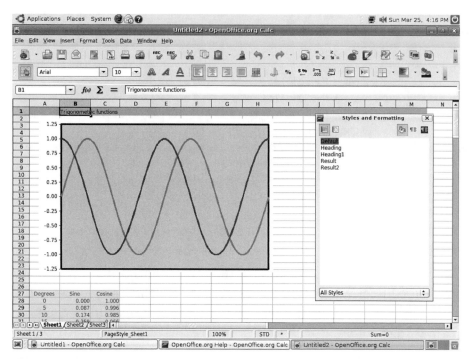

Figure 16.9
Calc's Default style may not be the same as the default style you've used in your spreadsheet.

7. Select a cell that contains data with your preferred default style of text.

8. Click the New Style from Selection button in the Styles and Formatting toolbar.

9. In the Create Style dialog box, enter Cell Text as a style name.

10. Click OK.

11. Apply the new Cell Text style to the Default style cell created in Step 6 using either the double-click or Fill Format mode methods.

The Navigator window is also nice to have around in Calc. As in Writer, the Navigator lists all of the objects within a spreadsheet and allows you to navigate to them with a few clicks of the mouse.

Figure 16.10 shows a typical Calc Navigator window. Right away you can see it is not as complex as the Navigator in Writer. It is no less useful, however.

Table 16.5 lists the functions of each of the buttons within the Navigator.

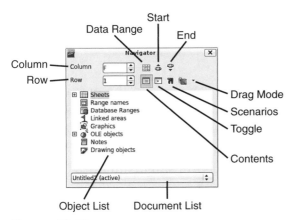

Figure 16.10
The Navigator in Calc is more streamlined than some of its OpenOffice.org counterparts.

Table 16.5 The Calc Navigator

Name	Function
Column	Lists the column letter of a selected cell. Values entered in this field (either directly or with the spin box controls) move the cursor to that column.
Row	Lists the row number of a selected cell. Values entered in this field (either directly or with the spin box controls) move the cursor to that row.
Data Range	Selects entire data area in the active spreadsheet.
Begin	Selects cell in upper-left corner of data area.
End	Selects cell in lower-right corner of data area.
Contents	Turns Object List in the Navigator on or off.
Toggle	Shifts Object List view to show only the current object type selected.
Scenarios	Changes Object List to a list of all scenarios associated with the active spreadsheet.
Drag Mode	Chooses the end result of click-and-drag actions of moving objects between documents.
Object List	Lists all elements contained within the active document.
Document List	Lists all open documents in Calc, distinguishing between active and inactive documents.

Not Just One Sheet

The perceived universe has three dimensions: length, height, and depth. Some people define time as the fourth dimension, and scientists have theorized about the existence of objects called superstrings that may vibrate through as many as 11 dimensions, which is enough to make nonscientists' heads hurt.

For now, we'll apply just the three-dimension analogy to Calc. Now that you have mastered the existence of the two-dimensional spreadsheet, it's time to venture into the third dimension: multiple spreadsheets.

The origin of multiple spreadsheets goes all the way back to the paper spreadsheets we talked about earlier in the book. When the early spreadsheets grew so large—with hundreds and thousands of rows and columns—some accountant-types got the idea to start layering some of the calculations onto other sheets. In this manner, spreadsheets didn't grow to huge sizes but still maintained the detail the accountants wanted.

When electronic spreadsheets were created, this methodology carried over. Even though size is a less pressing issue on a computer screen thanks to scrolling, most people still find it cumbersome not to see all of the data in a reasonable area. And, because we often print electronic spreadsheets, they still relate to the old paper medium.

When using multiple spreadsheets, it is important to remember how the sheets interconnect (if at all). Some people simply place unrelated datasets on each sheet, while others use related data with many cross-references. If you do use cross-references between multiple sheets, be careful that you don't inadvertently erase or change a piece of data that a cell on another sheet needs.

The use of multiple sheets is pretty simple. To view another sheet, simply click its sheet tab near the bottom of the screen. If you want to select more than one sheet (useful for printing), click a tab and hold the Shift key while clicking another tab. The two tabs and any in between them become selected. To select nonadjacent tabs, hold the Ctrl key while clicking.

New Calc documents have three sheets by default. Sometimes you may need more (or fewer) sheets. The next steps guide you through this procedure.

1. In an open Calc document, right-click the sheet tab adjacent to the location where you want to insert a new sheet.

2. Choose Insert Sheet from the context menu. The Insert Sheet dialog box will open.

3. In the Position area of the Insert Sheet dialog box (see Figure 16.11), select the After Current Sheet radio button.

4. Select the New Sheet radio button.

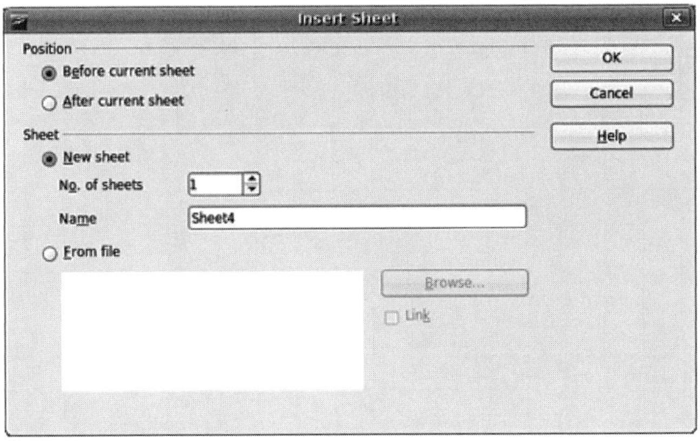

Figure 16.11
This dialog box allows you to create new sheets or borrow sheets from other documents.

5. Leave the No. of Sheets value at 1 and enter a new name for the sheet in the Name field.

6. Click OK. The new sheet appears, as seen in Figure 16.12.

7. Right-click another sheet tab.

8. Choose Delete Sheet from the context menu.

9. When asked if you are sure you want to delete the selected sheet, click Yes. The sheet is removed from the spreadsheet document.

Besides being able to create new sheets from scratch, Calc can import whole sheets from other documents. This is more effective and faster than cutting and pasting a data area from one document to another.

1. In an open Calc document, right-click the sheet tab adjacent to the location where you want to insert a new sheet.

2. Choose Insert Sheet from the context menu.

3. In the Position area of the Insert Sheet dialog box, select the After Current Sheet radio button.

4. Click the From File radio button.

5. Click the Browse button to locate the correct file in the Insert dialog box.

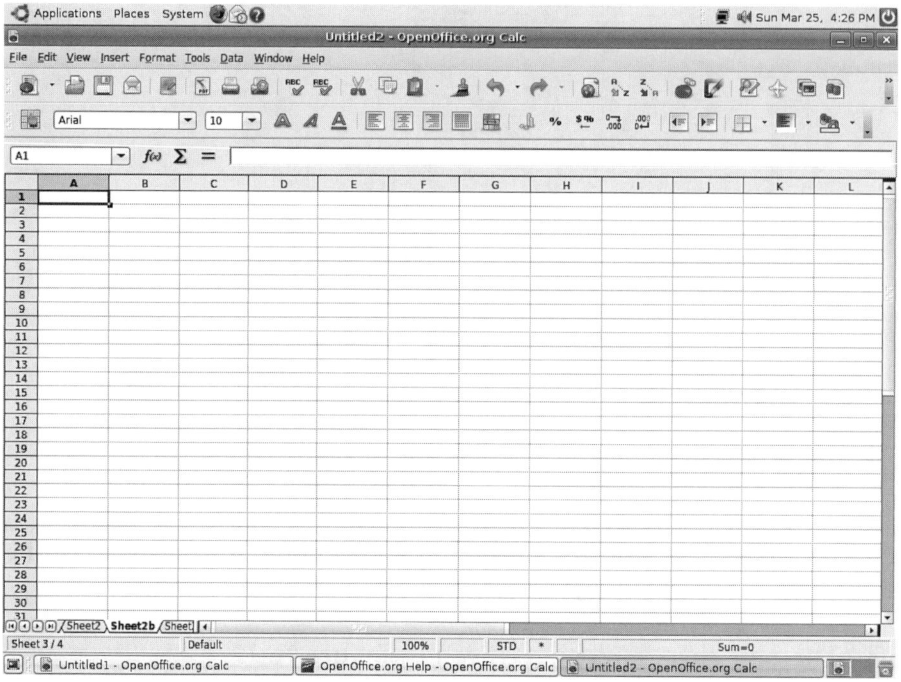

Figure 16.12
The new sheet, ready for data entry.

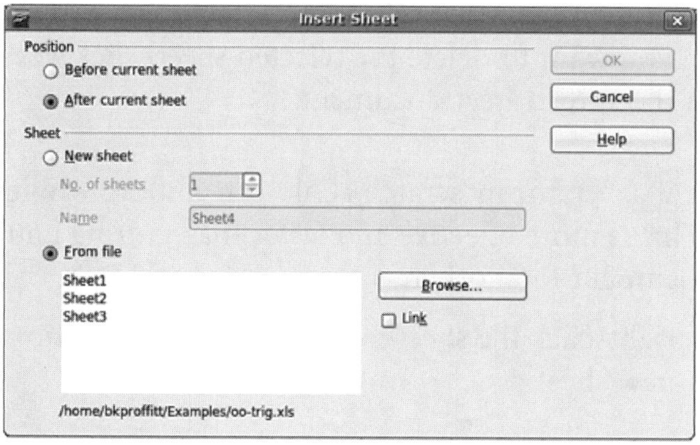

Figure 16.13
Choose from a list of sheets to place in your document.

6. Click Open in the Insert dialog box. The Insert Sheet dialog box now displays a list of the available sheets in the second file in the From File list (see Figure 16.13).

7. Select the desired sheet.

8. Click OK. The new sheet from the other document appears within the active document.

Cross-Reference Check

If your newly imported sheet has any cross-references to other sheets, particularly in its former home, those cross-references will become invalid. Check your new sheet thoroughly.

With all of these sheets flying around in the document, you likely need to perform some of the usual housekeeping functions to keep your documents looking neat and orderly.

Moving, copying, and renaming sheets is a piece of cake in Calc, as you will see in the next steps.

1. In an open Calc document, right-click the sheet tab you would like to move.

2. Click Move/Copy Sheet on the context menu.

3. In the Move/Copy Sheet dialog box (see Figure 16.14), be sure that the active document appears in the To Document field.

4. In the Insert Before list, select the sheet that you want to put your selected sheet in front of.

5. Click OK. The sheet moves to its new location.

To copy a sheet to another location in the spreadsheet, repeat Steps 1–4 and then continue with the following procedure.

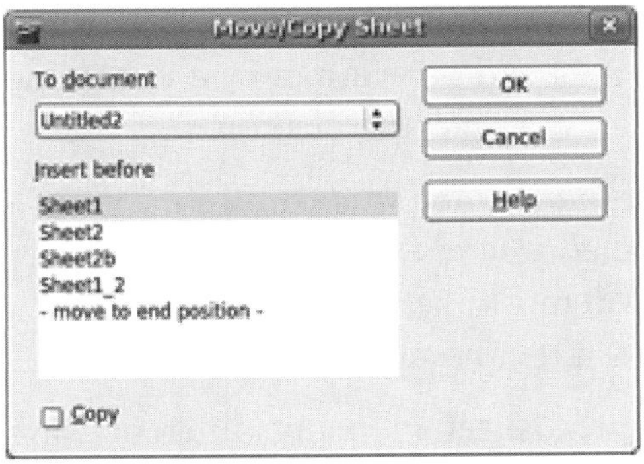

Figure 16.14
The Move/Copy Sheet dialog box.

1. Select the Copy check box.

2. Click OK. A copy of the sheet moves to its new location.

Sending Spreadsheets

To send a sheet or a copy of a sheet to another document, select the destination spreadsheet document in the To Document list, and then complete the steps to move or copy a sheet.

3. A copy of a sheet takes the name of the original sheet, followed by the copy number. To rename this copy, right-click the copied sheet's tab.

4. Click Rename Sheet in the context menu.

5. In the Rename Sheet dialog box, enter the new name in the Name field.

6. Click OK. The sheet now has the new name.

Good-Looking Data

The human body has several quirks that we have to put up with daily. One of them is the wandering eye. This is not the wandering eye that gets people in trouble. Rather, it is the inability of our eyes to stay focused in any one place for almost any length of time.

Our eyes, it seems, always have to be moving, soaking up the world around us. This translates into the need to create documents that attract our eyes so that they naturally want to look at the words on the page. It helps that in most cultures, lettering attracts the eye, even if we can't figure out the words. Though this is a learned response, the attraction doesn't keep the eyes there for long. It becomes necessary, therefore, to keep the interest with something other than just letters. Sometimes it's done by using outstanding content and other times by eye-catching colors (yellow fire trucks get more attention, for example, than red ones).

One thing that eyes—and the brain behind them—detest is confusion. Place a jumbled document or spreadsheet before someone, and the frustration level goes through the roof. At that point, the person will most likely ignore the document. Our visual system wants things to be simple and consistent.

You can establish consistency in a Calc spreadsheet in many different ways beyond the obvious use of colors and fills. One method is to use consistent formatting of data. In this context, the format of data refers to the way it appears.

For instance, time can be expressed in many different ways. Right now, as I write these words, it is Sunday, March 25, 2007, 4:37 in the afternoon, Eastern Daylight Time. Or is it 1637 hrs on 25/03/07? Time can be presented in thousands of different formats. You are free to choose whichever kind of format you want, but it is important to maintain consistency. If you use a 12:34 p.m. format in one cell with time data, then you should use the same format in other time data cells.

Time is just one of the values in Calc that can have different formats. Dates, text, numbers, and currency can all be displayed in different ways, as you will learn in the next sections.

Formatting Text

Text formats are perhaps the simplest to understand. Calc handles text in much the same way as Writer. Each cell can hold over 64,000 characters of text, so you can create whole documents within cells. But why would you want to?

You accomplish text formatting using the same tools found within Writer, with some additional functions designed specifically for cell use.

1. Within an open Calc spreadsheet, select a cell with data.

2. Click the Bold button on the Formatting toolbar.

3. Enter **24** into the Font Size field.

4. Choose Format | Cells.

5. Click the Alignment tab in the Format Cells dialog box (see Figure 16.15).

6. In the Text Orientation area, click the Vertically Stacked check box.

7. Click OK. Figure 16.16 shows the newly formatted text.

You can also have text auto-wrap within a cell.

1. In an empty cell within the spreadsheet, enter a lengthy text passage. A small red triangle indicates the presence of overflow text.

2. Choose Format | Cells.

3. Click the Alignment tab in the Format Cells dialog box.

4. Select the Wrap Text Automatically check box.

5. Click OK. The lengthy text passage appears in full within the cell.

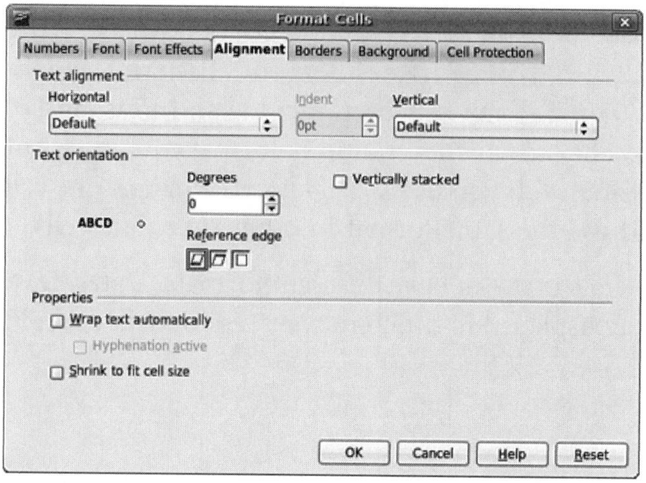

Figure 16.15
The Format Cells dialog box lets you choose the alignment of text within a cell.

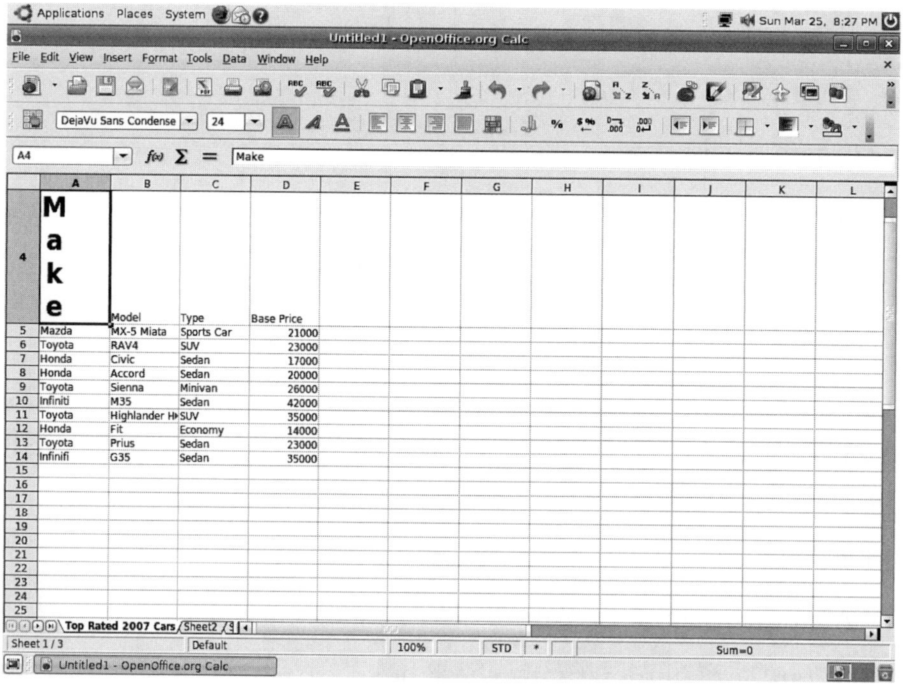

Figure 16.16
Vertical text in a spreadsheet.

Formatting Values

Politicians love to talk about values. We need to get back to traditional values, they say. But whose tradition? European? Asian? African? There is no one answer.

Nor is there one way to display data values. The different time formats have already been shown. Numbers, too, can be expressed in different ways. One dataset may project a significant value to the hundredths place, while another projects it to the thousandths place.

Even in the English-speaking cultures, numbers carry different names. In the United States, citizens refer to 1,000,000,000 as a billion. In the United Kingdom, a billion is officially 1,000,000,000,000,000,000. Advocates of the Queen's English refer to this as yet another example of the insidious U.S. corruption of the English language. Quite.

Within a spreadsheet, it may not be obvious to readers what is a data value and what is text. Is that 1999 in cell C3 indicative of a year, one short of 2,000 items, or the brand-name of a new company? The next steps show one quick way to find out.

1. With a Calc spreadsheet open, click Tools | Options.

2. In the Options dialog box, select the OpenOffice.org Calc | View menu tree options (see Figure 16.17).

3. Select the Value Highlighting check box in the Display section of the dialog box.

4. Click OK. The spreadsheet now displays all data values in a new color.

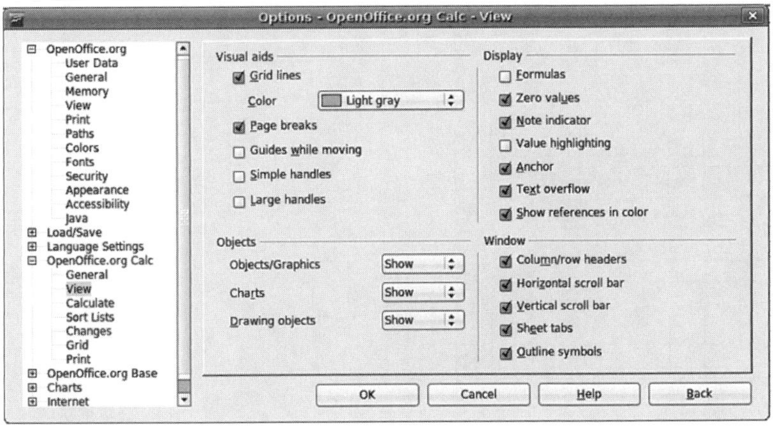

Figure 16.17
The View page of the Options dialog box.

Formatting Numbers

"Mathematics," Galileo Galilei once said, "is the alphabet with which God has written the universe." This means that we had better be really careful with how we present our numbers. You never know who might be checking your work.

One other thing: Number formats vary from nation to nation, so if you create a spreadsheet for readers in another country, try to accommodate their conventions as a courtesy. These steps demonstrate how to modify the format of a numeric value within a spreadsheet.

1. In an open Calc spreadsheet, select a cell with a numeric data value.

2. Choose Format | Cells.

3. In the Format Cells dialog box, click the Numbers tab (see Figure 16.18).

4. Select Currency in the Category list.

5. Select the −$1234.00 option in the Format list. A preview of the selected number appears in the Preview window, and the values in the Options area change to correspond to the selected format.

6. Click OK.

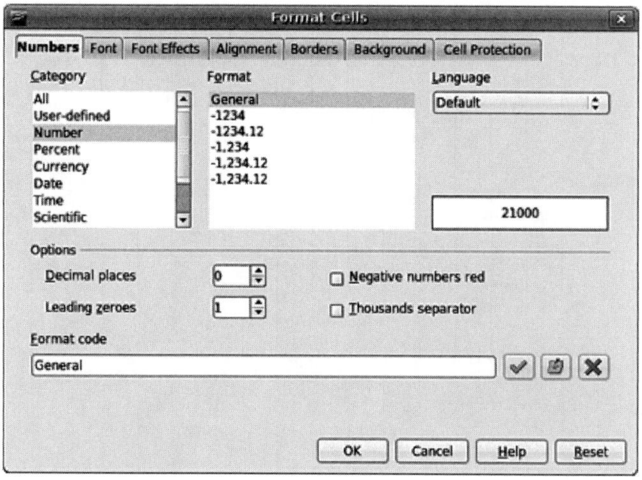

Figure 16.18
Setting numeric value formats.

Formatting Date and Time

Most people over the age of 30 remember the way they were taught to tell time. The little hand on the three and the big hand on the twelve meant 3:00.

These days, you can hardly find a clock that tells time in analog fashion.

Agreement on timekeeping is still a hot issue in international circles. While most countries have adopted the Gregorian calendar for trade purposes, many countries still have their own calendars and dates. And to make it more confusing, dates displayed from the same calendar can be shown in different ways. In the U.S., 4/19/07 translates to 19.4.07 in Europe.

Calc takes this all in stride and lets you choose your preferred method of displaying dates and times—at least those based on the Gregorian calendar. These steps show how to modify the format of date and time values within a spreadsheet.

1. Enter your date of birth into an empty cell within any open Calc document. Use any number-based format.

2. Select the cell.

3. Choose Format | Cells.

4. In the Format Cells dialog box, click the Numbers tab.

5. Select Date in the Category list.

6. Select the Friday, December 31, 1999 option in the Format list. In the Preview window, you can see the day of the week on which you were born.

7. To convert the date to an hour-based format, select Time in the Category list.

8. Select the 876613:37:46.00 option in the Format list.

9. Click OK. Now you can see the number of hours, minutes, and seconds that have passed between midnight, January 1, 1900, and your birthday.

Formatting Currency

Now for the nitty-gritty stuff. What do accountants, the originators of spreadsheets, count most of all?

Money.

The next steps show how Calc not only formats currency values, but also does so in a very cosmopolitan manner.

1. In an open Calc spreadsheet, select a cell with a numeric or currency data value.

2. Choose Format | Cells.

3. In the Format Cells dialog box, click the Numbers tab.

4. Select Currency in the Category list.

5. The Format list has two fields: a list of nations and a list of available formats for that nation. Select € Italian (Italy) in the top drop-down list.

6. Select the −€1234.− option.

7. Click OK. The value now appears in Euros.

Even though Calc offers a plethora of both common and esoteric formats, some day you may need to create your own, as the following steps demonstrate.

1. With any Calc spreadsheet open, select Format | Cells.

2. In the Format Cells dialog box, click the Numbers tab.

3. Select Percent in the Category list.

4. Select the −12.95% option in the Format list.

5. Select the Negative Numbers Red check box. Information now appears in the Format Code field.

6. Click the Edit Comment button, which has a note icon and is immediately to the right of the Format Code field.

7. Change the User-Defined value to Red Percent.

8. Click the Add button. You have now added the format to the Percent and User-Defined categories.

Formatting Cells

Thus far, the previous sections in this chapter have concerned themselves with formatting the data contained within a cell, but not the cell itself.

Formatting cells goes beyond just making the data look pretty. Recall that the human eye needs to have something to keep it focused. Following a long row of data across a screen is very difficult if nothing keeps the eye from wandering up or down into the adjacent rows.

With the judicious addition of fills and borders, you can help the eye track data across a screen.

All cells have borders. Sometimes the borders are invisible, but they are always there, like the air we breathe.

Cell borders can come in all of the available OpenOffice.org colors and can be as thick as 9 pts. I don't recommend that you use such an extreme width on individual cell borders, as you will obscure the cell's contents. But you may find uses for all of the various thicknesses.

Cell fills are also referred to as backgrounds for cells. These, too, come in a vast variety of colors. Care should be taken, however, to avoid the darker shades, as these obscure the text as well. But if you do use a dark fill color, you can change the text color to increase the contrast between text and background.

As you create your own fills, try to keep the number of different colors to a maximum of three shades. More than that could lead to confusing data representation and a frustrated brain.

1. Open a Calc document.

2. Select a range of cells one column wide.

3. Choose Format | Cells.

4. In the Format Cells dialog box, click the Borders tab, as seen in Figure 16.19.

5. In the Preview window, click the areas immediately to the right of and below the gray box. Solid lines appear in the Preview window.

6. In the Style list, select the 2.50 pt option.

7. In the Color field in the Line group, select Blue.

8. In the Shadow group, click the second Position preset button.

9. In the Color field in the Shadow group, select Orange 4.

10. Click OK. A partially blue box with an orange shadow appears around the selected range, as shown in Figure 16.20.

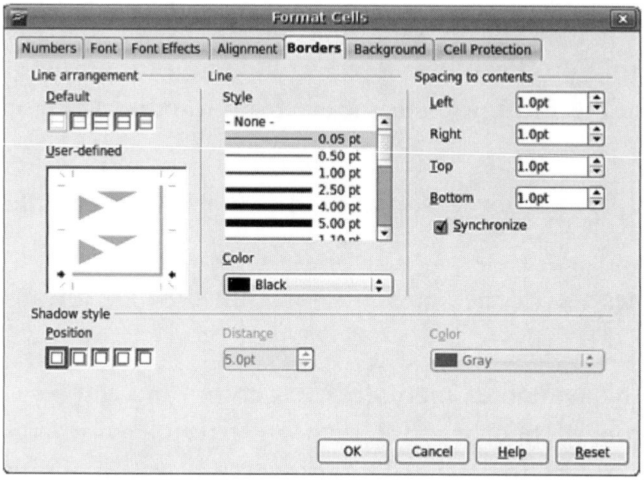

Figure 16.19
Making a run for the border.

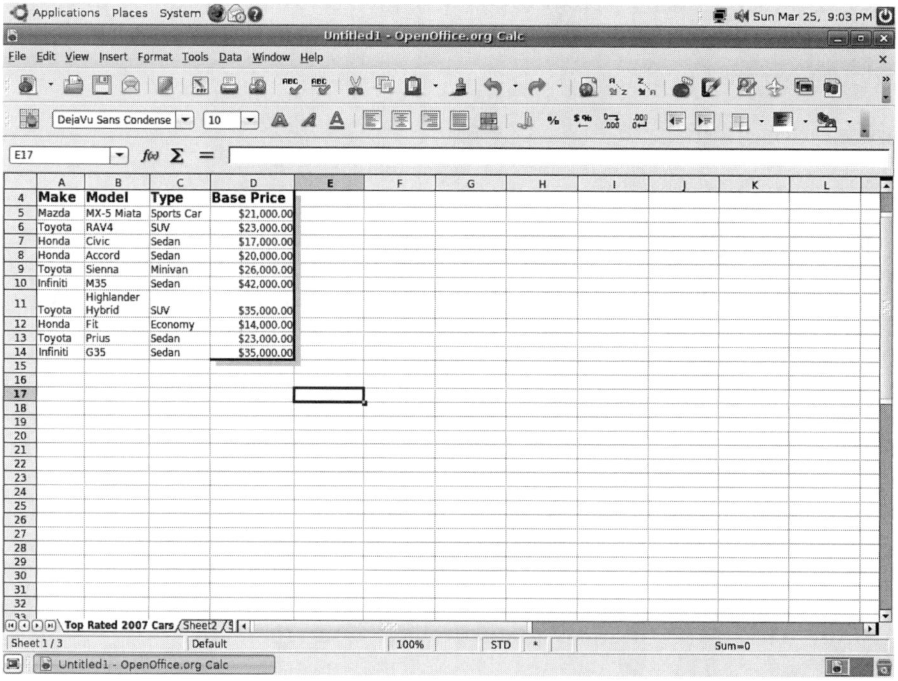

Figure 16.20
Interesting shadow effects can be achieved.

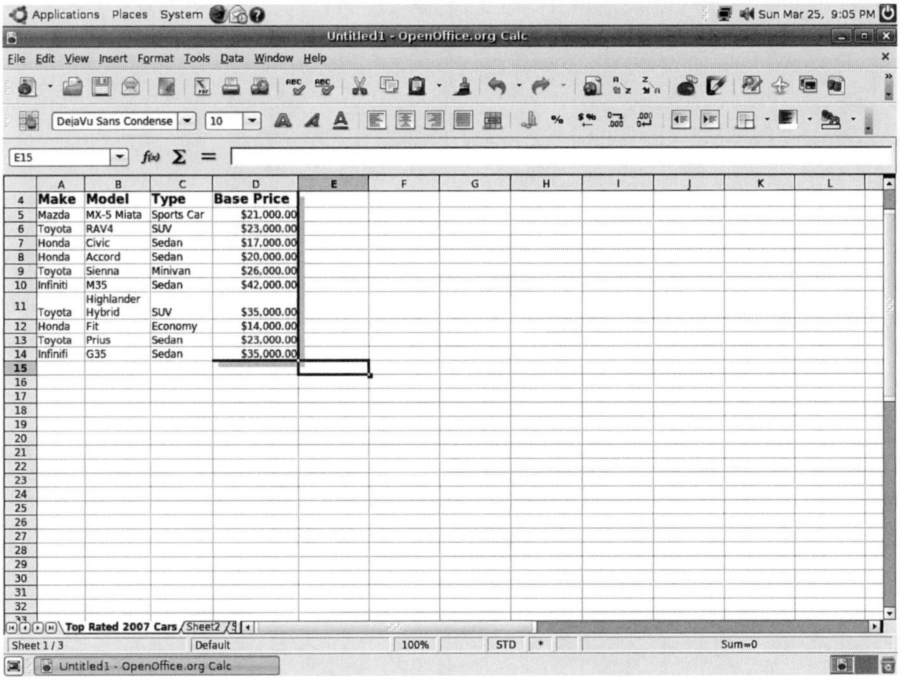

Figure 16.21
A cell range with no sense of style.

11. With the same range selected, repeat Steps 3 and 4, except this time click the Background tab.

12. Select Yellow.

13. Click OK. Figure 16.21 illustrates the end result of this task.

Formatting Ranges

To apply borders and fills quickly, click and hold the respective buttons on the Formatting toolbar.

Conclusion

Calc is an effective tool for the creation and management of data spreadsheets. This chapter reviewed many of the basic concepts of Calc, and as you explore this application in your continued use of Ubuntu, you will find it to be a very powerful tool.

Chapter 17, "Presenting with Impress," will move on to review an Open-Office.org component that will enable you to present your ideas to the world in new and attractive ways: Impress.

CHAPTER 17

PRESENTING WITH IMPRESS

They're not called meetings anymore, you know. The "in" business crowd refers to them as *collaboration sessions* or *team discussions*.

Nor are these discussions held in traditional conference rooms. More and more, corporations are turning away from the same old long table and swivel chairs in favor of more comfortable surroundings.

Corporations around the world have begun to recognize that how we meet is at least as important as why we meet.

Why we meet is to trade new ideas and improve the condition of the environment we share with others. (That, and free donuts.) And fancy collaborative fads aside, meetings work better when the many settle down and listen to one person every once in a while.

This means that one person has to get up and speak before the many. Oftentimes, this person speaks with informal, impromptu statements. But sometimes, the person will give a full-fledged presentation. And that is where OpenOffice.org's Impress application comes into play.

The Second Greatest Fear

Some people are good at presentations. They stand up in front of everyone else and mesmerize us with their logic, charisma, and charm. No notes, no slides—just the person and his vision.

The rest of us may require a little assistance. In a public speech, the power of the speaker's words is the only thing that can help people remember the speaker's message. Have you ever noticed how politicians always work some sort of catch phrase into their speeches? They are not trying to be trite—they're trying to give their audiences something to remember, because our memory and sense of hearing do not always work well together.

In a private business setting, where a lot of detail may be required, entirely verbal presentations would be impossible for others to remember later. So speakers have two choices: reduce the presentation to its mere essence to get the overall points across or rely on some other form of communication to get the finer points of the message to the audience.

Since many people fear public speaking second only to death, most would rather not become fiery orators in order to get their points across. Which leaves the second option: use another way to communicate. We simply remember things better if we have seen them with our own two eyes.

Thus, the corporate slide show was born.

It started off with placards at first, showing charts created by people whose job was to do nothing but show the charts. Overheads were used next, lending presenters the ability to support their points on the fly. Then came slides, which added color and speed to presentations. Finally, the slides were created directly on a computer and projected from there, as well.

Which brings us to the component in OpenOffice.org that gets this job done for you: Impress.

Learning the Tools to Use

The makers of Impress have loaded it with dozens of interesting tools that help you build incredible presentations with ease. This is readily apparent when looking at the Impress interface (see Figure 17.1).

Within Impress, you can choose from six views when working with your presentation. Five of these views enable you to edit your presentation in different ways. The sixth lets you view your presentation from start to finish. Figure 17.1 highlights the view controls in the center of the interface. Table 17.1 outlines the different views and their purposes.

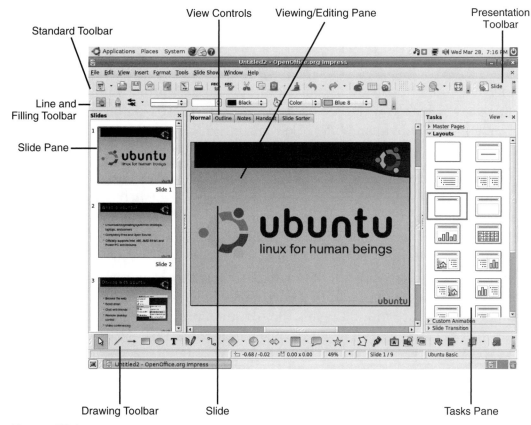

Figure 17.1
The Impress interface in Drawing view.

Table 17.1 The Impress Views

View	Function
Normal	The default (and primary) view in Impress where you edit slides on an individual level.
Outline	This view enables the creation and editing of the presentation's outline, which the slides directly reflect.
Notes	Many presenters need notes to guide them through their presentation. Use this view to create such notes.
Handout	Sometimes handouts accompany presentations so the audience can follow along and create their own notes. This view enables the creation of presentation handouts.
Slide Sorter	Use the Slide Sorter view to shift the slide order in a presentation, if needed.
Slide Show	This read-only view shows the presentation in its entirety.

Each of the five Edit views in Impress has a different set of tools to use. The following sections will examine these tools.

Normal View

If any view could be called the center of Impress, the Normal view would be it. In this view (which you can see back in Figure 17.1), you do all of the editing and creating of individual slides. You enter text, apply slide transitions, add pictures—anything that can be done to a slide, you do here.

This translates, of course, into a large number of tools you can use. There are too many tools to devote a lot of words to each. To help guide you in the right direction, the following sections will highlight the main tools within the Normal view.

Standard Toolbar

In all views of Impress, only the Standard toolbar is almost always present, and it retains many of the same tools you have already seen in Writer and Calc. Only two new buttons are found on this toolbar, the Spreadsheet and Display Grid buttons, as seen in Figure 17.2 and explained in Table 17.2.

Line and Filling Toolbar

In most of the OpenOffice.org applications, the Formatting toolbar usually appears right underneath the Standard toolbar. In Impress, however, this is not always a given. In fact, the toolbar you might be familiar with and call Formatting only appears when you are specifically editing text in Impress. At all other times, the Line and Filling toolbar will appear in its stead. Figure 17.3 illustrates the Line

Figure 17.2
The Impress Standard toolbar.

Table 17.2 The Impress-Specific Standard Toolbar Buttons

Name	Function
Spreadsheet	Inserts a full-powered Calc spreadsheet inside a slide.
Display Grid	Shows a placement grid on the slide to assist with object and text alignment.

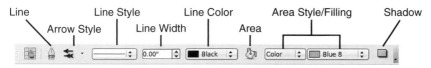

Figure 17.3
The Line and Filling toolbar.

Table 17.3 The Line and Filling Toolbar Buttons

Name	Function
Line	Opens the Line dialog box to control the attributes of a selected line.
Arrow Style	Applies arrow ends to a selected line or connector.
Line Style	Changes style of a selected line or connector.
Line Width	Changes width of a selected line or connector.
Line Color	Changes color of a selected line or connector.
Area	Opens the Area dialog box to control the attributes of a selected area.
Area Style/Filling	Two lists that control the fill type and color of a given area or background.
Shadow	Applies a shadow effect to a selected object.

and Filling toolbar as it appears when editing most Impress objects. Table 17.3 details the functions of the buttons within the Line and Filling toolbar.

Drawing Toolbar

The Drawing toolbar is a new toolbar for those of you reading this book cover to cover. You'll find it only within the Impress and Draw components. This toolbar contains a variety of features to customize the way you edit or create slides with Impress.

In the Drawing toolbar, the buttons focus on creating text and graphic objects on the slide. Many of the icons have submenus of options, vastly increasing the number of possible tools this single toolbar possesses. Figure 17.4 highlights the buttons on the Drawing toolbar, while Table 17.4 briefly explains the function of each button.

Presentation Toolbar

The Presentation toolbar is a control unique to Impress. Appropriately, it has unique properties. Unfortunately, in the default Impress view, this powerful toolbar is sort of shoved off to one side, as you saw back in Figure 17.1. To see it more clearly, let's undock it (see Figure 17.5). Like all docked toolbars, you can undock it by clicking and dragging the toolbar handle.

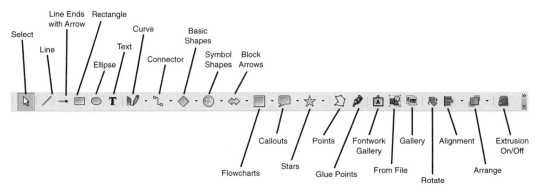

Figure 17.4
The Drawing toolbar.

Table 17.4 The Drawing Toolbar Buttons

Name	Function
Select	Activates the selection cursor.
Line	Accesses tools to create lines and filled lines in floating toolbar.
Line Ends with Arrow	Creates lines and arrows using floating toolbar.
Rectangle	Enables creation of rectangular graphic objects.
Ellipse	Enables creation of elliptical graphic objects.
Text	Activates the Text Formatting toolbar.
Curve	Enables creation of curved lines.
Connector	Enables creation of connectors between other graphic objects.
Basic Shapes	Enables creation of basic geometric shapes.
Symbol Shapes	Enables creation of symbols on slides.
Block Arrows	Enables creation of large, 2-D arrow shapes.
Flowcharts	Enables creation of standard flowchart shapes.
Callouts	Enables creation of callout shapes.
Stars	Enables creation of star shapes.
Points	Edits the control points of a selected object.
Glue Points	Edits the glue points of a selected connector.
Fontwork Gallery	Inserts stylized word-based artwork.
From File	Inserts artwork into a slide from a file.
Gallery	Activates the OpenOffice.org gallery of images and artwork.
Rotate	Enables the rotation of a selected object.
Alignment	Aligns selected object to the slide.
Position	Directs position of object layering with other objects on the slide.
Extrusion On/Off	Activates 3-D extrusion of a selected object.

Figure 17.5
The Presentation toolbar.

Table 17.5 The Presentation Toolbar Buttons

Name	Function
Slide	Inserts a new slide after the selected slide.
Slide Design	Allows a new slide design to be exchanged with the current slide's design.
Slide Show	Starts the Slide Show view of Impress.

All of the buttons on the Presentation toolbar have text labels, so you can easily ascertain which button does what. Table 17.5 details the purposes of the buttons on this small toolbar.

Outline View

The Outline view in Impress facilitates the entry of clean and well-organized text within the slides. Because all of the text in the slides belongs to one big outline, this is a key view to use in Impress. The points on the screen should support and organize your presentation, not repeat it word for word.

The tools and interface in the Outline view are rather simple, since the Normal view handles most of the formatting and special effects. Figure 17.6 reveals a look at the Outline view.

As you can see in Figure 17.6, the Standard toolbar remains the same, and the Line and Filling, Drawing, and Presentation toolbars are not present at all—nor is the Tasks pane. In place of the Line and Filling toolbar is the Text Formatting toolbar, and the Presentation toolbar has been swapped out by the Outline toolbar.

The way the Outline view functions is simple: When one of the slide icons is selected in the Slides pane, the corresponding top-level heading in the outline is highlighted.

The toolbars in this view also provide a unique set of tools to work with.

Outline Toolbar

The number of icons on the Outline toolbar has been heavily curtailed in the Outline view. Again, this is fine, since this view only needs a simple text editor.

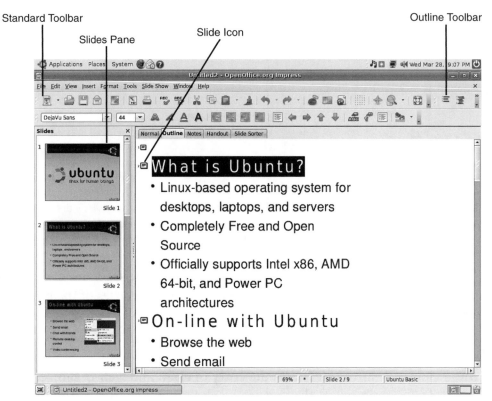

Figure 17.6
The Impress Outline view.

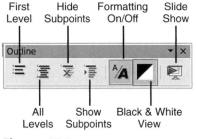

Figure 17.7
The Outline toolbar.

Figure 17.7 focuses on the Outline toolbar, and Table 17.6 details the buttons' functionality.

Text Formatting Toolbar

As mentioned previously, in the Outline View there is no Line and Filling toolbar. Instead, the Text Formatting toolbar takes its place. This toolbar is very

Table 17.6 The Outline Toolbar Buttons

Name	Function
First Level	Hides all levels in outline but first level.
All Levels	Shows all levels in outline.
Hide Subpoints	Hides any subpoints under selected outline paragraph.
Show Subpoints	Shows all subpoints under selected outline paragraph.
Formatting On/Off	Displays formatting of slide text in Outline view.
Black & White View	Displays all text in black and white, regardless of formatting.
Slide Show	Starts the Slide Show view.

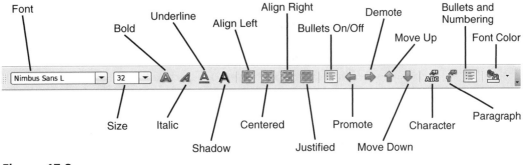

Figure 17.8
The Text Formatting toolbar.

similar in formation to the usual Formatting toolbar that appears in other OpenOffice.org applications. But it has enough new tools to warrant its own name and place in the Impress toolbar collection. As you can see in Figure 17.8, much is familiar about the Text Formatting toolbar. Table 17.7 discusses the new toolset.

Notes and Handout Views

The controls in the Notes and Handout views are nearly identical to the ones in the Normal view.

As you can see in Figures 17.9 and 17.10, the one significant difference in the controls is the disabling of buttons in the Presentation toolbar.

The Notes view presents each slide individually on a single sheet of paper. The slide covers the top half of the sheet, and the bottom half has a note box. Within this note box, you can enter any additional points or examples beyond your outline to assist during the actual presentation.

Table 17.7 The Text Formatting Toolbar Buttons

Name	Function
Font	Changes the font of selected text.
Size	Changes the font size of selected text.
Bold	Applies the bold style to selected text.
Italic	Applies the italic style to selected text.
Underline	Underlines selected text.
Shadow	Applies a shadow effect to selected text.
Align Left	Aligns selected paragraphs to left margin.
Centered	Centers selected paragraphs on page.
Align Right	Aligns selected paragraphs to right margin.
Justified	Justifies selected paragraphs to fill all space between margins.
Bullets On/Off	Changes selected paragraphs to a bulleted list.
Promote	Promotes selected paragraph to the next highest outline level.
Demote	Demotes selected paragraph to the next lowest outline level.
Move Up	Moves selected paragraph up in the text block.
Move Down	Moves selected paragraph down in the text block.
Character	Formats selected characters.
Paragraph	Formats selected paragraphs.
Bullets and Numbering	Formats bullets and numbering of selected list.
Font Color	Single-click applies displayed color to selected text. Click and hold reveals more colors to apply.

The Handout view is the simplest view of all. It simply displays a certain number of slides on a page that you can print and give to audience members to allow them to follow along. Handouts are very useful when giving a lot of detail in a presentation.

To change the number of slides displayed per page in the Handout view, click one of the alternative layouts displayed in the Tasks pane.

Slide Sort View

The Slide Sort view, illustrated in Figure 17.11, displays all of the slides in the presentation in miniature form. As the name suggests, this view offers an easy way to sort the order of the slides in the presentation.

The Slide View and Slide Sorter toolbars are something unique to this mode of Impress. Replacing the Line and Filling or Text Formatting toolbars, these small toolbars pack a lot of punch.

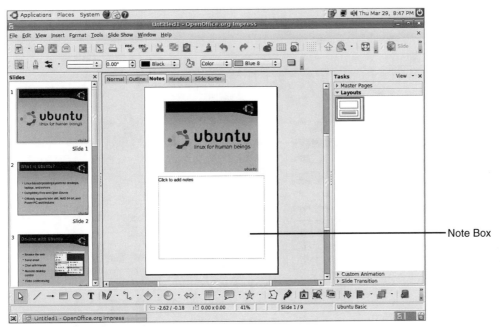

Figure 17.9
The Impress Notes view.

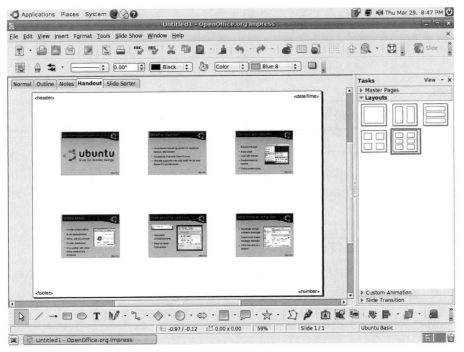

Figure 17.10
The Impress Handout view.

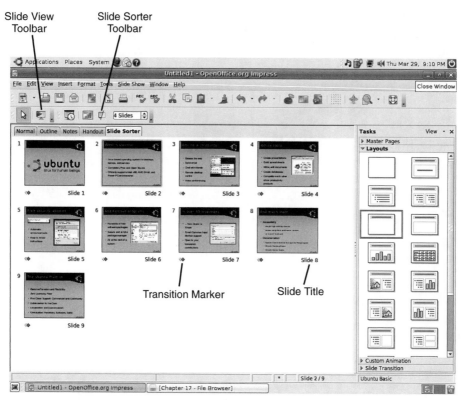

Figure 17.11
The Slide Sort view.

Back to Normal

Double-clicking any slide in the Slide Sort view opens that slide in the Normal view.

This view does more than just allow the sorting of slides. It also permits easy editing of the transitions between slides, among other things. The new Slide toolbars, which the next sections examine more closely, were created to accomplish these jobs.

Slide Sorter and Slide View Toolbars

Transitions are the effects that occur when moving from one slide to another, such as the sliding of one slide over the previous one.

Transition Beginnings

When editing transitions, bear in mind that you are editing the transition that *starts* the current slide.

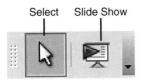

Figure 17.12
The Slide Sorter toolbar.

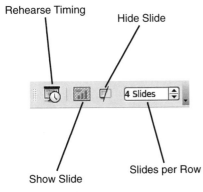

Figure 17.13
The Slide View toolbar.

Table 17.8 The Slide Sorter and View Toolbars Buttons

Name	Function
Select	Activates the selection cursor.
Slide Show	Activates the Slide Show view.
Rehearse Timing	Determines the timing for the slide by starting the Slide Show view with the addition of a timer that indicates the time to speak with this slide.
Show Slide	Shows the selected slide in the Slide Show view.
Hide Slide	Hides the selected slide in the Slide Show view.
Slides per Row	Enters the number of slides per row in this view.

Figure 17.12 shows the Slide Sorter toolbar in detail, while Figure 17.13 accomplishes the same thing for the Slide View toolbar. Table 17.8 explains the functionality of both of the toolbars' buttons.

Creating a Presentation

After you have figured out what to say, there are two opposing schools of thought when beginning a new presentation in Impress:

- Outline your presentation content first and worry about the design later.

- Create a blank design and fill in the text later.

There is no right way to do this, really. Each method has an equal number of pros and cons. It basically comes down to personal preferences: Do you like to organize your text first or your slides first?

If you are new to using Impress or a similar application, I recommend that you use the wizard to get things started. It's simple and quick. Plus, it's much easier to build a base of slide design and add content as needed.

1. From any application of OpenOffice.org, choose File | Wizards | Presentation. The Presentation Wizard dialog box will open (see Figure 17.14).

2. Select the From Template radio button. A list of presentation templates will appear.

3. Select the Recommendation of a Strategy option. The template will appear in the Preview window (see Figure 17.15).

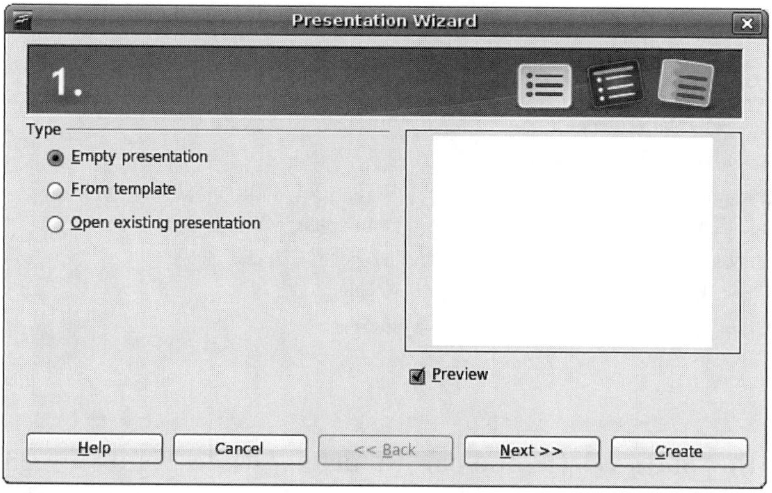

Figure 17.14
Starting the Presentation wizard.

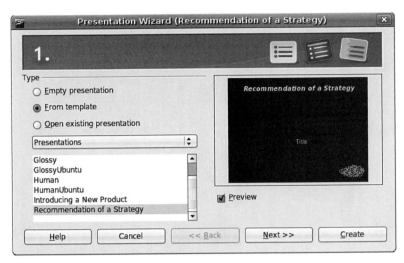

Figure 17.15
Impress has some nice templates to work with.

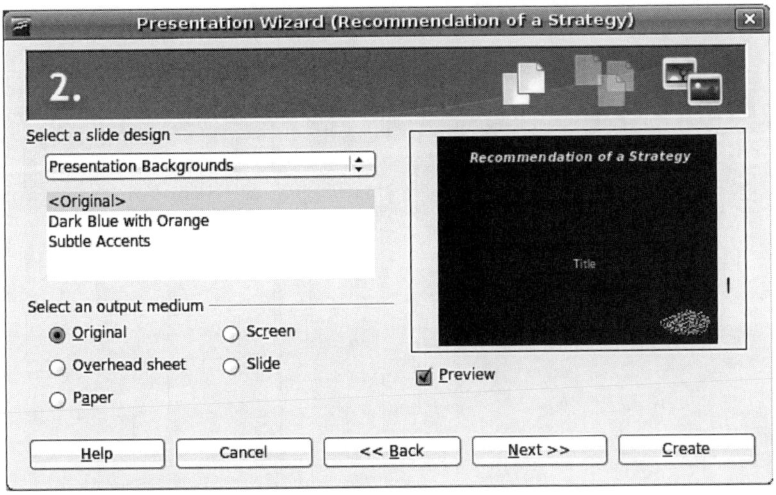

Figure 17.16
Choosing a background design.

4. Click Next. The Slide Design page will appear, as shown in Figure 17.16.

5. In the Select a Slide Design list, select the Subtle Accents option.

6. Select the Screen radio button for Select and Output Medium. A preview of the style appears in the Preview window (see Figure 17.17).

7. Click Next. The Transition page will appear (see Figure 17.18).

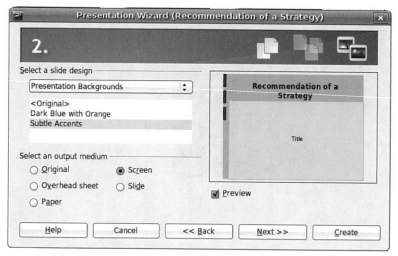

Figure 17.17
Different styles for the same template.

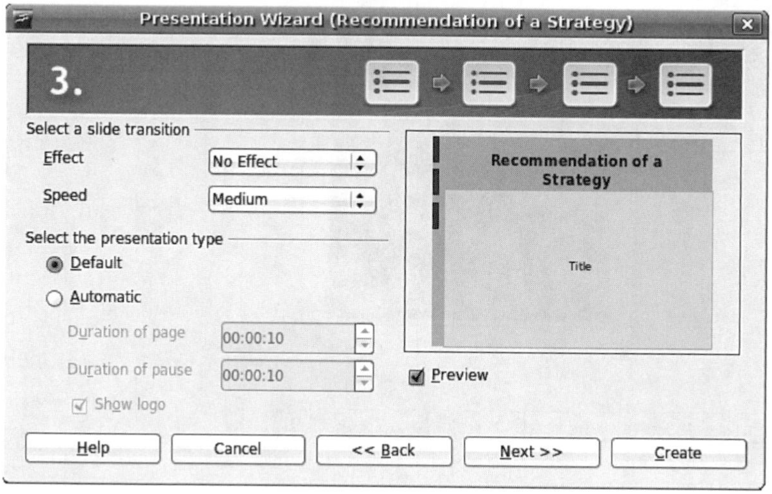

Figure 17.18
Transitions are configured here.

8. Select an option in the Effect drop-down list. An animation of the transition will appear in the Preview window for every effect you choose.

9. Select a Speed option. An animation of the transition will appear in the Preview window.

10. Click Next. The Content page will appear, as shown in Figure 17.19.

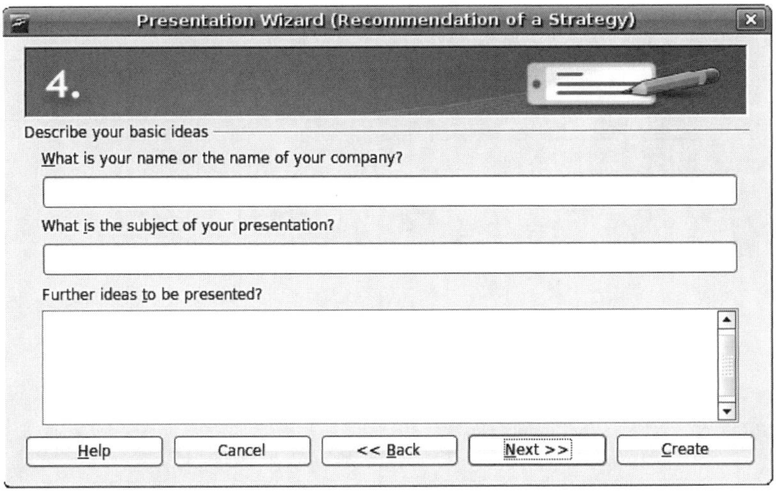

Figure 17.19
Basic content information can be entered here.

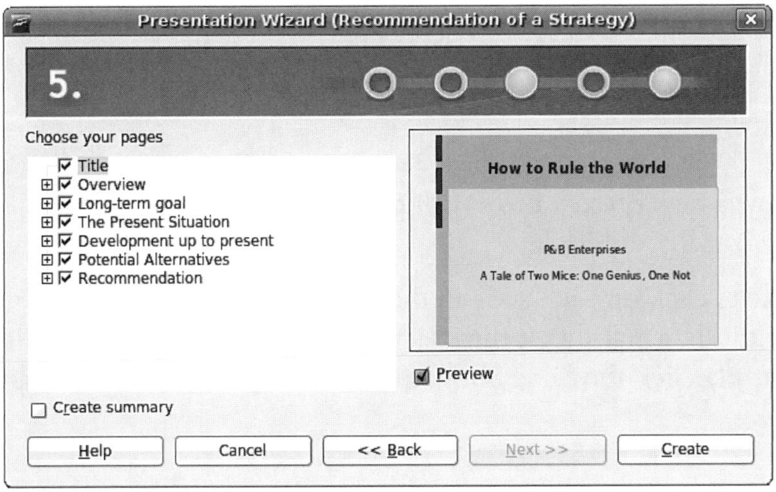

Figure 17.20
Choose the slides you want.

11. Enter the pertinent information in each field and then click Next. The Slide Selection page will appear (see Figure 17.20).

12. Use the expansion controls to see the contents of each slide. Select or clear the check boxes for the slides you do or do not need.

13. Click Create. The presentation will be created and displayed in Normal view.

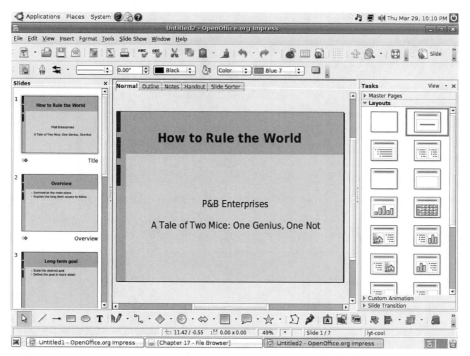

Figure 17.21
A new presentation for you to modify.

Figure 17.21 shows how a new presentation with placeholder slides based on the settings made in the wizard could look.

Now all you need to do is click on each slide in the Slide pane to view it and edit the slide's content in the Normal or Outline view. When your presentation is finished and saved, simply click the Slide Show icon in the Presentation toolbar to start the slide show.

Conclusion

In this chapter, you reviewed the wealth of tools contained within the Impress component.

In Chapter 18, we will take a look at one of the newest additions to the Open-Office.org application suite, one that you will definitely be able to use in your office or even home: the aptly named database application Base.

ORGANIZING WITH BASE

Fiction: Databases are big, evil, scary things. Somewhere in your professional career, you may have heard this rumor. Database administrators may be regarded with awe at your company. The simple truth is that anyone can make a database and understand how it works.

You will see for yourself in this chapter, as we explore the database component of OpenOffice.org, Base.

Database Concepts

Four different types of objects comprise databases. All of these objects working together make up the database. Any of them taken separately does not have much use.

These objects are tables, forms, queries, and reports. Before examining the workings of an actual database, it will help to review the functionality of each object.

You're probably already familiar with tables. They are essentially simplified spreadsheets. A database table is simpler because the purpose of the rows and columns is set, whereas a spreadsheet has more flexibility in how you can use rows and columns. Also, spreadsheets allow cells to interact with each other, whereas database tables don't. If you need mathematical comparisons made, put your data in a spreadsheet.

In a database table, each row is a database record. A database record is a collection of related data. In a database of books, for example, one record could be:

Ivanhoe, Sir Walter Scott, New American Library, September 1987

This record has five fields: Book Title, Author, Publisher, Published Month, and Published Year. All other records in this database table use the same fields. If a record needs to have more information, then the database table needs additional fields. In database programmer lingo, this is sometimes referred to as adding columns.

A form is the interface structure between the user and the table. Though you can directly enter data into a table (and some prefer this), a form gives the user visual cues to help enter data more quickly, rather than tediously tabbing across row after row of the database table.

At the very least, a good database needs tables and forms. If the database had just a table, it would be rather dull. If it had just a form, it would be only a shell surrounding nothingness.

Queries are little programming scripts that pull specific information out of a database. Don't panic if you don't think you can program anything. You can master queries once you understand the way they are structured. And Base has a wizard to help you with this.

Once a query has gathered information, it needs to be displayed. This is done in a report, the final piece of the database puzzle. Reports are, again, similar to spreadsheets, in that they typically present data in tabular form. Reports, however, are not interactive. They simply place the data requested by a query into a read-only file, which can be printed or displayed on screen. If data needs to be changed, it has to be done in the table (through the form).

Databases can have multiple versions of all of these objects. In a climatology database, you could have a table of known temperature highs and lows for a region and another table of rainfall amounts, each accessed by separate forms. The choices are limitless.

To start understanding databases at the day-to-day level, let's walk through the creation of a database to see how all of these components fit together.

Building Your Own Database

Databases are excellent tools to use in the business world. If you have a small business, creating a database to keep track of inventory or customers is a vital task. If you're using Ubuntu at home, a database could also come in handy. If you have a collection, you know how important it is to keep track of it. You may constantly acquire new items for the collection, trading with other hobbyists in order to finagle acquisition of the item you desire most.

Whether you use it for home or office, Base makes database creation simple.

To create a working database, you need to build the following items in this order:

1. Database file

2. Table

3. Form

You always need to build the database file first. You could, in theory, create the form before the table, but that would be cumbersome, and why do all the extra work?

The remainder of this chapter is devoted to the creation of a comic book collection database, which is, essentially, an inventory database. As you follow along, watch carefully and think about how you would like to build a database for your own needs.

Choosing Database Formats

OpenOffice.org is unique among office suites because of its compatibility with so many other programs. Base is no exception, having the capability to create and read databases in several formats beyond its native Base format:

- Adabas D

- dBASE

- Evolution LDAP

- Evolution Local

- Groupwise

- JDBC

- Microsoft Access

- MySQL

- ODBC

- Oracle JDBC

- Spreadsheet

- Text

Which format you choose depends on a couple of things. If you import data from another database in one of these formats, then you should select that format. You might also save a copy of the database in an alternate format if you intend to share the file with others who—heaven forbid—might not use OpenOffice.org or Ubuntu.

The following steps show the beginning of the database construction—specifically the first stage of creating a database in Base, which involves creating the main database file.

1. In any OpenOffice.org component, click File, New, Database. The Database wizard will open, as shown in Figure 18.1.

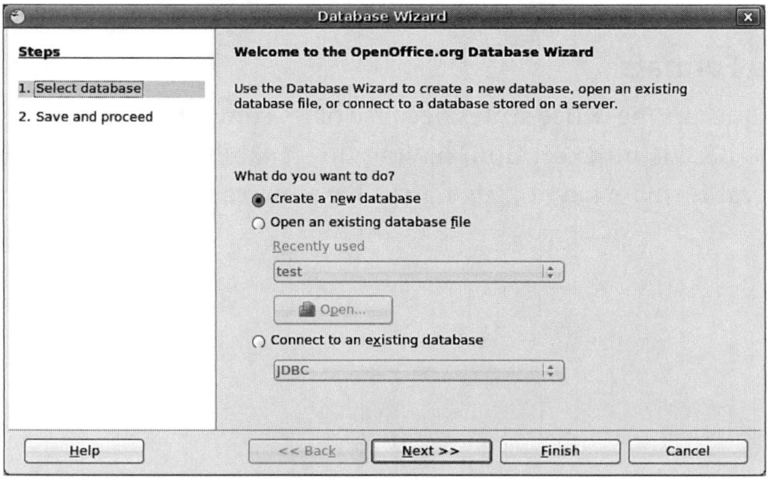

Figure 18.1
The first step in creating a database.

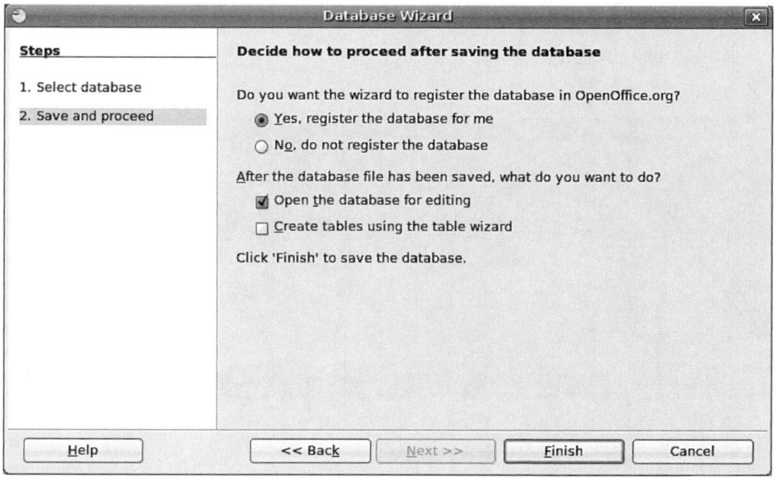

Figure 18.2
The second step in creating a database.

2. Click the Create a New Database radio button; then click Next. The Save and Proceed page will appear (see Figure 18.2).

Database Registration

Registering a database is something that all users should do with their database files. Registering will allow other applications to easily access your data when it is called upon. For instance, if you want to create a form letter and have a registered database of contact information, you will be able to refer to the data in that database much more easily.

3. Confirm that the Yes, Register the Database for Me radio button is selected.

4. Confirm that the Open the Database for Editing check box is selected.

5. Click Finish. The Save dialog box will open.

6. Type in a name for your new database file in the Name field.

7. Click Save. The Save dialog box will close, and the main Base window will open (see Figure 18.3).

Before we move on to create our database, it would be a good idea to examine the streamlined interface of Base. The window is divided into three primary areas, which were illustrated in Figure 18.3: the Database, Tasks, and Database Object panes.

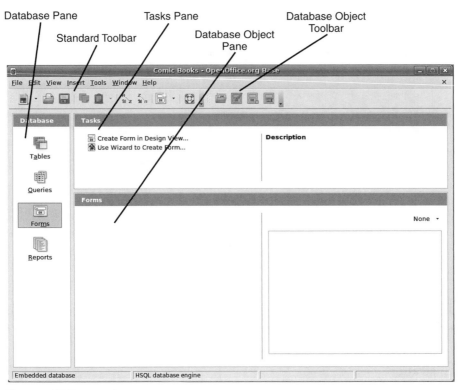

Figure 18.3
A new database, ready to begin.

In that same figure, you may have noticed that the Database Object pane is actually labeled "Forms." The fluid nature of the Base interface means that as certain database objects are worked with, the Database Object pane will change to reflect those objects. The Database Object toolbar and the contents of the Tasks pane will also be altered as different objects are handled. Try clicking on the different objects to see this in action.

In the Base window, only the Standard toolbar stays immutable, as shown in Figure 18.4.

Of these tools, the only one new to OpenOffice.org users is the Form button. Clicking it will begin the process of creating a form in the Design view of Writer, the application Base borrows to enable users to build forms by hand. Clicking the Form drop-down menu reveals a variety of tools, all designed to create various database components or view them.

The Database Objects toolbar has four versions, one for each object. It also has four buttons in each version: Open Database Object, Edit, Delete, and Rename,

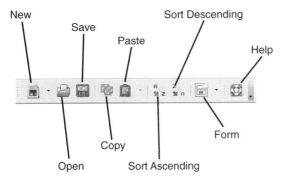

Figure 18.4
The Standard toolbar in Base.

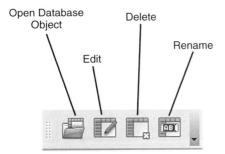

Figure 18.5
The Database Objects toolbar.

as seen in Figure 18.5. The functionality of these buttons is pretty straightforward, so we will not delve into them much further.

As you can see, the interface of Base is very simple. This is good because, as mentioned at the beginning of the chapter, traditionally database work has been regarded as complicated. And while it is true that manipulating data can be a complex process at times, Base's tools are not going to make it more complicated. In fact, the automated wizards in Base can create any component you need, which makes it even simpler.

Creating a Table

Now that you have created the database file and poked around the interface, it's time to put something in the database file. The logical place to start is creating the container to hold the data, which is the table. Using the Table wizard, here's how to create the database table.

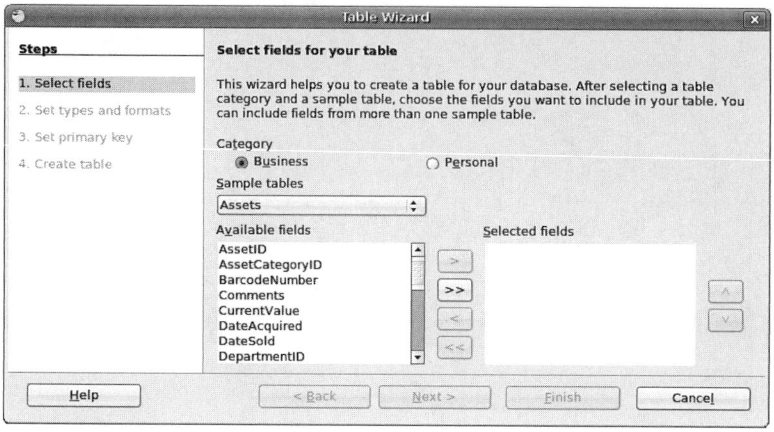

Figure 18.6
Select the table type you want to build.

1. Click the Tables object in the Database pane. The Base window will display table-oriented functions and objects.

2. Click Use Wizard to Create Table in the Tasks pane. The Table Wizard dialog box will open (see Figure 18.6).

3. In the Category section, select the Personal radio button.

4. In the drop-down list, select the Sample Tables option that most closely matches the kind of table you want to build. Don't worry if you don't see an exact match—you can modify the table in a moment. For this example, choose Library.

5. In the Available Fields box, click the fields that most closely match those you want to use.

6. Use the arrow keys to move the fields from the Available Fields box to the Selected Fields box.

Adding New Fields

If you do not see any fields close to your desired fields, add extra placeholder fields that you can rename. For this example, select the fields Title, Publisher, Edition Number, Copyright Year, Rating, Genre, and Notes.

7. Click the Next button. The Set Field Types and Formats page will appear (see Figure 18.7).

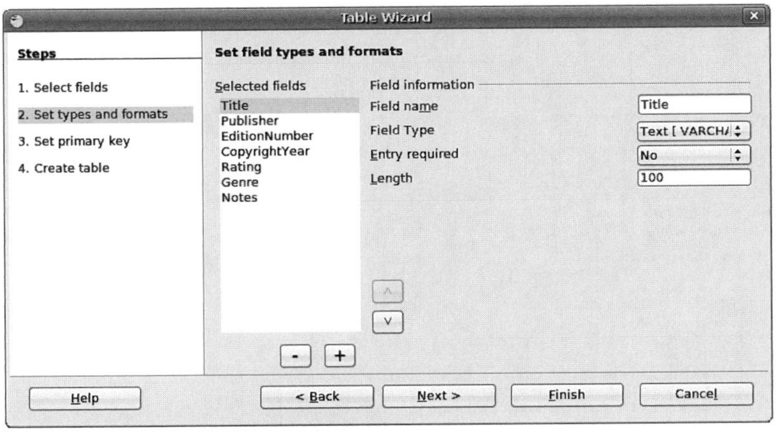

Figure 18.7
Modify the fields you have chosen.

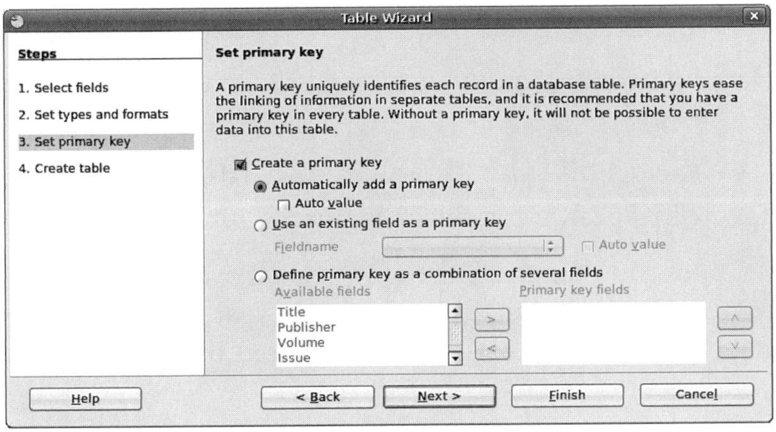

Figure 18.8
Confirming primary key selection.

8. Select EditionNumber in the Selected Fields box.

9. In the Field Name field, change EditionNumber to Volume.

10. Repeat Steps 7 and 8, changing CopyrightYear to Issue.

11. Click the Next button. The Set Primary Key page will appear (see Figure 18.8).

12. Confirm the Create a Primary Key and Automatically Add a Primary Key radio buttons are selected and click Next. The Create Table page will appear (see Figure 18.9).

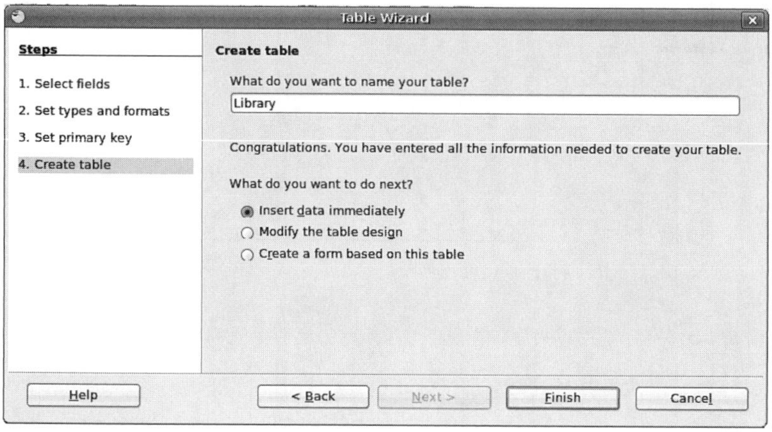

Figure 18.9
Putting the final touches on the table.

13. Type **Comics** into the What Do You Want to Name Your Table? field.

14. Click the Insert Data Immediately radio button and click Finish. The Table wizard will close.

To see the table you just created, double-click the Comics table in the Tables pane. The Table window will appear, as shown in Figure 18.10.

In addition to the field names you changed in the previous steps, other properties may need to be changed as well. For instance, the CopyrightYear field had a Date format by default, but under its new name of Issue, we need to change it to a Number format.

1. Click the Comics Table object in the Tables pane.

2. Click Edit in the Database Objects toolbar. The Table Design window for the Comics table will open (see Figure 18.11).

3. Select Integer from the Field Type list next to the Issue field.

4. Click Save.

5. Close the Table Design window.

Forms to Fill Out

You have created the heart of the database by making the table. You could stop right now and enter data to your heart's content. But after a while, it might become difficult to enter data in such a monotonous way.

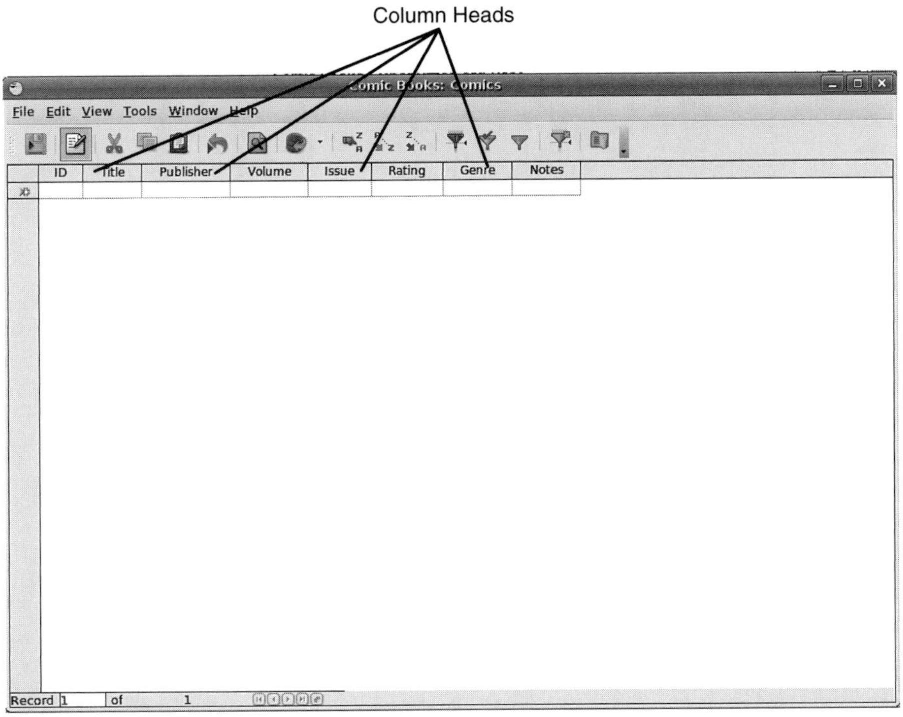

Column Heads

Figure 18.10
A fresh new database table.

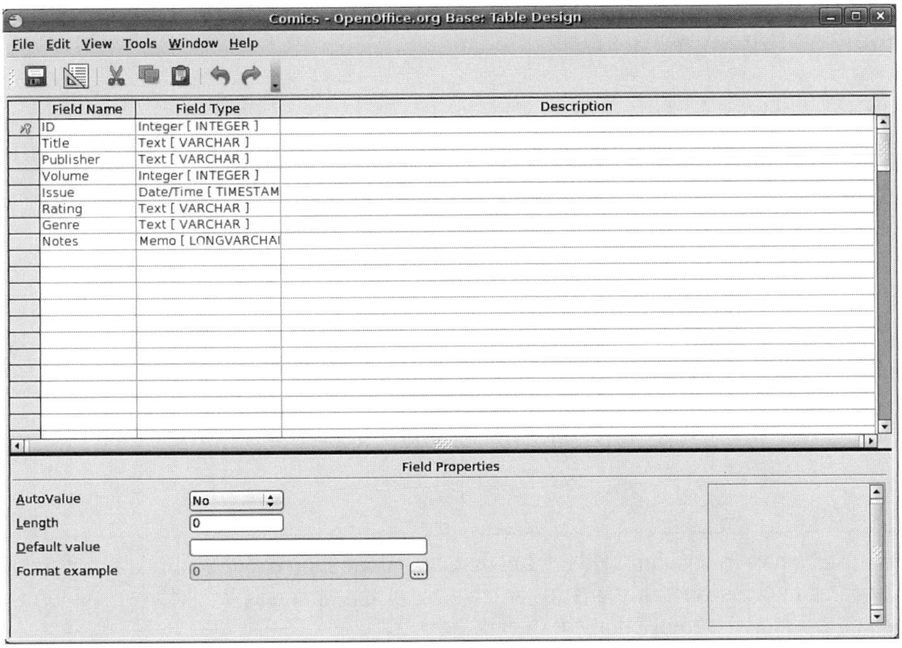

Figure 18.11
Edit and design table fields.

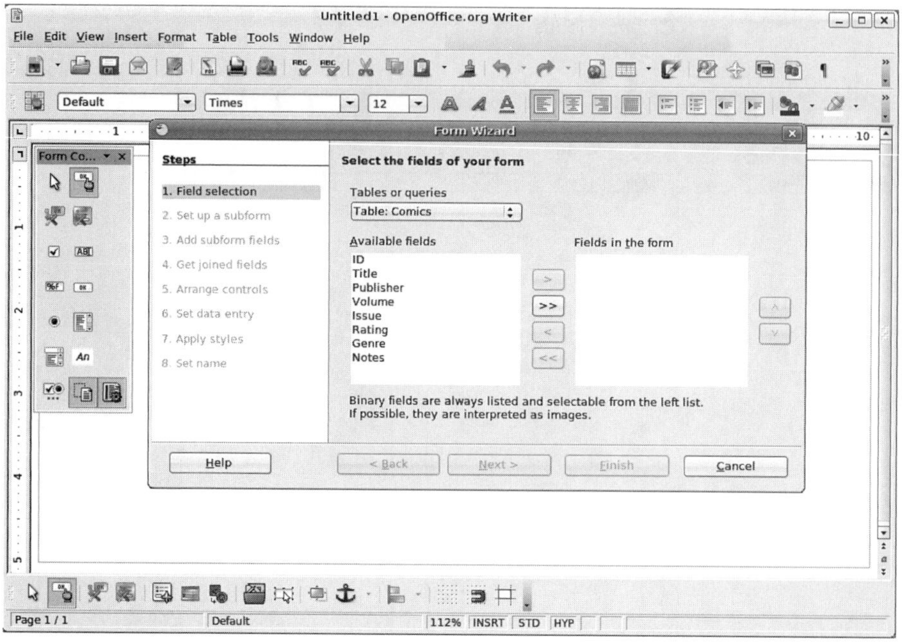

Figure 18.12
Starting the Form wizard.

So take the next step and create a form to enter your material.

1. Click the Forms object in the Database pane. The Base window will display form-oriented functions and objects.

2. Click Use Wizard to Create Form in the Tasks pane. The Form Wizard dialog box and the Form Design view of Writer will open (see Figure 18.12).

3. Confirm that the selected tables or queries are Table: Comics.

4. In the Available Fields box, click the fields that you want in your form.

5. Use the arrow keys to move the fields from the Available Fields box to the Fields in the Form box.

6. Click Next. The Set Up a Subform page will appear (see Figure 18.13).

Subforms and You

Subforms are used when you need to add a lot of detailed information about a particular aspect of your data, such as multiple classifications for an object. For this example, we'll forego subforms, since managing a simple inventory does not need them.

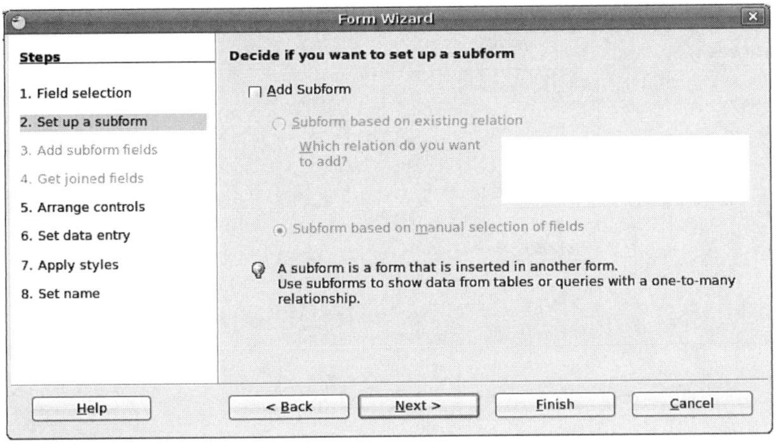

Figure 18.13
Decide to use subforms.

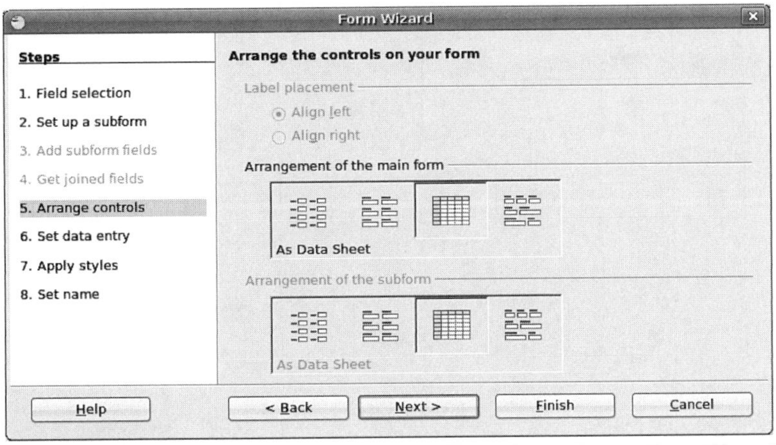

Figure 18.14
Choose the general structure of your form.

7. Click Next. The Arrange Controls page will appear (see Figure 18.14).

8. Click the In Blocks - Labels Above option; then click Next. The Set Data Entry page will appear, as shown in Figure 18.15.

9. If you want to just enter new data in a hurry, select the This Form Is to Be Used for Entering New Data Only radio button. Otherwise, leave the settings as is and click Next. The Apply Styles page will appear (see Figure 18.16).

10. Choose the Water option. The form being designed the Form wizard will change its color scheme.

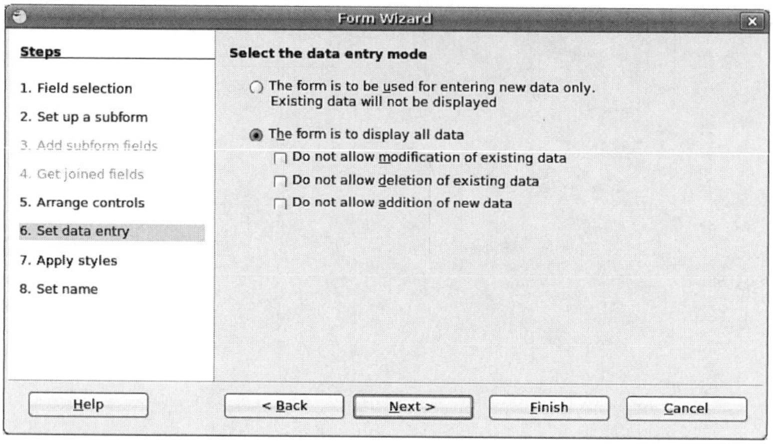

Figure 18.15
Decide how to enter data.

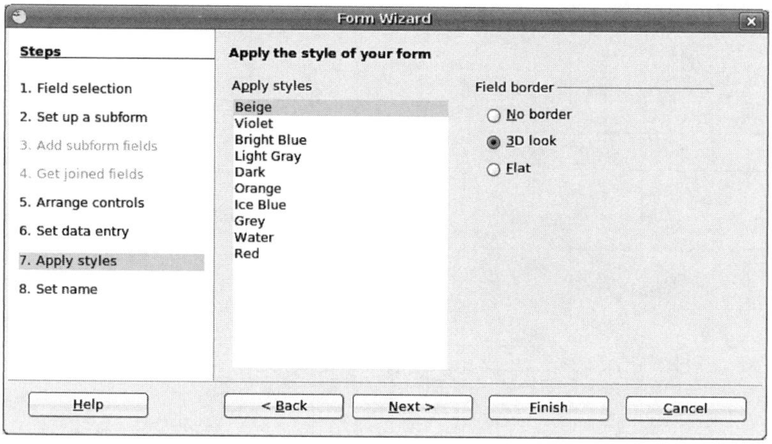

Figure 18.16
Get some style into your form.

11. Confirm the 3D Look radio button is selected and click Next. The Set Name page will appear, as seen in Figure 18.17.

12. Enter a new name on the form.

13. Select the Work with the Form radio button and click Finish. The form will be displayed in a Writer window (see Figure 18.18).

14. Close the form.

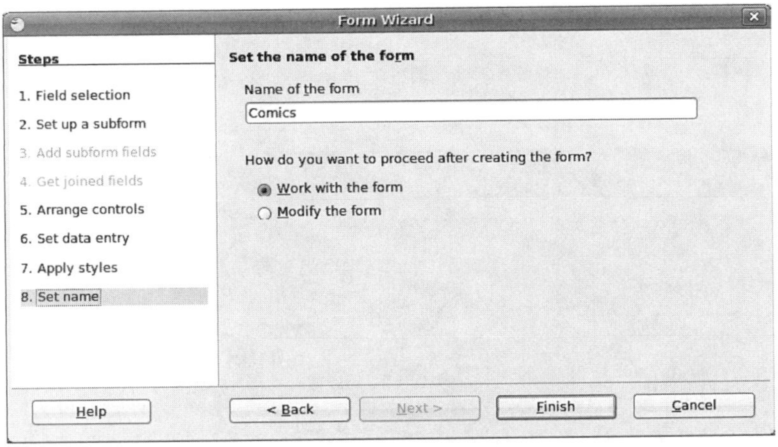

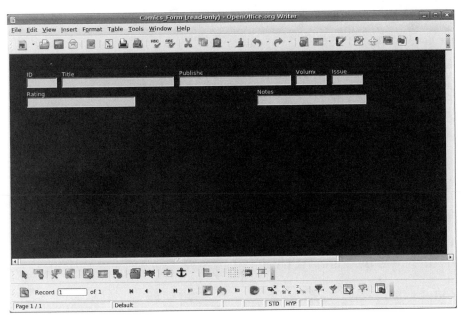

Figure 18.17
Polishing details on your form.

Figure 18.18
A pretty good start to a form.

The wizard does a good job of setting up a form, but it has its limitations. You can circumvent those limitations if you use the Form Design feature to tweak this form a bit.

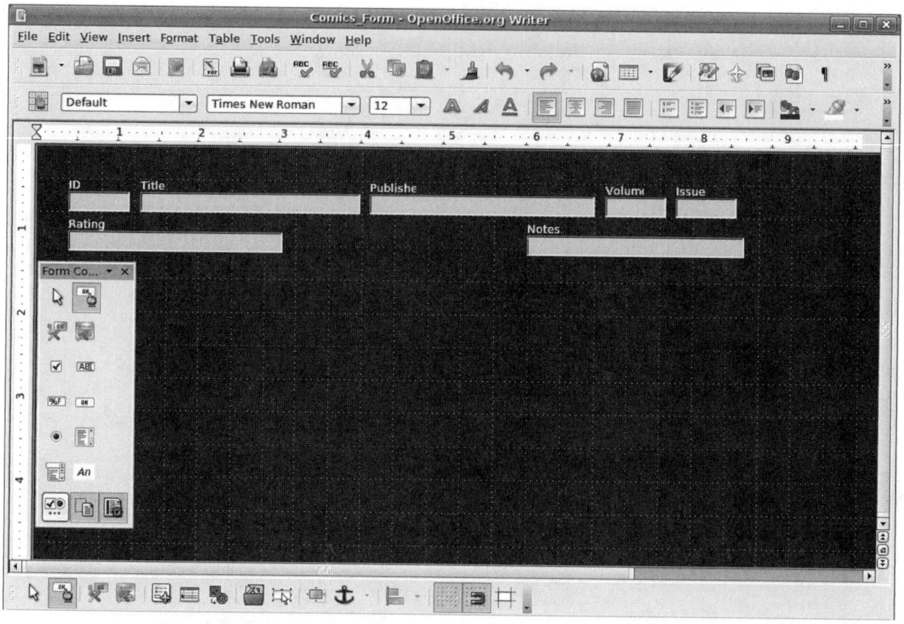

Figure 18.19
Form designing is done in Writer.

1. Click the Comics_Form form object in the Forms pane.

2. Click Edit in the Database Objects toolbar. The Form Design window in Writer will open (see Figure 18.19).

3. Click the Notes field. Anchor and Field handles will appear, as shown in Figure 18.20.

4. Right-click the Notes field. The context menu will appear.

5. Select the Group | Ungroup menu command. This will break the connection between the Notes field and its label.

Ungroup Encounter

Ungrouping fields and their labels is necessary because otherwise any resizing operation would resize both label and field, leaving you with a funny-looking form.

6. Drag the lower center field handle of the Notes field to increase the field size.

7. Right-click the field and choose Anchor | To Page from the context menu.

8. Drag the Notes field to another location on the form.

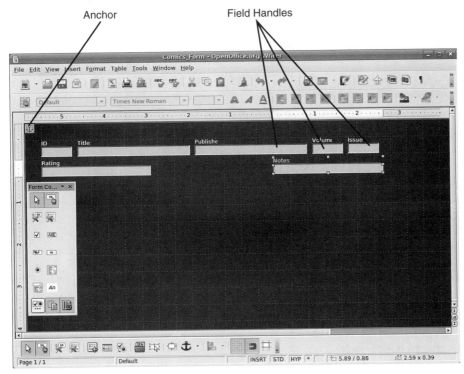

Figure 18.20
Additional elements make it clear you are in Form Design view.

9. Drag the Notes label to an adjacent position to the Notes field.

10. Add a title to the form by clicking in the main form area and entering the text in the first paragraph of the form. Figure 18.21 shows one possible finished look to the form.

11. Save your changes by clicking Save.

12. Close the Form Design window by clicking File | Close.

Queries to Ask

You enter data into the form, which in turn goes into the table. All is well and happy in the world.

Then you decide you want to know how many Spider-man comic books you have entered so far. You can't see this in the form, and after entering so many comic books, you find it impractical to scan the table for every Spider-man issue you have.

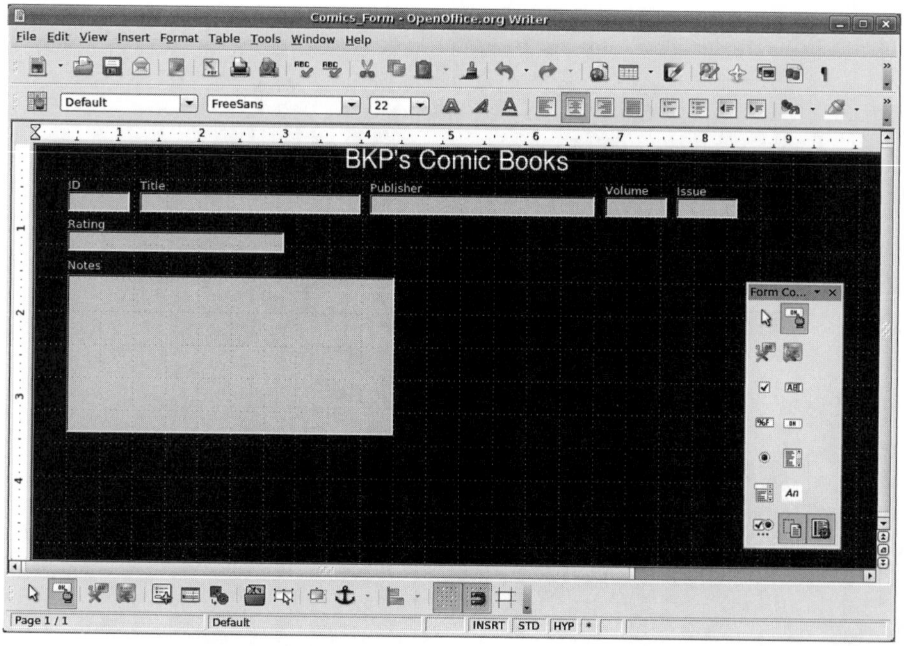

Figure 18.21
A form more customized to your needs.

So what do you do? Build a query!

A query is a set of instructions that tells the database to pull out certain pieces of information and store them in a query table, which is sort of like a subtable. You can even edit records from the query table and have those changes reflected in the main database table.

Working Ahead

In this example, several comic book records have been entered into the database already.

1. Click the Queries object in the Database pane. The Base window will display query-oriented functions and objects.

2. Click Use Wizard to Create Query in the Tasks pane. The Query Wizard dialog box will open.

3. In the Available Fields dialog box, choose the fields you want to have in the query. In this example, move all but Notes to the Fields in the Query box.

4. Click Next. The Sorting Order page will appear.

5. Select Comics.Publisher in the first Sort By field.

6. Select Comics.Title in the first Then By field.

7. Click Next. The Search Conditions page will appear.

8. Select Comics.Title as the first Field value.

9. Select Equal To for the first Condition value.

10. Enter Spider in the Value field.

11. Click Next. The Detail or Summary page will appear.

12. For most queries, leave the default settings and click Next. The Aliases page will appear.

13. Again, for most queries, leave the default alias settings and click Next. The Summary page will appear.

14. Review the query selections and click Finish. The Query wizard will close, and the Query Results window will appear.

The main database will reflect any changes made to the data in the query if you click the Refresh icon on the Database toolbar after making your edits.

Reports to Make

A query is nice for those occasions when you seek information for yourself on your Ubuntu PC. But if you want to share the information with others or want to transport the information, a report is the way to go.

A report differs from a query only in the type of output. Reports are read-only. Once information is in a report, you cannot change it there. You would have to change data in the database table and re-run the report to make changes on the report.

1. Click the Reports object in the Database pane. The Base window will display Report-oriented functions and objects.

2. Click Use Wizard to Create Report in the Tasks pane. The Report Wizard dialog box and a blank Writer window will open.

3. Confirm that the selected Tables or Queries are Table: Comics.

4. In the Available Fields box, click the fields that you want in your form.

5. Use the arrow keys to move the fields from the Available Fields box to the Fields in Report box.

6. Click Next. The Labeling Fields page will appear.

7. Confirm that the labels are the ones you want to use and click Next. The Grouping page will appear.

8. Click the arrow key to move desired fields to the Groupings box.

9. Click Next. The Sort Options page will appear.

10. Select Publisher in the first Sort By field.

11. Select Title in the first Then By field.

12. Click Next. The Choose Layout page will appear.

13. Choose an option in the Layout of Data field. The style will be reflected in the Writer window behind the Report wizard.

14. Choose an option in the Layout of Headers and Footers field. The style will be reflected in the Writer window behind the Report wizard.

15. Click Next. The Create Report page will appear.

16. Enter a name for your report, leaving all other options as is.

17. Click Finish. The report will be generated in the Writer window.

Conclusion

There is much more power to Base than just keeping track of collections, and this chapter was intended to give you a taste of this robust application. You are invited to experiment with Base on your own and create your own databases, which will help you at your job, business, or home projects.

We have come to the end of our introduction to Ubuntu. By now you should have a pretty good understanding of this popular operating system and be well on your way to making Ubuntu an integral part of your computing life. Thanks for coming along on this journey, and enjoy your Ubuntu!

INDEX